Identity Struggle of the People of Israel as Alien in the Pentateuch

Biblical Hermeneutics Rediscovered

The Series as the name suggests will focus on Biblical Hermeneutics, i.e., literary works concerned with methods of interpreting the Old and New Testaments of the Bible via different stream of topics like Literature and Poetry, Indigenous Philosophizing, Ethical response towards Ecology, Health and Healing, Science and Technology, Feminist Theology, Sociological approach towards Human Rights, Law and Politics, Arts, History of Ideas, Ancient Civilizations, Cultural Contiguity, Religious Cosmologies and Mysticism, Appraisal of various Theologians, World Peace and Harmony, Global Capitalism, Network Marketing, Cybertheology, Population and Demographics, Epigraphic Studies, Contextualized Education, and many others. We welcome a Mss. on any topic/s mentioned, whether they are original works, scholarly monographs, collections of conference papers, revised dissertations, or translations of historical documents. Through the Series we, the Publishers, are striving to put forward published works that may help Institutions, Academic Bodies, Researchers, Scholars and the World at large in furthering their respective knowledge and understanding on the concerned subject. We welcome your comments on our efforts and further suggestions on how we can enshrine new ray of analysing and explaining the written Texts through our upcoming books.

Biblical Hermeneutics Rediscovered - 30

Identity Struggle of the People of Israel as Alien in the Pentateuch

A North East Indian Tribal Reading

Imsu Longchar

Christian World Imprints

First Published in 2020 by

Christian World Imprints
Christian Publishing & Books from India
C-3, Wazirpur Industrial Area
Delhi-110052
cwidelhi2017@gmail.com
www.ChristianWorldImprints.com
Phone: +91 11 41526079

ISBN: 978-93-5148-451-6 (HB)
ISBN: 978-93-5148-452-3 (PB)

Printed in India.

DEDICATION

Dedicated to my beloved parents Lt.R.Temjen Longchar (1931-September 1993) and Lt.Talikala Longkumer (1944- December 2009) whose prayers and support led me to full time God's ministry

The book, in its original form, is the thesis submitted to the Senate of Serampore College, towards the Doctor of Theology degree, accepted in the Senate in December 2017. It is published with written permission. The original title of the thesis is unchanged. The candidate is solely responsible for the title, contents and opinions expressed in it.

Contents

Acknowledgement

I thank God for His unceasing guidance and providence throughout my research. In fact many are the persons to whom I am deeply indebted for the completion of this research.

My D.Th programme; Fr. Dr. Reji Mathew, the Registrar and Rev. Dr. Abraham, Dean of Doctoral Studies for their kind and valuable help on academic matters. Sincere thanks to P. G. George Dean, Department of Research/SATHRI and to Rev. Dr. P. C. Gine for his valuable suggestions and comments.

Grateful acknowledgement is made to the following Libraries and authorities of: Orthodox Theological Seminary, Kottayam; Mar Thoma Theological Seminary, Kottayam; St. Thomas Apostolic Seminary, Vadavathoor, Kerala; United Theological College, Bangalore; State Library Kohima; North East Zone Cultural Council Library, Dimapur.

Finally, my sincere thanks to my wife Sentila, son Sunep and daughter Penyu whose constant support and encouragement with prayer had helped me go through all the challenges and complete my research.

Abbreviations

AB	Anchor Bible
ABD	Anchor Bible Dictionary
AJT	Asian Journal of Theology
ANET	Ancient Near East Text
ATHANT	Abhandlungen Zur Theologie des Alten und Neuen Testaments
AUSS	Andrew University Seminary Studies
AWA	Ancient West Asia
BA	Biblical Archaeologist
BDB	F. Browns, S. R. Driver and C.A. Briggs, Hebrew and English Lexicon of the Old Testament
BHS	Biblica Herbraica Stuttgartensia
BI	Biblical Interpretation
BT	Bible Today
BZAW	Beiheft zur Zeitschrift fur die altestamentliche Wissenichaft
CBQ	Catholic Biblical Quarterly
FAT	Forchungen Zum Alten Testament
FOLT	Form of Old Testament Literature
HTR	Harvard Theological Review
IDB	Interpreter's Dictionary of the Bible
ITC	International Theological Commentary
JAOS	Journal of American Oriental Studies
JBL	Journal of Biblical Studies
JSOT	Journal for the Study of the Old Testament
JSOTSup	Journal for the Study of the Old Testament Supplement Series

JPS	Jewish Publication Society
JTS	Journal of Tribal Studies
LHBOTS	Library for Hebrew Bible Old Testament series
NCB	New Century Bible
NIB	New Interpreter's Bible
NICOT	New International Commentary on the Old Testament
OTA	Old Testament Abstract
OTE	Old Testament Essay
OTS	Old Testament Studies
OTL	Old Testament Library
SBL	Society of Biblical Literature
SBLDS	Society of Biblical Literature Dissertation Series
ST	Studia Theologica
TDOT	Theological Dictionary of the Old Testament
TSC	Tribal Studies Centre
TS	Theological Studies
TT	Theology Today
TynB	Tyndale Bulletin
VT	Vetus Testamendum
WBC	Word Biblical Commentary
ZAW	Zeitschrift fur die alttestamentliche Wissenschaft
ZABR	Zeitschrft fur altorentalische und biblische Rechtsgeschichte

Introduction

1. Statement of the Problem

The ancestors of Israel were known as "aliens" in the ancestral narrative. An alien is associated with each of the stories of Abraham, Isaac, Jacob, and Joseph, and with all the major geographical settings of the narrative-Canaan, Egypt, and Paddan-aram. In a narrative concerned with instituting a strong tie between the ancestors of Israel and their divinely homeland, alien sounds a note of discord. Recurring emphasis on aliens within Canaan suggest alienation from the land that is supposed to be Israel's home. Although the Israelites' ancestors were regarded as father/mother figures in the Old Testament period, yet the ancestor were alienated as a pattern repeated through time. Aliens seems unpleasant and troubling counter-note to the establishment of an ancestral claim in Canaan. Therefore, the question arises- in whose interest? That becomes the question for this research. Remembering the past alienation in Canaan and Egypt by the ancestors, the tribals of the North East India also experience alienation and oppression within one's own land. "Alien" becomes their identity. This research work will be made from ideological perspective.

2. Elaboration of the Problem

Biblical terms *gër* (גר = alien) is understood as "resident alien". גר (alien) in the Pentateuch connotes the one who does not belong to a particular group or considered to be a second-class citizen with limited rights and opportunities. The label "alien" has the opposite quality; it is used to separate off one group from those who do not, and are not supposed to have belonged to it. They lives among people who are not their blood relatives, and thus they lacks the protection and the privileges which usually come from blood relationship and the place of birth.[1] The term alienation is thus used primarily to express something negative: not belonging to, exclusion from, aliens to, and barbarianin. The ancestors too are members of a tribe who stood in the central position. The "stranger and alien" as are seen in the biblical text, they were identified.

The term "alien" appears 30 times in the Patriarchal narratives of the Pentateuch, nine times in its verbal form √גור (*gur* = sojourn) and 21 times in its nominal form מגור (*magur* = sojourning-place/ dwelling-place).[2] An alien is associated with each of the stories of Abraham, Isaac, Jacob, and Joseph, and with all the major geographical settings of the narrative - Canaan, Egypt, and Paddan-aram. It is often situated in high-visibility positions at the start, climax, or at the close of the stories. It occurs in a variety of literary forms, ranging from narrative report to dialogue between characters in a variety of literary forms, ranging from narrative report to dialogue between characters.

In the so-called 'historical Creed,'[3] (Deut. 26: 5b-9) this conveys the sense of "vulnerable" or "destitute," since a landless person was without security of food and protection.[4] Already in Exodus 12: 49, the legal prescription pertaining to the relatively equal status of גר (*gër* = alien) and the אזרח (*'zarah* = a native of the land)[5] are mentioned. אזרח refers to someone who is part of the established and dominant kinship group of the sons or house of Israel, and thus has access to the family-landed property. An expression גר in contrast, live in the same territory but is not a member of this dominant kinship group. In the ancestors' stories it often includes the story of a paradigmatic leader or hero who goes through an identity crisis.

Leviticus consistently calls for equal responsibility and equal treatment of these two socio-economic groups. Leviticus goes beyond the stipulation in

---

1 D. Kellermann, "גור *gur*; גר *gër*; גרות *geruth;* מגוּרים *meghurim,*" in *Theological Dictionary of the Old Testament,* Vol-11, edited by G. Johannes Botterweck and Helmer Ringgren (Grand Rapids, Michigan: William B. Eerdmans Publishing Company, 1975), 439-449. (Hereby *TDOT).*

2 √גור; Gen 12:10; 19:9; 20:1; 21:23, 34; 26:3; 32:5; 35:27; 47:4. גֵר; Gen 15:13; 23:4; 35:27. Exo 2:22; 12:4; 18:3. Lev 19: 33; 25:35; 25:47. Num 9: 14; 15: 14. Deut 10:18; 18:6; 23:8; 24: 17; 27:19. מגוֹר; Gen 17:8; 28:4; 36:7; 37:1; 47:9.

3 Gerhard Von Rad, *The Problem of the Hexateuch and other essays,* translated by Rev. E. W. Trueman Dicken (Edinburgh and London: Oliver and Boyd, 1966), 5. This prayer is to be said at the handing over of the tithes in the so-called year of tithing.

4 Ronald E. Clements, "The Book of Deuteronomy," in *The New Interpreter's Bible A Commentary,* Vol-2, (Nashville: Abingdon Press, 1998), 480.

5 Francis Brown Driver, and Charles A. Briggs, *A Hebrew and English Lexicon of the Old Testament* (Oxford: Clarendon press, 1979), 280. (Hereby *BDB).*

Exodus (22:20-21; 23:9) to refrain from oppressing the resident aliens, in that Israel is to love the resident alien as if he is or she were native Israelites:

> When an alien resides with you in your land, you shall not oppress the alien; the alien who resides with you shall be to you as the citizen among you; you shall love the alien as yourself, for you were aliens in the land of Egypt: I am YHWH your God (Lev. 19:32-34).

Only with the beginning of exodus does the Pentateuchal narrative actually portray Israel as one who has gone through the oppression, exploitation, cultural and national alienation which the ancestors experienced in Egypt as residential aliens is interpreted as a negative example; (Ex. 1:11-14; 2:11; 3:7-9; 4:31; 5:4-23; 6:6-9). YHWH's prophecy to Abram in Gen.15:13 is "Then the Lord said to Abram, 'know for certain that your offspring shall be residential aliens in a land that is not theirs, and shall be slaves there, and they shall be oppressed for four hundred years." It inclined the reader of the Pentateuch narrative to identify Egypt negatively. However, the ancestors' experience in Egypt as residential aliens can be interpreted as positive example as found in Genesis. 12:10-20; 20:1-18; Abraham is enriched by Egypt and through Joseph, Israel received a bountiful welcome in Egypt. However, this explicit portrayal of Egyptian oppression does not appear again in the subsequent stories of wilderness, wandering or in the legal material until Deut. 26.

In other words, the tradition of the ancestors in Genesis, and much of the legal material, especially in Exodus, Leviticus and Numbers, does not necessarily presuppose a negative experience of Israel in Egypt. And yet, by framing the Pentateuchal narrative at the beginning with anticipation of Egypt as oppressive (Gen. 15:13) and at the end with retrospect of Egypt as oppressive "A wandering Aramean was my ancestor; he went down into Egypt and lived there as an alien,...When the Egyptian treated us harshly and afflicted us by imposing hard labor on us." (Deut. 26:5-7), the narrative informs the reader an overpowering view of Egypt largely as a negative experience and example.

As from the above passages, Israel portrayed as resident aliens in Egypt supports the Pentateuch's dominant view that the people from whom Israel was formed were never indigenous to Egypt. However, by insisting the same time that the distinction between native aliens and residential aliens is to be disregarded or erased. The text also implicitly undermines the distinction between Israel as resident aliens in Egypt and the native Egyptians. The categories presented in the text as 'native' and 'resident alien' are fluid and dependent upon the ideological interests of the users of these terms. To portray Israel as resident aliens in Egypt and as indigenous in Canaan may suggest Israel's lack of roots in Egypt and its claim to ownership of Canaan, but that ideology trips over its inherent contradiction, not least with an Identity of origin in Mesopotamia.

Even in Leviticus 25 the sale of property and debt-slavery offers an interesting view how Leviticus understood the status of the resident aliens and the native in relation to the Exodus in Egypt. The chapter contains references to a number of socio-economic strata, one finds reference to אבדים *('bdim* = slaves) both male and female (25:6, 39, 42, 44), the season labourer, (25:23, 35, 40,45, 47, 50, 53), then the residential aliens (25: 23, 35, 47), and finally, the landholders by references to their inalienable property (25:10, 13, 24, 25, 27, 28, 32, 33, 34, 41, 45, 46). Overlapping with this list are references to categorize kinship or kin such as brothers or close relatives (25:25, 35, 36, 39, 46, 47, 48), and relatives or associates (25:14, 15, 17). The main purpose of this chapter is to stress that the property held by the families in Israel, as well as individual Israelites themselves are inalienable, even when Israelites sell property or their own selves in times of economic needs, such sales are to be seen as temporary. In the Jubilee Year will reverts to its original owner.

These rules of inalienable property apply to the land holding Israelites alone. While Israelites out of need are forced to sell property and so take the status of residential aliens, a tenant or seasonal workers, such a situation is not viewed as being permanent (25:25-28). When the Israelite out of need similarly sell him into and render his service for a particular period of time, they shall serve until the year of Jubilee (25:39-41). This law is in contrast with Exodus 21:1-6 where it is laid down that a Hebrew shall serve for six years after that one is set free. Furthermore in contrast, slaves taken by Israel from the surrounding nations, or from the residential aliens born in their midst, are considered slaves in perpetuity, but the property may be possessed for the children for inheritance (25:45-46). Thus the earlier passages mentioned above in Exodus and Leviticus to mandate the equal treatment of resident aliens here breaks down. The contradiction is especially evident if one compares the earlier invocation of Egypt to justify the equal treatment of the residence aliens "love the residence aliens as yourself for you were residence aliens in Egypt" (Lev 19:34) with the innovation of Egypt here to justify the differential treatment of the Israelites and the residential alien. The kinship group of the children of Israel (25:46) is immune to enslavement because YHWH claims, "they are my slaves whom I brought out from the land of Egypt; (therefore) they shall not be sold as slaves are sold." (25:42, 55). Residence aliens, in contrast are liable to permanent slavery because they do not belong to YHWH not having been acquired by slaves in Egypt.

Thus Leviticus 25 presents tensions both internal to the chapter and externally with previous material in the text. Internally, the prohibition against charging interest or profit from one kin (25:36-37) conflicts with the provision of the Jubilee Year. Secondly, the prohibition of selling property in perpetuity, because the property in the final analysis belongs to YHWH (25:23), conflicts with exemption of urban property (25:29-30). Thirdly, the very notion that

YHWH owns land (25:23) conflicts with the repeated recognition of, and emphasis on, the inheritable and inalienable of the family or clan (references above). And externally the difference between the treatment of the residential alien and the landholding Israelite in Leviticus 25 conflicts with the earlier mandate in Leviticus to erase such differentiation in status and in treatment.

The passages chosen above is an essential element of the construction of the ethnic identity- a contrast between "us" and "them", ethnic identity is the contrast over against "us" and "them", and the ethnic identity is contrast over against an 'other' or 'others'. In fact, at times the Pentateuch insists with great force on the difference between Israel and Egypt or גר (*gër* = aliens) and, אזרה (*'zarah* = native aliens). It preserves a memory of the struggle at a given time between the powerful (Egyptians) and the powerless (Hebrews). It describes the efforts of the powerful to dominate, and the power of the powerless to resist: the power of the powerful to define reality and the power of the powerless to redefine reality. The book of Leviticus exists because it is in someone's interest for it to exist. In whose interest, then are they? Since the ancient Israelites society like other societies, for example, is not homogeneous, the question that usually comes into our mind. In which group's interest are these laws? And since groups are usually in some kind of conflict with other groups the question arises: On what kind of social conflict is alluded to or repressed, by the text? It is usually the victors in any social conflict whose texts get preserved. The researcher will look narrowly at the elites and power holders in Israelite society for the matrix of this law.

Accenting ideology, however, raises a question related to the source distribution of the texts. While sojourn may show a strong presence across the lines of source divisions, does it serve similar ideological ends in the different sources? Here a number of scholars, primarily German, have made a case for a distinctive sojourn ideas in the Priestly source.[6] P, they contend, introduce the idea of patriarchal sojourn in Canaan; this novel and intriguing notion is not shared by the "older" sources.

Therefore doing a research on גר will provide essential information as to the 'identity politics' of the producer of the text. Special references of alienation in Egypt in Genesis, Exodus, and Leviticus through Deuteronomy

6 Theodore Hiebert, *The Yahwist's Landscape: Nature and Religion in Early Israel* (Oxford: Oxford University Press, 1996), 88-89; Gerhard Von Rad, *Old Testament Theology Volume 1: The Theology of Israel's historical Origins*, trans. D. G. M. Stalker (San Francisco: Harper Collins, 1962), 169; Gerhard Von Rad, *Genesis: A Commentary,* trans. John H. Marks, OTL (Philadelphia: Westminster, 1961), 195, 245,402-03; K. Schmid, "The So Called Yahwist and the Literary Gap between Genesis and Exodus," in *A Farwell to the Yahwist? The Composition of the Pentateuch in recent European Interpretation,* edited by T. B. Dozeman and K. Schmid, SBL Symposium Series 34 (Atlanta: Society of Biblical Literature, 2006), 43.

will be analysed, paying particular attention to their narrative context and development, and thus to both their significance as the narrative of the Pentateuch and their thematic significance in the Pentateuch as a whole.

Similarly, social contempt for the Tribals of The North East India is also a kind of alienation. The Tribals in the North East India are in a more advantageous position, having land, people, government, etc., of their own. But there is a sense of feeling of no longer at home, or of not yet being at home, in its own land living as undervalued minorities. The unrest in the North East India is rooted in the classic factors of deprivation or social and cultural injustice with a deep fear of the loss of identity, and it is this fear that animates one of the most serious insurgency in North East India.

Peter Haokip expresses a similar opinion that "The hill tribes of Manipur (till recently or still today in some places and by some) were called *hao* = untouchable (which is a derogatory designation) and were not allowed to enter the houses of Manipur Hindus. It was considered to be defilement. If a tribal wanted to meet a Manipuri Hindu, he could only shout from a distance in front of the court yard of the house.[7] That is the way tribals are looked upon in Indian society. They are always treated as low caste people who are poor, illiterate, simple people and impure.

The North East India tribal communities are considered as "aliens" because of the following reasons: (a) they do not belong to the dominant racial groups of the Aryans and Dravidians; (b) they do not belong to the major religious communities of the Hindus and the Muslim; (c) they are vulnerable minority; (e) they are dependent upon the assistance of the Central Government, and (f) they are the victims of land alienation, oppression and exploitation.

What pricks the researcher to do this study, as being from the tribal community, various tribes and sub-tribes inhabiting Nagaland, Mizoram, Manipur, Arunachal Pradesh and Sikkim, have taken their decision to venture out and live in and work at Delhi, Mumbai, Chennai and elsewhere had been one of the best examples of national integration. For a group of people who used to say that they were "going to India" while travelling to Kolkata from their region, this was indeed a giant step forward in understanding their country and their rights as citizens to live and work anywhere in the country. When venturing out from the region to the mainland India, tribals are alienated. They are referred to as chinkies, junglees, Coronavirus, primitive, backward, their looks, habits, culture and the food habit has come to acquire derogatory connotation. The authorities, be it at the centre or in the states, failed miserably to reassure the panic-stricken people that their lives and properties are safe in any part of the country. And that leaves the tribals of the North East India

7 Peter Haokip, "The tribal People of the Northeast: A Liberating Quest for Identity, Equality and Respect," *Janadeepa* 2/2 (1999), 69.

uneasy. One might therefore conclude that the ideological impulse is at the very heart of this passage. The researcher would assert that this is true of all literary texts. This ideological material is hidden, but may be exposed by examining the cracks or fault lines in the text; the point of conflict. In the case of the text the primary fault lies between the alienation and the texts it seeks to interpret.[8]

3. Hypothesis

The research work will operate with the basic assumption that alienation was the identity of the Israelites in the land of Egypt, so also the Tribals of North East India seem to be having "alien" status in the present day situation. Therefore it demands re-reading and re-interpreting the portrayal of aliens in Pentateuch in relation to the tribal situation in today's context.

4. Importance of the Study

The main purpose of the research is to seek to answer that question by a thorough investigation of the contribution made by the reference of alien's in the pentateuchal narrative. To bring definition to the project, the researcher has selected a specific text that provides a distinctive lens through which to view the texts. The tool the researcher has selected to shape the textual reading is a sociological reading of Anthony D. Smith, a contemporary scholar working in the areas of ethnicity. His categories accord well with the principal themes of the patriarch narrative, and offer a helpful medium for relating ideas of the land and community.

Secondly, land decides and creates the time and history for the tribals. The environment, festivals and religious activities are centered on the soil-cycle. Therefore the land is very crucial to the understanding of the tribals' worldview. Many of the tribals have been reduced to landless wanderers. In this context, tribals may re-read the following biblical passages concerning the promised Land: they may put themselves into the role of the Israelites who have been afflicted and humiliated (Deut. 26:5ff); they also might receive the promise of God which came through Josephs: "God will visit you one day, bring you back to the land which he swore to your fathers, Abraham and Isaac and Jacob" (Gen. 50:24). The tribal should see an analogy with their own experience when God call the tribal leader Moses and asked, "Go and gather the elders of your own tribes, and say to them, "The Lord, the God of your father has appeared to me saying, I have observed you and what has been done to you in this land, and, I promise that I will bring you out of this affliction" (Exod. 3:16-17). To preserve the identity of the tribals at the same

8 Another fault line that would bear examination concerns the reason for the deliverance, alternately the sincere repentance Israelites or God's gracious activity. Likewise, the purpose of the oppression is described as punishment and test. A close examination of these "cracks" in the narrative would reveal other ideological intentions.

time, an attempt will be made in contributing to the biblical understanding of "nationhood" and promote a harmonious living and national integration.

5. Definition of Terms and Terminologies

Identity: the term "identity" in the Oxford Advanced Learner's Dictionary means characteristic, feeling or beliefs that distinguish people from others: a sense of national/cultural/personal/group identity.[9] Sociologist Zygmunt Bauman[10] posits that the very notion of identity is a modern preoccupation. Only when human being begins to be dis-embedded from traditional spaces and relationship, long accepted rhythms of time and well-established activities of survival do we begin to ask "Who am I?" and "Where do I belong?" For Bauman "identity 'becomes' a problem; it was a 'problem' from its birth-was born as a problem…, could exist only as a problem; it was a problem, and thus ready to be born, precisely because of that experience of under-determination and free floating-ness which came to be articulated *ex post facto* as 'dis-embeddedment.'"

6. Scope and Limitation

The study will confine to the limited chapters from the book of Genesis 12:10-20; 20:1-18; 26:1-11; Exodus 22:21-24; 23:9; Deuteronomy 24:17-22; Leviticus 17:8-15 and 24:16, 22 and 25; and Numbers 15:13-16; 26, 29, and 30. It might consider other relevant texts from the Pentateuch when it would become absolutely necessary. It may be argued that these biblical chapters are not completely self-contained units of tradition and that many historical and literary questions go beyond these limits to include the other patriarchal narratives and even the rest of the Pentateuch. The research will be limited to the tribals of the North East India.

7. Previous Studies

Historically speaking, ideological criticism emerged into biblical studies in the late 1970s and early 1980s from several different but not unrelated new

---

9 A. S. Hornby, ed. *Oxford Advanced Learner's Dictionary,* 8th edition (Oxford: University Press, 2010), 770.

10 Zygmunt Bauman, "From Pilgrim to Tourist-or a Short History of Identity," in *Questions of Cultural Identity,* edited by Stuart Hall and Paul du Gay (New Delhi: SAGE Publications, 1997), 18 Disembeddedment refers to the way in which contemporary social practices can be no longer be primarily defined by the grounding, or embeddedness, in the local context of a restricted place and time. Social practices are now, in large part removed from the immediacies of context with the relations they involve typically being stretched over large tracts of time and space. Local experiences and events are shaped by processes taking place on the other side of the world, and vice versa. These are processes, moreover, that are primarily impersonal and abstract.

perspectives. The earliest and in some ways the most determinative was the impact of Latin American liberation theology, with its intellectual indebtedness to Marxist/materialist forms of analysis. This trajectory of influence was mediated in Hebrew Bible studies above all by Gottwald's work, in particular *The Tribes of Yahweh: A Sociology of the Religion of Liberated Israel, 1250–1050 B.C.E.* Although primarily concerned with a reconstruction of a peasant revolt model for the formation of the nation of Israel, it analysed a historical series of "horizons" of interpretation, recoverable from the biblical text that delineated different ideological construal of the events of the Late Bronze/ Early Iron Age. Although in many ways independent of Gottwald, both African Mosala, *Biblical Hermeneutics and Black Theology in South Africa* and feminist Yee, *Poor Banished Children of Eve* Marxist/materialist forms of interpretation have been significant in ideological criticism of the Hebrew Bible.

Greifenhagen, *Egypt on the Pentateuchal Map* argues that Egypt shadows are particularly long in the Pentateuch, which contains over half of the explicit references to מצרים (*mitz-rah-'yim* = Egyptian) or מצרי (*mitz-ree* = Egypt) in the Hebrew Bible. The scrolls of Leviticus, Numbers and Deuteronomy fairly consistently present Egypt in negative terms and support the ideology of Exodus that insists on a separation of Israel from Egypt that allows for no possibility of return. Greifenhagen main focus is to explore this topos and to inquire as to its particular significance in the ideology embodied in the rhetoric of the Pentateuch.[11]

Douglas and anthropologist, she argues that the ostensibly priestly concern with ethnic purity that underpins the prohibition on foreign marriage cannot be derived directly from the Pentateuch. In particular, the book of Numbers stands against the idea that the 'holy seed' was a clearly defined group, established by legitimate birth. Drawing attention to Numbers 15:22-31 and 19:10, for example, she points out that the purity system is there specifically designed to include the non-native גרים (*gerim* = aliens or sojourners), and unlike the tendency of Deutronomy (e.g. 23:3), there is no blanket ruling against strangers simply by virtue of their ethnicity.[12] Douglas concludes that Numbers opposed the separatism of Ezra and Nehemiah: 'the concern of the priestly editor is to constrain a populist xenophobia'. Recent biblical scholarship is perhaps less willing to speak of Priestly texts in Numbers and Leviticus have declared

---

11 F. V. Greifenhagen, *Egypt on the Pentateuch's Ideological Map Constructing Biblical Israel's Identity*, JSOT Supplement Series 361 (Sheffield: Sheffield Academic Press, 2002), 15.

12 Mary Douglas, *In the Wilderness: The Doctrine of Defilement in the Book of Numbers* (Sheffield: JSOT Press, 1993), 155.

aliens to be on the same legal footing as native-born Israelites.[13] Rolf Rendtorff similarly has raised the possibility that the Priestly laws concerning the *gerim* were shaped and edited in opposition to the marriage policies of Ezra.[14]

Patric D. Miller, in *The Religion of Ancient Israel,* in his topical approach on the "exclusion of foreigners" asserts that the situation is different with regard to the resident alien גר (*gër* = alien) who resides in Israel on a relatively permanent basis.[15] Milgrom has summarized the situation for the alien as follows:

> Though the *ger* enjoyed equal protection with the Israelite under the law, he was not the same legal status; he neither enjoyed the same privileges nor was bound by the same obligation. Whereas the civil law held the citizen and the *ger* to be equal status (e.g. Lev 24:22; Num 35:15), the religious law made distinctions according to the following underlying principle: The *gër* is bound by the prohibitive commandments but not by the performative one. For example, the *gër* is under no requirement to observe the festivals. The paschal sacrifice is explicitly declared a voluntary observation for the *gër*: Whereas an Israelite abstains from the sacrifice on pain of *karet*, the *gër* may observe it provided he is circumcised (Exod 12:47-48; Num 9:13-14). In fact, the injunction to dwell in sukkot is explicitly directed to the "Israelite citizen" (Lev 23:42), which by implication, excludes the *gër*. Similarly, the *gër* may participate in the voluntary sacrificial cult if he follows its prescription (Num 15:14-16); Lev 22: 17ff).[16]

Awabdy article encourages Christians to revisit and reinterpret the Bible in order in more faithfully align themselves with God's mission in the world. As a text case Awabdy offer's Leviticus and concludes with some suggestion for reforming mission theology and praxis.[17]

---

13 Knohl I, *The Sanctuary of Silence: The Priestly Torah and the Holiness School* (Minneapolis, MN: Fortress, 1995), 21, 53, 93. Knohl draws a distinction between the earliest layer of the Priestly tradition, which he calls the Priestly Torah, and a later Holiness School, to whom he ascribed the ethical concern with aliens. Knohl asserts that the Holiness School influenced Priestly tradition even before the exile in Babylon.

14 R. Rendorff, "The *Ger* in the Priestly Laws of the Pentateuch," in *Ethnicity and the Bible*, edited by M. G. Brett (Leiden: E.J.Brill, 1996), 86-87.

15 Patric D. Miller, *The Religion of Ancient Israel,*(Louisville, Kentucky: Westminster John Knox Press, 2000), 201.

16 Jacob, Milgrom, *Numbers: The Traditional Hebrew Text with the New JPS Translation.* JPS Torah Commentary, (Philadelphia: Jewish Publication Society, 1990), 399.

17 Mark A. Awabdy, "Green Eggs and Shawarma: Reinterpreting the Bible, Reforming Mission with Leviticus גר as Test case," *Asbury Journal* 66 (2011), 31-45.

Mauch shows that the root meaning of "sojourner" is especially evident in early texts, and that this basic meaning persists in the later stages of biblical history and literature. Two further connotations developed in the Covenant code and D, and in the postexilic period. In the Covenant code (Ex 20:23-33) and preceding Decalogue (20:1-17) and D, גר (*gër* = "so-journer," "stranger") designates, not the immigrant Hebrew, but the indigenous population of Palestine conquered by the Hebrews. He further states that postexilic period Deutro-Isaiah takes up the promise to Abraham ("by you all the families of the earth will bless themselves" (Gen 12:3b)) and set forth the universal scope of Yahweh and Israel: "This one will say, "I am the Lord's" another will be called by the name of Jacob yet another will write on his hand, "The Lord's" and adopt the name of Israel" (Isa 44:5; 42:1-4; 49:6; 55:4-5).[18]

Albertz paper concludes that there are markedly different concepts about the treatment of "strangers" in the Pentateuch, ranging from social integration of poor resident aliens and their religious assimilation in the covenant code and Deuteronomy to the legally regulated co-existence of foreign inhabitants of the province of yehud in the Holiness code. Furthermore, one finds a controlled integration of "stranger" in the Holiness redaction and the later priestly legislation. This difference has to do with different theological concepts of the Deutronomic and priestly legislators and the very different social and political challenges that the legislators had to cope with. Given those challenges, the biblical legislators tried to limit social and political conflicts with different kinds of "strangers" without giving up Israel's distinct religious and ethnic identity.[19]

Evident in the early text as *ger* experienced by the ancestors in Gen 12, 20 can be interpreted as alienation of the ancestors. The real problem lies behind this that of a small group confronted by a superpower is also read negatively. Coats, on the other hand, has defined Genesis 12:10-20 as a "tale" in that it is simply told with the focus on the plot. He has pointed out that the "tales themselves do not mention the promise of progeny and that in each case the issue raised in the plot is the patriarch's deception, selfish self-protection, and separation," which result in "plagues on the one who caused disruption" and eventually in "an appropriate remedy for the problem". This issue finds analogy in the context only in Gen 12:3. The central argument of these stories is that strife with the patriarch brings curse, no matter who may be at fault: "The focus of the genre on event, not theological proposition, shows the intention of the story to be a description of circumstances that obtain for people who

18 T. M. Mauch, "Sojourner," *The Interpreter's Dictionary of the Bible* (New York: Abingdon Press, 1962), 397-399. (Hereby IDB).

19 Victor, H. Matthews, abstract of *From Aliens to Proselytes: Non-Priestly and Priestly Legislation Concerning Stranger,* by Rainer Albertz, *Old Testament Abstract* 35 (February 2012), 75-85.

support the patriarch in contrast to circumstances that obtain for people who deny support for the patriarch."[20]

Cohn discusses the depiction of the relationship between the Patriarchs and native inhabitants of Canaan as portrayed in the stories of Genesis. The focus of his analysis is on the social and economic boundaries drawn between the two groups. Cohn suggests that these distinctions without recourse to religious differentiation as in the subsequent traditions provide the meaning for Israelite identity construction in the material studies.[21]

Lenchak, *Israel's Refugee Ancestor,* bases on (Deut 26:5).[22] In his article he argues that, Israel's own ancestors were also displaced person, that is, they were refugees. The story of those refugee ancestors can be found in the book of Genesis.

Kidd's monograph *Alterity and Identity in Israel: The גר in the Old Testament* follows a word-study approach.[23] Ramírez Kidd argues for a sharp distinction between the noun גר (*gër*=alien) and the verb √גור (*gur* = sojourn), however, and on this basis launches an exclusive study of the noun form alone. The distinction is overdrawn, and leads Kidd to an overly selective approach where texts that are proximate are alternately included in his analysis or excluded based solely on the criterion of noun vs. verb form.[24] The overall picture he paints thus exhibits substantial lacunae. Three examples highlight a need to attend to these gaps. First, Kidd suggests that a positive depiction of sojourn in Egypt, connected with the patriarchal stories, becomes significant during the exilic period.[25]

This proposal warrants exegetical attention to the patriarchal narratives, but because Ramírez Kidd has excluded the verb √גור (*gur* = sojourn) from his study he is not free to pursue such an analysis. Second, Kidd notes a

20 G.W. Coats, "A Threat to the Host," in *Saga, legend, Tale, Novella, Fable: Narrative Forms in the Old Testament Literature*, JSOT Sup 35 (Sheffield: JSOT Press, 1985), 72, 75, 81; Cf G. W. Coats, *Genesis with an Introduction to Narrative Literature*, Vol-1 (Grand Rapids, Michigan: William B. Eerdmans Publishing Company, 1983), 3ff.

21 Robert L. Cohn, "Negotiating (with) the Native: Ancestors and Identity in Genesis," *Harvard Theological Review* 96 (2003), 147-66.

22 Timothy A. Lenchak, "Israel's Refugee Ancestors," *The Bible Today* 35/1 (January 1997), 11-15. (Hereby *BT*).

23 José E. Ramírez Kidd, *Alterity and Identity in Israel: The גר in the Old Testament*, BZAW 283 (Berlin: Walter de Gruyter, 1999), 10.

24 For example, he excludes Deut. 26:5 from his primary analysis while including other texts in Deuteronomy, and cites Gen. 15:13 and 23:4 but disregards the numerous other references to sojourn in Genesis. The 19 references that couple noun and verb forms together in one verse, Ramírez Kidd simply analyzes as instances of the noun, dismissing the accompanying verbal forms as dependent. Kidd, *Alterity and Identity in Israel: The גר in the Old Testament,* 17.

25 Kidd, *Alterity and Identity in Israel: The גר in the Old Testament,* 91-98.

connection between pilgrim theology in the Psalms and ancestral sojourn in Canaan, but again does not treat the relevant Genesis texts.[26] Third, Kidd briefly outlines the connection between the LXX translation of sojourn texts and the development of the idea of sojourn in the New Testament.[27] He highlights the sojourn of the patriarchs as foundational to Christians' self-identification as an alien people, while neglecting direct analysis of these influential texts. In all, Kidd's analysis suggests a greater significance for the sojourn texts in Genesis than the parameters of his study allow. My study aims to correct this omission, and the integration of verbal and nominal forms of sojourn in one study is an essential element of method serving this end. A full examination of references to patriarchal sojourn in texts *beyond* Genesis is beyond the scope of this study, but a thorough treatment of the Genesis texts themselves lays a solid foundation for further investigation of the larger connections Kidd suggests.

All the studies assessed above do not address the issue of the proposed title. Reading Pentateuch from the Tribal worldview is yet to receive proper attention. Therefore, the present topic is quite different from the above said works.

8. Method of the Study

The method, which is proposed to be used in this research, is ideological approach. The researcher has engaged in multiple approaches like socio-historical critical approach, hermeneutical and exegetical analysis in order to expose textual aggression in a particular biblical passage.

No single method of doing ideological criticism exists. As Gottwald remarked, "it comes in many voices, speaks many languages, and resides in many different disciplines and critical approaches, including psychoanalytic theory, cultural criticism, sociolinguistics, subaltern studies, feminist theory, and deconstruction, to name a few."[28] Consequently, the practice of ideological criticism is often seen as a form of resistance to unacknowledged and oppressive power and thus as raising issues of the ethics of interpretation. One chooses to interpret in a way that supports or opposes the power dynamics at work in the text. Ideology as the general material production of ideas, beliefs, and values in social life. Secondly, ideology can refer to (true or false) ideas and beliefs that symbolize the circumstances and life experiences of a particular; socially significant group of class. According to Clines:

> "Ideological criticism systematically asks about the ideological interests inscribed in the text. That is to say, it does not view the texts

26 Kidd, *Alterity and Identity in Israel: The* גר *in the Old Testament*, 104.

27 Kidd, *Alterity and Identity in Israel: The* גר *in the Old Testament,* 118-29.

28 Norman Gottwald, *The Tribes of Yahweh: A Sociology of the Religion of Liberated Israel, 1250–1050 B.C.E.* (Maryknoll, N.Y.: Orbis, 1979).

> primarily as historical documents...nor as theological documents... nor as purely literary texts with the status of works of art, but as ideological documents that serve some particular or group interest. Such a criticism is of course not entirely new... What is new is the emphasis on the partisanship of every text, on the role of conflict among various groups as a model of ancient society, on a foregrounding of the ideological issue, and especially, on the demand to press beyond mere description of the ideology of the text to a critique of it."[29]

The ideological criticism that informs reseracher investigation requires a twofold task. Using an *extrinsic analysis*, I determine the complex interrelationship between material modes of production and ideologies in the society that produces the biblical text. Secondly, *intrinsic analysis* investigates the rhetorical strategies of the text itself to ascertain the different ways in which the text inscribes and reworks ideology. In this process both extrinsic and intrinsic method of biblical exegesis and hermeneutics will be employed.

Since the researcher will be taking up Gottwald's understanding of ancient Israelite modes of production; I offer his definition of "mode of production":

> In a narrower sense, mode of production...refers to the way human capacities and technology are socially organized for the labor necessary to meet basic human needs and to allocate what is produced. In a broader sense, mode of production includes the social ramifications of the labor process in class and status divisions, in political process, in family organization, and in juridical procedures.[30]

Yee[31] the extrinsic analysis utilizes social-scientific methods to help shed light on the sociohistorical circumstances of a text's production. Extrinsic

---

29 J. A. Clines, "Biblical Interpretation in an international Perspective," *Biblical Interpretation,* 1 (1993), 67-87.

30 Norman K. Gottwald, "Sociology (Ancient Israel)." *Anchor Bible Dictionary* 6. New York: Doubleday, (1992), 83.

31 Gale A. Yee, "Ideological Criticism: Judges 17-21 and the Dismembered Body," *Judges and Method New Approaches in Biblical Studies,* edited by Gale A. Yee (Minneapolis: Fortress Press, 1995), 147; Cf. David J. A. Clines, *Interested Parties: The Ideology of Writers and Readers of the Hebrew Bible* (Sheffield: Sheffield Academic Press, 1995). Clines asserts: "On the surface, their texts lay claim to coherence and rationality, and they give the appearance of sincerity and either moral fervor or objectivity. But beneath the surface there are issues of power, of self-identity and security, of group solidarity, of fear and desire, of need and greed that have also played a role in the production of the text, sometimes a leading role." This is the concern of ideological criticism of the text. Text

analyses are the social locations of power, their conflicts and their ideologies. Taking the opposing perspective, intrinsic analysis asks about those voices that are excluded; perhaps those of other tribal groups, of women, or the poor. Intrinsic analysis uncovers competing voices, marginalized by the society's power structures, which are encoded in the text by their very absence. The text conceals and repressed these voices in its attempts to resolve the contradictory opinion they pose.

The researcher has selected a specific approach that provides a distinctive lens through which to view the texts. Tribal hermeneutics is a part of liberation hermeneutics, but the tribal people read the bible in the context of identity crisis, alienation from their land and culture, exploitation and economic dependency. All this require a re-interpretation of the Bible, the Bible will not only lose its significance, and Christianity will remain superficial without really taking root into the tribal cultures

I have chosen the translation "aliens" for the word cluster √גורג (*gur*)/ גר (*gër*)/מגור (*megur);* which is translated as "Sojourn" in English. The reason is because it is a modern social and political connotations evoked by some alternative translation proposed such as "resident alien," "immigrant," or "client."[32] This has a wider meaning "Sojourn" may be an old-fashion word.

9. Structure

The first chapter gives special attention on the question of how the legal status of the alien and the understanding of the culture and literature of Ancient West Asia help us better understands specific elements of the narratives.

The second chapter is to investigate ancient Israel from the perspective of ethnic identity. The researcher's agenda in this area derives from the approached formulated by Hutchinson and Smith. The researcher has opted for identity as ideology.

The third chapter attentions are given on Alien and Ethnic Identity in ancestral narratives of Genesis. An attempt is made to offer a helpful matrix for relating ideas of identity, land and community.

The fourth chapter is the Ideological contestation concerning Israel's being alien in Egypt. Treatment of Aliens in the Book of Exodus and Deuteronomy law is the subject of this study. This study presumes that biblical law construct

---

and readers are fair game for ideological critics, and especially when texts are used by the readers in the service of power and of social control. Cf. Jonathan E. CycK, "A map of Ideology for Biblical Critics" *Rethinking Contexts, Rereading Texts Contribution from the Social Sciences to Biblical Interpretation, e*dited by M, Daniel Carroll R (Sheffield, England: Sheffield Academic press, 2000), 108-145.

32 Robert Alter, *Genesis: Translation and Commentary* (New York: W.W. Norton and co., 1996), 109.

identity and therefore builds on earlier work that identifies such a function in the Deuteronomic history.

The fifth chapter is to study the text of Leviticus 17, 24, and 25 anew to tell whether and to what extend it deserves its status in constructing the identity of the land. What kind of justice does it offer and to whom; whose interests are represented by the text; what understanding of the social world does it embody, and how close is that to anything we might recognize.

The sixth chapter attempts to delineate how tribal communities and individuals negotiate their identities within the nation. Racial discrimination against the people of North East India is most felt at the institution where their Indian-ness is question. The tribals always regard the land as the symbol of unity and it is the land that gives them an identity. The development is viewed within the paradigm of colonial contradictions historical events and differential development.

Chapter 1

The Status of Alien in Ancient West Asia

1. Introduction

In order to evaluate the historical and theological significance of the laws pertaining to the aliens in Old Testament, first we need to put them in the context of ancient Near Eastern legal texts.[33] These texts can provide a framework within which we can appreciate the distinct nuances of the Old Testament laws, as well as the traditions which they have in common with their neighbours. There are two aspects of Near Eastern culture which are of importance to a study of the legal status of the alien. (1) The nature of ancient legal collections: their purpose intended audience, literary and subsequent historical values; and (2) the social and legal status of aliens in these cultures. Aliens are a phenomenon that all societies, both ancient and modern, must deal with. We can expect that some societies will include their treatment in legal precepts, & in other societies, social moves regarding aliens will not become inscribed in law. The ancient Near East is based on texts rather than a direct study of living peoples; we are limited by what the texts tell us. This means that the task of penetrating to identity and ethnicity is often complicated. For example, the biblical text tells us what was distinctive about Israelites and Judahites that made them different from the surrounding peoples, but what we have are the views of the biblical writers, not necessarily of the average Israelite or Judahite who might have seen his or her identity in quite different terms. We will study when data permits how other ancient Mediterranean societies dealt

33 The Ancient Near Text will be hereby referred to as Ancient West Asia.

with aliens. The researcher will pay special attention to the legal provisions of the גר (*gër* = alien) in the Ancient West. Asia and how the stipulation related to the people of Israel. We shall now briefly discuss them.

1.1. Ancient West Asia Legal Collection

In looking at the history of the Ancient West Asia one can know that the protection of the widow, orphan, and the poor was their common policy. Protecting orphans and widows was a theologically grounded social concern in second millennium Egyptian and Mesopotamian texts. Protecting the גר became a specifically Israelites concern as it is evidence in one of Israel's earliest legal traditions, the Book of the Covenant (BC Exod 20-23). An harmony occurs in Exod 22:20-21: (1) גר (*gër* = alien); (2) יתום (*yathowm*= orphan); (3) אלמנה (*'almanah* = widow). After this the גר-orphan-widow becomes distinctive triad of the so called Deuteronomic code (Deut 12-26).

For example, Egypt, held responsible its hierarchs for the welfare of those under them, but as a closed society. As for Ramirez: "the principle of solidarity applied primarily to its members. This may explain why, although the protection of the weak was a common policy in the legal and wisdom tradition of the ancient Near Eastern societies, the stranger was very seldom mentioned among them."[34] This is presumably at odds with Van Houten, who asserts that the Israelite community denied the גר full religious status, on the other hand T. R. Hobbs, contends that Israel did not show hospitality to the גר because the גר was no stranger, but already a covenant members.[35] Their openion differs but aliens were mentioned among them.

1.1.1. Historical Connection

The law of Ancient West Asia is by no means that of a single system; it is the product of many societies, with different languages and cultures, that flourished, declined, and were replaced by others over the course of thousand of years. The people of Israel were late comer in the scenario of the ancient West Asia therefore, they learn from the earlier settlers.

Although the main aim is to draw on comparative material to elucidate biblical law as "the law of ancient Israel was an integral part of a much wider legal tradition,"[36] the rational for studying Old Testament laws in the context of ancient oriental law presupposes that the laws in the Old Testament are in some way related to other legal collections in the ancient West Asia, and that

34 Jose E. Ramirez Kidd, *Alterity and Identity in Israel: The* גר *in the Old Testament,* BZAW 282 (Berlin/New York: Walter de Gruyter, 1999), 39.

35 T. R. Hobbs, "Hospitality in the First Testament and the 'Telological Fallacy,'" *JSOT* 95 (2001), 20-24.

36 Postgate J. N. Review of the *Studies in Biblical and Cuneiform Law*, by Westbrook, Raymond, *Vetus Testamendum* 40/3 (July 1992), 431-432.

there are historical collections between the people of Israel and other people of the fertile Crescent. Speiser asserts that, "there was much contact between the peoples of the Fertile Crescent, that there was a common culture in ancient Mesopotamia, and that this is reflected in customary law."[37]

However, for Postgate, "Old Testament law does not seem to have been influenced by Egyptian legal practice."[38] Egypt has left behind no body of law which is analogous to the law collection of Mesopotamia or those in the Old Testament. Wilson asserts that, "There are no textual references to laws, nor accounts of law-giving by the king or an official until the tradition of king Bocchoris, c.700 B.C."[39] Since Pharaoh was believed to be divine, law proceeded from his mouth. The codification of law was neither necessary nor proper. Since each new Pharaoh was a new god, it would not be fitting for him to be heir to a standing tradition outside of himself.

Similarly, the laws of the Hittites do not seem to have had much influence on Old Testament laws. Meek rightly said: "the content of the Hittite laws is quite distinct from Old Testament laws and reflects a different traditional culture."[40] Nor did Syria-Palestine have a separate legal tradition which exerted much influence on Old Testament law. This conclusion is based partly on arguments from silence since no codes of laws have been recovered in Syria, and because there is evidence that Syrian Palestinian law was itself influenced by the ideology of the Babylonian legal tradition indeed, there appears to have much contact with the influence from Mesopotamia.

Referring to the Mesopotamian law Roland de Vaux feels that, "there are many similarities between Mesopotamia law and Old Testament laws are to be explained by a common legal tradition which was an integral part of a similar underlying culture."[41] Kensky pointed out that, "the judicial principles, such as retribution, which underlie the laws, produced a similar customary

---

37 E. A. Speiser, "Cuneiform law and the history of Civilization," *Proceedings of the American Philosophical Society* 107 (1963), 538-39 argues that the strength of Mesopotamia law is indicated by its use in Assyria at a time when Assyria was an enemy of Babylon and by its existence in Ugarit.

38 H. J. Boecker, *Law and the Administration of Justice in the Old Testament and Ancient East,* translated by J. Moiser (Minneapolis: Augsburg, 1980), 17.

39 J. A. Wilson, "Authority and Law in Ancient Egypt," *Journal of American Oriental Society*, Supp 17 (1954), 5. Hereby *JAOS.*

40 T. J. Meek, "The origin in Hebrew law," in *Hebrew Origins* (New York: Harper & Row, 1936), 62. There is one Hittite law which is close to the Old Testament law i.e. Deut 22:23-27. Both laws deal with the rape of a women, and make a distinction between a woman raped in the city and a woman raped in the country, and declare her innocent if rape outside the city.

41 Roland de Vaux, *Ancient Israel: Its life and Institutions,* translated by John McHugh (London: Darton, Longman & Todd, 1961), 146.

law."[42] Westbrooke argue that, "all the ancient West Asia system belonged in varying degree to a common legal culture, one very different from any that obtain today. At the very least, they shared a legal ontology: a way of looking at the law that reflected their view of the world and determined the horizon of the lawmaker."[43] The question is bound up with the fundamental issues of the nature of the ancient legal source.

1.1.2. A Comparison of Mesopotamia and Biblical Law

The importance of discussion for this study of the legal status of the גר to keep in mind the nature, purpose and scope of these ancient Mesopotamian law codes. What kind of comparison can be drawn between ancient Mesopotamian legal and collection and Biblical law? There are Old Testament parallels laws and stories from the ancient West Asia and at other time the differences between the traditions. Mathews and Benjamin argues, "the Book of the Covenant and the Laws of Hammurabi has been the focus of the discussion. In the Bible, the Covenant Code (Exod 21-23), the Holiness Code (Lev 17-26) and the Deuteronomic Code (Deut 12-26) are parallel to the Code of Shulgi."[44] Shulgi (2094-2047) ruled during the Third Dynasty of Ur. The Book of Covenant and the Law of Hammurabi have been the focus of the discussion, since the greatest parallel exist between the laws of these two codes. Mendenhall point out that Law of Hammurabi reflects, "a class society which values human life on the bases of class, whereas the Covenant Code, with one exception, advocates impartial justice."[45] As the laws of Hammurabi were not referred to in legal practice, so also the biblical laws are not referred to by the judges, or any other practitioners of the law in the biblical text.

1.2. The Literary Genre of Ancient West Asia Law

Having made the case that our understanding of the Old Testament law will be enriched and refined by examining other law collections from the ancient West

42 See the discussion of the principle of equal retribution in Near Eastern law and Old Testament law by T. Frymer-Kensky, "Tit for Tat: The principles of equal Retribution in Near Eastern and biblical Law," *Biblical Archaeologist* 43 (1980), 230-34.

43 Raymond Westbrooke, "The Character of Ancient Near Eastern law," in *A History of Ancient Near Eastern Law,* edited by Ramond West brook, Vol. 1 (Leiden, Boston: Brill, 2003), 4.

44 Victor H. Mathews and Don C. Benjamin, *Old Testament Parallels Laws and Stories from the Ancient Near East* (New York/Mahwah, New Jesey: Paulist Press, 2006), 101-2. The Code of Shulgi is the oldest system of laws recovered by archaeologist from the world of the Bible. The Book of the Covenant.

45 G. E. Mendenhall, "Ancient Oriental and Biblical Law," *Biblical Archaeologist* 17/2 (May, 1954), 26-46.

Asia, the researcher need to investigate what the nature of those law codes was. The law codes to which the researcher comparing the Old Testament laws are:

1. Laws of Eshnunna, dated to c.1930 B.C.[46]
2. Lipil-Ishtar Law code, dated to c. 1868-1857 B.C.[47]
3. Code of Hammurabi, dated to, c. 1728-1686 B.C.[48]
4. Middle Assyrian Laws dated to c. 1112-1074 B.C.[49]

If we define a law code as a body of law which seeks to be comprehensive and to which judges are bound when deciding cases, then none of the law collections qualify as a law code. Firstly, it is clear that they are not intended to be exhaustive. For example, the Laws of Hammurabi contain no laws pertaining to murder or the giving of loans, yet evidence from contract tablets of the time indicate that these were dealt with according to a known legal procedure.

The function of Mesopotamia legal collections is difficult to ascertain. The only statement within the law codes about the intended human audience is found in the epilogue to the laws of Hammurabi:

> Let any wronged man who has a lawsuit come before the statute of me, the king of justice, and let him have my inscribed stela read aloud to him, thus may he hear my precious pronouncements and let my stela reveal the lawsuit for him . . . May any king who will appear in the land in the future, at any time, observe the pronouncements of justice that I inscribed upon my stela. May he not alter the judgments that I rendered and the verdicts that I gave.[50]

On the basis of the prologue and epilogue sections Paul has suggested that, "these documents are a royal *apologia.* Prologue and epilogue are extant for the laws of Hammurabi and in part for the Lipit-Ishtar collection, and it has been argued that all the Mesopotamian law collection evinced this three-part structure."[51]They indicate that the legal collections have been promulgated soon after a change in government. The main purpose of publication would be to give legal credence to the new state. Whitelam asserts, "The law codes

46 Albrecht Goetze, "The Laws of Eshunna," in *Ancient Near Eastern Texts Relating to the Old Testament*, edited by James B. Pritchard (Princeton, New Jersey: Princeton University Press, 1969), 161-63. Hereby *ANET.*

47 S. N. Kramer, "Lipit-Ishtar Lawcode" in *ANET...*, 159-61.

48 Theophil J. Meek, "The Code of Hammurabi" in *ANET...*, 163-80.

49 Theophil J. Meek, " The Middle Assyrian Laws" in *ANET...*, 180-88.

50 Martha T. Roth, *Law Collections from Mesopotamia and Asia Minor,* Society of Biblical Literature (Atlanta: Scholar Press, 1995), 134.

51 S. M. Paul, *Studies in the Book of the Covenant in the Light of Cuniform and Biblical Law* (Leiden: Brill, 1970), 11.

would serve to justify the King's position as the head of state."[52] The code of Hammurabi articulated in the prologue: "When Marduk commissioned me to guide the people aright, to direct the land, I established law and justice in the language of the land, thereby promoting the welfare of the people."[53] They emphasize that he has fulfilled his divine mandate as the faithful shepherd and judge of his people.

There are growing number of scholars who have argued that the so-called Mesopotamian "law codes" or cuneiform collections consist of different meanings extended over long time-periods and exhibit social, political, economic and ethnic differences. In determining whether the Mesopotamian cuneiform collections are an authentic source for Mesopotamian law traditions, scholars have developed different theories each of which has different variations. It is argued that in the light of the existing theories, if the Mesopotamian cuneiform collections are not an authentic source of law and therefore not a law code, the generic naming of the cuneiform collections of Mesopotamia as "codes" or "law codes" encompasses a certain meaning, which may obscure and confuse the debate with regards to their true meaning and correct application in the study of ancient Mesopotamian law traditions.

The fact that the Code of Hammurabi was recopied for more than a millennium with no significant changes indicates to him that at some point it has changed its genre. It has become canonical literature and was recopied in scribal schools for its own sake. In conclusion, Westbrook claims that, "when the legal texts are copied without changes being made, then they are no longer functioning as references for judges, but that when legal collections are being revised, this indicates that they are being applied in the courts."[54] This indicates that when the laws are preserved without the prologue and epilogue, there is evidence that they are being copied with changes and addition being made, and when they are exposed in a location at which legal disputes are settled, then the laws are functioning as a set of precedents which are referred to in the process of negotiation.

1.2.1. Mesopotamia Law

In the Mesopotamia law there is a record of the earliest law collection (ca. 2100) from the city of Ur in Mesopotamia has been attributed to King Ur-Namma or his son Shulgi. Following the collapse of the Akkad Dynasty (ca. 2334-2193), Ur-Namma founded the Ur-III dynasty and united the city-states

52 K. W. Whitelam, *The Just King: Monarchical Judicial Authority in Ancient Israel,* JSOT Sup 12 (Sheffield: JSOT Press, 1979), 22.

53 Theophil J. Meek, "The Code of Hammurabi," 165.

54 Christiana Van Houten, *Alien in Israelite Law: A Study of the Changing Legal Status of Strangers in Ancient Israel,* JSOT Suplt 107 (Sheffield: Sheffield Academic Press, 1991), 29.

of Sumer and Akkad, south and northern Mesopotamia, respectively. The prologue reads: "… Ur-Namma, the mighty warrior, lord of the city of Ur, king of the lands of Sumer and Akkad…[by the might] of the god Nanna, my lord, [by the true command of god Utu(?)], I established [justice in the land (?)]."[55] It was Shulgi, however, who was known for his administrative and judicial reforms and may have used his father's legacy to advance his own. Whether the laws originated from Ur-Namma or Shulgi, the royal intent was to maintain the land's equilibrium and to receive honor for doing so. In the prologue "Ur-Namma" isolates at least three groups from whom he liberated Sumer and Akkad: one, "the *nisku*-people"[56] who "had-control of the fields"; two, the 'sea-captains" who "had control of the foreign maritime trade"; three, "those who appropriate (?) [the oxen]… those who appropriate(?) [the sheep …]." Later he recounts that he, by the strength of god Nanna, "liberated Akshak, Marad, Girkal, Kazallu, and their settlements, and for Uṣarum, whatever (territories) were under the subjugation of Anshan."[57] Apropos to our study is this statement of liberation that follows a lacuna in the cuneiform tablet:

> "[…] I returned. I established freedom for the Akkadians and foreigners (?) in the lands of Sumer and Akkad, for those conducting foreign maritime trade (free from) the sea-captains, for the herdsmen (free from) those who appropriate (?) oxen, sheep, and donkeys."[58] While "foreigners" (*gi* [*rs-ra*]) is a restored reading of a broken text, they are paired with the Akkadians as those "in the lands of Sumer and Akkad" who benefited from the king's liberation program. In contrast to the *nisku*-people and Anshan, who were a negative presence supplanted by the king, the *gi*[*rs-ra*] "foreigners" were granted residence and freedom in Sumero-Akkadian city-states. The final words of the prologue read, 'I establish justice in the land."[59]

This probably functions as a synopsis of Ur-Namma's (or Shulgi's) record of actions, beginning with his care for Ur's subclasses: "I did not deliver the orphan to the rich. I did not deliver the widow to the mighty. I did not deliver the man with but one shekel to the man with one mina (i.e., 60 shekels). I did not deliver the man with but one sheep to the man with one ox."[60] The above

55 Roth, *Law Collections from Mesopotamia and Asia Minor,* 15.

56 The *nisku* people were probably a menial or lower-class of persons. Cf. Roth, *Law Collections from Mesopotamia and Asia Minor,* 271.

57 Roth, *Law Collections from Mesopotamia and Asia Minor,* 5-16.

58 Roth, *Law Collections from Mesopotamia and Asia Minor,* 15.

59 Roth, *Law Collections from Mesopotamia and Asia Minor,* 17.

60 Roth, *Law Collections from Mesopotamia and Asia Minor,* 16.

example shows that the Mesopotamian law has a place for the alien, orphan and the widow proper care and justice is maintained.

Four centuries after Ur-Namma, and two centuries after Lipit-Ishtar,[61] the law collection attributed to Eshnunna (ca. 1770) likely emerged during the reign of Dadusha, who later fell to King Hammurabi. Although more than one law may relate to our topic,[62] one stands out: "If a foreigner [*ubārum*], a *napṭaru*, or a *mudû* wishes to sell his beer, the woman innkeeper shall sell the beer for him at the current rate."[63] *Ubārum*, translated by Roth as "foreigner," is probably more precisely rendered "resident alien."

A non-citizen has no protection under the local law, except insofar that as a foreign citizen of a friendly state, he was protected by the rules of international law. A citizen, by contrast, was entitled in theory to expect protection under the law and the respect of his legal rights even by his monarch. A ruler could grand special protection to resident aliens (Akk. *Ubaru/;* Heb. *ger*). Once granted resident status, foreigners appear to have had equal access to the local courts.

A foreigner could acquire a protected status from the local ruler and thus become a resident alien (*ubarum*). Law of Eshunna 41 protects the "resident alien along with other categories of outsider from economic exploitation by a taverneress."[64] Such a law may suggest that the *ubārum* (and *napṭaru* and *mudû* classes) was at times unjustly denied the right of selling their beer at the inn, or was permitted to sell their beer only at a lower price, or was required to pay innkeepers a larger fee to sell their beer. They were, in any case, by this law protected from a type of unfair trade.

---

61 In the prologue of the laws of Lipit-Ishtar (ca. 1930), fifth dynast of Isin, Lipit-Ishtar announces that he liberated Sumer and Akkad, established justice, eradicated violence, restored children and fathers to each other, among other beneficent deeds. The first laws of possible relevance relate to the *miqtu*-person whom Roth defines as a "palace dependent or client" (Roth, *Law Collections…* 24, 29, cf. Deut 24:14 and prologue-epilogue). Another law reads: "If he [a father?] takes a slave […] he dies […] an outsider […] marries (?) […]" ("Laws of Lipit-Ishtar" [Roth, *Law Collections*, 30]). Unfortunately, this tablet is irreparable.

62 A second law from Eshnunna may be relevant, but not demonstrably. This law protects a man, captured and residing in a foreign land, from losing his wife to another: "If a man should be captured or abducted during a raiding expedition or while on patrol (?), even should he reside in a foreign land for a long time, should someone else marry his wife and even should she bear a child, whenever he returns he shall take back his wife:" "Laws of Eshunna." Roth, *Law Collections…* 63.

63 Roth, *Law Collections from Mesopotamia and Asia Minor,* 65.

64 Raymond Westbrooke, "Old Babylonian Period," in *A History of Ancient Near Eastern Law,* edited by Ramond West brook, Vol. 1 (Leiden, Boston: Brill, 2003), 377.

1.2.2. Societal Tensions Produced by Ethnic Differences or Alienness

Tensions out of ethnic differences were rarely detected, a tendency toward coexistence and assimilation more often emerged. For example, there is evidence of ethnic tension between the Sumerians and Akkadians in early Mesopotamia. Likewise, Amorites appear to have settled peacefully among Sumerians and Akkadians as early as the late third millennium BCE, and the Kassites who ruled Babylonia after the fall of Hammurabi's dynasty became so thoroughly assimilated that we still have little knowledge of their language. Nuzi's population around 1500 BCE included several possibly ethnic groups with no evidence of friction among them. In New Kingdom Egypt, Asiatics who had arrived as nomads or slaves were assimilated, individuals bearing Asiatic names entered the ranks of officialdom, and Asiatic deities were absorbed into the Egyptian pantheon. Nubians and Libyans also were incorporated into the ranks of the Egyptian military.

Complicating this assessment, according to an Akkadian proverb: "Flesh is flesh, blood is blood, alien is alien, foreigner is foreigner."[65] Being a foreigner could indeed make a person "other" if a foreigner did not adopt local norms and customs. Thus, in Mesopotamia, to the extent that they remained beyond the pale of civilized behavior, Gutians and Amorites were seen as barbarians. Until they actually began to reside in Egypt, surrounding peoples were similarly regarded as despicable and uncivilized. The Hebrew Bible also revealed that resident aliens might be subject to exclusion. Robertson remarks, "resident alien were forbidden to own land."[66] Especially notable is the stigma that was imposed on foreigners from Syria and southern Babylonia whom the Assyrians brought to Samaria to replenish its population after deporting the Israelites. According to Lemche the foreigners who were brought from Syria and Babylon, "Centuries later, the Jews regarded their descendants, the Samaritans, as pariahs who were not allowed membership in the Jewish community."[67] By and large, being of different ethnicity did not necessarily entail social disadvantage.

1.2.3. Egypt

With the eighteenth Dynasty arrive the new kingdom, the period during which the *Instruction of Amenemope* was written. Material concerning widow,

65 Benjamin R. Foster, *Before the Muses: An Anthology of Akkadian Literature* (Bethesda, MD: CDL Press, 1996), 346.

66 John F. Robertson, "Social Tensions in the Ancient Near East," in *A Companion To the Ancient Near East*, edited by Daniel C. Snell (Malden: Blackwell Publishing Ltd., 2005), 209.

67 N. Lemche, "The History of Ancient Syria and Palestine: An Overview," in *Civilization of the Ancient Near East,* edited by Sasson J., Vol. 11 (New York: Charles Scribner's sons, 1995), 1213.

orphan and the poor is much restricted in Egyptian literature. This is due to the fact that no legal code has as yet been discovered. The protection of the weak was also the ideal of kings and monarchs (rulers of a district). In the "instruction(s) /Wisdom of Amenemope(t)," a wisdom collection dating originally to the Ramesside period (ca. 1300-1075), the twenty eight chapter includes imperatives to act beneficently towards the widow, stranger, brothers and the poor:

> Do not pounce on a *widow* when you find her in the fields and then fail to be patient with her reply. Do not refuse your oil jar to *stranger,* double it before *your brother*. God prefers him honors the *poor* to him who worships the wealthy.[68]

Thus, perhaps it is surprising to find in this context a wisdom imperative commanding generous towards the stranger in Egypt.

Gardiner explain, "at the beginning of the Dynasty XII there lived a nomarch named Ameny who boasted that he ruled his province with justice, respecting the poor man's daughter and the widow."[69] If we take a glance at the occurrence of this ideology and policy in the wisdom Literature it is obvious that the ideal of respecting the right of the weak, widow, and the orphan flourished in times of decay or at the beginning of a new period. There is ample evidence of this policy at the end of the First Intermediate period and the beginning of the middle kingdom (2000 B.C.). In the didactic discourses of the eloquent peasant, the peasant says to Rensi, the chief steward: "Because thou art the father of the orphan, the husband of the widow..."[70] this statement by the peasant is of the utmost importance, because a married woman had no legal personality after her husband death, as was also the case with minor orphans. It was the duty of the king or monarch to protect their rights in the same way as the father of the family should have done.

In the instruction of Marikare the conduct of a king against his people is prescribed. One of the maxims indicates that, if the King desires long life on earth, he must not oppress the widow and annex the property which someone has inherited from his father. Another text which originated not long after this is the instruction of King Amenemhet. One of these is charity to the poor and the elevation of minors. Emphasis on this policy and ideal is quite understandable

68 Mark A. Awabdy, *Immigrants and Innovative Law* (Tubingen, Germany: Mohr Siebeck, 2014), 236, Citing "Instruction of Amenemope," translated by Miriam Lichtheim (COS 1. 47:121).

69 Cf. Sir Alan H. Gardiner, *Egypt of the Pharaohs* (Oxford: Oxford University Press, 1961), 129.

70 Pritchard, *ANET,* 408.

when we take into consideration the confusion and abuse of the general rights of the people during the First Intermediate period.

This period of increased infertility coincided in Egypt with the transition from the highly organized Old Kingdom to the decentralized, chaotic conditions of the First Intermediate Period. Increased infertility and consequently diminished rainfall in central Africa probably produced a series of low Nile floods. The Egyptian state's survival was linked to the effectiveness of those floods. The literary composition known as the Admonitions of Ipuwer provided eloquent, if hyperbolic, testimony to the chaos of this calamitous time:

> . . . A man looks upon his son as his enemy. . .
> The virtuous man goes in mourning because of what has happened in the land . . .
> Foreigners have become Egyptians everywhere . . .
> The land is full of gangs; a man goes to plough with his shield . . .
> Indeed, the ways are blocked, the roads are watched,
> Men sit in the bushes, until the night traveller comes, in order to plunder his load.
> What is upon him is taken away; he is thrashed with blows of a stick and criminally slain . . .
> Indeed, the scribes of the land-register – their writings are destroyed; the grain of Egypt is common property.
> Indeed, the laws of the council-chamber are thrown out,
> Men walk on them in public places,
> Beggars break them up in the streets . . .
> Beggars come and go in the Great Houses [law courts].
> Indeed, the children of princes are cast out in the streets . . .
> The king has been disposed of by beggars.[71]

This description might have been used for didactic (teaching purpose) or to add legitimacy to the coming of new ruler. Nonetheless, it clearly recounts the chaos caused when the law of the society broke down and people's survival was threatened.

The famous instruction of Amenemopet originated ca.1000 B.C. Here again there is concern for the oppressed and disabled. A maxim declares that, "the oppressed must not be robbed and that no harshness may be inflicted on

71 W. W. Hallow and K. L. Younger, eds., *The Context of Scripture: Canonical Composition from the Biblical World* (Leiden: Brill, 1997), 94-96, Cf. F. Charles Fensham, "Widow, orphan, and the poor in Ancient near Eastern legal and Wisdom Literature," *Journal of near Eastern Studies* 21/2 (April 1962), 129-137.

the disabled."[72] We have ample evidence that kings and rulers were encouraged to protect the weak and the needy people.

In spite of the lack of legal material and the fact that we have mainly used wisdom literature as our source, the parallel trend between Mesopotamian policies of the protection of the weak and that of Egypt is clear. It is regarded as a virtue of kings and rulers an as an important part of the duty of the sun-god. As in Mesopotamia the religious ethics are closely intertwined in Egypt with the social ethics. It is to a certain extent, however possible to trace the social policy of protection back to its very roots in Egyptian history.

1.2.4. The Alien in Bedouin Society

Old Testament Scholars have drawn analogies between the alien referred to in the Old Testament and other fringe peoples. Since there are no helpful comparisons to be drawn from the legal material, they have turned to other material and other societies when making analogies. For example, when discussing the practice of hospitality in the Old Testament, shown, for example, Old Testament parallels spring to mind. Abraham's gives a lavish reception to the three 'men' at Mambre (Gen 18: 1-8) and Laban is eager welcoming Abraham's servant (Gen 24: 28-32), refers to the customs of nomads. The law of asylum which he sees operative in modern Bedouin societies is reflected, he claims, in the Old Testament institution of protecting the alien. V. H. Kooy describes, "the duty of hospitality to a stranger in terms of present-day Bedouin customs."[73]

In assumption made by Kooy above Rogerson argues: "they have assumed that the desert has somehow preserved for thousand years the sort of life lived by the Patriarchs."[74] Secondly, they have identified the Patriarchs as Bedouins, nomads or semi-nomads. This description has come under attack. J. W. Rogerson concludes that "we know too little about mobility and livestock breeding and their relationship to be able to described ancient people as nomadic or semi-nomadic, and that the meaning of 'Bedouin' is also so vague as not to be helpful."[75] Both of these scholars have assumptions which are questionable.

72 Pritchard, *ANET*, 421-24.

73 V. H. Kooy, "Hospitality," *Interpreter's Dictionary of the Bible*, Vol. 11 (Nashville: Abingdon Press, 1976), 654. Hereby IDB.

74 John W. Rogerson, *Anthropology and the Old Testament* (Oxford Blackwell, 1978), 1-4, 37, for a description of the history of the anthropological study of the Old Testament, and the need to rethink much assumption.

75 Rogerson, *Anthropology and the Old Testament,* 42-45.

1.3. Critique

After much study of the collection, it is justifiable that the code was created to justify and legitimize Hammurabi's reign. Simply put, Law of Hammurabi is political propaganda. Its target audience was the gods and the ruling elite, and its provisions were meant to show the wisdom, fairness, and equity of the king. The prologue to Law Hammurabi virtually says as much. As Bruce rightly comments "Hammurabi himself probably had little to do with composing the individual provisions in Law Hammurabi and most likely assigned the task to a group of his officials and scribes."[76]

The other law collections are subject to the same basic critique. Based on their own prologues, Law of Ur-Namma and Law of Lipit-ishtar also appear to be propagandistic tools in the hands of their respective kings. The biblical codes are used in the service of a religious agenda. Law of Eshnunna and Neo-Babylonian Law come to us on scribal exercise tablets.[77] They may well have been copied from larger monumental inscriptions and, thus, may be interpreted in the same manner as Law of Hammurabi, though it is conceivable that they were really nothing more than scribal exercises. Thus, it is likely that the primary purpose of each of the codes had little or nothing to do with establishing societal law. To be sure, they yield important insights into the various ancient West Asia societies from which they come – insights into royal ideology, politics, scribal training, and religion. But do they tell us anything about law?

This question is still one of sources, but it takes us one level deeper. These ideologies make a further contribution to the on-going debate about the writing of the history of ancient Israel. What come into the mind of the reader what were the sources for the provisions in these law collections. This is where scholarship diverges and disagreements are keen. The starting point is usually the idea that the codes are the product of the same pseudo-scientific (terms use to describe a claim, belief, or practice presented as scientific but which does not adher to the scientific method) efforts that gave us other collections or lists. As explained above different societies of ancient West Asia reacted differently to the challenge of incorporating newcomers.

It is, however, open to question as to at what early stage in the history of ancient West Asia was the compulsion felt to protect the גר. It may not be right to say that Israelites borrowed such ideas and principles from their neighbours. F. Charles Fensham may be right when he states that "it was the common policy, and the Israelites later on inherited the concept from their ancestors, some of whom had come from Mesopotamia, some had been captive

76 Bruce Wells, "Law and Practice" in *A Companion to Ancient Near East,* edited by Daniel Snell (Oxford: Blackwell Publishing Ltd., 2005), 185.

77 Wells, "Law and Practice," 185.

in Egypt, and other had grown up in the Canaanites world."[78] In the Israelite community this policy was extended through the encouragement of the high ethical religion of Yahweh, to become a definite part of their religion, later to be inherited by Christians and Muslims.[79] The narrative of any history depends upon the specific historical situation upon which the interpretation is offered. From the above study we can ascertain that biblical tradition has lots of its significance but ancient West Asia readings in relation to Israelite background allow us to see a longer, larger and vivid tradition of all major tradition and literatures. Thus without the ancient West Asia traditional background many of the Israelites literary genres and traditions cannot be properly understood and studied. Further comparative studies have perhaps helped us to show that the Old Testament is significant and authentic as it is originated within its own environment.

In the following chapter the researcher portrays ethnicity and identity in ancient Israel the recent archaeological debate, issues and problem, and see what aspects of ethnicity would serve as possible identifiers of an ethnic group 'Israel' and as a boundary markers between members belonging to Israel and members belonging to some other possible group during the Late Bronze-Iron Age transition and in the Early Iron Age.

78 F. Charles Fensham, "Widow, Orphan, and the poor in the Ancient Near Eastern Legal and Wisdom Literature," *Journal of Near Eastern Studies,* Vol. XXI (January-October, 1962), 137.

79 Gnuse, *You shall Not Steal,* 139.

Chapter 2

Ethnicity and Identity in Ancient Israel An Ideological Reading

2. Introduction

Recent years have witnessed the rise of studies analysing ethnic dynamics within biblical documents. As with other areas of focus in biblical studies, this trend reflects larger developments in the culture of the interpreter, in this case, the increased salience ethnic identity in modern societies. Increasingly forced to grapple with issues of ethnicity as part of our own experience within a multicultural world, biblical scholars today bring a new set of questions to our investigation of biblical texts.

The Hebrew Bible itself also begs for such investigation. Within the over arching narrative, the 'tribe' Israel consists of twelve 'clans', kinship groups that each trace their ancestry back to one of the sons of Jacob/Israel. The central human character running through this narrative, then, consists of an 'ethnic' group.

The aim of this chapter is to investigate Ancient Israel from the perspective of ethnic identity. Firstly, the researcher will look into definition and basic features of ethnicity from the stand point of ethnic studies. The researcher's agenda in this area derives from the approach formulated by John Hutchinson and Anthony D. Smith. Secondly, we will make a review the current status of scholarship about the origin of Israel. Thirdly, after summarizing the development in the study of ethnicity, the researcher analysis three broad eras of the biblical narrative; pre-monarchic, and exilic/post-exilic and review how studying of ethnicity have been applied to Old Testament studies. Further apply this insight to determine basic features of ethnicity and ethnic boundaries in early Israel. The researcher has opted for identity as ideology so as to conceptualise, and explore its forms and expression in a variety of context in Ancient Israel.

As with the ideological method, Gottwald remark "no single method of doing ideological criticism exists. As one survey remarked, "it comes in many voices, speaks many languages, and resides in many different disciplines and critical approaches, including psychoanalytic theory, cultural criticism, sociolinguistics, subaltern studies, feminist theory, and deconstruction, to name a few."[80] Consequently, the practice of ideological criticism is often seen as a form of resistance to unacknowledged and oppressive power and thus as raising issues of the ethics of interpretation. One chooses to interpret in a way that supports or opposes the power dynamics at work in the text. For David Clines ideology means "to reach beneath the surface of the text of the Hebrew Bible and the texts of biblical scholars and to expose what it is 'really' going on underneath the claims and commands and statements of the biblical and the scholarly texts-at the level of big ideas."[81]

2.1. Definition

Scholarship often uses identity to mean ethnicity.[82] Although the term 'ethnicity' has its roots in the Greek term *ethnos*/*ethnikos*, which was commonly used to describe pagans, that is non-Hellenic and, later, non-Jewish (Gentile) or non-Christian, second-class peoples, its academic and popular use is fairly modern. Sociologically speaking, the term was coined by Riesman in 1953 and it gained wider use only during the 1960s and 1970s.[83] However, from its inception ethnicity has remained a 'hot potato' of sociology. Although, the term was coined to make sense of a specific form of cultural difference, it acquired a rather different set of meanings. While the Anglo-American tradition adopted 'ethnicity' mostly as a "substitute for minority groups within a larger society of the nation-state,"[84] the European

80 Gottwald, *The Tribes of Yahweh,* 65-66.

81 Clines, *Interested Parties: The Ideology of Writers and Readers of the Hebrew Bible*, 12.

82 Sinisa Malesevic, *Identity as Ideology Understanding Ethnicity and Nationalism* (New York: Palgrave Macmillan, 2006), 1.

83 R. Bartlett indicates that the term 'ethnicity' was in sporadic use long before the 1950s, it still referred only to 'paganism', as in the following quote from 1782. R. Bartlett, "Medieval and modern concepts of race and ethnicity," *Journal of Medieval and Early Modern Studies* 31/1 (2001), 39–40.

84 R. A. Schermerhorn defines an ethnic group as 'a *collectivity within a larger society* having real or putative common ancestry, memories of a shared historical past, and a cultural focus on one or more symbolic elements defined as the epitome of their peoplehood'. R. A.

tradition regularly opted to use ethnicity as a synonym for nationhood defined historically by descent or territory.

There have been different approaches to ethnicity not only in biblical scholarship[85] Sociologists Hutchinson and Smith view that:

> "ethnicity should be seen mainly in biological terms (ethnic group have a common ancestry or kinship or genetic pool) is widely rejected but has contributed the importance insight that ethnic group generally define themselves in kinship or quasi-kinship term. Other saw the question in terms of distinct cultures, but this was problematic in that cultural groups do not always develop an ethnic identity or group consciousness. There is also the fact that there is a 'primordial' quality to ethnic identity in which the group's distinctiveness- 'we/they' is essential."[86]

The classic study is that of Barth[87] who pointed to the importance of inter group boundary mechanisms: ethnic groups define themselves in contrast with other groups ('self-ascription'), often by a minimum of explicit (even trivial) differences.

The reason behind this is because our knowledge of groups in the ancient West Asia is based on texts rather than a direct study of living peoples, we are limited by what the texts tell us. This means that the task of penetrating to identity and ethnicity is often complicated. For example, the biblical text tells us what was distinctive about Israelites and Judahites that made them different from the surrounding peoples, but what we have are the views of the biblical writers, not necessarily of the average Israelite or Judahite who might have seen his or her identity in quite different terms. An interesting example shared by Grabbe: "the situation in the Persian period, with the text of Ezra making a sharp distinction between 'Israel' and the 'people of the land(s)', but there is reason to think that both groups were Judahites and did not necessarily regard themselves as separate in the way that the textual writer portrays it."[88]

Schermerhorn, *Comparative Ethnic Relations: A Framework for Theory* and Research (New York: Random House, 1970), 34.

85 Ann E. Killebrew, *Biblical People and Ethnicity: An Archaeological Study of Egyptians, Canaanites, Philistines, and Early Israel, 1300-1100 B.C.E* (Atlanta: Society of Biblical Literature, 2005), 8-16.

86 Geertz Clifford, *The Interpretation of Culture* (New York: Basic Books, 1973), 255-310.

87 Frederik Barth, "Introduction," in *Ethnic Groups and Boundaries: The Social Organization of Culture Difference,* edited by Frederik Barth (Boston: Little Brown and Company, 1969), 1-38.

88 Lester L. Grabbe, *A History of the Jews and Judaism in the Second Temple Period 1; Yehud: A History of the Persian Province of Judah* (London and New York: T&T Clark International, 2004), 285-8.

Trying to find a definition of an ethnic group is still not easy. Killebrew begin with a basic definition of ethnicity as "group identity."[89] This definition is general enough to include the variety of human relationships that can lead to ethnic formation within the specific historic context of the biblical world. Social scientists have attempted to explain the phenomenon of ethnic group solidarity as having either primordial or circumstantial origins. According to the former, genetically based explanation for group membership, one belongs to a particular group because of birth or blood ties; that is, one's parents or ancestors were members of the same group. There is often a historical depth to a group's identity, usually supported by a rhetorical and mythical or religious language that may detail the origin of the group and support social or political structures. These ties based on kinship often are quite conservative, reflected in a great continuity in the group's cultural expression, and can persist for many generations while remaining stable and resistant to change.

A second major approach to ethnicity, termed "circumstantial" or "situational,"[90] sees ethnic allegiance as a result of political and economic interests and strategies. Bently asserts: "if a situation should change so that members of a group feel it is to their advantage to align their "ethnic" identity differently, the boundaries of the group will also change. This flexibility means that the typical behavioural characteristics of an ethnic group cannot be treated as fixed and static indicators of identity."[91] It varies from time, space and context.

This study uses a more fluid middle ground that combines the primordial and circumstantial approaches as a more appropriate approach to ethnicity. Although one may question whether ethnicity existed in antiquity, Researcher's definition of ethnicity as group identity approaches the concept in its broadest meaning and takes into account the phenomenon of "bounded groups" or social borders. Scotts interprets "ethnicity as resulting from a variety of diverse forces that can bind individuals into a social grouping. Thus, ethnicity is a dynamic and ongoing process of interaction

---

89 Killebrew, *Biblical People and Ethnicity...*, 8.

90 Frederik Barth ed., *Ethnic Groups and Boundaries: The Social Organization of Culture Difference* (Boston: Little Brown and Company, 1969), 7-38. Regarding the social circumstantial or structural conditions, responsible for ethnic solidarity, see David L. Horowitz, "Ethnic identity," in *Ethnicity: Theory and Experience,* edited by N. Glazer and D. P. Moynihan (Cambridge, Massachusets: Harvard University Press, 1975), 111-40.

91 For a cogent discussion of these two approaches, which he terms "primordial" and "instrumentalist," see Carter Bentley G. "Ethnicity and Practice," *Comparative Studies in Society and History* 29 (1987), 24-27.

or ethnogenesis that can take place on many levels between various groups of people."[92]

Scholarship often uses *identity* to mean *ethnicity.*[93] *Berquest remarks: "identity, ethnicity has several noticeable benefits. Firstly, it reflects the biblical texts' interest in genealogy. Second, the theory of identity fits both the ancient and modern interests in telling history as a story of peoples, races, and ethnoi.* Thirdly, an ethnicity theory reflects the cross-generational aspects of the biblical representation of Judean identity. Lastly, this theory of ethnic identity creates a clear connection between the ancient biblical story and the contemporary world; the story of Judah is not just a story of ancient people but a story of ancestors and thus, for some peoples today, a story of their own ethnicity."[94] Secondly, according to Malesevic, "'ethnicity' in its full sociological meaning is a very recent term which was not in general use in the nineteenth and early twentieth century's and, with the clear exception of Weber, no other classical sociologist employed this term in their works."[95] To begin with the term ethnicity let us start with the cross-disciplinary investigation by looking at how people conceive ethnicity. Hutchinson and Smith terms "ethnicity, ethnic identity and ethnic group or community can be somewhat slippery and lack any agreed definition,"[96] we will follow the well formulated definition, comprehensive and helpful definition given by sociologist Hutchinson and Smith.[97] According to them ethnic communities or *ethnies*[98] *habitually exhibit, albeit in varying degrees, six main features:*

---

92 For combination of both approaches see M. Scott George, Jr. "A Resynthesis of the Primordial & Circumstantial Approaches to Ethnic groups Solidarity: Towards an Explanatory Model," *Ethnic and Racial Studies* 13/2 (1990), 147-71.

93 Jon L. Berquest, "Constructions of Identity in Postcolonial Yehud," in *Judah and the Judeans in the Persian Period,* edited by Oded Lipschits and Manfred Oeming (Winona Lake, Indiana: Eisenbrauns, 2006), 54.

94 Berquest, "Constructions of Identity in Postcolonial Yehud," 55.

95 Sinisa Malesevic, *The Sociology of Ethnicity* (London, New Delhi: Sage Publications, 2004), 13.

96 J. Hutchinson and Anthony D. Smith, eds., *Ethnicity* (Oxford Readers: Oxford University press, 1996), 4-7. Cf. T. Parsons, "Some Theoretical Consideration on the Nature and Trends of change in Ethnicity," in *Ethnicity: Theory and Experience,* edited by N. Glazer and D. P. Moynihan (Cambridge: Harvard University Press, 1975), 53.

97 Hutchinson and Anthony D. Smith, *Ethnicity*, 5-6.

98 The term used by Hutchinson and Smith. Smith defines an *ethnie* as "a named human population with myths of common ancestry, shared historical memories, one or more elements of common culture, a link with a homeland and a sense of solidarity among at least some of its members." By 'sense of solidarity' Smith means deep feelings of group commitment expressed in altruistic values and actions. This includes a sense of belonging to a common ethnic group, which is conceptualised as active and in times of crises as superior to other forms of collective identification. Anthony D. Smith and John Hutchinson,

1. a *collective proper name,* to identify and express the 'essence' of the community;
2. a myth of *common ancestry,* a myth rather than a fact, a myth that includes the idea of a common origin in time and place, and that gives an ethnie a sense of fictive kinship, what Horowitz terms a 'super-family';
3. shared *historical memories,* or better, shared memories of a common past or pasts, including heroes, events and their commemoration;
4. one or more *elements of common culture,* which need not be specified but normally include religion, customs, or language;
5. a *link* with a *homeland,* not necessarily its physical occupation by the *ethnie,* only its symbolic attachment to the ancestral land, as with diaspora peoples;
6. a *sense of solidarity* for significant sector of the population.[99]

According to Hutchinson and Smith there are two basic approaches to their associated proponents, namely *Premordialism* and *Instrumentalism.* In addition to these, there are other approaches which play on further related issues.[100] Ideological criticism *extrinsic* analysis of literary texts necessarily involves the social sciences in reconstructing the social world of gender relationship in the biblical period.[101]

For Smith, an *ethnie* is defined by its ancestry myths but also by its possession or loss of a "homeland," a historic territory.[102] "Ethnicity is defined, first of all, by a collective belief in common origins and descent, however fictive, and thereafter by shared historical memories associated with a specific

---

"Introduction," in *Ethnicity*, edited by John Hutchinson and Anthony D. Smith (Oxford: Oxford University Press, 1996), 6-7. Sinisa Malesevic argued that: "Smith's theory can be properly understood only when one engaged more directly with the broader sociological worldview that his position is an integral part of–Durkheimianism." Cf. Malesevic, *Identity as Ideology,* 8.

99 Hutchinson and Smith, *Ethnicity*, 6-7. Cf. Anthony D. Smith, *National Identity* (London: Penguin Books, 1991), 21.

100 See Hutchinson and Smith, *Ethnicity,* 9-10 for summaries of the approaches of Barth ('transactionalist'), Horowitz ('social psychological'), and Armstrong ('ethno-symbolic').

101 Regarding the social-scientific study of the Bible see Norman K. Gottwald, "Sociological method in the Study of Ancient Israel," in *The Bible and Liberation: Political and Social Hermeneutics,* edited by Norman K. Gottwald (Maryknoll, New York.: Orbis, 1983), 26-37. Ronald Clement, ed., *The World of Ancient Israel: Sociological Anthropological & Political perspective* (Cambridge: Cambridge University Press, 1989).

102 Anthony D. Smith, *Myth and Memories of the Nation* (Oxford: Oxford University Press, 1999), 127.

territory which they regard as their 'homeland.'"[103] Once again, subjective attachment is far more important than actual possession of the territory in question. Smith observes:

> *Ethnie* do not cease to be *ethnie* when they are dispersed and have lost their homeland; for ethnicity is a matter of myths, memories, values and symbols, and not of material possessions or political power, both of which require a habitat for their realization … Territory is relevant to ethnicity, therefore, not because it is actually possessed, nor even for its 'objective' characteristics of climate, terrain and location, though they influence ethnic conceptions, but because of an alleged and felt symbiosis between a certain piece of earth and 'its' community. Again, poetic and symbolic qualities possess greater potency than everyday attributes; a land of dreams is far more significant than any actual terrain.[104]

Smith calls the process by which an association forms between the *ethnie* and the land the *territorialization of memory*. This term refers to the process by which a terrain acquires moral and aesthetic significance for a group through the rooting of memories in particular locations, so that the place evokes "a field or zone of powerful and peculiar attachments" [105] by its association with memories handed down through generations of the *ethnie*. The land comes to be viewed as "the unique and indispensable setting of events and experiences that moulded the community."[106] In practice, this connection is achieved by:

> …attaching specific memories of 'our ancestors' and forebears, particularly if they are saintly or heroic, to particular stretches of territory. For example, leaders and educators of the community may locate the deeds of heroes and great men at specific sites, 'poetic spaces' eulogized in the chronicles and ballads recited down the generations, thereby binding their descendants to a distinct landscape endowed with ethno-historical significance. Across the landscape lie the 'sites of memory'; the fields of battle, the monuments to the fallen, the places of peace treaties, the temples of priests, the last resting places of saints and heroes, the sacred groves of spirits and gods who guard the land.[107]

---

103 Smith, *Myth and Memories of the Nation,* 208.

104 Anthony D. Smith, *The Ethnic Origin of Nations,* 28. See also Smith, *National Identity*, 22-23.

105 Smith, *Chosen People* (Oxford: Oxford University Press, 2003), 134-35.

106 Smith, *Myth and Memories of the Nation,* 269.

107 Smith, *Myth and Memories of the Nation,* 151-52.

After reviewing the current trends in the study of ethnicity, we now turn to studies of Israelite ethnicity according to three broad eras of Israelites history: pre-monarchic, monarchic, and exilic/post-exilic. The 'pre-monarchic Israel' involves one in a host of controversial, issue in contemporary studies related to the Hebrew Bible. For instance, archaeological work has demonstrated that new settlement spread throughout the central highlands during the transition from the Late Bronze Age to Iron 1.[108] Scholars remain divided, however, over who these early settlers were, where they came from, and whether or not we can refer to them as 'Israelites.'

2.2. Pre-Monarchic Israelites Ethnicity

There are disagreement persists regarding the nature of the evidence concerning Israel during this time period. Other than selected materials in Judges or I Samuel, most scholars working specifically on Israelite ethnicity in the pre-monarchic period regard the biblical narrative portraying this era as late and historically unreliable. Studies reviewed within this section concern highland settlers within the transition from Late Bronze Age (LBA) to Iron 1, roughly the thirteenth to early eleventh centuries BCE. Because archaeological evidence serves as the primary source material for the pre-monarchic period, it is necessary to first present a brief overview of a recent archaeology.

The treatment of Israelites ethnicity during the pre-monarchic era concerns the highland settlements that arose during the transition from the Late Bronze Age (LBA) to Iron 1. Killebrew examines four major peoples who play significant roles in the biblical narrative-Egyptian, Canaanites, Philistines, and early Israel, during the transition from LBA to Iron 1. As the title indicates, Killebrew focuses on 'ethnic' identity for each of these peoples. Although her work is interdisciplinary and makes use of biblical materials as well as contemporaneous non-biblical texts, Killebrew relies primarily on archaeological evidence. She confidently states that "ethnicity in its diverse manifestations can be identified under certain circumstances in the archaeological record."[109] She defines ethnicity as 'group identity.'[110]

Killebrew first reviews the textual evidence related to Israel's origins and presence in the land of Canaan. She regards the Exodus narrative as reflecting collective memory of Egyptian occupation and enslavement of Canaan during the thirteenth to twelfth centuries BCE, rather than an account of an actual departure of group of people from Egypt itself. According to Kellebrew "the

108 W. G. Dever, "Archaeology and the Emergence of Early Israel," in *Archaeology and Biblical Interpretation*, edited by J. R. Bartlett (London: Routledge, 1997), 26-30.

109 Kellebrew, *Biblical Peoples and Ethnicity* (Atlanta: SBL, 2005), 2.

110 Kellebrew, *Biblical Peoples and Ethnicit,* 8.

conquest narratives of Joshua must be regarded as historically suspicious. She notes that both Joshua and Judges portray Israel as a non-indigenous group distinct from the native Canaanites."[111] Among non-biblical texts, she cites the Merneptah (or 'Israel') stele, an Egyptian victory stele commemorating Pharaoh Merneptah's triumphant military campaigns, which mentions a people named 'Israel' in this region. Though not all scholar agrees.

Killebrew chronicles archaeological evidence demonstrating major changes in settlement patterns throughout Canaan and, in particular, a marked increase in small village in the central highlands during this time. On the basis of her survey of archaeological work on these highland sites, she identifies the twelve-eleven century as typical of these settlements, characteristics that others have noted as well:

> Villages are characterized by modest numbers of domestic structures, usually a version of the three-or four-room pillared house; few, if any, public structures or fortifications; a proliferation of silos; the appearance of cistern and agriculture terraces; absence of big bones; paucity of burial; and most notably, a very limited repertoire of utilitarian ceramic container that continue the tradition of Late Bronze Age pottery shapes.[112]

Killebrew's main concern lies with Israel's ethnogenesis during this era. She contends that 'Israel' in this era can only be understood in the context of regional developments. The decline of LBA empires, especially Egyptian imperial hegemony over the eastern Mediterranean, resulted in a social and political fragmentation that allowed for the development of more kinship based society. In particular, these changes allowed for greater movement of indigenous Canaanite populations. This accounted for the migrations of urban dwellers into the central highlands and thus, the rapid growth of new settlements. Killebrew concludes that "what became known as Israel gradually emerged during the infiltration of diverse people into these highland areas."[113] Her argument, however, deals more with constructing a reasonable scenario in which a new social collectivity could emerge in the highland areas than in demonstrating something particularly ethnic about this group's identity.

Dever [114]an American archaeologist has given good reasons which rather affirm that the archaeological record speaks for a distinct Israelite identity in

111 Kellebrew, *Biblical Peoples and Ethnicity,* 153-54.

112 Kellebrew, *Biblical Peoples and Ethnicity,* 157.

113 Kellebrew, *Biblical Peoples and Ethnicity*, 37-42, 184-85.

114 W. G. Dever, *Who Were the Early Israelites and Where Did They Come* From? (Grand Rapids, Michigan: Eerdmans, 2003), 191-200.

Early Iron Age 1. In addition, Dever[115] suggests that the archaeological record speaks for the birth of a new identity. Dever's observations need further attention. First of all, there is an increase in rural settlement, with a population explosion most notably in the hill country. Accompanying site and house layouts indicate an emphasis on extended family and clan. Moreover, the archaeological record speaks for an agrarian mode of production and communitarian and tribal organisation. Dever point out "one small but significant potential boundary marker, Pork bones are almost entirely absent from the Iron 1 highlands, in contrast to the lowlands."[116]

According to Dever, these people originated from Canaanites stock and had moved from urban areas to the highlands out of economic necessity. At some point, as a result of changes that took place over time as they adapted to their new environment, and as a 'motley' assortment of other marginal peoples joined them, a new group identity emerged that set them apart from their Canaanite neighbours. Dever says:

> The inescapable conclusion-only likely to be enhanced by future archaeological research-is that the Israelite settlement in Canaan was part of the larger transition from the Late Bronze to the Iron Age. It was a gradual, exceedingly complex process, involving social, economic, and political-as well as religious-change, with many regional variations.[117]

Dever also make a number of doubtful claims about our ability to detect 'consciousness,'[118] ethnic or otherwise, on the basis of material remains. Dever stands on better ground when he refers to twelfth-century "'Israel' having a general sense of 'peoplehood.'"[119] Yet in a related problem, he claims that ethnicity is the same thing as peoplehood.

Block-Smith, in contrast to Killebrew and Dever, contends that the search for Israel in the late thirteenth and twelfth-century central highland. Block-Smith contends that the search for Israel in the late thirteenth- and twelfth-

115 Dever, *Who Were the Early Israelites and Where Did They Come From?*, 193.

116 Dever, *Who Were the Early Israelites and Where Did They Come From?*, 108. While Leviticus and Deuteronomy date from the exilic period or later, the distinction between the Iron I highlands, where pig was rare, and the pork-purveying Philistines along the coast provided a meaningful context for pork abstinence as an Israelite trait in the twelfth and eleventh centuries B.C.E. Cf. Bloch Smith, "Israelite Ethnicity in Iron Age 1: Archaeological Preserves what is Remembered and what is Forgotten in Israel's History," *JBL* 112/3 (2003), 423.

117 W. G. Dever, *Recent Archaeological Discoveries and Biblical Research* (Seattle: University of Washington Press, 1990), 79.

118 Dever, "Archaeology and the Emergence of Early Israel," 42.

119 Dever, "Archaeology and the Emergence of Early Israel," 42.

century central highland stands at an 'impasse.'[120] In her view, "all the typical features used to argue for Israelites ethnicity in this period-the pillared or four room house, the 'collared-rim, and abstinence from pork-have been shown to be without foundation. None can be conclusively identified as exclusively "Israelite" or as distinguishing "Israelites" from neighbouring people."[121]

Block-Smith brings together multiple means of analysis in order to detect what she sees as "faint traces of Iron 1 Israelites *ethnos.*"[122] This include use of a 'Meaningful Boundaries' approach to ethnicity, an emphasis on the role of collective memory in the process of ethnogenesis, an integration of biblical and archaeological evidence that she calls a 'Tell-Tale' approach to ethno-archaeology. She also said that ethnic groups arise out of shared interests between peoples, typically political or economic.

A 'Tell-Tale' approach poses several questions regarding ethnic identity. What primordial features or "common heritage" unified the *ethnos*?[123] Bloch-Smith identifies worship of the god 'El', along with a sense of Kinship, as distinctive features of this early era. The second questions ask, 'What circumstantial features including shared interest fostered the formation of ethnic Israel?'[124] In Bloch-Smith's view, "the key for answering this question lies in seeing the philistines as the primary people over against whom Israel identity took shape. Both biblical and archaeological evidence supports cultural and material distinctions between these peoples. Earlier scholars made the mistake of trying to distinguish early Israel from the Canaanites, a task doomed from the beginning, since cultural differences between the two are not supported by the material record."[125]

Scholars like Pitkänen review the six characteristic of ethnic group specified by Hutchinson and Smith which the researchers have cited above in

120 Elizabeth Block-Smith, "Israelites Ethnicity in Iron 1: Archaeology Preserves What is Remembered and what is Forgotten in Israel's History," *JBL* 122/3 (2003), 402.

121 Block-Smith, "Israelites Ethnicity in Iron 1: Archaeology Preserves What is Remembered and what is Forgotten in Israel's History," 406. As James C. Miller rightly said in relation to 'Tel-Tale' approach to ethno-archaeology Bloch-Smith's 'Tell-Tale' integration of biblical evidence with archaeology forms a central pillar of her work. Biblical text, however, remain notoriously difficult to date. Archaeology, on the other hand, cannot determine the significance of traits appearing in the material remains, but it can provide means of dating some traits that have been tagged as significant by biblical evidence. So, even though Bloch-Smith regards the biblical narratives as products of the exilic era, she believes they contain remnants of ancient material that can in some cases be dated by archaeology.

122 Block-Smith, "Israelites Ethnicity in Iron 1 Archaeology Preserves What is Remembered and what is Forgotten in Israel's History," 425.

123 Miller, "Ethnicity and the Hebrew Bible: Problems and Prospects," 420.

124 Block-Smith, "Israelites Ethnicity in Iron 1: Archaeology Preserves What is Remembered and what is Forgotten in Israel's History," 421.

125 Miller, "Ethnicity and the Hebrew Bible: Problems and Prospects," 185.

the definition. Pitkänen proceeds to collect biblical evidences regarding Israel that fits within each of these categories. Although he recognizes the disputes dating of biblical texts, he contends that the amount of evidence at least presents the possibility of a 'distinctive Israelite identity and the existence of ethnic boundaries' during the LBA-Iron 1 transition period.[126] Minimal possible boundaries which have possible boundaries being called as 'Israelites' believing in the descent from the patriarchs or like believing in common history of the Patriarch and the Egyptian sojourn and Exodus, having an egalitarian ideology, certain food restrictions such as a pork taboo, male circumcision, and solidarity with other Israelite. Pitkänen suggests that such early Israelite ethnicity could have come about through a group of slaves who escaped from Egypt and made their way to Canaan. Called by name 'Israel' and bearing the characteristics outline above, their company grew as individual Canaanites joined the group and became assimilated to Israel's beliefs and practices.

Finkelstein insist that the term 'Israelite' is nothing more than a designation for those individuals and groups settling in the hill country during the Iron 1 period. In fact, Finkelstein[127] has stated he might be willing to omit the term 'Israelite' from the discussion of Iron 1 settlement and refer instead to 'hill country settlers' until the period of the monarchy. Whitelam[128] in support writes: Finklelstein's own presentation of his archaeological findings makes clear, it is not possible to attach ethnic labels to the various sites at the end of the Late Bronze Age and beginning of the early Iron Age. Thus, Finkelstein's adoption of the more neutral term 'hill country settlers' is much more prudent.

There are general tendency to see the development of Israelite identity as a later phenomenon. Lemche asserts that "there is more confusion which arises because of the difference between the modern notions of ethnicity and the one current in ancient societies, is that we possess very definite ideas about the identity of people and nation which accords well with the division of our world into nation-state."[129] Most people in ancient times did not have our notions of ethnicity and nationality.

---

126 P. Pitkänen, "Ethnicity, Assimilation and the Israelite Settlement," *TynB* 55/2 (2004), 174.

127 Israel Finkelstein, "The Emergence of Israel in Canaan: Consensus, Mainstream and Dispute," *JSOT* 2 (1991), 49-59.

128 Keith W. Whitelam, "The Identity of Early Israel: The Realignment and Transformation of Late Bronze-Iron Age Palestine," *JSOT* 63 (1994), 57-87. Thompson puts it, 'It has become exceedingly misleading to speak of the term "Israelite" in an archaeological context of Iron 1 Palestine". Cf. T. L. Thompson, *Early History of the Israelite People: From the Written and Archaeological Sources* (Leiden: Brill, 1992b), 310. Also Cf. Whitelam, "Israel's traditions of origin reclaiming the land," *JSOT* 44 (1989), 19-42.

129 N. P. Lemche, *The Cannanites and their Land: The Tradition of the Canaanites* (Sheffield England: Sheffield Academic Press, 1991), 52.

2.3. Monarchic Era

In contrast to the pre-monarchic and exilic/post-exilic eras about which studies of ethnicity abound, few scholars have studied Israelite ethnicity in the monarchical period. Sparks, *Ethnicity and Identity in Ancient Israel,* analysis Israelite ethnicity from its dim pre-monarchic manifestations through the post-exilic era, but he devote the bulk of his attention to the period of monarchy. Sparks reconstruct Israelite ethnicity during different historical periods. Sparks adopted minimalist perspective.

In defining ethnicity itself, Sparks contends that what distinguishes ethnic social identity from other overlapping from of identity is perceived genealogical links among group members. Sparks, therefore defines the role of ethnicity in his project as follows:

> We are researching ethnic when it serves as: (1) a concept of sociocultural integration ('we are the children of Abraham'); (2) as a tool for sociocultural delimitation (*they* are not children of Abraham'); and (3) as a model for explaining the origins of other peoples ('*they* are the children of lot').[130]

Sparks endeavours to bypass certain controversies surrounding the dating of biblical material, such as the Pentateuchal narratives most concerned with issues of ethnicity, by deriving his basic data from sources datable with relative certainty. These include the prophets Amos, Hosea, Isaiah, Jeremiah, and Ezekiel, and the book of Deuteronomy.

The eight-century prophets presuppose existing ethnic identity in the form of ancestor traditions (Jacob) and a migration tradition (exodus from Egypt). Sparks claims: "the details and salience of such identity, however, vary between the north and the south, and from prophet to prophet. For example, Hosea and his 'proto-Deuteronomic community' sought to intensify ethnic sentiment in favour of a religious, 'mono-Yahwistic' national agenda that rejected all other gods as foreign."[131] Sparks declares this outlook to be a distinctively northern means to construing ethnic identity, since Hosea does not apply his message to Judah, and the southern prophets Amos and Isaiah uphold a more universalistic outlook. Finally, for Sparks, it was in the exile that ethnic boundaries became most clearly defined. Rituals connected with purity, the rite of circumcision, and Sabbath observance helped to identify those who were "in" from those who were "out."

---

130 Kentron L. Sparks, *Ethnicity and Identity in Ancient Israel: Prolegomena to the Study of Ethnic sentiments and their Expression in the Hebrew Bible* (Winona Lake, Indiana: Eisenbrauns, 1998), 3.

131 Sparks, *Ethnicity and Identity in Ancient Israel*, 322.

2.4. Exilic/Post–exilic Eras

The exilic/post-exilic have attracted in academic circles for several reasons. First, the Israel shock of defeat and survival at the hands of the Babylonians, the destruction of the Solomonic Temple, and exile of its leaders to Babylon, came away deeply transformed. Furthermore, most scholars date the finalization of the Hebrew Bible to the exilic and post-exilic eras. Thus, it is in some sense a response to and, therefore, a reflection of the needs of people and a nation attempting to redefine itself after the trauma of military destruction and exile. Efforts to read the Hebrew Bible in such a context have brought renewed attention to these time periods.

Small but quite vocal group of scholars like (Lemche, Davies, Thompson) claim that the Hebrew Bible, especially its historical narratives, was created in the post exilic period in order to address the need of Persian era Judeans. The 'biblical Israel' portrayed in these narratives is thus a literary fiction meant to serve as part of the collective memory for a newly formulated people.

Mullen contends that, Deuteronomistic History (DtrH) in its function as ideological narratives, a "Social drama"[132] reflecting the concerns of Yahwists in the first half of the sixth century BCE. Mullen is concerned with the final form of the written text, and he subjects it to a closer reading. The goal is not historical reconstruction of Israelites and Judean-history in a diachronic sense. Mullen employs sociological studies of ethnic identity and boundaries to interpret the concern of the Deuteronomistic Historian.

Mullen takes up segments of the DtrH in literary order. Deuteronomy is an ideological definition of what Israel should be, a "social manifesto of Israelite ethnic identity"[133] or a "ritual manifesto of ethnic boundary formation for ancient Israel identity."[134] Mullen also interprets Deut 18:15f, to the effect that: "prophecy is a central Israelite social institution for the biblical writers. The book of Judges depicts the narrative dissolution of that community (depicted in Joshua) through a series of vignettes that illustrate the dangers of failing to appropriate and maintain the ethnic boundaries established by Deuteronomy."[135]

The Deuteronomic Historian refines his interpretation of the ideal 'Israel.' Mullen describes: "the covenant laid out in Deuteronomy was not a static description of Israel's character and behaviour; rather, the historical narrative that follows demonstrates how it required interpretation and implementation

132 E. Theodore Mullen. Jr, *Narrative History and Ethnic Boundaries: The Deuteronomistic Historian and the Creation of Israelite National Identity* (Atlanta: Scholar Press, 1993), 37-47.

133 Mullen Jr, *Narrative History and Ethnic Boundaries*, 55.

134 Mullen Jr, *Narrative History and Ethnic Boundaries,* 87.

135 Mullen Jr, *Narrative History and Ethnic Boundaries,* 112.

in new situations."[136] The Israel's experience depicted in such situations in Joshua-2 Kings offered help for the exiles in understanding how to respond in their current circumstances as they looked towards the future. If their current circumstances result from the failure of covenant faithfulness among their ancestors, the situation can only be remedied by a decisive return to the covenant with their God. The restoration of the Davidic kingdom and of this people to their land, therefore, requires renewed devotion to YHWH expressed through obedience to the command of the covenant.

Berquist examines the term 'Judah' and 'Judeans' in Persian period. A 'Judean' was apparently someone who had something to do with Judah. But Berquist question, "Who, then, counts as Judean? What criteria can we use to ascertain who is a Judean and who is not? What are the limits of this group, and what kind of group would they be?"[137] Later, he examines five different ways in which these questions have been tackled. Berquist pointed two problems in this approach (1) he regards the application of the modern construct of ethnicity to an ancient society as anachronistic. (2) He contrasts 'racial and ethnic theories of identity as 'unclear' and 'always contested.'[138] He asserts that: "a theory of identity that accurately reflects the biblical interest will emphasise that identity is problematic, unobvious, and highly contested."[139] He further pointed out that: "Nehemiah 5:7-8 depicts Nehemiah's perception that the deep divides between different groups in Judah were between kin."[140] Berquist rightly question of the term 'Judean.' But why arguments involving kin cannot be about ethnic identity he does not explain. The researchers will explain more in Chapter v about Golah returnees in the context of the complex landscape of Yahwism in the Persian era.

Thompson suggested the distinctive Israelite ethnicity cannot be trace in Palestine until the Persian era. He argues that: "the late Bronze-early Iron transition is not related to ethnicity but is about socio economic change and indigenous impulses."[141] Especially, Thompson's reconstruction denies any historical reminiscences from the biblical text for the time before the exile and attempts to explain the origins of Israel completely independent from the biblical texts.[142]

---

136 Mullen Jr, *Narrative History and Ethnic Boundaries,* 284.

137 Berquist, "Constructions of Identity in Postcolonial Yehud," 53.

138 Berquist, "Constructions of Identity in Postcolonial Yehud," 54.

139 Berquist, "Constructions of Identity in Postcolonial Yehud," 56.

140 Berquist, "Constructions of Identity in Postcolonial Yehud," 55.

141 T. L. Thompson, *Early History of the Israelite People: From the Written and Archaeological Sources,* Studies in the History of the Ancient Near East, 4 (Leiden: Brill, 1992), 210.

142 Thompson, together with scholars like Lemche and Davies, have raised a major controversy during recent years, as these scholars have suggested that nothing can be reconstructed about the history of Israel before the Babylonian exile based on biblical

2.5. The Identity of Israel and Recent Archaeology

Together with new critical reading of written sources, archaeological and epigraphic evidence have played a key role in these recent developments, being used to support arguments that Judaism and Jewish culture was indeed heterogeneous in both Palestine and the Diaspora, and that Jewish communities in the Diaspora maintained their Judaism and a distinct Jewish identity.

Sian Jones explores the broad theme of the relationship between Jewish identity and patriotism in the period between the destruction of the first temple and late antiquity, with special attention to the Graeco-Roman period. Jones argues that: "the material world is intricately involved in the perception and expression of group identity, but at the same time there is no straightforward relationship between particular types of material culture and particular identities. Moreover, there are qualitative differences in the ways in which material and literary traditions are involved in processes of self-identification, and identification by others-difference which have important implication for the interpretation of group identities in the past."[143]

On the issue of how should we approach the relationship between material culture and identity if it is not a fixed and intrinsic one? For Jones this issue is obviously of "crucial importance for archaeologist if we are to analyse cultural identity from the material remains of past societies, as we do not have direct access to people's beliefs and ideas."[144] It is also central to the development of a critical approach to the relationship between the archaeological materials and various cultural identities referred to historical sources.

Within the archaeology transformation that have taken place in many ways which resembles in the study of ethnicity. These developments carry significant implications for discerning ethnic symbolism in the archaeological record. Dever, American archaeologiest who promoted the adoption on new archaelogy by archaeologist of the holy Land, noted that by the 1970's several aspect of the new archaeology were being incorporated into the discipline, which includes collecting and analysing artifact, such as animals bones and

---

texts. The 'minimalist' scholars have in been adequately responded to by such works as W. G. Dever, *What Did the Biblical Writers Know and When Did They Know It? What Archaeology Can Tell Us about the Reality of Ancient Israel* (Grand Rapids, Michigan: Eerdmans, 2001) and V. P. Long, D. W. Baker and G. J. Wenham, ed., *Windows into Old Testament History: Evidence, Argument, and the Crisis of 'Biblical Israel'* (Grand Rapids, Michigan: Eerdmans, 2002).

143 Sian Jones, "Identities in practice: Towards an Archaeological Perspective on Jewish Identity and in Antiquity," in *Jewish Local Patriotism and Self-Identification in the Graeco-Roman Period,* edited by Sian Jones and Sarah Pearce (Sheffield Academic Press, 1998), 31.

144 Jones, "Identities in practice: Towards an Archaeological Perspective on Jewish Identity and in Antiquity," 42.

plants (zooarchealogy) remains (botanical archaeology) in order to paint the picture of how ancient people lived and the relationship of their culture practice to the natural world around them. Dever holding his view writes: "the biblical text we have is indeed a "literary construct," the product not of any historical consciousness in the modern sense, but rather of the literary imagination of late, elitist, nationalist religious parties who finally edited various materials into our Hebrew Bible."[145] He readily acknowledges that many of the Biblical "stories" are just that i.e. myth and legend interwoven with some factual material, or "historized fiction."[146] Dever confronts the "revisionists" and their ideology poses a threat to biblical studies, to syro-palestine archaeology, to theological and religious studies, to the life of synagogue and church, and even to the political situation in the Middle East.[147] How ideology has always plagued Biblical and Syro-palestinian archeology. Revisionist historian according to Dever, produce 'constant caricatures of "biblical archaeology."[148] Their work consists, he tells us, of 'misinformed, ill-tempered and increasingly ideological monologues'. He writes,

> we do insist, however, that to ignore the biblical texts when dealing with the Iron Age of ancient Palestine, or to deny correlations of texts and artefacts when they occur, is not only methodologically unsound but reckless and ultimately defeatist. If positivism is *passe* today, so is nihilism. As for the fad of deconstruction, belatedly discovered by the revisionists, it has already run its course in many other disciplines.[149]

German and American biblical scholarship, which has dominated the study of the 'history of Israel' for most of the last century, is founded upon a concept of history based on the study of the origins and development of nation states and the great statement who determined the course of history.

---

145 Dever, *What Did the Biblical Writers Know & When Did they Know It?*, 30.

146 Dever, *What Did the Biblical Writers Know& When Did they Know It?*, 32.

147 Dever, "Archaeology, Ideology and the Quest for an 'Ancient' or 'Biblical' Israel," *Near Eastern Archaeology* 61/1 (1998), 47.

148 The older 'biblical archaeology' commonly worked with a correlation of biblical text and archaeological discovery. Much criticism later argued that archaeological finds had been much too easily and swiftly identified with biblical references, and the tendency moved quite strongly towards a quite autonomous archaeology of Palestine, working independently of biblical evidences. This movement has been, obviously, one of the wellsprings of the revisionist approach to biblical history. Hence Dever, thought critical of 'biblical archaeology,' is critical also to what he calls the 'nonbiblical archaeology' of the revisionists, who as he sees it, refuse to recognized plain evidences of correlation between Bible and archaeology when these evidences are present.

149 Dever, *What Did the Biblical Writer Know & When Did they Know It?*, 247.

Modern historiographer has worked in the shadow of ideas of nationalism which emerged in the eighteenth century and have become the dominating force of politics in the nineteenth and twentieth centuries.[150] On the dominan writing on the history of Israel, AhlstrÖm writes: "Because the author of the Bible were historiographers and used stylistic pattern to create a 'dogmatic' and as such tendentious literature, one many question the reliability of their product."[151] He continues: "Biblical historiography is not a product build on facts. It reflects the narrator-outlook and ideology rather than known facts."[152] Ideology is played off against facts. And again: "the biblical narrators were not really concerned about historical truth. Their goal was not that of modern historian - the idea of 'objectivity' has not yet been invented."[153]

Scottish scholar Provan, reflection on writings on the History of Israel asserts the increase emphasis on 'the Bible as literature' along with the tendency to a late dating of the text."[154] Why then, he ask, 'assume that the narrative world thus portrayed has anything to do with the "real" world of the past ? Why not regard it as a "fictive world," an ideological construct created by its authors for their own purposes?[155] Provan does not dispute that: "biblical historiography is, in at least a very general sense, ideological literature, or that ideology has partially shaped the litearure of the last century or two on the history of Israel."[156] Provan concludes with an expression that different approaches to the subject, deriving from these beliefs and philosophies, are accepted as valid. To this end he pleads for greather 'awareness of one's own presuppositions and dispositions.'

As it has been indicated above, the great historical importance of the ideology of early Israel lies not so much in itself but in the set of later developments through which it was adapted and preserved.

---

150 J. P. Taylor, *Political Geography World Economy, Nation State and Locality* (London: Longman, 1985), 125.

151 Gosta W. Ahlstrom, "The Role of Archaeological and Literary Remains in Reconstructing Israel," in *The Fabric of History: Text, Artifact and Israel's Past,* edited by D. V. Edelman, JSOT Sup127 (Sheffield: JSOT Press, 1991), 116-41.

152 Gosta W. Ahlstrom, "The Role of Archaeological and Literary Remains in Reconstructing Israel," 136.

153 Gosta W. Ahlstrom, *The History of Ancient Palestine from the Palaeolithic Period to Alexander's Conquest,* edited by D. V. Edelman, JSOT Sup 146 (Sheffield: JSOT Press, 1993), 50.

154 Iain W. Provan, "Ideologies, Literary and Critical Reflection on Recent Writing on the History of Israel," *JBL* 114/4 (1995), 585.

155 Provan, "Ideologies, Literary and Critical Reflection on Recent Writing on the History of Israel," 586.

156 Provan, "Ideologies, Literary and Critical Reflection on Recent Writing on the History of Israel," 605.

2.6. Israel's Ethnic Identity: Issues and Problems

It is something of truism to point out that ethnicity had played an important role in the history of Judaism both in the post biblical era and prior to it.[157] More specifically with respect to ancient Israel recent biblical scholarly activity both literary and historical has raised a serious doubt about the supposed origins and antiquity of Israelites ethnicity.[158] So there is growing consensus that these issues need to be revisited. Israel ethnicity represents a special problem in biblical studies. In decades past, the "American school" in the Albright tradition,[159] the "German school" in Alt tradition[160] and the "Sociological school" associated with Mendenhall[161] could despite their importance differences, suggest a *Sitz im Leben* for the emergence of Israelite ethnic sentiments. For the American school, the Israelites represented the conquering outsider who, upon entrance into palestine, met a foreign culture that could be viewed as ethnically distinct from Israel. In the case of the German School, the popular "amphictyony hypothesis" suggested a united Israel that stood over against the surrounding peoples, again a context of "otherness" suitable for ethnic sentiment to emerge. For Mendenhall and Gottwald, the original opposition pitted village dwellers against residents of the palestinian city-states. However, literary study of the Hebrew text and archeological work in Palestine have raised considerable problems for all of these paradigms over the last few decades. In defence to amphictyony hypothesis Von Rad has suggested that: "despite the apparent lateness of deutronomic thought, early credal statements from the

157 Breet, "Interpreting Ethnicity," in *Ethnicity and the Bible*, edited by M.G.Breet, Biblical interpretation Series 19 (Leden: Brill, 1996), 11. Cf. H. G. M. Williamson, "The concept of Israel in Transition," in *The World of Ancient Israel*, edited by R. E. Clements (Cambridge: Cambridge University Press, 1989), 141-61.

158 M. Skjeggestads, "Ethnic Groups in Early Iron Age Palestine: Some Remarks on the Use of the Term 'Israelite' in Recent Research," *JSOT* 6 (1992), 159-186.

159 W. F. Albright, *Yahweh and the Gods of Canaan* (London: University of London Press, 1978), 73; F. M. Cross, *Canaanite Myth and Hebrew Epic: Essay in the History of tjr Religion of Israel* (Cambridge: Harvard University Press, 1973), 47.

160 For Alt and scholars accepting his amphictyonic model of early Israel, the tribal groups involved stood in opposition to native Canaanite people: "these neighbours were the inhabitants' people of Palestine before the Israelite settlement." Albrecht Alt, *Essay on Old Testament History and Religion* (Garden City, New York: Doubleday, 1968), 125. Cf. Peter Machinist, "outsider or Insiders: The Biblical View of Emergent Israel and its Contexts," in *The Other in Jewish Thought and History Constructions of Jewish Culture and Identity,* edited by Laurence J, Silberstein and Robert L. Cohn (New York: University Press, 1994), 35.

161 G. E. Mendenhall, *The Tenth Generation* (Baltimore: Johns Hopkins University press, 1973), 78; Cf, N. K. Gottwald, *The Tribes of Yahweh*, 232-233.

amphictyonic period could be isolated within the later Dt/Dtr corpus."[162] There is no convincing evidence for a early amphictyonic Israel and therefore such a context for the apperance of a distinct, Israelite ethnic identity can be no longer confidently maintained.

The conquest model as a context for the emergence of ethnic Israel has faced a similar. First, there were those who wished to affirm the basic historicity of the biblical text, even if the date of the conquest was to be lowered to the 13th century and the time of the Late Bronze-Early Iron Age transition instead of the 15th century as suggested by the biblical chronology. Finkelstein has adopted conservative approach for determining the dates. For Finkelstein "Late Bronze 111: twelve century until circa 1130 B.C.E. Early Iron 1: Late twelve century and first half of the eleventh B.C.E."[163] The most illustrious proponent of this view was Albright, and his work was continued by his disciples, the most notable of whom was John Bright.[164] Firstly archeological study have failed to uncover evidence for a unified conquest of Palestine that could be connected with a group of Israelites. As Miller has noted, "were we dependent upon archaeological and other non-biblical evidence alone, we could have no reason even to support that such a conquest ever occured."[165] The question raised by the archeological evidence extend beyond the question of later period in Israel's history. AhlstrÖm suggest, "because to this point, the evidence derived from the source has failed to provide any clear distinction between a supposed Israelite material culture and competing material cultures that might be identified with the other ethnic group."[166] Despise support in some quaters, the "peasant revolt" model of the Sociological school have been heavily criticized.

Gottwald point out that: "the model is informed by a modern sociological scheme that is highly questionable value, particularly in its tendency to use

162 Particularly Deuteronomy 6:20-24 and Josh 24:2b-13. See von Rad "The Form Critical Problem of the Hexateuch," in *The Problem of Hexateuch and other Essay*, translated by E. W. T. Dickens (Edinburgh, London: Oliver and Boyd, 1966), 43.

163 Israel Finkelstein, *The Forgotten Kingdom: The Archaeology and History of Northern Israel,* 7.

164 For a summary, including bibliographical references to Albright and Bright see W. G. Dever, *Who Were the Early Israelites,* 41-49.

165 J. M. Miller, "Israelite History," in *Hebrew Bible and Its Modern Interpreters,* edited by D. A. Knight and G. M. Tucker (Philadelphia: Fortress, 1985), 11.

166 G. W. Ahlstrom, *Who is the Israelites?* (Winona Lake, Ind: Eisenbrauns, 1986). Supporting this position are most theorists. Cf. N. Lemche, *Early Israel: anthropological and Historical Studies on the Israelites Society before the Monarchy,* Vetus Testamentum Sup 37 (Leiden: Brill, 1995), 386-406; J. M. Miller and J. H. Hayes, *A History of Ancient Israel and Judah* (Philadelphia: Westminster, 1986), 72.

comparative "ideal types" in the analysis of quite disparate social and historical contexts".[167] The whole approach is governed by his Marxist ideology.

The assumption, shared by many historian and archaeologist, that the emergence of numerous rural sites in the highlands and margins of Palestine during the transition from the Late Bronze to the early Iron Age is to be identified with a single people, 'Israel', itself begs the question. Most importantly, assumptions about the unity of premonarchic Israel are brought into question. The prevailing understandings of the identities of the many Israel's of history and of the ideas of Israel that corresponds to those identities are tied closely to the problem of the nature and functions of the religious traditions preserved in the Hebrew Bible and the ways in which they have been interpreted by various communities from their inception to the present day.

Because of the serious questions surrounding the amphictyonic hypothesis, the conquest model, and the peasant-revolt theory, we are left without a convincing historical context that could produce or foster ethnic distinctions between ancient Israelites and other groups. The question then remains how and why ethnic sentiments became such a powerful form of identity in ancient Israel. Furthermore, the matter is complicated by the fact that, despite an overarching concern for ethnic identity in the Hebrew source, the sentiments are not uniform in character, as several examples show.

Today Pentateuchal narratives, or pentateuch's components, have been increasingly viewed as literary products from the late morarchy, the exile, or even from the Persian era. Whitelam writes: "the dramatic effect that the Davidic court must have had upon shaping the idea of Israel and its origin."[168] And even if one is not fully convinced of such a late date for the materials. Knight asserts that: "it is now difficult to hold to an early date with unshaken confidence."[169] Neither an amphictyonic context, nor the conquest model nor a supposed patriarchal age can be established with any certainty, and so they

167 For a brief example of this sociological philosophy in action, see N. K. Gottwald, "Early Israel and the Canaanite Sociological System," *Palestine in Transition: The Emergence of Ancient Israel,* edited by D. N. Freedman and D. F. Graf (Sheffield: Almond, 1983), 25-37.

168 Robert B. Coote and Keith W. Whitelam, *The Emergence of Early Israel in Historical Perspective* (Sheffield: Sheffield Phoenix Pres, 2010), 170.

169 D. A. Knight, "The Pentateuch," in *The Hebrew Bible and the Modern Interpreters,* edited by D. A. Knight and G. M. Tucker (Philadelphia: Fortress, 1985), 281-282. Most scholars agree that the first five books of the Hebrew Bible, Genesis through Deuteronomy, were in much of their final form early in the Persian period. Since this block of literary material contains almost all of legal codes of the Hebrew Bible, it seems reasonable to assume that Darius' interest would have focused here. Cf. Jon L. Berquist, *Judaism in Persia's Shadow a Social and Historical Approach* (Eugene, Oregon: Wipf and Stock Publishers, 1995), 138. Cf. Joseph Blenkinsopp, "The Pentateuch," in *The Cambridge Companion to Biblical Interpretation,* edited by John Barton (Cambridge: University press, 2011), 184. James Barr argues that the main body of Hebrew text had its origins in a late period, say in the

cannot serve as stable context for the emergence of a distinct ethnic identity in ancient Israel.

Today, the phenomenal changes which have taken place in biblical studies in recent years means that serious questions needs to be raised about the relationship between biblical studies and the study of the early Israel. The three dominion conceptual model of Israel's ethnic distinctiveness (amphictyony, conquest, peasant-revolt cannot get a clear picture of Israelite origins and hence queries should be focus on more tangible literary sources and historical periods. Before dealing with ethnicity and boundary marker, it is necessary that a more thorough definition of ethnicity is needed.

Before going any further, something must be said about the definition of sociology, especially as it relates to anthropology. The two terms have come to be used almost interchangeably, and satisfactory distinctions are difficult to pin down. This is partly because the terms are used differently on opposite side of the Atlantic,[170] and partly because older definition and partly because older definitions no longer hold. The use of contemporary comparatives material became even more common in the 18th and 19th centuries, when the social sciences began to establish themselves in universities throughout Europe. Sociologist such as, "Herbert Spencer (1820-1903) is best known as a proponent of social Darwinism. Karl Marx (1818-1883) associated with Political science and economics, but his voluminous writings embracing all the social science. Max Weber (1864-1920) an opposition of Marx's dialectical materialism held that history is shaped not by economic interests but by a society's commonly held value orientations. Emile Durkheim (1858-1917) who was an original theorist but also a major force in shaping sociological method."[171] As noted

Persian Empire or even, more extremely, in the Hellenistic period. Cf. James Barr, *History and Ideology the Old Testament: Biblical Studies of the end of a Millennium*, 59.

170 See John W. Rogerson, *Anthropology and the Old Testament* (Oxford: Blackwell, 1978), 9-10. It is said that anthropology was the study of "primitive "or preindustrial society, while sociology was concerned with modern, industrial society. Distinctions are made by different scholars with these two approaches. In Britain these subject have traditionally fallen under the heading of social anthropology, which is roughly equivalent to cultural anthropology in the United States; see John W. Rogerson, "Anthropology," *A Dictionary of Biblical Interpretation*, edited by R. J. Coggins and J. L. Houlden (London: SCM, 1990), 26.

171 Robert R. Wilson, *Sociological Approaches to the Old Testament* (Philadelphia: Fortress Press, 1984), 13-16; Cf. Robert R.Wilson, "Sociology of Old Testament," *Harper Colins Bible Dictionary*, edited by Paul J. Achtemeier (Bangalore: Theological Publication in India, 2009), 1040. Social-scientific models have a variety of sociological and anthropological method. The principal method that has been employed is structural-*functional approach* the tradition of E. Durkheim. Cf Gottwald, *The Tribes of Yahweh*, 608. Secondly the *Conflict theory* was originally formulated by George Hegel and Karl Marx and adapted by Max Weber. Cf Victor H. Matthews, *Studying the Ancient Israelites* Matthews, Victor H. Mathew, *Studying the Ancient Israelites A Guide to Source and Methods,* (Grand Rapids,

above, social sciences have often influenced Old Testament scholars, who have applied social scientific approaches both to the study of Israelite religion and to the study of biblical literature. However, within a generation such experimental cross-disciplinary research was severely shortened and biblical scholars employed the social science primarily when they made comparative use of archaeological techniques.[172] Even the ancient Near Eastern textual data were also included.

Sociological approach can deal with social dimensions of Biblical studies. Interpreting the Biblical texts with the sociological approach is very effective to our contemporary religious and secular life. Gracia writes: "They are understandings, or texts aimed to produce understandings, of text in terms of sociological factors, be it economic, psychological, cultural, political, or historical."[173]According to Chalcraft, "it involves sociological and anthropological 'way of thinking'. These are all used to illuminate the worlds within the texts which, moreover, span the whole breath of ancient Israelite social forms and production."[174] As Massey remarks, "the social-scientific method enabled biblical scholars to gain a fuller and more accurate understanding of the social environment and cultural dimension of the biblical world."[175] According to Elliott, "Social-scientific criticism of the Bible is that phrase of the exegetical task which analyzes the social and cultural dimensions of the text and of its environmental context through the utilization of the perspective, theory, models, and research of the social science. As a component of the historical-critical method of exegesis, social-scientific criticism investigates biblical texts as meaningful configurations of language intended to communicate between composer and audience."[176] The above definition is true in the sense that the history interweaves with social science.

Sociological methods and theories were initially employed to understand the religion of ancient Israel. This initial sociological research on the Hebrew

---

Machigan: Baker Academic, 2007), 130. Thirdly, *Cultural Materialist Theories,* based on subsidence.

172 Archaeological techniques to the study of ancient Israel were employed William Foxwell Albright. He was a specialist in archeological and linguistic approach. From the Albright stream of scholarship have come G. E. Mendenhall's proposals that the Israelites covenant was a religious analogue of a suzerain-vassal political treaty and that the Israelites conquest was a peasants' revolt. See N. K. Gottwald, *The Tribes of Yahweh,* 14.

173 George J. E. Gracia, *How Can We Know What God Means? The Interpretation of Revelation* (New York: Palgrave, 2001), 99.

174 David J. Chalcraft, *Social-Scientific Old Testament Criticism: A Sheffield Reader* (Sheffield: Academic Press, 1997), 17.

175 James Earl Massey "Reading the Bible from particular social locations: An Introduction" *The New Interpreters Bible*, Vol-1 (Nashville: Abingdon Press, 1994), 150-151.

176 John H. Elliott, *What is Social-Scientific Criticism*? (Minneapolis: Fortress Press, 1993), 7.

Bible maintained that: "religion was the key to recovering the social origins of the Hebrew Bible and that the religion of earliest Israel described in the Hebrew Bible was an expression of the character of its social structure. In addition, these studies also considered the economic motivations that might account for the development of biblical Israel."[177] In this short space, it is impossible to provide an exhaustive history of the application of social-scientific approaches to the Hebrew Bible. The following discussion will trace, side by side, the development of sociological theory and methods with respect to the interpretive study of the Hebrew Bible.

As discussed above, research in the social sciences has often influenced Old Testament scholars, who have applied social scientific approaches both to the study of Israelite religion and to the study of biblical literature. However, sociological approach is still in its infancy and scholars are still debating the question of methodology.

2.7. Ethnicity and Ethnic Boundary Markers in Early Israel

Having outlined a number of features of ethnicity above, let us see how they can be applied to the early Israelites. First of all, let us see what aspects of ethnicity would serve as possible identifiers of an ethnic group 'Israel' and as boundary markers between members belonging to Israel and members belonging to some other possible group during the Late Bronze-Iron Age transition and in the Early Iron Age. To do this, the researcher will work on the basis of the definition given by Hutchinson and Smith as quoted above.

First of all, there is the question of a common name. The Bible itself is replete with expressions, which distinguish the Israelites from other groups inhabiting the land. While the exact ethnic composition of Canaan during Late Bronze Age-Iron Age 1 is not clear, Mendenhall speaks about such groups as the "Canaanites, Hittites, Amorites, Perizzites, Hivites and Jebusites (e.g. Judg.3:5)."[178] In addition, the Merneptah stele clearly indicates that there was an entity called Israel somewhere in the region of Canaan about 1200 BC,[179] and there is no doubt that an Egyptian, Assyrian and Hittite identity existed in a wider ancient Near Eastern context. So there are very good reasons to conclude that a group which was called Israel and was distinct in an inscriptive sense existed in Canaan during Late Bronze Age-Iron Age 1.[180] Dever dealing

177 Naomi Steinberg, "Sociological Approaches: Toward A Sociology of Childhood in the Hebrew Bible," *Method Matters Essays on the Interpretation of the Hebrew Bible in Honor of David L. Petersen*, edited by Joel M. Lemon and Kent Herold Richards (Atlanta: Society of Biblical Literature, 2009), 251-52.

178 G. E. Mendenhall, *Ancient Israel's Faith and History: An Introduction to the Bible in Context,* edited by Gary A. Herion (Louisville: Westminster John Knox, 2001), 11.

179 Sparks, *Ethnicity and Identity in Ancient Israel,* 94-109.

180 Dever, *Who Were the Early Israelites?*, 216-21.

with archaeology and "ethnicity" asserts "there are many universal "Iron 1" material traits that are common to all sites simply because they are universal in this period, such as typical cooking pots springing off the local Bronze 11 repertoire. It is the clear cut and consistent differences from side to side, however, that are diagnostic of cultural and thus of "ethnic" identity. These differences include: side-type; settlement plan; technology; subsistence; social organization; ceramic repertoire; religion and ideology; and even, one might argue, language, the latter surely an "ethnic marker."[181]

Secondly, the Bible is packed with descriptions of a belief in common ancestry for the Israelites. Stories that, Israelites are descendants of patriarchs Abraham, Isaac, Jacob and Joseph form a backbone of Israelite self-consciousness according to the Hebrew Scriptures. It is of course another matter how early such beliefs originated and when they were committed to writing. While there are scholars who would date the documents to the time "before the monarchy, estimates for the time of writing generally vary from the early monarchy to the Persian period, in line with various views of the dating of the Old Testament documents."[182]

Thirdly and closely related to the previous point, the Bible is full of historical memories of a common past. The stories about the patriarchs and the Egyptian sojourn and slavery and the subsequent Exodus provide a foundation for a shared history. As already indicated above and as is well known, the origin and historicity of these stories is much disputed, but again, there is the *possibility* that a group of slaves had escaped from Egypt and entered the land of Canaan during the time of the early Israelites, whatever the historical circumstances surrounding them might be as opposed to what the biblical sources attest. These people might also have had at least some kind of historical reminiscences about the patriarchs. It would be very possible that the combination of historical memories about the patriarchs and the Exodus would distinguish the adherents of this group from other people in Canaan.

Fourthly, there is the question of a common culture. In relation to this, it is unlikely that language, which is always intertwined with culture, is an issue as Hebrew is a Semitic language and is likely to have had mainly dialectal differences with other languages in the area.[183] According to Cook, "Yahwism" coexisting in ancient Israel was an initially small minority stream of theological tradition composed of geographical and socially diverse groups in northern & southern Israel. These groups shared a religious commitment to a covenantal

181 Dever, "Archaeology, Ideology and the Quest for an 'Ancient' or 'Biblical' Israel," 47.

182 G. J. Wenham, "Pondering the Pentateuch: the Search for a New Paradigm," in *The Face of Old Testament Studies: A Survey of Contemporary Approaches,* edited by D. W. Baker and B. T. Arnold (Grand Rapids: Baker, 1999), 116-44.

183 Cf. The Sibboleth incident in Judg. 12:1-6 which indicates dialectal differences even within different regions in Israel.

village-based, land-oriented Yahwism that arose before the emergence of Israelite kingship."[184] Cook argues for the early origins of biblical Yahwism. As regards religion, the Bible of course clearly distinguishes Yahwism from the surrounding religions. However, the origins of Yahwism are debated.[185] In a broad sense, these fall along the lines of other views of Israelite origins. If the Israelites originated from the Canaanites indigenously, then it is likely that the origin of Yahwism lies in Canaanite religion. On the other hand, if at least some of the Israelites came from outside, bringing a belief in YHWH with them, it is possible to see Yahwism as a development more or less external to Canaan. It must also be kept in mind that there may have been a big gap between the Yahwism advocated by the canonical documents and that of popular religion. The biblical documents themselves clearly indicate that this was the case, and archaeological evidence from the time of the monarchy confirms cases where YHWH was put on a par with another deity.[186] Whatever the complications, for the sake of our argument, there is nevertheless a possibility that some of the early Israelites believed in a deity called YHWH. How widespread this belief may have been and whether, when and how much it distinguished an Israelite from surrounding peoples in practice is a matter about which we cannot be certain. As for Yee "Yahwism was the dominant religious ideology, which unified the tribes under a familial idiom of mutuality and Kinship that expressed itself in the economic and social interest of the people."[187]

We still have one important aspect of common culture to consider, namely, circumcision. According to the biblical tradition, circumcision was a boundary marker (Gen. 17; 1 Sam. 31:4). As Stager remarks: "however, one may not assume that all people around Israel were uncircumcised, and the biblical tradition itself seems to hint that not all Israelites were necessarily circumcised in actuality (Josh. 5: l-9)."[188] Therefore, circumcision may have been a boundary marker in early Israel, but if so, it is difficult to say to what extent.

Coming to the fifth point of the main features of ethnies according to Hutchinson and Smith, a link with a homeland, the land of Canaan features

184 Stephen L. Cook, *The Social Roots of Biblical Yahwism* (Atlanta: SBL, 2004), 18.

185 R. Gnuse, "The Emergence of Monotheism in Ancient Israel: A Survey of Recent Scholarship," *Religion* 29 (1999), 315-36.

186 J. S. Holladay, "Religion in Israel and Judah Under the Monarchy: An Explicitly Archaeological Approach" in *Ancient Israelite Religion: Essays in honor of Frank Moore Cross,* edited by P. D. Miller, Jr., P. D. Hanson, S. D. McBride (Philadelphia: Fortress, 1987), 249-99.

187 Gale A. Yee, *Poor Banished Children of the Eve Woman as Evil in the Hebrew Bible* (Minneapolis: Fortress Press, 2003), 32.

188 Cf. P. J. King and L. E. Stager, *Life in Biblical Israel* (Library of Ancient Israel; Louisville, Kentucky: Westminster John Knox, 2001), 43-45.

as a particularly strong concept in the biblical tradition. Certainly, this is the case with the Babylonian exiles. Examples throughout history also indicate that people who have been displaced from their country of birth often long to be back there. From the standpoint of ethnicity, it would not be likely that land would be a distinguishing feature between the early Israelites and non-Israelites, as both would be essentially living in the same area, even though with the distinction between the highlands and the lowlands.

Finally, we come to the sixth of Hutchinson and Smith's points, a sense of solidarity among at least part of the people constituting the ethnie. This point is very much linked to all the previous points. And, according to the Old Testament, such solidarity existed during the premonarchical period. In particular, leaving aside the books of Exodus-Joshua, according to the books of Judges and Samuel the Israelites could assemble together if threatened.[189]

2.8. Implication and Conclusion

The three divisions which are made in this chapter concern more on sources. The first, establishing agreed upon dates for biblical texts and discerning the social settings reflected by them remains a persistent problem. Secondly, despite these advantages to an ethnic theory of identity, scholarship has often recognized the substantial problems with the categories of ethnicity. For example, archaeologists have difficulty discerning the ethnicity of a given artifact's maker or use. Historians find reconstruction ancient lineages to be problematic and uncertain. On the other hand as stated above ethnicity is essentially a modern concept and does not fit well with descriptions of the premodern world and so investigation into ancient Israelite ethnicity require a more definition of ethnic identity. Thirdly, scholarship on ethnicity emphasizes the subject character of ethnic boundaries as discussed above; they are largely the product of the mind and imagination. Fourthly, such theories ignore too much of the biblical textual evidence. Fifthly, historical importance of the ideology of early Israel lies not so much in itself but in the set of later developments through which it was adapted and preserved. Ideological criticism according to Clines, agrees with the requirement (see introduction for definition). Ideological criticism as I see it, systematically asks about the ideological interests inscribed in the texts. That is to say it does not view the texts primarily as historical document, nor as theological documents, nor as purely literary texts with the status of works of art, but as ideological documents that serve some particular or group interest.

189 See e.g. Judg. 3-4 (Deborah) and other judges; Judg. 19-21 (the crime of the men of Gibeah); 1 Sam. 11 (Saul and the Ammonites).

With the change of identity, the new entrants, setting aside their original background, would also be likely to adopt Israelite foundation stories.[190] The fact that the patriarchal stories take place in Canaan would no doubt make it easier to associate with them, even if the stories also speak about the alienation and exodus from Egypt. Moreover, on the survival issue Dever explain: "the new entrants would adopt an egalitarian ideology like the Israelites. While the justification for this ideology would ostensibly be liberation from Egypt, it would fit the conditions of the highland frontier where everyone needed to cooperate in order to survive."[191] As Gottwald rightly said, "oppressed people looking for a better life at the highland frontier would undoubtedly associate with such an ideology."[192] The frontier would help facilitate the acceptance of a common Israelite solidarity for the new entrance.

Thus, all of the minimal boundary markers of being called an Israelite, believing in a descent from the patriarchs or the like, believing in a common history of the patriarchs and in an Egyptian sojourn and exodus, having an egalitarian ideology, accepting some food restrictions, such as abstaining from eating pork, the practice of circumcision, and having some sense of obligation towards fellow Israelites would have been crossed by the new entrants.

In summary, there are significant differences among the positions discussed in this chapter. They all say that the early Israelites were indigenous to Canaan, but not withstanding the same archaeological and textual evidence, they come up with vastly different descriptions of the process by which the Israelites became a people. Despite their differences, these scholars are in agreement that the Israelites came from multiple backgrounds. The model discussed above acknowledges that no one model is adequate. This explanation highlights different aspects of the first Israelites. Further research is needed to determine which explanation best describes who the majority of these Israelites were and what the principles process was that led to their emergence in the land of Canaan.

In investigating long term settlement patterns Braudel has termed *la longue duree.* No interpretation can claim to be definitive. It requires long-term research in order to verify or negate their assumptions and conclusion. The researcher has no intention to follow any of this models stated above but to have a general understanding of investigation how identity develops over the human lifespan and throughout social change. Much further work remains in investigating of legal texts dealing with boundary issues, treatment of aliens, and cleanliness/uncleanness regulation will be discussed in the following

190 An immigrant to the Western countries would be likely to adopt West foundation stories, or at least his or her children would, as part of growing up in the society.

191 Cf. W. G. Dever, *Who Were the Early Israelites?*, 185.

192 Cf. N. K. Gottwald, *The Tribes of Yahweh,* 647.

chapters. Since the majority of the texts that the researcher examines come from the Hebrew Bible, the frame of reference at this point is to identify ethnic boundary markers distinct to the ethnic group "Israel" which is based on the text. *Intrinsic* analysis will be in the following chapters.

Smith's understanding of sacred ethnoscapes offers rich resources for the analysis of alienation. The processes of territorialization of memory by which the *ethnie* and the land come to be associated are clearly evident in the narratives of Pentateuch. Ancestral alienation is a striking part of this process of territorialization, as Chapter three will show aliens and ethnic identity in ancestorial narratives of Genesis.

The exposition above has shown how Smith's work provides both theoretical and methodological structure to my investigation of aliens in Genesis. Thus Smith's notion of ethnoscrapes set up correlation between attachment to land and the intensification of ethnic bonds. If the land of Canaan is Israel's ethnoscrape, it is clear from the primary trust of the Hebrew Bible that Israel developed an intense identity association with the land. The identity struggle of the people of Israel as alien in the Pentateuch downplays the territorial component of Israel collective identity, stressing instead that the ancestors of Israel originally were, and in some sense continued to be, alienated from the land which was their ethnoscrape. The theme of the Patriarch as גר in the land poses an interpretive challenge when viewed in comparison with the prominent territorial commitment portrayed in the biblical texts.

Therefore, גר = *ger* 'aliens" is a problem for ethnic identity. The ethnic ideal is represented by what is authentic, rooted, original, pristine, autochthonous, native, primordial, and ancient.[193] גר in contrast, represent rootlessness, alienation, dispossession, foreignness, and anxiety. It negates the possibility of a natural, organic connection of Israel to its territory. Thus an understanding of the varied components of ethnic myth helps illuminate the diverse ways in which גר functions, and clarify its helpful role in constructing ethnic identity. Both elements Smith identifies, territorial and election, are key for the interpretation of aliens' in Pentateuch.

193 Smith, *Chosen People,* 39.

Chapter 3

Alien and Ethnic Identity in Ancestral Narratives of Genesis

3. Introduction

The author of Hebrew describes the heroes of the book of Genesis as aliens in the land of promise. Christian tradition looks to the alien of the patriarchs as exemplary; the author of Hebrews depicts their alien existence in Canaan as a faith standpoint for belivers to immitiate. In the Hebrew Bible, 1 Chro 29:15 and Psa 39:13 reference the alien of the fathers as a pattern repeated through time, and several motive clauses attached to laws about treatment of the alien urge the remembrance of past alien in Egypt.[194]

Turning the spotlight on the book of Genesis itself reveals a textual emphasis on alien that confirms the impression facts from the allusions throughout the canon. Alien appears 17 times in the patriarchal narratives of Genesis. גר occurs eight times in Genesis in its nominal form and nine times in its verbal form גור "to tarry as a sojourner,"[195] indicating that the character is going or staying somewhere where the character is a stranger (12:10; 20: 1;

194 Exod 22:20-23; 23:9; Lev 19:34; Deut 10:19; 23:8. These text may refer to the alien experience of the exodus generation, but some author have argued that ut refers to the experience of earlier generation starting with Jacob and sons. See Kidd, *Alterity and Identity in Israel,* 90-98.

195 D. Kellermann, "גּוּר *gur;* גר *ger;* גרוּת *geruth;* מְגוּרִים *meghurim,*" *TDOT*, Vol. II, edited by G. Johannes Botterweck and Helmer Ringgren (Grand Rapids, Michigan: William B. Eerdmans Publishing Company, 1975), 439.

21:34; 35:27). Alternatively, the location itself may be described using a noun מָגוֹר; identifying it as a place of alien; this noun always occurs in construct form connected with a genitive pronoun or a noun that indicates the character(s) who experience this location as a place of alien (36: 7; 37: 1).
The accent on alien in Genesis is, however, somewhat surprising. In a narrative concerned with instituting a strong tie between the ancestors of Israel and their divinely appointed homeland, alien sound a note of discord. In this chapter, the researcher will investigate the alien references to the Genesis narrative, and offer a helpful matrix for relating ideas of identity, land and community.

3.1. Overviews of Scholarly Approach on Gen 12:10-20; 20:1-18; 26:1-11

Firstly before turning to the textual exegesis, overviews of scholarly approach to the alien highlight the reason for the neglect and explain why a focus on them is appropriate for this particular study.

Martin Noth classifies patriarchal itineraries as secondary literary forms used to bind together independent unit of tradition.[196] Westermann contends in response that the itineraries reflect migrant life and thus originate at an earlier stage of oral tradition; he assigns them to "the oldest layer" of Gen. 12-50.[197] Thompson argues against a historical foundation for the wandering of patriarchs, suggesting literary origins for the form instead as either "a traditional folk-tale motif (so, Gen. 12: 10) or a secondary editorial technique of linking original distinctive narrative (so, Gen. 13: 1f)."[198]

In classical formulations of the documentary hypothesis of the Pentateuch, this triplet has been seen to demonstrate the existence of distinct documentary sources for the book of Genesis. Two versions of the story are conventionally assigned to J (Gen 12, 26), and the third (Gen 20), which is considered more sophisticated theologically and ethically, is assigned to the E source. Noth, an advocate of such a classical view, argued that not only these ideological

196 Noth argues that Pentateuch contains "secondary itineraries" which originated by virtues of the locale centers to which the individual narratives were attracted. Secondly "authentic itineraries" would be understood list of stations along a route which serve no other purpose than to establish this route, irrespective of events which might have occurred at the place mentioned. Noth allows for a few individual exceptions where a short journey may represent an "authentic itinerary" preserving the historical memory of a travel route. In these cases Noth believes the itinerary is independent from the development of narrative material. Martin Noth, *A History of Pentateuchal Traditions,* translated by Bernhard W. Anderson (Englewood Cliffs: Prentice-Hall, 1972), 220-23.

197 Claus Westermann, *Genesis 12-36: A Commentary,* translated by John J. Scullion (London: SPCK, 1985), 47

198 Thomas L. Thompson, *The Origin Tradition of Ancient Israel, 1: The Literary Formation of Genesis and Exodus 1-23,* JSOT Sup, Vol. 55 (Sheffield: Sheffield Academic Press, 1987), 33.

distinctions and certain vocabulary items but, more important, the very existence of multiple versions of a given story requires the presupposition that documentary sources underlie the present patriarchal narrative. Noth assert: "... secondary accretions usually add new materials, not the same materials in new versions... I do not know how this situation could be explained except by the assumption of two sources..."[199]

Speiser felt that all three stories (Gen 21:10-20; 20:1-18; 26:1-11) reflected a misunderstanding of a socio-legal institution which allowed a favoured wife to be considered by her husband as his sister.[200] Brettler, explore two examples in Genesis which exhibit typological thinking. As in Chronicles, the patterns should not be viewed as decorative, but their purposes must be explored. Giving the early place of Genesis within the canon, the events are not "types" or re-enactments of earlier occurrences, but foreshadow later events; for this reason, Brettler refer to them as "pre-enactments."[201] Clines question about the fulfilment or otherwise of the promise lays the significance of the triple narrative of the 'ancestress in danger.'[202] Goldingay suggests a picture of non-fulfilment or (anti-fulfilment).[203] Rosenberg's treatment of the Patriarchal

199 M. Noth, *A History of Pentateuchal...*,22 In view of Noth's opinion that doublets must be explained by the existence of separate documentary source, how does he explain the presence of a doublet (12 and 26) within J? "In (Gen 26) we find a concatenation of various units and tradition which in part are merely sketched and are really not complete in themselves... The chapter appears to be an artificial literary composition... With the aid of a narrative thread running through the whole, J has gathered up here in a compendium like fashion everything that the oral tradition known to him had to say about Isaac" (p.104)

200 E. A. Speiser, "The Wife-Sister Motif in the Pentateuch Narratives," in *Biblical and Other Studies,* edited by Alexander Altmann (Cambridge, MA: Harvard University Press, 1963), 15-28.

201 Marc Zvi Brettler, *The Creation of History in Ancient Israel* (London and New York: Routledge, 1995), 50.

202 David J. A. Clines, *The Theme of the Pentateuch,* JSOT Supt 10 (Sheffield: Sheffield Academic Press, 2004), 48. See David J. A Clines, *What does Eve Do to Help? And other Readerly Question to the Old Testament* (Sheffield: JSOT Press, 1990), 67. Cf. Robert Polzin, "The Ancestress of Israel in Danger," *SEMEIA* 3 (1975), 81-97. See also Mark E. Biddle, "The 'Endangered Ancestress' And Blessing for the Nation," *JBL* 109/4 (1990), 599-611. T. D. Alexander, "Are the Wife/Sister of Genesis Literary Composition Variant? *Vêtus Testamentum* XLII/ 2 (1992), 145-153. Cf. J. Cheryl Exum, "Who is Afraid of the Endangered Ancestress? Edited by J. Cheryl Exum and David J. A. Clines in *The New Literary Criticism and the Hebrew Bible,* JSOT Supt 143 (Sheffield: JSOT Press, 1993), 91. Cf. Gordon J. Wenham, "Pondering the Pentateuch: The Search for a New Paradigm," edited by David W.Baker and Bill T. Arnold in *The Face of Old testament Studies A Survey of Contemporary Approaches* (Grand Rapids, Michigan: Bakers Books, 1999), 123.

203 J. Goldingay, "The Patriarchs in Scripture and Tradition," in *Essay on the Patriarchal Narrative,* edited by A. R. Millard & D. J. Wiseman (Leicester: IVP, 1980), 13. Yahweh intent to make Abram a great nation, to make him a blessing to the nation, and to give the

narratives offer no new interpretation for the 'wife-sister' stories, claiming that the meaning is 'obscure' and will continue to elude us. However in a footnote he suggests that there must be some 'socio-economic factors involved.[204] Hoffmeir asserts that: "wife-sister' stories to be separate events. He argues in the light of ancient West Asia practice of "diplomatic marriage."[205] However, stories can develop in many unexpected ways, and the criteria used by Koch to decide which plot elements are original are subjective. As Niditch points out, folklorists who study parallel versions of the same story "would suggest that such searches for originals are fruitless."[206] Instead, it is best to treat each story on its own terms, using the other variants to help highlight significant elements that might otherwise escape notice.

Seter cites parallels with mythological sources from the classical world to argue for a genre of ethnographic history in which ancestral travels or wanderings are a central element in the account of national origins.[207] Seter's concludes with the late dating of the Yahwist. For Albertz the final editing of the book took place only in the fifth century BCE, during the period of Persian rule.[208] In the history of scholarship concerning the Pentateuch the book of Genesis has played a pivotal role. From the source-theory of Graf and Wellhausen,[209] to the form-critical work of Gunkel, and to the tradition histories of von Rad and Noth: time and again the different methods of these preeminent scholars have found fertile ground for analysis and application in the textual data of Genesis. There has been no shortage of essays, monographs,

---

land of Canaan to his descendants. But as a result of an entirely human response to a real crisis, each element in his promise receives a kind of anti-fulfilment.

204 Joel Rosenberg, *King and Kin: Political Allegory in the Hebrew Bible* (Bloomington: Indiana University Press, 1986), 77.

205 James K. Hoffmeier, "'The Wives' Tales of Genesis 12, 20 & 26 and the Covenants at Beer-Sheba" *Tyndale Bulletin* 43/1(1992). 81-99.

206 Susan Niditch, *Underdogs and Tricksters: A Prelude to Biblical Folklore* (San Francisco: Harper & Row, 1987), 23. For an additional critique of Koch approach, see David Peterson, "A Thrice-Told Tale," *Biblical Research* 18 (1973), 3-43.

207 Van Seters, *Prologue to History: The Yahwist as Historian in Genesis* (Louisville: Westminster John Knox, 1992), 209-13.

208 Rainer Albertz, *A History of Israelite Religion in the Old Testament Period,* Vol. 1 (London: SCM, 1992), 29. Van Seters dated the Patriarchal stories to Monarchy or later. John Van Seters, *Abraham in History,* 152.

209 Description and analyses of the recent history of scholarship on the compositional origins of the Pentateuch abound; some reliable and thorough efforts include Rolf Rendorff, "The paradigm is changing Hopes-and Fears," *Biblical Interpretation* 1/1 (1993), 34-53. Whybray, *Introduction of the Pentateuch* (Grand Rapids: Eerdmans, 1995). Greifenhagen, *Egypt on the Pentateuch's..* 213. Greifenhagen argues the final text form the Pentateuch within the late fifth or early fourth century BCE. Cf. Frank Crüsemann, *The Torah Theology,* 333.

thesis, and dissertations; it would simply not be possible to engage every study. As historical-critical scholarship has shown, the Pentateuch incorporates various earlier traditions. However, the exact nature of the composition of the Pentateuch, and the sources and traditions upon which it draws, are today hotly debated, disrupting the earlier virtual scholarly consensus around the documentary hypothesis associated with Wellhausen.

Questioning about the authorship of Genesis, renewed in recent years by the so-called minimalists, the researcher attempts to focus on Genesis as a repository of collective memory rather than to view either the book as a whole or its putative sources as the expression of the ideology of a particular group or period in the history of Israel.[210] Writers wove into Genesis their imaginative constructions of the origins of their people, basing their constructions on received traditions, but modelling and reinventing them according to the needs of the present. So, without specifying the date of the "editorial present"[211] of Genesis, the researcher attempts to encounters ethnic identity present in the book.

3.2. Extrinsic Analysis of Genesis 12:10-20; 20:1-18; 26:1-11

It is now generally recognized that the convergence of so-called sociological approaches to the study of Israelites history and literary approaches to the study of Hebrew Bible has resulted in a major paradigm shift in biblical studies.[212] Today most scholars agree that first five books of the Hebrew Bible, Genesis through Deuteronomy, were in much of their final form early in the Persian period. Since this block of literary material contains almost all the legal codes of the Hebrew Bible, it seems reasonable to assume that Darius' interest would have focused here.[213] Albertz argues that Genesis

---

210 For a rigorous historical approach to biblical expressions of ethnicity, see Kenton L. Sparks, *Ethnicity and Identity in Ancient Israel* (Winona Lake, Ind.: Eisenbrauns, 1998). In his account of the development of ethnic sentiments, however, Sparks does not deal with the Pentateuch, since he considers it to be a late, Persian-period document.

211 I borrow the phrase "editorial present" from Seth Daniel Kunin, *The Logic of Incest A Structuralist Analysis of Hebrew Mythology,* JSOT Sup 185 (Sheffield: Sheffield Academic Press, 1995), 50, to refer to the final form of the text. Kunin, however, uses the term in a more strictly structural sense, suggesting that this form reflects the structures of the editorial process though not the structures of the antecedent texts that comprise it.

212 P. R. Davies, *In Search of 'Ancient Israel*, JSOT Sup 148 (Sheffield: JSOT Press, 1992), 47, Davies set out self consciously to author a 'savage' attack against history writing that he flogs as theological apologetic, and to stimulate a paradigm shift in the writing of history of ancient Israel. Additionally, he offers his own reconstruction of who, where, how and why biblical literature was authored as an agenda for new scholarship.

213 Jon L. Berquist, *Judaism in Persia's Shadow,* 138. Cf. Jon L. Berquist, "Constructions of Identity in Postcolonial Yehud," edited by Oded Lipschits and Manfred Oeming in *Judah and the Judeans in the Persian Period* (Eisenbrauns: Winona Lake, Indiana, 2006), 53-65.

should be understood "not as a preliminary stage but as a substratum of Yahweh religion."[214] Albertz argues that the triplets story of Genesis seek to describe the small group of the family and the religion associated with it. Instead of assuming that the sources of Genesis survive relatively intact and that biblical interpretation should focus on their reconstruction, that the received Hebrew version of Genesis can be quite directly related to the politics of the Persian period.

Researcher exegetical analysis of the alien however, presupposes neither an early nor a late dating. Instead my approach is an experiment in certain type of reading which I undertake because of it appropriateness for interpretation of the puzzling aspects of the alien texts in the Hebrew bible. This research is based on the method proposed by Yee[215] on Ideological criticism which includes a two part analysis- an extrinsic analysis and an intrinsic analysis. An extrinsic analysis 'investigates the social and historical worlds, in which these texts are produce,' and in intrinsic analysis 'focuses on what the text actually says (content) and how it says it rhetoric'(for more detail cf. introduction).

3.2.1. Mode of Production

In his analysis of the ancient West Asian economic systems that undergird biblical societies. Jobling adopts Carol Meyers use of the term "household" mode of production for pre-monarchic Israel (rather than Marx's "primitive commune),"[216] and Gottwald's notion of the "Asiatic" mode of production (following Marx),[217] though he prefers the term "tributary" for this mode of production, because "many important examples are not Asian."[218] As Jobling

214 Albertz, *A History of Israelite Religion*, 29. Barr argues that the main body of Hebrew text had its origins in a late period, the Persian period or even, more extremely, in the Hellenistic period. Barr, *History and Ideology*, 59. Cf also Keith W. Whitelam, "Introduction: General Problems of Studying the text of the Bible in order to reconstruct History and Social background," edited by J. W. Rogerson and Judith M. Lieu, in *The Oxford Hand Book of Biblical Studies* (Oxford: University Press, 2006), 256-58. F. V. Greifenhagen argues that the final text form of the Pentateuch within the late fifth or early fourth century BCE has been suggested. F. V. Greifenhagen, *Egypt on the Pentateuch's Ideological Map,* 213.

215 Gale A. Yee, *Poor Banished Children* ...9-27. Cf. Gale A. Yee, "Ideological Criticism: Judges 17-21 and the Dismembered Body," 146-167.

216 Carol Meyers, *Discovering Eve: Ancient Israelite Women in Context* (Oxford: Oxford University Press, 1988), 142.

217 Norman K. Gottwald, *The Hebrew Bible in Its Social World and in Ours* (Atlanta: Scholars Press, 1993), xxv-xxvii.

218 David Jobling, "'Very Limited Ideological Options:' Marxism and Biblical Studies in Postcolonial Scenes," in *Postcolonial Biblical Criticism: Interdisciplinary Intersections*, edited by Stephen D. Moore and Fernando F. Segovia (London and New York: T&T Clark, 2005), 193.

goes on to state, the household and tributary modes of production, together with the slave-based mode of production (relevant mainly to the economic world behind the New Testament), "provide a most effective large-scale historical framework for the Bible."

According to Marx and Engels, for individuals, the mode of production is "a definite form of expressing their life, a defined *mode of life* on their part. As individual express their life, so they are. What they are, therefore, coincide with their production, both with *what* they produce, and *how* they produce."[219] Thus, a society, innately economic, is formed through the exchange and corroboration of its people who employ such forces and relations, denotes as a mode of production. According to Engels, the ultimate cause of social change lay not in people's beliefs and ideas but in changes from one mode of production to another.

The greatest theoretical debt which Biblical Studies owes to Marxism, in the opinion of Jobling, is the understanding of historical modes of production (MPs). Postcolonialism also has a great deal to learn from MP theory.[220] The archaeological and textual artifact only has meaning within a model. In collection of essays entitled, *The Ancient Economy: Evidence and Models*, the editors and authors carefully demonstrate the power of explanatory models in our construal of the economic past.[221] In the previous chapter we have seen in ancient West Asia and Egypt there is a clear recognition of certain basic common structures that were shared in the ancient Egyptian and Mesopotamian empires and Canaanite city states.

As Jobling argues: "'Mode of production' is a concept of the utmost comprehensiveness. Based on the model of base and superstructure, it extends the latter to include every aspect or 'sector' of the workings of a society (law, art, religion, etc.) considered in terms of the systems of implication that them together."[222] Jameson moves away from the idea that a given society

219 Karl Marx and Friedrich Engels, "The German Ideology," (1845), in *Cultural And Theory: An Anthology*, edited by Imre Szeman and Timothy Kaposy (West Sussex: Wiley-Blackwell, 2011), 162. Cf. G. E. M. De Ste. Croix, *The Class Struggle in Ancient Greek World from the Archaic Age to the Arab Conquests* (Ithaca, New York: Cornell University Press, 1981), 32. Croix discussed Marx concepts of the 'relations of production: The social relation on whom men enter in the process of production: which finds legal expression to a large degree either as property relations or as labour relations.

220 David Jobling, "'Very Limited Ideological Options:' Marxism and Biblical Studies in Postcolonial Scenes," 93.

221 Ian Morris and Joseph G. Manning, "Introduction," in *The Ancient Economy: Evidence and Models*, edited by Joseph G. Manning and Ian Morris (Stanford California: Stanford University Press, 2005).

222 Jobling, "'Very Limited Ideological Options:' Marxism and Biblical Studies in Postcolonial Scenes," 193.

at a given time exemplifies just one mode of production. Instead, Jameson argues:

> every social formation or historically existing society has in fact consisted in the overlay and structural co-existence of several modes of production all at once, including vestiges and survivals of older modes of production, ... as well as anticipatory tendencies which are potentially inconsistent with the existing system but have not yet generated an autonomous space of their own.[223]

West asserts: "… any proposed analogy needs to be brought to the bar of mode of production theory in order to test the limits of 'translating' between societies which worked in fundamentally different ways."[224]

Most scholars who use "mode of production" terminology do so with a clear recognition that they are using a Marxist economic category. For those doing biblical scholarship in "third world" or postcolonial contexts, the mode of production model is particularly important. The debt to Marx in this model is apparent; indeed, as Jobling acknowledges, "The greatest theoretical debt which Biblical Studies owes to Marxism ... is the understanding of historical modes of production."[225] But, precisely because of its debt to Marxist analysis, there is the very real danger that the modes of production model has fallen into disuse or, worse, disregard. But, the researcher will attempt by using the tools especially in dealing with ethnicity and Identity.

3.2.2. From Tributary to Familial Mode of Production: Pre-monarchic Israel

The tributary mode of production, characterize of the empirical political economy of the ancient West Asia, tracing its trajectory across biblical text and time. The productive processes that generate wealth and power in the biblical world centered on land and were pre-capitalist. The vast majority of people produced food and other life necessities from the earth working in household or village teams. Since technology and transport were not sufficiently developed to create a large consumer market for manufactured goods, the route to concentrating wealth and power in such circumstances was to gain control over agrarian and products which the operator could themselves consume or assign to retainers at their discretion or convert into other valuables through trade and acquisition of land. This has been achieved in the ancient West Asia

---

223 Fredric Jameson, *The Political Unconscious: Narrative as a Socially Symbolic Act* (Ithaca: Cornell University Press, 1981), 95.

224 Gerald West, "Tracking an Ancient Near Eastern Economic System: The Tributary Mode of Production and the Temple State," *OTE* 24/2 (2011), 511-532.

225 Jobling, "Marxism and Biblical Studies in Postcolonial Scenes," 192.

by the so-called down of civilization, distinguished by the emergence of strong centralized states that siphoned off agrarian and pastoral surpluses through taxation, produce landholding and merchant groups who profited from peasant indebtedness and high level international trade, and engaged in war-fare and conquest of neighboring land.

Amin called this a 'tributary" [226] it laid heavy tribute on fruits of their labour. Developments in the western Mediterranean and Aegean areas appear to have been broadly similar to those in the immediate biblical world, although by Greco-Roman times slave labor began to produce the critical mass of surplus labor values. Gottwald asserts: "tributary relations of production imposed on the agrarian multitudes continued among much of the populace dominated by Rome, since in the long run slave production did not prove successful in agriculture.'[227] On the other hand, the dominated tribute-bearing class consisted of peasants, pastoralist, artisans, priests, slaves, and unskilled workers-all those who did not draw surplus from any other workers but who were structurally subjects to their own surplus being taken by members of the dominant class, or who were themselves dependent wage laborers.[228] Resistance or avoidance strategies by the dominated could reduce the intensity of the exploitation. The peculiarity of earliest Israel is that it enjoyed the longest stretch of tribute-free communal life known to us from AWA source.

The dramatic change in highland settlement pattern, which witnessed a rapid expansion of agriculture settlement in the Palestinian highland and steppes during the thirteenth to the eleventh centuries BCE, generally acknowledged by archaeologist and historians as evidence of the emergence of Israel, needs to be reviewed in the light of long-term settlement patterns.[229] The material culture and economic arrangements of these sites further suggest that the settlement expansion was primarily a result of internal development. It is clear that the economy of these sites was agriculture with a varying pastoral

226 Samir Amin, *Class and Nation, Historically and in the Present Crisis* (New York/ London: Monthly Review, 1980), 46-70. "Tributary" is a more descriptive term for this mode of production than the older label "Asiatic," which in employing the name of the continent where it has more often appeared, fails to characterize the nature of the mode of production as such.

227 Norman K. Gottwald, "Social Class as an Analytic and Hermeneutical Category in Biblical Studies," *JBL* 112/1 (1993), 6

228 Gottwald, "Social Class as an Analytic and Hermeneutical Category in Biblical Studies," 6.

229 Cf. Robert B. Coote and Keith W. Whitelam, *The Emergence of Early Israel...* 119; William G. Dever, "Israel, History of (Archaeology and the Conquest)," *ABD,* Vol. 3 (New York: Doubleday, 1992) 545-53; Robert B. Coote and Keith W.Whitelam, "The Emergence of Israel Social Transformation and State Formation following the Decline in Late Bronze Age Trade," *Semeia* 37 (1986), 107-47. Norman K. Gottwald, *The Tribes of Yahweh* (Maryknoll, New York: Orbis, 1979), 584-87.

component. Alongside the domestic pottery, such sites also included large numbers of saddle stones, querns, mortars and pestles necessary for carrying out agriculture tasks. The major technological achievement of the hill country sites was the development of terracing to produce agricultural land and protect against erosion.[230] This shows that the villagers were more interested in short-term measure of producing food, rather than long-term investment in commercial crops.

Under this tributary mode of production, the peasant bore the heaviest tax burden of the state vis-a-vis other social groups. A considerable percentage of the peasant population escaped their oppressive situation by fleeing to the highland areas and becoming nomads, refugees, or outlaws, outside the jurisdiction of the urban centres and Egyptian authority.[231] This withdrawal of the peasant population has a negative impact on the city-states, which lost a significant portion of their tax base and were confronted with populations beyond their control that threatened trade relations with surrounding nations.

The early ones have little if anything to do with real kinship systems, but are the record of all sorts of tribes and clans which constituted the extremely complex social structure of early Israel and of Pre-Israelite populations of the region.[232] It is difficult to say much about the identity of the peoples of the first part of the period (Iron 1, 1200-1000 B.C.E).[233] The early Iron Age in Canaan witnessed a dramatic growth and cultivation in the highland areas and the rise of village life. Settlement in the "frontier" regions of the land was made possible by the technology in cistern building and terracing that the peasants brought with them. Scholars correlate the emergence of Israel with this push into the hill country and the development of a new mode of production. Lemche argues: "in the course of time, it became possible for this 'outlaw' population group to consolidate their toehold in the highlands and, through socio-political integration, to achieve such a degree of independence that they were able, as

---

230 L. Stager, "Agriculture," *IDBSV;* 13, cited by Robert B.Coote and Keith W. Whitelam, *The Emergence of Israel*...123.

231 Coote and Whitelam, "*Emergence of Israel*,"..., 118-25. Both Mendenhall and Gottwald envision a "peasant revolt" against the urban elite. Although this theory is attractive, particularly in light of the present study, arguments against such a deliberate uprising are convincing. See Frank S. Frick, *The City in Ancient Israel* (Missoula, Montana: The Society of Biblical Literature, 1977), 186. Frick discusses various theories on the Israelites occupation of Palestine.

232 George E. Mendenhall, *The Tenth Generation The Origin of biblical Tradition* (London: The John Hopkins University Press, 1973), 179.

233 Jonathan M. Golden, *Ancient Canaan and Israel An Introduction* (Oxford: Oxford University Press, 2004), 63. Golden attempting to define and ethnic identity one of the most importance feature that anthropologist considering cuisine and the various practices surrounding food consumption. Cf. Samuel Rocca, *The Fortification of Ancient Israel and Judah 1200-586 BC* (Oxford: Osprey Publishing Ltd, 2010), 6.

tribes, to administer their own territories, settled in them, clear new land for a growing population, and defend them against outside interference."[234] From tributary to familial mode of production premonarchic Israel Yee remarks: "the organization of this new society was strongly kinship-based, consisting of "the father house," "lineage" and "tribe." Operating under a familial mode of production, the family household was the basic socioeconomic unit. As self sufficient, mutually supporting, and protecting entities, the households, lineages and tribes were tributary-free, having no state mechanisms to appropriate their surpluses."[235] So the tribes remained in a familial mode of production as free agrarians for about two centuries.

Since this nineteenth-century idea of cultural evolution has thus been successfully challenged by the work of other 'disciplines, its continuing use in OT historiography is seriously called into question: and one should ask whether a nomadic stage should be posited in the history of the Israelites. Such a stage has usually been posited in connection with two periods--the patriarchal age and the period of the Israelite settlement in Palestine in the thirteenth century. In both instances the model for understanding the historical process has been the sedentarization of nomadic groups.

So why should the highland settlers of Iron 1 all are nomads or pastoralists settling down? The settlers were likely a mixture of peoples: former nomads and pastoralists, former city dwellers, immigrants, refugees from the lowlands. Since the vast majority of people made their living from agriculture, why should we expect a difference in material culture between the different groups? Fritz remarks: "there was a variety of settlement but nothing that says "Israelite" versus "Canaanite."[236]

The alien in Gen.12: 10; 20: 1-18; 26: 1-11 was a product of this traumatic time, encoding the inconsistencies and ruptures of this period. It responded to a particular socioeconomic contradiction: to maintain national unity and security against the threats of the invaders, the confederated tribes of Israel reverted back to an oppressive political system and mode of production that they rejected when they became a confederacy. Once again, the story in Genesis 12 witnesses to and is a product of social conflict. It preserves a memory of the struggle at a given time between the powerful (Egyptians) and the powerless (Hebrews). It describes the efforts of the powerful to dominate, and the power of the powerless to resist: the power of the powerful to define reality and the power of the powerless to redefine reality. Clines in his book *Interested Parties*

234 Lemche, "Israel History of"... 539.

235 Gale A. Yee, *Poor Banished Children of Eve: Women as Evil in Hebrew Bible*, 61. Cf David L. Petersen, "Genesis & Family Values," *JBL* 124/1 (2005), 5-23. Petersen focuses family as the primary importance in Genesis.

236 Volkmar Fritz, *The Emergence of Israel in the Twelve and Eleventh Century BCE,* Biblical Encyclopedia 2 (Atlanta: SBL, 2011), 129.

asserts: "On the surface, their texts lay claim to coherence and rationality, and they give the appearance of sincerity and either moral fervour or objectivity. But beneath the surface there are issues of power, of self-identity and security, of group solidarity, of fear and desire, of need and greed that have also played a role in the production of the text, sometimes a leading role."[237] This is the concern of ideological criticism of the text. Text and readers are fair game for ideological critics, and especially when texts are used by the readers in the service of power and of social control.

3.2.3. Effects on Family and Gender Relationship or Strategy to Escape Insecurity and Exploitation

For the most part, the texts handed down in the Old Testament are not 'literature' in the sense that they were set down in writing from the beginning and indented for 'literary' use. Rendtorff suggests: "Many texts were primarily composed for a particular occasion within the life of Israelite society and also used there. Only in the course of time did they then grow together into the books that we now have, or were fitted together in the course of systematic work."[238]

Scholars who have worked on the Genesis originate in the migrant lifestyle of the communities among whom the patriarch tale originated. Westermann asserts: "if a women is infertile (Gen 11:35), the constant course of event is interrupted: something extraordinary happens, which the narrative takes up. If a group is morally threatened by a famine on its way, the constant course of journey is interrupted; something extraordinary happens, which the narrative takes up.[239] Gottwald on migrant movement states that:

> "there remain embedded in the several traditions reports of movements which cannot be easily reduced to any single type. Some of the data suggest circumstances typical of transhumant seasonal treks. On the other hand, most of the movement are described with reference to circumstances of famine, intermarriages, pilgrimages, or inter-group conflict, factors which tend to be better understood as evidence of migration than of nomadism."[240]

The continual struggle of the family household to provide for its own subsistence was by no means its only concern. The peasantry were under

---

237 David J. A. Clines, *Interested Parties: The Ideology of Writers and Readers of the Hebrew Bible,* 24.

238 Rolf Rendtorff, *The Old Testament An Introduction* (Philadelphia: Fortress Press, 1983), 77.

239 Claus Westermann, *Genesis: An Introduction,* translated by John J. Scullion S.J (Minneapolis: Fortress Press, 1992), 146.

240 Gottwald, *Tribes of Yahweh,* 451.

extreme pressure to provide for the needs of the exploitative urban elite, militarily superior Bedouin and bandits. Thornier pointed out that: "it is quite common for peasant families to grow two groups: the first being the cereal on which their own subsistence and that of others depend, and the second often being some kind of non-food grain, such as fruit, fibre or oilseed. The peasantry were thus able to participate in the local trade economy to only limited extend."[241]

Taxation was the most important form of redistribution in relation to the peasant economy. According to Owen the agrarian societies highlights the tremendous burden this could place upon the village communities. In theory each cultivator's major liability was a land tax amounting to anywhere between10-50 percent of their annual production, or a similar tax of his animals.[242] Under certain circumstances, taxation might also include cash and so force the peasantry into growing cash crops and coming even further under the influence of market forces. This almost certainly meant that the peasants would have to seek credit from wealthy families in the towns, either to pay off taxes or to procure capital in order to work the land. This inevitably led to debt and the loss of land. Thus the two basic resources of labour and land were subject to the control of those elements of society, such as the urban elite or powerful nomads, who had access to a greater resources base and were able to control the means of force. The peasant's most basic economic resources were likely to be in someone else's credit.[243] The agrarian community highlights the tremendous burden this could place upon the village communities which could be forced to part with their crops.

Just as the small villages or tiny hamlets of early Israel can be linked with the lineage or kinship group מִשְׁפָּחָה refers to an "entity that stands between tribe and family or household."[244] Although, usually translated "father's house" or "house of the father," this term is better rendered "family house" or "house of the father," which more successfully reflects the integral

241 D. Thornier, "Peasant Economy as a Category in Economic History," edited by T. Shanin, in *Peasants and Peasant Economies* (Harmondsworth: Penguin, 1971), 206. Cf. Roger Owen, *The Middle East in the World Economy 1800-1914* (London, NY: I.B. Tauris, 2009), 41.

242 Roger Owen, *The Middle East in the World Economy 1800-1914*, 35. According to Lenski agrarian societies highlights the tremendous burden this could place upon the village communities who could be forced to part with anything between 30-70 percent of their crops. Cf. G. E. Lenski, *Power and Privilege. A Theory of Social Stratification* (New York: McGraw-Hill, 1966), 266.

243 Coote and Whitelam, *The Emergence of Early Israel in Historical Perspective*, 112.

244 H. J. Zobel, "מִשְׁפָּחָה; mispaha," *TDOT*, Vol. IX. edited by G. Johannes Botterweck, Helmer Ringgren, Heinz-Josef Fabry (Grand Rapids, Michigan: William B. Eerdmann Publishing Company, 1998), 80.

relationship between kinship-linked persons and the material basis for their survival. In terms *bet ab* denotes the extended or compound family that inhabited a residential family group or even to a schematized social-genealogies fiction. In many texts, however, especially those stemming form or reflecting the premonarchical period,[245] the term probably denotes a multigenerational living group. As Meyer argues:

> the term probably denotes a multigenerational living group. The structure of these groups, as has been noted, was in flux as families expanded or contracted as the result of births, marriages, death, or other circumstances that augmented or depleted family size. Still, whatever the configuration of the *bet ab* at a given moment, the governing kinship relationship was father-son-descent, or patrilineality; and the governing territorial determinant was patrilocality-males inheriting family land from their parents and females move out to the *bet ab* of their husbands.[246]

For Wright the kingship structure had three tiers:

1. "Bet 'ab (father's house) this is an important Kinship structure of Israel and the one in which the individual Israelite felt the strongest sense of inclusion, identity, protection, and responsibility. The "father's house" was an extended family comprising all the descendants of a single living ancestor (the head ro's-bet-'ab) in a single lineage, excluding marriage daughters (who entered their husbands 'bet'ab along with their families, resident labourers, and sometimes resident Levites. Thus, the bet'ab included the head of the house and his wife (or wives), his sons and their wives, his grandson and their wives, plus and unmarried sons or daughters in the generations below him, along with all the non related dependence."
2. *The clan* (*mispaha)* which functioned as a protective association of families, with a variety of economic, social, judicial and military duties.
3. *The tribes* (*sebet/matteh)* the largest kinship grouping. The tribes major significant was in territorial landholding.[247] But the principles did not work out consistently in practice. Israelites were frequently in contact with aliens, or foreigners with whom it became necessary to assume close relationship of different kinds.

In this Louis Wallis asserts:

245 Gottwald, *Tribes of Yahweh,* 285-92.

246 Carol Meyers, "The Family in Early Israel," in *Families in Ancient Israel*, edited by Don S. Browning and Ian S. Evison (Louisville, Kentucky: Westminster John Knox Press, 1997), 19.

247 Christopher J. H. Wright, *Old Testament Ethics for the People of God* (Leicester, England: Inter-Varsity Press, 2004), 339. C. J. H. Wright, "Family," *ABD* 2, 762.

> "If the original Kinship theory were literally followed out, it would have excluded all foreigner blood from Israel. As a matter of fact, the society called Israel was the product of an ethnic mixture equal to that which has occurred in the history of the nations. It was, in the first place, the result of union between the incoming deserts clans and earlier Canaanites inhabitants; and subsequently other outsiders were grafted into the social body. Where these aliens were women they came in, of course, as the property of their husbands. Where they were of the male sex, they came either as chattels or as adopted freemen, according to the circumstances of the case. An outsider, thus adopted was known as a *ger,* גר. The Bible has much to say about the 'stranger' and the "sojourner." It is usually the *gerim* (plural) that are thus designated."[248]

Free foreigners became a part of Israelite society by adoption into some native family, after which they were treated as blood-members of the kin. The inclusion of free foreigners involved a special agreement, or ברית (*berith*= Covenant) and acceptance of the family cult by the incomer.

Max Weber contends that: "the *gerim* of the cities as well as among the Bedouins of the deserts were a great many artisans and merchants. To judge from Arabic conditions the tribal organization did not grant them full membership."[249] The pre-exile metic (*ger*) was sharply differentiated form the total foreigner; *nokri.* The later was without rights. The *ger* was of foreign stock, but was legally protected.[250]

Land like labor, was a major features of an Israelite family household. The specific identification of each family household with its inherited domain (נַחֲלָה -*nahala*) "patrimony" or "inheritance,"[251] was exceptionally strong; family land was to be held in perpetuity. Thus we see that the kinship theory of society, not only in Israel but throughout the ancient world, could not be consistently put into practice. Although the society structure of ancient Israel was largely determined by actual blood kinship.

248 Louis Wallis, "Biblical Sociology 11," *American Journal of sociology* 14/3 (November 1908), 327.

249 Max Weber, *Ancient Judaism,* translated and edited by Hans H. Gerth and Don Martindate (London: Collier Macmillan Publishers, 1952), 28.

250 Weber, *Ancient Judaism*, 28.

251 E. Lipinski, "נָחַל *nahal;* נַחֲלָה *nahala,*" *TDOT,* Vol. XI, edited by G. Johannes Botterweck, Helmer Ringgren and Heinz-Josef Fabry (Grand Rapids, Michigan: William Eerdmans Publishing Company, 2001), 319-334.

3.2.4. Family Identity

Just as the family was inextricable connected with its landholdings, so also were individual family members economically and psychologically embedded in the domestic group. As is widely recognized by anyone looking at premodern societies, the concept of the individual and of individual identity as we know it today did not yet exist in the biblical world. Whatever sense of individual agency a person may have had derived from his or her contribution of household survival rather than from individual accomplishment. The profound independence of family thus created an atmosphere of corporate family identity, in which one could conceive not of person goal and ventures but only of familial ones. On family identity Osterud observe: "People located themselves on the superimposed domains of land and kin group and did not view themselves as independent actors in domains of their own choice or making. In the merging of the self with family, one can observe a collective, group-oriented mind-set, with the welfare of the individual inseparable from that of the living group."[252]

In premodern agrarian settings such as early Israel, therefore, individualistic elements in human existence, including a person's range of psychological processes and feeling states, were characteristically subordinated to the person's role in the family unit.[253] Accepted and adaptive role behaviour determined the character of the component family members. A גר was not an autonomous entity but someone's *father, mother, daughter, son, grandparent,* and so forth.

גר represent rootlessness, alienation, dispossession, foreignness, and anxiety. It negates the possibility of a natural, organic connection of Israel to its territory. Thus an understanding of the varied components of ethnic identity illuminates the diverse ways in which גר functions, and clarifies its helpful role in constructing ethnic identity.

3.3. Intrinsic Analysis of Genesis 12:10; 20:1; 21:34; 26:3-5

גר occurs three times in reference to Abraham three times in reference to Jacob (of which one reference includes Esau as well). The first mention of Abraham as גר is also the first גר in the Hebrew Bible. The reference occurs in Gen.12:10 at the start of Abraham's visit to Egypt designating his time in Egypt as alien. The second and third references 20:1 and 21:34, frame Abraham's time in

252 Nancy Grey Osterud, "Land, Identity, and Agency in the Oral Autobiography of Farm Women," in *Women and Farming: Changing Roles, Changing Structures,* Rural Studies Series, edited by Wava G. Haney and Jane B. Knowles (Boulder, Colo: Westview Press, 1988), 77-79.

253 Teodor Shonin, "Peasantry as a Political Factor," in *Peasants and peasant Society,* edited by Teodor Shonin (Harmondsworth, Middlex: Penguin Books, 1971), 240-43.

Gerar, also describing this visit as a time of גר. The fourth and sixth occurrences, 35:27 and 37:1, note that Jacob lived in Hebron or Canaan and describes these locations as place where his father's lived as alien. These above references will be brought into the discussion of the primary references in this chapter and to see what is the rhetorical and ideological purpose of this text within the context of the initial production and circulation of Genesis.

3.3.1. The Ur to Egypt

The Abraham-Sarah stories are collection of stories and notices of diverse origins. About the origin, growth, and arrangement of the traditions scholarly opinion varies widely according to methodologies and assumptions about the history of Israelites religion. No details are given of the route, method, or time of travel. There is no reason to assume that a journey from southern Mesopotamia to Syro-Palestine was undertaken only by semi-nomads in antiquity. Movements in stages by groups of persons, possibly merchants, are attested by records of Old Babylonian itineraries.[254]

Canaan is portrayed in the route periscope as the land of divine grant and ancestral history. The subsequent journey in Egypt, placed in juxtaposition with the time in Canaan described here, occupies the position of negative counterpart on the ideological map of the text. The structure of this section further supports the establishment of Canaan as Israel's ethno scrape[255] and of Egypt as its foil. Tracking the place names as they appear in order in the text, the movements of Abraham and his family including the journey after their return from Egypt may be charted as follows:

Ur (11:28, 31) -> Haran (11:31; 12:4) ->Canaan (12:5)[256]

-> Shechem (12:6)

->Bethel and Ai (12:8)

->the Negev (12:9)

->Egypt (12:10)

254 William W. Hallo, "The Road to Emar," *Journal of Cuneiform Studies* 18 (1964), 57-88. Cited by Donald J. Wiseman, "History and Tradition" *Bibliotheca Sacra* (April-June 1977), 125.

255 An ethnoscape may acquire additional significance from religious forms of ethnic myths and memories, and so develop into a *sacred* territory. Smith identifies this further religious dimension as both moral and ritual; "the historic homeland becomes sacred partly through the same process of myth-making and shared remembering as occurs in all ethnic communities, but also through the special heroic acts of moral and ritual conduct of a community of believers and its religious heroes." See Anthony D. Smith, *Myth and Memories of the Nation* (Oxford: Oxford University Press, 2003), 270.

256 Canaan is also mentioned as the intended destination of Terah in 11:31, but it is not yet an actual stopping point on the itinerary.

->the Negev (13:1)

->Bethel and Ai (13:3)

->Hebron (13:8)

Two types of movement appear in this diagram. The first is linear, starting with the departure from Ur and ending with the arrival in Canaan. The second circular,[257] beginning with Canaan, progressing to Egypt, then returning to Canaan. In the first sequence, Canaan is the destination and the end point of the journey, set up in the text (12: 5) as the place which Abraham's family aims for and the place in which they arrive. Elisabeth Robertson Kennedy shows a symmetrical structure of departure and return portrayed in the diagram below. In the itineraries framing the Egypt story (12:8-9; 13:3-4):

12:8 A וַיִּקְרָא בְּשֵׁם יְהוָה tent & alter at Bethel; Abraham called on the name of Yahweh

12:9 B וַיִּסַּע אַבְרָם הָלוֹךְ וְנָסוֹעַ journeyed by stages (√נסע and √הלך)

12:10 C וַיֵּרֶד אַבְרָם מִצְרַיְמָה Abram went down to Egypt

12:14 D כְּבוֹא entered

12:15 E וַתֻּקַּח הָאִשָּׁה the women was taken

12:16 F הֵיטִיב dealt well with

12:17 F' וַיְנַגַּע afflicted

12:19 E' אִשְׁתְּךָ קַח take your woman

12:20 D' וַיְשַׁלְּחוּ send away

13:1 C' וַיַּעַל אַבְרָם מִמִּצְרַיִם Abram went up from Egypt

13:3 B' וַיֵּלֶךְ לְמַסָּעָיו journeyed by stage √נסע and √הלך)

13:3-4 A וַיִּקְרָא...בְּשֵׁם יְהוָה' tent & alter at Behel; Abram called on the name of Yahweh.[258]

Once Abraham has arrived in Canaan, however, his movement take on a new shape. His journey follows a symmetrical out-and-back loop, travelling to Egypt and then back in a series of carefully reversed stages. When Abraham returns to Bethel, the narrative stresses that it was the place where he had been

257 The argument for symmetry is weakened by the dissimilarity between Shechem and Hebron, on the ground that the two locations are still within Canaan. J. J, Scullion plots a concentric structure that is similar, but begins and ends at Bethel and Ai. Cf. J. J. Scullion, *Genesis: A Commentary for Students, Teachers, and preachers,* OTS 6 (Collegeville: Liturgical, 1992), 112.

258 Elisabeth Robertson Kennedy. *Seeking A Homeland: Sojourn and Ethnic Identity in the Ancestral Narratives of Genesis*. (Leiden: Brill, 2011), 51.

at the beginning (בַּתְּחִלָּה), and where he had made and altar *at the first* (בָרִאשֹׁנָה) (13:3-4). According to Jansen "Abram's arrival at Bethel has the character of a return and a recognition...The stranger has begun to become familiar."[259] Abraham's journey to Egypt traces a loop which lands him back where he started, in Canaan, his original destination and destiny. Aliens in Egypt, then, are quite decidedly temporary. The journey to Egypt is emphatically reversed with a journey back to Canaan; an גר outside the land resolves into belonging within it. The reference to alien in the itinerary periscope contributes to the construction of an ethnoscape. Canaan the land of promise, Egypt, the land of גר, is the negative counterpart.

3.3.2. Aliens in Egypt

The end of the periscope it is difficult to decide whether the episode ends at 13:1 or at 12:20. The main arguments in favour of 13:1 are that Abram's going up from Egypt matches his going down to Egypt in 12:10 and that the verbal parallel (12: 20 // 13:1) "him his wife, and all who belonged to him" tie these two verses tightly together.[260] However, it seems slightly more natural to view the expulsion from Egypt as marking, the conclusion of one scene, and the journeying to the Negeb as signalling the start of a new episode.

The movement of the patriarch Abram in and out of Egypt in Gen. 12 sets the pattern for the first narrative movement. When famine threatens, Abraham resides there as an alien in Egypt, the verb accompanying the reference to alien is "he went down"[261] ירד (*yarad* = travel from North to South)[262] to settle there as a resident alien (12:10). The story ends with an antonym denoting the reverse movement, "he went up," וַיַּעַל (*waya'al*) the √אָלָה (*'alah*) in (13:1) the root is found in all Semitic languages with the basic meaning indicating movement upward: "go up."[263] Elsewhere in Genesis as it is here, גר in Egypt is clearly bracketed on either side with antonyms denoting descent and ascent.[264] The

259 J. Gerald Janzen, *Abraham and all the Families of the Earth: A Commentary on the Book of Genesis 12-50* (Grand Rapids: Wm. B. Eerdmans Publishing Co., 1993), 28.

260 Gordon J. Wenham, *Genesis 1-15,* WBC, Vol. 1 (Waco, Texas: Word books, publisher, 1987), 285.

261 Francis Brown, S. R. Driver, and Charles A. Briggs, *A Hebrew and English Lexicon of the Old Testament* (Oxford: Clarendon Press, 1979). 432. (Hereby *BDB*).

262 G.Mayer, "יָרַד; yarad," *Theological Dictionary of the Old Testament,* Vol. V1, edited by G. Johannes Botterweck and Helmer Ringgrenn (Grand Rapids, Michigan: William B. Eerdmans Publishing Company, 1990), 318.

263 H. F. Fuhs, "לָעָלָה," *TDOT*, Vol. V1, edited by G. Johannes Botterweck, Helmer Ringgrenn and Heinz-Josef Fabry (Grand Rapids, Michigan: William B. Eerdmans Publishing Company, 2001), 77.

264 The terminology as aliens is not used in the itinerary notice of Joseph's story. But with dialogue with Pharaoh "have come to reside as aliens in Egypt" is described (Gen 47: 4).

first visit of Joseph's brothers to Egypt opens with וַיֵּרְדוּ (*weyir^edu* = they went down) in (42:3) and closes with the less-precise mirror word, וַיֵּלְכוּ (*wayil^eku*) from the √הָלַךְ (*halak* = go from, departed from),[265] (42:26). In later re-tellings of the visit, however the descent is once again described by יָרַדְנוּ (*yarad^enu* = we went down), (43:20) and the ascent by עָלִינוּ (*'alinu* = we went up), (44:24). The brothers' second visit is clearly bracketed with the verbs וירדו (*wiredu* = went down), (43:15) and וַיַּעֲלוּ (*'alinu* = we went up), (45:25). Much anxiety surrounds the יָרַד (yarad = going down), of Benjamin to Egypt (42:38; 43:4,5,7; 44:21,23,26) with the urgent need that he complete the circuit and עָלָה (*'alah* = go up) from Egypt (44:33,34).[266] The vocabulary used of Abram's journey anticipates the same vocabulary used to describe Israel's entrance into and exit from Egypt. McAfee asserts: "resident alien" reflects his self-conscious awareness of himself as an outsider, without legal or moral claim to insider status. Though Abraham and his line are referred to as 'alien' in Canaan as well (Gen. 17: 8; 23: 4; 28:4)."[267] But this status is understood temporary, until Abraham's descendants have taken possession of the land as its new divinely appointed 'insiders.'

Egypt has an initial positive survey as a place of food and survival. But then Egypt becomes an uncertain place that both threatens danger and promises. At the border Abram is anxious that Egypt may mean death for him; so he prevails upon Sarai to present herself as his sister in order to reverse the perceived threat and to claim not only life but also enrichment (12:11-13).[268] One of the more noteworthy features of the book of Genesis is the presence of three accounts in which a patriarch pretends that his wife is his sister (12: 10-13: 1 [A], 20: 1-18 [B], 26: 1-13 [C]).[269] Their close proximity in Genesis and the complete absence of such incidents elsewhere in the Old Testament has naturally led scholars to consider their relationship to one another. As Skinner writes: "with the development of source-criticism it was suggested that the accounts reflected the existence of parallel documents in Genesis accounts A

---

265 *BDB,* 231.

266 The overall Josephs narrative sets up several literary patterns of descent and ascent paralleling the "going down" and "coming up" to and from Egypt, such as the pit in Dothan and the several instances of jailing. In all these places, a descent with no chance of ascent threatens death. Cf Donald A. Seybold, "Paradox and symmetry in the Joseph Narrative," in *Literary Interpretations of Biblical narratives,* edited by Kenneth R. R. Gros Louis, James S. Ackerman, and Thayer S. Warshaw (Nashville: Abingdon, 1974), 61-65, 70.

267 Gene McAfee, "Chosen People in a Chosen Land: Theology and Ecology in the Story of Israel's Origins, in *The Earth Story in Genesis,* edited by Norman C. Habel & Shirley Wurst (Sheffield: Sheffield Academic press, 2000), 165.

268 Abram's words "that it may go well (יטב) with me" (12:13). Cf. *BDB,* 405 in view of the goods he will gain in Egypt, can be understood as a reference to his hopes of enrichment.

269 T. D. Alexander, "The Wife/Sister Incidents in Genesis Oral Variants," 145-153.

and C were widely held to originate from J, and account B from E."[270] Gunkel have even suggested that the parallel narratives A and C indicate that J itself was comprised of two separate sources.[271] Under the influence of form-criticism it was Koch who proposed that: "three incidents developed as oval variants of one original story."[272] Some scholars have tended towards the opinion that accounts B and C were literary compositions based upon and presupposing knowledge of account A.[273] Clines, calling these stories: "'The Ancestor in Danger' seems to be more appropriate focus, since that is the complication that sets each of these stories in motion. We might, nevertheless, wonder whether in fact the biggest danger is to either the ancestress or the ancestor, and not rather to some other element in the story, like the plot or else the achievement of what is supposed to be happening in Genesis."[274] For Petersen these three narratives are 'really' one narrative, a "thrice-told tale."[275]

The strategy works; Abram lives and is indeed enriched (12:16), but Pharaoh and his household are stuck with plague (12:17). Thus a fundamental ambivalence is associated with Egypt; it is simultaneously a place of potential great enrichment-note that Abram's wealth is not detailed until he reside there as an alien in Egypt[276] and also place that raises fears, entices to deception, and so threatens death and plague.

The danger associated with Egypt eventually outweighs the benefits, and so Egypt cannot be a place of permanent settlement for Abraham. The patriarch is expelled שָׁלַח "send"[277] and "goes up" to (עלה) from Egypt, albeit far wealthier than before. Thus, from the very beginning of the story cycles that narrate the origins of Israel, the audience of the Pentateuch encounters a proto-exodus movement: a pattern of entering Egypt because it is clearly advantageous to do so, but also leaving or being expelled from Egypt because

---

270 J. Skinner, *A Critical and Exegetical Commentary on Genesis,* 2nd edn (Edinburgh, 1930), 232-3, 315. E. A. Speiser, *Genesis* (Garden City, New York, 1964), 91, G. Von Rad, *Genesis A Commentary,* 2nd edn. (London: SCM Press Ltd., 1972), 226-270.

271 H. Gunkel, *Genesis,* 3rd edn. (Gottingen, 1910), 168-9, 299,

272 K. Koch, *The Growth of the Biblical Tradition* (London, 1969), pp. 111-32.

273 J. Van Seters, *Abraham in History and Tradition* (New Haven, Conn , and London, 1975), pp. 167-91.

274 Clines, *What does Eve do to Help?,* 67-84.

275 Petersen, "A Thrice -Told Tale," 30-43.

276 Gen. 12:16; 13:2. It seems that his nephew Lot was similarly enriched since after the Egyptian experience they could no longer live together because their possessions were so great (13:5-7). The notice of Abram's possessions acquired before all this in Haran (12:5) does not give the same picture of impressive wealth.

277 *BDB,* 1018.

it cannot become a permanent home.[278] Thus, the ideological pattern around the term 'Egypt' is being established, which will influence the reading of the following narratives.

The narrative of Abram and Sarai's experience in Egypt is the first of three sequential incidents in Genesis expressing the so called "wife -as- sister' or endangered ancestress' motif. The same motif appears twice more in Gen.20 and 26. However, these further instances show an interesting from Egypt. In neither Gen 20 nor 26 does the story takes place in Egypt itself; the action happens rather in Gerar, an area between Egypt and Canaan; that is, a luminal or transitional area.[279] However, an Egyptian connection remains; Gerar is Philistine (26:1), and the Philistines, according to the Table of Nations, are the second generation offspring of Egypt (10:13). The same pattern of deception and subsequent enrichment is repeated both times, but by the third instance, which involves Isaac, the Egyptian connection is repudiated. The deity tells Isaac explicitly not to go down to Egypt as his father Abraham had done (26:2), Isaac is still enriched; however, in this case not by the foreign king, but by Gen 26 this particular danger exist only as a potential. As discussed above, the first incidence of גר and return establish Canaan as the homeland, in which destiny is realized. The alien in Genesis set the scene for the defining event on several levels.

Firstly, the text established that the final return of the people to Canaan will be a "homecoming," a return to a land inscribed with ethnic significance. As Thompson states: "the patriarchal narratives have as one of their functions that of explicating story the perception that the Israel which came out of Egypt was coming back home to the land given to Abraham, Isaac, and Jacob in the very beginning by God himself."[280] The narrative has established Canaan as the site of divine promise and sacred ancestral memory, in contrast with alien in Egypt.

Secondly, the repetition of the גר and return pattern shows that in returning to Canaan from Egypt residing there as an alien, the Israelites repeat the pattern of history and walk in the footsteps of Abraham, Jacob, and Jacob's sons, their ethnic father.[281]This association of the exodus with the acts of the ancestors

---

278 The vocabulary used for Abram journey to (ירד) and from (עלהשלח), anticipates the same vocabulary used to described Israel's entry and exit from Egypt.

279 Gerar was located on the way to Egypt and is mentioned in connection with Kardesh (identified in ancient with Petra and now mainly with 'Ayn Qudayrat) and Shur (the fortification on the Egyptian frontier). In the north it is bordered on the territories of Beersheba and Gaza (Gen 10:19; 26:1-2; 11 Chron 14:12-13). Cf Yehoshua M. Grintz, "Gerar," *Encyclopaedia Judaica,* Vol. 7 (New York: Thomas Gales, 2007), 505.

280 L. Thompson, *The Origin Tradition of Ancient Israel...*, 33.

281 Greifenhagen focuses his attention on the ideological construction of Canaan as an ethnic homeland. He describes Abraham's movement as "proto-exodus." Cf F. V. Greifenhagen,

strengthen ethnic identification by attaching to the return from Egypt a sense of continuity between past and the present. For Jansen "the territorialisation of memory thus occurs not only in the movements of the patriarchs within Canaan, but also foreshadowing the Exodus story in its main lines and even in some of its detail."[282]

Thirdly, Genesis portrays גר in Egypt as a temporary state of alienation, the positive pole to the divine promise of belonging in Canaan, and then shows that the same God who originally grants the land also guarantees the termination of this גר outside it. This relationship is found in the promise speech of chapter 15. There Yahweh promises Abraham the possession of Canaan (15:7), then foretells the alien of the Israelites in Egypt, (15:13), and also promise that they will "come back here" out of alien in a land after the time span of "the fourth generation" (15:16). Westermann argues that: "it is not to be equated with the "400 years." The lengthy period rests on God's plan in history which also encompasses the other nation."[283] Genesis shows that the will of Yahweh is behind both the original journey to Canaan and the land of origin and later return to Canaan once again from the land of גר. Both ethnic migrations are directed towards Canaan, the divinely appointed. As from the above example we have seen that reference to alien help to define both the divine land promise and the exodus event.

3.3.3. Wives-sisters Narrative

In Genesis account of their wandering, the ancestors are pictured negotiating around and with the natives of Canaan proper, as well as with those of the border areas of Egypt and Philistia. These encounters identify the points between the patriarch and the locals, and their resolutions define a boundary between them. What is immediately striking about this boundary is that it is never defined in religious terms. Cohn notes:

> In Deuteronomy and the Deuteronomistic literature, Moses and the Deuteronomistic editors repeatedly distinguish Israel's God and Israel's mode of worship from the idolatry and ritual practices of the Canaanites, forbidding the latter to the Israelites and demanding the destruction of the local sacred places. Genesis, by contrast, is remarkably silent about religious differences. If Israelite identity in Deuteronomy hinges on the people's exclusive devotion to YHWH

Egypt on the Pentateuch's Ideological Map, 44.

282 J. Gerald Janzen, *Abraham and all the Families*, 26. Cf. U. Cassuto, *A Commentary on the Book of Genesis* (Jerusalem: The Magnes Press, 1984), 334.

283 Westermann, *Genesis 12-26: A Commentary*, 227.

and absolute rejection of the deities, images, and practices of the natives.[284]

The tales of the ancestors' meetings with the local population, though seeming to delay the movement toward the fulfillment of the divine promises, are critical to understanding how Genesis constructs Israelite identity. In every one of these tales, the natives are shown to be a threat to the very existence of the ancestral line. If the keynote of the ancestor tales is the repeated promise of nationhood and land, the encounters between the ancestors and the natives threaten to destroy both elements of that promise. In these encounters, the locals are shown wielding sexual and economic power over the ancestors and aiming to use this power to dominate and assimilate them, thus aborting the divine intention.

The researcher examines the ancestors' encounters with the locals in order to explore the nature of the boundary between the two groups and what that boundary reveals about Israelite identity as constructed by the writers of Genesis.

The three well-studied wife-sister episodes form one clear trajectory of danger. In their travels, first Abraham and then Isaac stand to lose their lives and their wives to local kings, the unnamed Pharaoh of Egypt and the Philistine Abimelech of Gerar. What lies behind this literary topos, says anthropologist Pitt-Rivers, "is the ancient Mediterranean custom of "sexual hospitality," the use of women to establish patron-client bonds between host and guest. On this reading, the patriarch gives over his woman in order to dwell in the land unmolested (though molestation is precisely the fate of the woman herself), protected by the 'king' and permitted to graze his flocks and herds."[285] Abraham and Isaac, however, seem unfamiliar with the Mediterranean custom, for they both assume that in order to have the wife; the foreign ruler would have to kill the husband, avoiding adultery at the cost of murder. Thus, Abraham and Isaac pass off their wives as their sisters to secure their own safety. Behind the tales, however, is the assumption that the fathers would have found it acceptable to use their sisters to establish alliances.

---

284 Robert L. Cohn, "The Second Coming of Moses: Deuteronomy and the Construction of Israelite Identity," *Proceeding of the Twelfth World Congress of Jewish Studies* (Jerusalem: World Union of Jewish Studies, 1999), 59-71.

285 Julian Pitt-Rivers, *The Fate of Shechem or The Politics of Sex: Essays in the Anthropology of the Mediterranean* (Cambridge: Cambridge University Press, 1977), 159-61. J. K. Hoffmeier suggests instead that the wife-sister stories reflect the practice of diplomatic marriages, a proposal that serves to place the sexual relations offered under the umbrella of socially sanctioned marriage, but maintains the same pattern of exchanging women belonging to the household of a sojourner for safety and rights to settle in the land. James K. Hoffmeier, "The Wives' Tales of Genesis 12, 20 & 26 and the Covenants at Beer-sheba," *TynBul* 43, No. 1 (1992), 81-99.

The researcher, however, reject this practice: the sequence of the three wife-sister narratives an increasing resistance to sexual hospitality as well as the in-creasing recognition that God, not sexual exchange, brings about the enrichment of the chosen family. In the first narrative (12:10-20), Pharaoh's found Sarah attractive (vv. 11, 14) and take her into Pharaoh's harem, and Pharaoh duly rewards Abraham with flocks, herds, and slaves. But a divinely sent plague and Pharaoh's expulsion of the couple, foreshadowing the exodus, rescue the fore-mother. The same motif appears twice more in Gen 20 and 26. In the second narrative (20:1-17), Sarah, now pregnant, remains untouched by King Abimelech, to whom God reveals Sarah's status as wife in a dream. Now Abraham's reward from Abimelech comes after Sarah's release as compensation for the indignity caused her. Here, Abraham's after-the-fact explanation that Sarah really is his sister can be read either as vindication or as a lame excuse. In the third version (26:6-11), the matriarch, now Rebekah, never even enters the king's palace. The reader knows that Isaac and Rebekah are ambiguously not brother and sister, but cousins, and so Isaac cannot make any such excuse to the king, admitting rather to a lie based on fear. This time the patriarch's reward comes directly from God, quite independently of the aggrieved Abimelech. In Gen 12 the ancestress is clearly in danger of being absorbed into the house of the foreign king, but by Gen 26 this particular danger exists only as a potential.

In comparison with the other two wife sister tales, this is the only tale that includes a promise. The promise of Isaac in 26:2-5 is generally viewed as conditional, although many commentators focus on the second portion which cites Abraham's obedience, rather than the first portion containing the commands of Isaac.[286] Mullen argues that the promise to Isaac in 26:2-5 was clearly not unconditional,[287] and voices an objection to the scholarly position that the promise to Abraham were unconditional, arguing instead for the presence of a dialectic: "Yahweh will remain faithful to his promise, but always has the power to revoke it if Abraham or his descendants fail to follow Yahweh's commands."[288] Mullen finds this dialectic be a basic tension which he believes is "endemic to the narrative presentation of the ways in which the human and divine realms interacts in the biblical material."[289] It appears for the first time in Genesis here, in 26:3. The promise is well suited to accompany the command to גר for it pledges a better situation inherent in life as an alien,

---

286 Moshe Weinfeld, "The Covenant of Grant in the Old Testament and the Ancient Near East,"*JAOS* 90/2 (1970), 195

287 E. Theodore Mullen, Jr, *Ethnic Myths and Pentateuchal Foundation: A new Approach to the Formation of the Pentateuch* (St. Atlanta: Scholars, 1997), 149.

288 Mullen, *Ethnic Myths and Pentateuchal Foundation*, 147.

289 Mullen, *Ethnic Myths and Pentateuchal Foundation*, 147.

offering protection by an authority higher than the local sovereign to whose power the גר will be vulnerable.

The wife-sister stories demonstrate the dangers that threaten the integrity of this outsider family as it wanders in lands occupied by others. What these tales demonstrate is that wives cannot be exchanged for security, how much their patriarchal husbands may try to arrange it. In each case God intervenes with a plague (12:17), dream (20:3-7), or blessing (26:12) to redeem the wife and thus keep the first family intact.

How does the representation of the relationship between ancestors and natives in Genesis shape Israelite identity? Firstly, by representing the fathers as outsiders, as immigrants to a land currently occupied by others, Genesis validates outsider over native. As kunin remarks: "Each of the two is associated with a qualifier: wife with danger and the sister with safety. It is likely that this opposition relates to one that is implied in the first section, that is, insider-outsider."[290] Machinist rightly pointed out in Mesopotamia and Egypt, "outsiders -Amorites for Mesopotamia, Asiatics for Egypt--were perceived to be threatening, in Genesis, outsiderhood is a badge of distinction, a mark of divine chosenness."[291] The indigenous peoples stand by and watch but do not actively resist, even if some attempt to dominate the ancestors. Interestingly, by giving voice to native spokesmen like Abimelech and Hamor, biblical writers show how their ancestors as outsiders were themselves seen as Other by local folk. This imaginative representation of foreign discourse grants the natives greater human depth and makes the threat posed by the outsider ancestors all the more convincing.

Secondly, practice endogamy and economic independence by the ancestors' separates from the native, the ancestor traditions construct a memory of family purity and territorial separation. The repeated challenge of the native peoples to each succeeding generation establishes that separation as one not easy to achieve. Finkelstein remarks: "each generation, the message would seem to be, must overcome both the threat and the temptation of being submerged matrimonially and economically. By depicting those recipients, moreover, as four generations of a single family whose descendants spread geographically through Israel and Judah, Genesis sets forth a "pan-Israelite" ideology that would have served to express an all-Israel national consciousness."[292] Whether

290 Seth Daniel Kunin, *The Logic of Incest A Structuralist Analysis of Hebrew Mythology*, JSOT Suplt Series 185 (Sheffield: Sheffield Academic Press, 1995), 66.

291 Peter Machinist, "Outsiders or Insiders: The Biblical View of Emergent Israel and Its Contexts," in *The Other in Jewish History and Thought*, edited by Laurence J. Silberstein and Robert L. Cohn (New York: New York University Press, 1994), 51.

292 Israel Finkelstein and Neil Asher Silberman argue that these pan-Israelite traditions that are nevertheless centered. Israel Finkelstein and Neil Asher Silberman, *The Bible Unearthed: Archaeology's New Vision of Ancient Israel and the Origin of Its Sacred Texts* (New York:

that consciousness is to be assigned originally to the Josian period or to a later one, its important function in the development of Jewish collective memory is clear.

The natives in Genesis constitute an Other different from the Others in subsequent books. They alienate the first family not by design but by doing what comes naturally: extending sexual hospitality, offering economic integration, selling and protecting real estate. Recognizing themselves as outsiders, the fathers also come to understand the peculiar divinely imposed requirements of their identity vis-a-vis the natives: endogamy and land holdings apart from the local scene. Even voluntary circumcision, the fathers' ethnic marking, cannot domesticate the natives as marriage partners or residential neighbors. Though the ancestors walk softly in a land not yet their own, their tales establish a firm ethnic boundary between themselves and the local populations on the basis of which future enmities easily develop.

Why are גר a context for blessing and the fulfilment of the promises? The fulfilment of promise for the patriarch through a miraculous birth follows upon the reception of the same blessing by the people amongst whom he resides as aliens, and who receive it through his intercession.[293] It may be suggested that an ethic of positive interaction with others is related somehow to aliens, but the connection is not made clear in the text.

Divine promise in Genesis functions as the agreement for Israel's ethnic identity. In Genesis, this promise involves a departure from both land and kin in order to establish an alternative identity, through the possession of a God given land and the production of God-given offspring. The land of origin and the community of birth are both ceased, and a new land and new family are guaranteed by divine grant. The divine promise thus both defines and provides the new grounds of being for the emerging *ethnie.* The narrative then tells the story of the aliens who comes to belong in the land *by the action of God,* and the barren one who miraculously gives birth *by divine intervention.* The

---

Simon and Schuster, 2001), 43-47. Around Judah fit the Josian period when Judah saw itself as the heir to the Israelite territories and people that remained after the Assyrian conquest. The traditions embrace North and South yet stress the superiority of Judah and constitute a "powerful expression of seventh-century Judahite dreams." While this pan-Israelite ideology fits the Josian period, given a different interpretation of archaeological, linguistic, and historical data, one could equally well imagine it as the product of the Solomonic era, or the exilic or postexilic periods.

293 According to Biddle all three of these stories relate primarily to the promise that the patriarch will bring blessing to the nations. Gen 12 illustrates only that the nation will be punished for ill-treating the patriarch, *even if the patriarch at fault.* Genesis 20 refines this definition of the promise in two ways, both of which have to do with the blessing element in Yahweh's promise and which stress that the patriarch can bring concrete benefit to one outside the covenant. Cf. Mark E. Briddle, "The 'Endangered Ancestress,'" 608-09. Cf. G. W. Coats, "A threat to the Host," 75, 81.

barrenness and alien are in one sense the counterpart to the blessing desired. They are the necessary route to a new ethnic identity in which land and descendants are clearly granted by God, in accordance with a charter promise.

3.3.4. Alien and Territorial Boundaries in Chs. 12-13, 20-21, and 26

This analysis will highlight only a few of the similarities in the larger narrative sequences around the wife-sister narratives, focusing especially on aspects relevant for the interpretation of the territorial negotiations that follow after the wife-sister material. The analysis is not in-depth; rather, it is specifically centered on issues of alien and boundaries as they relate to the oath in 21:23.

It is striking that all three wife-sister tales commence with an explicit reference to alien.[294] All three narrative sequences situate the character of alien in relation to their settings, both physically and socially. The local monarchs, Pharaoh and Abimelech, are characterized by contrast as the way they exercised power in their respective lands, the native authorities with whom the patriarchs have to deal in their attempts to establish security and territorial holdings for themselves in lands where their rights are in question.

In all three stories the patriarchs resort to a deception, portraying their wives as their sisters (12:13; 20:2; 26:7), presumably with the intention of gaining physical safety (12:12; 20:11; 26:7, 9). Allowing for variations in the details of the deception and its discovery, there are a few key similarities in the trick and its results. As Hoffmeir explain: "in the plot development of each story, the discovery of the ploy is followed by a confrontation with the native monarch, who reproaches the patriarch for his misdeed (12:18-19; 20:9-10; 26:9-10)."[295] The confrontation between monarch and patriarch is the high point of the stories' drama. After the confrontation, the conflict subsides into a level of harmony as two elements form the end of the plot: the patriarch receives material wealth, and the patriarch moves his habitation away from the wronged monarch. Thus, the promises both restate and in some respect enhance those made to Abraham. The promises is however, thrice repeated to Jacob (28:15; 31:3; 46:4).

It is thus an entirely appropriate reassurance for someone who has just been instructed to live as a גר, i.e., without full citizenship rights.[296] Scharbert regards "bless" can always be translated in the sense of "giving vitality,

294 Several commentators highlight the danger to an alien in strange territory as the central plot crisis of the stories. See Patrick Miller D., Jr., "Israel as Host to Strangers," in *Israelite Religion and Biblical Theology: Collected Essay* (Sheffield: Sheffield Academic Press, 2000), 553-54; Thompson, *The Origin Tradition of Ancient Israel,* 53.

295 Anthropological patterns of "sexual hospitality." Cf. J. K. Hoffmeier, "The Wives...." 81ff.

296 N. M. Sarna, *Genesis,* The JPS Torah Commentary (Philadelphia: Jewish Publication Society, 1989), 183.

prosperity, abundance, or fertility."[297] However, blessing does regularly include the gaining of progeny, personal fertility, as well as that of one's animals and crops also included in prosperity. This is not particularly an implication of Yahweh's being with a person. Nicol argues that: "the question relating to Isaac's progeny do not seem a major issue in Genesis 26."[298]

While there are differences in the timing of the acquisition, the motivation for the enrichment, and even the stated source of the wealth, it nevertheless remains a common outcome that the Patriarchs emerge from the deception episodes richer (12:16 and 20:14; 26:12-14).

Likewise, there are variations in the extent and stated motivation of the relocation that ends the narrative, but a monarchical order regarding a change of residence is clear in each incident.[299] In 12:19-20 Abraham is forcibly expelled from Egypt and leaves the circle of Pharaoh's authority; the remainder of the narrative sequence locates him in Canaan, and his territorial negotiations are not with Pharaoh but Lot. In 26:16-17 Abimelech asks Isaac to leave, which he does. Here, however, Isaac's move takes him only from Gerar to the valley of Gerar, and in the subsequent negotiations over wells he continues to deal with Abimelech, whose authority extends over Isaac's new location as well. In 20:15 Abraham is invited to settle anywhere in Abimelech's land that pleases him. While this may be interpreted positively, and it is true that Abraham is not expelled from Abimelech's land, the speech nevertheless implies a request that he change his location from the place where he resides at the time of the wife-sister deception. It seems that Abimelech wants Abraham a little further away perhaps in his land, but not in his city. It is unclear when it is that Abraham moves out of Gerar and where exactly he is located in the episodes from 21:1 to

---

297 Joseph Scharbert, "ברך *brk*; בְּרָכָה *berakhah,*" *TDOT,* Vol. II, edited by G. Johannes Botterweck, Helmer Ringgren (Grand Rapids, Michigan: William B. Eerdmans Publishing Company, 1975), 294.

298 G. G. Nicol, "Studies in the Interpretation of Genesis 26:1-33" (D. Phil Thesis, Faculty of Theology, University of Oxford, 1987), 17-31.

299 In 26:16 Abimelech tells Isaac to move away because they have become 'too powerful". Coats maintains that the breach in the relationship has nothing to do with the wife-sister deception and is only related to Isaac's ability to wrest wealth from the land (26:12-14), it is possible to interpret Isaac's "power" in a broader sense that also includes his deception and the resulting decree for his protection. Fretheim, for example, argues that Isaac's wealth is due in part to Abimelech's edict protecting him, and thus is related closely to the wife-sister incident. See Coats, *Genesis, with and Introduction,* 190-91, 194; Fretheim, "The Book of Genesis," *The Interpreter's Bible,* edited by Leander E, Keck, Thomas G. Long, David L. Petersen et al., (Nashville: Abingdon, 1994), 527. The theme of wealth creating division and necessitating separation also appears in 13:5-7, where the separation between Abraham and Lot is attributed to the increase in their wealth. In chs. 12-13 the expulsion from Egypt results from the wife-sister deception, and the separation from Lot results from material prosperity; in ch. 26, both themes are evident in Isaac's expulsion from Gerar.

21:24, but at least by 21:25 he is located further away, in Beer-sheba. The well negotiations take place with Abimelech, who is represented by the narrative as having some sort of territorial authority in the area of Beer-sheba.

In all three sequences, an alien scenario unfolds with similar features. The territorial negotiations that follow, then, happen against this complex backdrop: firstly, an offer by a sojourner of an exchange of "'goods (sex for safety) that is judged ethically reprehensible by the local monarch when the sex offered is revealed to be adulterous;"[300] secondly, an end to the transaction between גר and monarch and a return (or preservation) of the "goods" in undamaged form; thirdly the enrichment of the patriarch by possessions of the land where he sojourns; and fourthly, a move by the patriarch to a location further from the local monarch's central habitation.

Seter argues that: "the territorial negotiations following the wife-sister material in each sequence also share common patterns and themes, although chs. 21 and 26 offer far closer parallels than those in ch. 13."[301] In all three sequences, the patriarch moves away from the direct circle of the native monarch and, by stages, deeper into territory more traditionally identified as the land promised to Israel. The three agreements have reciprocal structures, with an equality of obligation required of the two sides in each. The three dialogues involved in 13:9; 21:23; 26:29 makes use of words carrying ethical connotations refrain from harm to one another.

The above mentioned, taken together with the preceding summary of the wife sister material, shows why the land negotiations are to be interpreted in continuity with the wife-sister stories. First, the thematic unity between the narratives is strong. Both involve negotiations over commodities that are in question for a גר: safety, territorial rights, and wealth gleaned from the land. Both involve the definition of territorial boundaries and the movement of the protagonists across these boundaries toward positions where peaceful existence is possible. Both end in the affirmation of land rights for one or both sides. Both, finally, reflect on ethical obligations with a strong affirmation of expected "right" behaviour. The key distinction in this regard is that the patriarch in his interaction with the other party does not meet the ethical standard of right behaviour in the first case, but does in the second.

300 The moral sensitivity displayed by the local monarch, highlighted by a contrast with the indifference evidenced by the patriarchs is a striking element of all three tales. See discussions in Alter, "Sodom as Nexus: The Web of Design in Biblical Narrative," in *The Book and the Text: The Bible and Literary Theory*, edited by Regina Schwartz (Cambridge: Basil Blackwell, 1986), 155-56; Polzin, "The Ancestress in Danger," 93.

301 Van Seters, and Hauge offers an overarching motif analysis that spans the wife-sister stories and the territorial negotiations following them. See Van Seters, *Abraham in History and Tradition,* 189-91; Martin Ravndal Hauge, "Struggles of the Blessed in Estrangement II," *Studia Theologica* 29 (1995), 114-15.

3.3.5. Motifs of Death and the God of the Impossible

Genesis expressed in themes motifs of life. These conditions form the backdrop for God's promises to Abraham. The researchers have mentioned two: famine and landlessness.

1. Famine occurs in the times of each patriarch Abraham, Isaac, and Jacob. Famines in Genesis function like barrenness, for neither land nor people are able to reproduce. Famines occurred in the ancient world due to drought or crop failure. In Genesis they create a threat to the very existence of the people. It may be true that the frequency of famines in Genesis implies that the patriarchal period was drier than later times,[302] but the famines here are symbolic. Humans are helpless to control conditions that will give them life, health, and survival. Death of the people is a likely result, except that God provides food and nourishment in the first generation when Abram and his wife/sister go to Pharaoh's court in Egypt, and when Isaac and his wife/sister go to Abimelech and the Philistines, and then when, against all odds, Joseph becomes ruler in Egypt. Each of these stories stands on its own, but together they portray a crisis of survival, where God then provides.
2. The second motif is landless aliens. The only land and the family owns in Genesis is a grave, the cave at Macphelah that Abraham buys to bury his wife. The ancestors are גר, wanderers who, even when they dwell in the land, do not control it. They see land as their identity, their place of rootedness in the world, But they seek it, are displaced from it, and return to it repeatedly, but only in promising fashion. The ancestors live in dangerous conditions, face armies, neighbors who stop up wells and hostile natives who see them as threats to survival. They have nowhere to be, but God promises them land. These two motifs portray limited situations, conditions in which Judah's life is gravely challenged, and the future appears uncertain, even impossible. God's promises are set against these motifs and catastrophic back-stories. The God who does impossible things in Genesis is the product of human wrestling to claim God in their particular situation. These motifs of death and divine responses to them are not systematic indications of how God is. God does not always reverse barrenness, nor feed the hungry, nor provide land for the landless, nor homes for גר. The portrayals of God in Genesis are pastoral interventions, theological efforts to support the flagging spirits of people on the knife-edge between life and death. They are apperceptions of the divine, partial seeing, expressions of faith in the unseen.

302 William H. Shea, "Famine," *ABD* 2 (New York: Double day, 1992), 770–71.

In Genesis the ancestors are גר from beginning to end. Their only grasp on the land comes from the buried bones of Sarah, Abraham, and Isaac. Wanderings are continual, settlements temporary, and dislocation characterizes their existence, but it will not be so forever. Being "strangers" or "aliens" is not permanent because God has promised them land from the beginning. The primary recipients of the promise are not Abraham but his offspring, the audience during the Persian period.

3.4. Conclusion

How then, finally, does the representation of the relationship between ancestors and natives in Genesis shape Israelite identity? First, by representing the patriach as outsiders, as alien to a land currently occupied by others, Genesis validates outsiderhood over Native. By moving through the land and establishing links with its major cities-Shechem, Bethel, Hebron, Beersheba-the outsiders make their claim on the land that they stand to inherit. The indigenous peoples stand by and watch but do not actively resist, even if some attempt to dominate the ancestors. Interestingly, by giving voice to native spokesmen like Abimelech, biblical writers show how their ancestors as outsiders were themselves seen as other by local folk.

Therefore, to reside as an alien in its ordinary definition means life in a land not possessed, presence without belonging. Isaac, a father of the *ethnie*, is commanded to reside as an alien. His life as an alien brings him the benefits of divine election, blessing and protection, but the promise of land remain unfulfilled. He is to live in expectation, waiting on the fulfilment of the promise. His life as an alien is a life of obedience to the divine command, and is thus rewarded with signs of promise fulfilment. The text shows that not only land possession but also reside as an alien are part of the divine plan for Israel, and sketches the shape a life an alien might take.

The three story that has been discussed above Gen 12, 20, and 26, this rhetorical style is characteristic of each incident. It creates complex interlocking sets of relationship whose function is not to advance the story but to state conviction, confirm principles or prove a point. The thematic unity between the narratives is strong. Both involve negotiations over commodities that are in question for a גר: safety, territorial rights, and wealth gleaned from the land. Both involve the definition of territorial boundaries and the movement of the protagonists across these boundaries toward positions where peaceful existence is possible. Both end in the affirmation of land rights for one or both sides. Alien in Genesis serves an important function in the construction of an *ethnie,* helping to clarify the ideological map of the text by colouring certain locations with shades of alienation and others with shades of belonging.

In the promise speeches of Genesis, residing as alien contributes to ethnic identity. Here alien is expanded beyond a memory to a model, offering a paradigm for a relationship to the land that emphasizes symbolic connection over concrete possession. Alien brings benefits of divine election, blessing and protection. His life as an alien is a life of obedience to the divine command, and is thus rewarded with signs of promise fulfilment.

Chapter 4

Ideological Contestation Concerning Israel's Being Alien in Egypt

4. Introduction

Just as Genesis 12 is the bridge between creation and patriarch, so also Exodus is the bridge between the patriarchs and the Deutronomic Covenant (DC).[303] Generally, the Book of the Covenant (BC)[304] (Exod. 20: 23-23:19) is traced conventionally to the premonarchic period (1200-1000 BCE) because it contains no references to a king.[305] The Deuteronomic Law (DL)[306], however, has been associated with the "book of the law" discovered in the Jerusalem temple (2 Kings 22-23) in the course of King Josiah reforms (640-609 BCE). It contains to be debated whether the story of the discovery of the "book of the law" reflects actual historical events or a story created to support King's

303 Ryan O' Dowd, *The Wisdom of Torah: Epistemology in Deuteronomy and the Wisdom Literature* (Gottingen: Vandenhoeck & Ruprecht, 2009), 17. (Hereby DC is used in Deuteronomic Covenant).

304 Hereby BC is used in place of Book of the Covenant.

305 Later dates for the BC have been proposed. See for example, Douglas A. Knight, "Village Law and the Book of the Covenant," in *A Wise and Discerning Mind: Essay in Honor of Burke O.Long,* edited by Saul M. Olyan and Robert C. Culley (Province RI: Brown Judaic Studies, 2000), 163-79 (Monarchic period). And John Van Seters, *A Law Book of Diaspora: Revision in the Covenant Book* (Oxford, New York: Oxford University Press, 2003), (exilic period). Cf. Lawrence Boadt, *Reading the Old Testament An Introduction* (New York: Paulist Press, 1984), 184.

306 Hereby DL is used instead of Deuteronomic Law.

Josiah's reform. The DL has been described as 'a direct descendant of the Book of the Covenant' because many of its provisions are 'restatements' of those found in the BC.[307] A comparison between the laws in Deuteronomy and those in the Covenant code of Exodus reveals a striking degree of overlap in terms of content. The Book of the Covenant has some striking statements on social issues, but their number is small. There is a great increase in the number of such laws in the Deuteronomic code. The following text Exod 22: 21-24 and Deuteronomy 24:17-22 will be looked into. The treatment of Alien in the Book of Exodus and Deuteronomic law (DL) is the subject of this study. This study presumes that biblical law construct identity and therefore builds on earlier work that identifies such a function in the Deuteronomistic History. Ideological criticism can include a two part analysis-an extrinsic analysis 'investigates the social and historical worlds in which these texts were produced', and an intrinsic analysis 'focus on what the text actually says (content) and how it says it (rhetoric).[308] The *extrinsic analysis* highlights the Independent Monarchy a native-tributary mode of production in Monarchy and its effect on the life of the peasant. The *intrinsic analysis* underscores the ideological identity of Israel vis-a-vis Egypt, the inclusive law: widow and Deuteronomy and the rights of Indigenous people.

4.1. Extrinsic Analysis Exodus 22:21-24 and Deuteronomy 24:17-22

Different arguments are given for dating the covenant code in the monarchical period:

(1) The traditional dating based on the documentary hypothesis argues for a date in the early period of monarchy. This theory is based partly on the incorporation of the legal material into E source, and partly on the connection of the polemic law of the alter (Exod 20: 24-26) with the reforms of Jehu or Elizah (1 Kgs 16:1-4, 18:1-40).[309]

---

307 Dale Patrick, *Old Testament Law* (Atlanta: John Knox Press, 1985), 97. It is believed that the similarities between the Book of the Covenant and the Deuteronomic Law are due to the reworking of the chronologically earlier provisions of the Book of the Covenant in the later law. However, an alternative explanation for these similarities has been proposed, that there was a deuteronomistic revision of the Book of the Covenant's provision after the premonarchic period. Lohfnik and Levinson have rejected that explanation. See Lohfink, "Poverty in the Laws of the Ancient Near East," 34-50; and Bernard M. Levinson, *Deuteronomy and the Hermeneutics of Legal Innovation* (New York: Oxford University Press, 1997), 11-13.

308 Yee, 'Ideological Criticism: Judges 17-21and the Dismembered Body," 146-70.

309 Eissfeld, *The Old Testament: An Introduction,* translated by P. R. Ackroyd (Oxford: Basil Blackwell, 1966), 219. Cf. Fohrer, *Introduction to the Old Testament,* translated by David Green (London: SPCK, 1970), 136-37.

(2) Another theory is based on the connection of the Covenant code with the Deuteronomic code. Since Wellhausen,[310] there has been a suspicion that certain elements of this corpus are later additions by Deutoronomic hands and unfortunately part of the laws on the poor belongs to the so-called "Deuteronomic code." For example, the laws dealing with aliens, widow and orphans have been described as belonging to a later stage of development in the Covenant code, showing signs of Deuteronomic redaction. Smith, support this view.[311] Against this view Patrick presents that the Deuteronomy relies on and adapts the Covenant code.[312]

In the Covenant code, widow, orphan and alien are mentioned in separate laws and the fixed formula 'alien, widow and orphan which is prevalent in and typical of Deuteronomy do not occur. Lohfink argues: "to be sure, it has had its stages of literary development. The law on the poor does not belong to the earliest parts, and in addition, they themselves seem to be stratified. But the final stage is older than the code of Deuteronomy."[313] For Lohfink, the theme of the poor is anything but accidental. Crusemann while accepting the earlier existence of some of the laws in oral forms, argues for a date in the period of monarchy.[314]

The identification of the Book of Deuteronomy with the law of the book of Josiah (640-609 B.C.E.) by Wilhelm Martin Laberecht de Wette (1805) received prime importance after Graf had suggested in 1866 the probability of an earlier date for Deuteronomy than the priestly source and also Wellhausen had successfully led this hypothesis in the following two decades.[315] De Wette reached this view, having observed a correspondence between the legislation in Deuteronomy, where the law book is first introduced and the legal reforms of Josiah in 2 Kings 23. Since the time of De Wette, the vast majority of scholars have accepted that the book of Deuteronomy.[316] It was de Wette who

310 J. Wellhausen, *Prolegomena to the History of Ancient Israel* (Cleveland & New York: meridian Books, 1957).

311 Mark S. Smith, *The Pilgrimage Pattern in Exodus,* JSOT Sup 239 (Sheffield: Sheffield Academic Press, 1997), 173.

312 Patrick, *Old Testament Laws,* 65.

313 Lofnik, "Poverty in Biblical Law," 39 and 42.

314 F. Crusemann, *The Torah: Theology and Social History* ...152.

315 G. T. Manley, *The Book of Law: Studies in Date of Deuteronomy* (London: The Tyndale Press, 1957), 1-10. His book is an excellent study on date of Deuteronomy. Cf. Joy Joseph, "'Re-Lecturing' of Deuteronomy (Chapter 12-26) in the Post Exilic period." (D.Th Dissertation, Munchen University, 1997), 11. See Gerhard Von Rad, *Deuteronomy: A Commentary* (Philadelphia: Westminster Press, 1966), 11. See also R. E. Clements, *Deuteronomy Old Testament Guides* (Sheffield: JSOT Press, 1976), 70.

316 Katherine Stott, "Finding the Lost Book of the Law: Re-reaching the story of 'The Book of the Law' (Deuteronomy-2 Kings) in Light of Classic Literature." *JSOT 30*/2 (2005), 155. (155-169).

propounded the theory that Deuteronomy reflects the reform of Josiah, a theory which was considered a great discovery and was used as a key to understand the process of the composition of the Pentateuch.[317] His theory stood firm and unshaken during the period of over 100 years.[318]

The problem surrounding the date, authorship and provenance of Deuteronomy are amongst the most controversial in the study of the Old Testament.[319] For Gressmann[320] Deuteronomium was probably given its literary form sometimes between the middle of eight century and the middle of seventh century in the Northern kingdom. And they also assumed that, after the fall of Samaria, the book might have been brought to the southern kingdom and deposited in the temple of Jerusalem and forgotten till the restoration of the temple in the eighteenth year of Josiah. Since the Enlightenment, however, scientific biblical scholarship has advocated a large variety of hypothesis regarding the date and authorship of the work.[321] The Book has been Moses,[322] Samuel or Judges,[323] Priest,[324] prophets,[325] scribes and wisemen;[326] it has been dated in various periods from the time of Moses to the time of the exile, a time span of seven centuries.[327] M. G. Kline,[328] K. A. Kitchen,[329] and others have argued that the treaty-covenant structure of Deuteronomy indicates that it must be dated in the Mosaic age. The thrust of argument rests on several bases.

---

317 Moshe Weinfeld, "Deuteronomy-The Present State of Inquiry," *JBL* LXXXV1 (Sept, 1967), 249.

318 Weinfeld, "Deuteronomy- The Present State of Inquiry," 250.

319 E. W. Nicholson, *Deuteronomy and Tradition* (Oxford: Basil Blackwell, 1967), 37.

320 H. Gressmann, "Josiah und das Deuteronomiun," *ZAW* 42 (1924), 313-337.

321 Peter C. Craigie, *The Book of Deuteronomy, The New International Commentary on the Old Testament* (Grand Rapids, Michigan: Wm. B. Eerdmans Publishing Company, 1976), 24.

322 R. K. Harrison, *Introduction to the Old Testament with a Comprehensive review of Old Testament Studies and a Special Supplement on the Apocrypha* (Grand Rapids, Michigan: William B. Eerdmans Publishing Company, 1969), 636-640.

323 Scholars like T. Oestreicher, A. C. Welch ascribe the date of the origin of Deuteronomy to the period of Samuel or the Judges.

324 Von Rad, *Deuteronomy: A Commentary,* 25.

325 E. W. Nicholson, *Deuteronomy and Tradition...,* 69.

326 Moshe Weinfeld, *Deuteronomy and Deuteronomic School* (Oxford: Clarendon Press, 1972), 67. Cf. M. Weinfeld, "Deuteronomy-The present state ..., 254.

327 Peter C. Craigie, *The Book of Deuteronomy...,* 25.

328 Meridith G. Kline, *Treaty of the Great King-The Covenant Structure of Deuteronomy: Studies and Commentary* (Grand Rapids, Michigan: William B. Eerdmans Publishing Company, 1963), 35.

329 K. A. Kitchen, *Ancient Orient and Old Testament* (London: The Tyndale Press, 1966), 25. He seeks to use form-critical studies to prove a second millennium date for Deuteronomy.

The impression given here is that, with regard to the question of the date and authorship of the book of Deuteronomy, there is no general consensus in modern critical research. It should be noted that scholarly suggestions regarding the date of origins are different and can be referred back to the periods from the time of Moses to the post exilic era.[330] It means that the present law book of Deuteronomy may contain materials of different periods from Exodus to the post-exilic period.

4.1.1. Independent Monarchy: A Native-Tributary Mode of Production

The tribes remained in a familial mode of production as free agrarians for about two centuries. The transition to a monarchy and tributary mode of production resulted from complex external and internal pressures affecting Israel. The biblical texts describe Philistine military incursions into Israelite territories as the chief force for the tribes' demand for a king. For one thing, Israel's growth and prosperity in the highland areas posed a political threat to Philistine strongholds along the coast, and to the Amalekites in the south and the Ammonites in the east. In addition, the highland tribes cultivated agriculture products less available in the lands belonging to these peoples, providing an economic attraction for Philistine, Amalekite, and Ammonite expansion.[331]

Coote and Whitelam delineate three areas in the shift in highland infrastructure that facilitated state formation. First, the expansion of horticulture and the population increase in highland regions were crucial for the emergence of Israel. Nevertheless, once the frontier was "tamed," there was no more room for further economic expansion, and population growth put considerable stress on limited natural resources. "Under these conditions the rise of kingship may have been largely a self-generating process."[332]

The second factor that expedited state formation was the increasing socio-economic stratification in the Israelite population.[333] The limits put on available land for cultivation, the increased population growth, and the

330 Scholars like Gerhard Von Rad and P. C. Craigie the sanctuaries of Northern Israel (Shechem or Bethel) to be Deuteronomy's place of origin, and the century before 621 must be its date. There is no sufficient reason for going farther back. Cf. Von Rad, *Deuteronomy: A Commentary,* 26; Peter C. Craigie, *The Book of Deuteronomy,* 124-29.

331 Israel Finkelstein, "The Emergence of the Monarchy in Israel: The Environmental and Socio-Economic Aspects," *JSOT* 44 (1989): 61. Cf. Norman K. Gottwald, "The Participation of Free Agrarians in the Introduction of Monarchy to Ancient Israel: An Application of H. A. Landsberger's Framework for the Analysis of Peasants," *Semeia* 37 (1986), 87-88.

332 Coote and Whitelam, "Emergence of Israel," 135. Lemche, "Israel History of"..., 542.

333 David Hopkins, "Bare Bones: Putting Flesh on the Economic of Ancient Israel," in *Origin of the Ancient Israelite States,* edited by Volkmar Fritz and Philip R. Davies, JSOT Sup 228 (Sheffield: Sheffield Academic Press, 1996), 129-32.

depletion of resources created a disproportionate degree of inequity among Israelite social group. Lemce asserts: "Its consequence would have been that the more fortunate Israelites were in a position to bind their poorer kinsmen to them by means of contracts which transformed what were originally independent peasants into indentured peasants in the service of their fellow countrymen. Over the course of time the latter took on the character of local petty nobles or wealthy farmers."[334]

Weber sees in the emergence of the Israelite monarchy, a ruling class of wealth urban families who, by the accumulation of wealth, became 'economically expendable' thus able to devote themselves to politics and war. The ancient free peasantry was disarmed in the process, as Weber illustrates with his comparison of the peasantry summons in the Song of Deborah with the chariot of Solomon. In this situation which gave rise to typical class antagonisms, urban patricians were pitted against socially, economically, and militarily descending peasants. The so-called "biblical social evils" which the prophets chastise are then connected with this social tension.[335] It is Weber analysis which has set the tone for most of the subsequent analyses of the Israelites social structure.

Increasing political centralization promoted the rise of the monarchy. While most free agrarians supported the move toward a monarchy to defend themselves against Philistines hegemony, prosperous landholders within Israel saw in the monarchy a way to advance their own economic and political interests. The monarchy represented the "means by which a subgroup of emergent landed elite in Israel imposed greater costs of national defence upon village small holders and retained political control over their participation in trade among themselves."[336]

Through foreign conquests and the taxation of non-Israelite land in Canaan, Wittenberg argues that: "King David was able to forestall the extraction of tribute from free agrarians. However, he initiated an array of political and economic structure that, under the rule of his son Solomon, assimilated the tribes back into a tributary economy and exacerbated the social stratification among free agrarians."[337] Those among the landed elite part of the ruling class or otherwise profited from tax concessions and latifundiary arrangements, for the majority of Israel's free agrarians. However for Holladay, this was not the

334 Niels Peter Lemche, "Israel, History of (premonarchic Period)," *Anchor Bible Dictionary,* Vol. 3 (New York: Doubleday, 1992), 542.

335 Max Weber, *Ancient Judaism* (Glencoe, Ill.: Free Press, 1952), 18. Cited by Frank S. Frick, *The City in Ancient Israel* (Missoula, Montana: Scholars Press, 1970), 100.

336 Coote and Whitelam, "Emergence of Israel"..., 141. See Marvin L. Chaney, "Systemic Study of the Israelite Monarchy," *Semeia* 37 (1986), 67-68.

337 Günther Wittenberg, "King Solomon and the Theologians," *Journal of Theology for Southern Africa* 63 (1988), 16-17.

case: "The King and the ruling elite began to demand their surpluses, in both human and natural resources, to pay for the centralize bureaucracy, ambitious building projects, and luxurious courts lifestyle."[338] Thus, these farmers became progressively more impoverished. Over time, they fell to peasant status as they were increasingly taxed. Often, this taxation resulted in the loss of their ancestral lands to the state in order to pay their debt.[339] Gottwald's comments on Israel's relation to the state from the time of its inception are insightful:

> "Although Israel arose in opposition to the state system and in time survived apart from any particular state structure, its history and ethos were fashioned in intimate response to the commanding position of the state. In both native and foreign guises, the state intruded insistently upon the economy and ideology of the villages which constitute the heart land of Israel."[340]

The expansion of agriculture and the growth of population, supporting each other hand in hand, were the foundation of the adaptive success of early Israel. There existed powerful and uninhibited practical and ideological incentives for each. Coote and Whithelam rightly states that:

> The effects of depletion and overpopulation would lead to the political forms created by landed interests for the furtherance of their power. Along with ecological pressure in favour of the cultivation of the vine and olives, richer people, those with more land, have less incentive to grow food and move to grow cash crops for market. It is impossible to understand early Israel without realizing that the market component of its product was continuously increasing, and that there was a probable correlation between expansion and market avoidance on the one hand and intensification and market acceptance on the other hand.[341]

The shift from local consumption to urban marketing hastened the social integration of wealthier Israelites farmers with the left behind urban elites in the highland cities.

---

338 John S. Holladay Jr., "The Kingdoms of Israel and Judah: Political and Economic Centralization in the Iron 11 A-B (ca. 1000-750 B.C.E)," in *The Archaeology of Society in the Holy Land,* edited by Thomas E. Levy (New York: Facts and File, 1995), 382.

339 Gottwald, "Social Class as an Analytic and Hermeneutical Category," 6-9.

340 Norman K. Gottwald, "Sociology (Ancient Israel)," in *ABD* 6 (New York: Doubleday, 1992), 82-83.

341 Coote, Robert B, and Keith W. Whitelam, "The Emergence of Israel, social Transformation and State Formation following the Decline in Late Bronze Age Trade," *SEMEIA* 37 (1986): 134.

In shifting from local to urban cities Kessler remarks: "Those whose economic existence was thus threatened do not appear to have been the classic biblical oppressed persons; the book of Amos never speaks of widows and orphans. Rather, these are small farmers who are expected to hand over more and more and when nothing more to be taken from them, fall into slavery. And the "girl" to whom, according to Amos 2:7, "father and son go in," is apparently a daughter already given into debt slavery and is sexually abused by her owners and overseers."[342] Since the upper class were closely attached to the power of the state.

Therefore, with the introduction of monarchy the egalitarian mode of life gradually disappeared from the face of Israelite society. The Israelite society underwent radical changes in the economic realm. There was a shift in the mode of production distribution. Market economy was also introduced. With the shift in domain under monarchy, lands once freely held by the peasants began to fall into the hands of rich land owners.

4.1.2. Internal and External State Politics

Social, political, and economic developments in both Israel and Judah often resulted from external influences and pressures from the wider Ancient West Asia context. By the eight century B.C.E during the reign of Jeroboam 11 (786-746 B.C.E) Israel and Judah reached heights of climax in terms of their economic prosperity. For the first time Israel enjoyed political freedom which help them in the development of their economy in terms of new markets and new sources of income. As a result, there was rapid organization and there was a radical shift from barter system to monetary economy. However, the consequences were severe to the peasants. They not only lost their piece of land but also were forced to sell themselves as slaves (Amos 2:6, 8:6). The upper class is accused not only of exploiting the lower class, but of unbridled luxury in architecture (3:10-11, 15; 5:11), furnishing (3:15; 6:4), and banqueting (2:8; 4:1; 6:4-6), since they were closely attached to the power of the state.

Egalitarian values which were followed during the period of tribal confederation were practice of this system in rural/village areas, whereas in urban areas new system was more prevalent. Many people think that both these systems continued simultaneously. There are indications that certain features of the Bronze age system were adopted and adapted by Israel in the early monarchy, coinciding with the period of intensified urbanization in Israel. Bright observes:

> Early Israel had been...a class society with none of the feudalism of the Canaanites states; she had no ruling class, no social distinction

342 Rainer Kessler, *The social History of Ancient Israel An Introduction,* translated by Linda M. Maloney (Minneapolis: Fortress Press, 2008), 109.

> or extremes of wealth and poverty. This was all changed (in the Monarchy) Solomon's commercial and industrial ventures, though state monopolies, raised the living standard of the nation allowed some...to grow rich. The court grew very rich. As royal projects drew people to the cities, urban population grew apace, with an attendant weakening the tribal ties and tradition... plagued hid subjects into forced labour for the state (1 Kings 5:13-18) a wholly 'un-Israelites' measure. As life was regulated under the crown, and as Canaanites with a feudal background and no conception of the covenant order were absorbed, notion of aristocracy and class distinction began to intrude (1 Kings 2:1-15).[343]

Weber views are commendable as he sees the emergence of the Israelite monarchy, a ruling class of wealthy becomes "economically expandable" and thus able to devote themselves to politics and war. The ancient free peasantry was disarmed in the process, as Weber illustrates with his comparison of the peasantry was disarmed in the process, as Weber illustrates with his comparison of the peasants summons in the Song of Deborah with the chariot cities of Solomon. In this situation which gave rise to typical class antagonism, urban patricians were pitted against socially, economically, and militarily descending peasants. The so-called "biblical social evil" which the prophets chastise is then connected with this social tension.[344] It was Weber analysis which has set the tone for most of the subsequent analyses of the Israelite social structure.

Gottwald asserts that the emergence of strong centralized states siphoned off agrarian and pastoral surpluses through taxation and merchant groups profited from peasant indebtedness and high level international trade and the monarchy engaged in warfare and conquest of neighbouring lands.[345] The socio-economic situation of Judah on the eve of the reign of Josiah may be rightly observed by Gottwald as he states: "Judah had been a shrunken vassal kingdom of Assyria for seventy five years, reduced in size, with its ruling class members-both those in and out of government-pushed to writing all they could out of the peasant economic base in order to survive and prosper marginally Imperial? To solidify its precarious position, further alienating its members from those exploited."[346] It was at this very juncture; Josiah came to the throne,

343 John Bright, "Hebrew Religion, History of," in *IDB,* 11 (Nashville: Abingdon Press, 1962), 564.

344 Max Weber, *Ancient Judaism*, translated and edited by Hans H.Gerth and Don Martindale (New York: Collier Macmillan Publisher, 1952), 18.

345 N. K. Gottwald, "Social class as Analytical and Hermeneutical Categories in Biblical Studies," *JBL* 112/1 (1993), 4-6.

346 N. K. Gottwald, "Social class as Analytical and Hermeneutical Categories in Biblical Studies," 12.

when the entire structure of society was at a complete breakdown. The very fabric of the society was very much interwoven with corruption except for the few elites with consumerist life-style while the majority of the population were at the receiving end. In fact, politically, economically, socially and even religiously the society was at the point of total disintegration.

Lenski, as a part of his larger study on social stratification, has reviewed the social structure of agrarian societies, a type of society marked by relatively advanced agricultural technology but no industrialization. His thoroughly researched study highlights the typical pattern of societal interactions, roles and power relationship in these agrarian cultures.

Lenski further notes that 'the unequal distribution of power, privilege, and honor in (agrarian societies) arises largely from the functioning of their political system.[347] He goes on to explain that this is not an unexpected finding:

> Given the nature of man and society...we should logically anticipate an increase in social inequality as the economic surplus expands, as military technology expands to the point where to the average man can no longer equip himself as well as certain others, and as the powers of the state increase. Furthermore, we should expect that the actions of men of power, who act in the name of the state, would be the primary source of this increase of social inequality.[348]

He goes on to explain that the highest and most powerful class in such a society is made up of the ruler and the various state officers, advisors to the king, civil and military officials and the landed elites by inheritance of royal grant.[349] This class makes up of tiny minority of the population, yet owns or controls most of the resources, power and wealth.

The next most powerful class is made up of various people. Foremost among these are members of the retainer group dependent on the political elite [350]people such as servants, soldiers and lower level civil officials. By and large, their tasks are the maintenance of the distributive economic system whereby goods and wealth are redistributed from the lower classes to the higher, in particular to the crown, through taxes, rent and fees.[351] Finally, Lenski notes that: "The merchant class, despite its humble origins, has a source of accruing wealth and therefore some political power through its trade. Its stands in a market relationship with the government, not an authority relationship, and so

347 Gerherd Lenski, *Power and Privilege: A Theory of Social Stratification* (New York: McGrw-Hill, 1966), 210.

348 Lenski, *Power and Privilege,* 210.

349 Lenski, *Power and Privilege*, 220.

350 Lenski, *Power and Privilege*, 243.

351 Lenski, *Power and Privilege*, 246.

maximize these market forces and minimize the effects of royal authority and elite control."[352]

In the vast underclass, making up the large majority of the population, stand the peasants. On their labor falls the burden of supporting the whole state apparatus and the privileged class.[353] This they do through the payment of land taxes and rents, and by supplying labor services, all of which often constitute a large portion of their production. Lenski notes the bare subsistence level and condition of their life: "to compound the misery created by their economic situation, the peasants were often subjected to cruel and inhumane treatment by their superior."[354] According to Yee "tax cycle demanding goods and resources as well as forced labor siphoned off the peasants' surplus production. When they could not meet their tax payment because of crop failure or war, a debt cycle in the form of credit held at high interest rates was imposed, resulting in an endless circle of debt."[355] However, the consequences were severe to the peasants. They not only lost their piece of land but also were forced to sell themselves as slaves. Egalitarian values which were followed during the period of tribal confederation were never practice during the monarchic period.

4.1.3. Urban Social Structure

Attempt to analysis the social structure of the Israelites must certainly reckon with the problematic expression *'am-ha'arets,* which is applied to a group of people seventy times in the OT. The problem is to ascertain to what particular group, the term is applied. In the use of this term in the OT, the researcher in this section is interested only in the monarchy. In this period, the use of this expression is mainly in three books: 2 Kings, Jeremiah and Ezekiel. In these books, the "people of the land" is distinguished from, or contrasted with: (1) the king or prince; (2) the king and his servants; (3) the chiefs and the priests; and (4) the chiefs, the priests and the prophets.[356] The different witness in these texts is basically one between subjects and the ruling element, including the priests and prophets associated with the latter. In those instances where a rural-urban cleavage has been suggested, another explanation is preferable. In 2 Kgs 11:20 there appears the phrase: "So all the people of the land rejoiced; but the city was quiet after Athaliah had been slain with the sword in the king's house." Vaux in his suggestion that the contrast implied here is nothing more than a distinction between the city as the seat of the regime which had just been

352 Lenski, *Power and Privilege*, 250-54.

353 Lenski, *Power and Privilege*, 266.

354 Lenski, *Power and Privilege*, 271.

355 Gale A. Yee, *Poor Banished Children of Eve Woman as Evil in the Hebrew Bible,* 32.

356 (1) 2 Kgs 16:15; Ezek 7:27; 45:22; (2) Jer 37:2; (3) Jer 1:18; 34:19; 44:21; (4) Ezek 22:24-29.

overthrown and the rest of the country which had remained loyal to the Davidic house.[357] Thus, the expression *'am ha'ares* here used as a general meaning and does not refer to a particular class or group within the population. Looking into Ezek 22:23-31, reflecting back to the fallen kingdom of Judah, names as those responsible for the catastrophe not only kings, priest, officials, and prophets, but also the *'am-ha'arets,* for having oppressed the needy, the poor, and the גר (v.29). As Keller comments: "it is clear that here *'am-ha'arets* does not mean the population as a whole, but its economically powerful upper class."[358] The translation "landed aristocracy" is entirely appropriate in this case.

Another instance where a rural-urban cleavage has been suggested is in 2 Kgs 25:3: "the famine was so severe in the city that there was no food for the people of the land." There is again no need for reading into this verse a rural urban split. A simpler interpretation of this verse is to take the second half of the verse as standing in opposition to the first half so that both refer to the same location "The famine was so severe in the city that there was no food for the people living there." One other passage in 2 Kings is instructive for our purpose here: "But the people of the land killed all those who had conspired against King Amon, and the people of the land made his son Josiah King in place of him" (21:24). Frick remarks: "The expression has a political significance here, in that the action of the "people of the land" represents a movement on the part of the native free Israelites over against the action of the "servants" of King Amon who had put him to death."[359]

The "people of the land" thus most generally represents the free Israelite community, constituted on the basis of kinship as the etymology of *'am* suggests, as distinct from the royal entourage, Israelite or גר, who owed their status not to membership in the kinship group of Israel, but to the royal favor. Nicholson's conclusion is worth mentioning:

> ... the term has no fixed and rigid meaning but is used rather in a purely general and fluid manner and varies in meaning from context to context. To regard it as a technical term designating a specific class or group within the population of Judah is to read far too much into its meaning.[360]

357 Roland de Vaux, *Ancient Israel* (New York: Mc Graw-Hill, 1961), 71.

358 Rainer Kessler, *The Social History of Ancient Israel An Introduction,* 99.

359 Frank S. Frick, *The City in Ancient Israel* (Missoula, Montana: Scholar Press, 1970), 101. The "people of the land" thus most generally represents the free Israelite community, constituted on the basis of kinship as the etymology of '*am* suggests, as distinct from the royal entourage, Israelite or alien, who owed their status not to membership in the kinship group of Israel, but to the royal favor.

360 E. W. Nicholson, "The Meaning of the Expression *'m h'rs* in the Old Testament," *Journal of Semitic Studies* X (1965), 60.

The above example tells us not only about the book's vision for the people of God, but about the existence of a well-to-do upper class and an often impoverished lower class. Fricks concludes saying "the rise of the monarchy brought with it a hierarchy social structure. It created a royal family, a national cult, a patrician class centred in the cities, and a semi-free artisan and peasant class."[361]

In Deuteronomy 24 there are five references to the alien, in vv.14, 17, 19, 20, and 21. It seems that the concern of the alien dominates, and that is true to some extent. These references are found in a section of the law code, Deut. 24:5-25:4, which has been characterized by its concern for the needy. However, contained within this collection are laws which do not conform to that concern, such as Deut 26:16 which will not discuss in this chapter. Most of the laws appear to be ancient, and many have parallels in the Book of the Covenant. The hands of the author are noticeable mostly in the organization of the chapter, and in the motivational clauses which have been attached to the law. Deuteronomy is well-known for its humanitarian concern for the marginalized.

4.2. Intrinsic Analysis Exod 22:21-23:9 and Deut 14:21; 24:17-22

Most scholar agree that these laws do not date to Mosaic period of the wilderness but originate for the most part sometime after the settlement in Canaan and perhaps before the rise of the monarchy in Israel. The goal of studying biblical laws, then, does not have to be learning more about ancient Israelite judicial administration or about a sociohistorical context purportedly giving rise to these laws. Instead, these laws can be studied for their ideological content. That content is important because, by expressing appropriate behaviour, it constructs identities.[362]

In the "Book of the Covenant" as well as in Deuteronomy, The גר is mentioned exclusively in a social connection. "You shall not wrong or oppress a resident alien, for you were aliens in the land of Egypt."(Exod 22: 21; 23:9). The גר is close to widows, orphans, and the poor (Exod 22:21, 24; cf. also Deut 14:19; 16:11, 14; 24:14, 17,19,21; 26:13; 27:19). Class differences are also constructed through the laws on the widow, orphan, and stranger-groups that are devoid of the economic support of a privileged Israelite male.[363] The

361 F. S. Frick, *The City in Ancient Israel,* 205.

362 Craig Calhoun, *Critical Social Theory: Culture, History, and the Challenge of Difference* (Oxford: Basil Blackwell, 1995), 213.

363 The widow is not just a woman whose husband has died. She is also a woman whose sons or her husband's family are not willing or able to support her. Bennett Harold V. *Injustice Made Legal: Deutronomic law and the Plight of Widows, Strangers, and Orphans in Ancient Israel* (Grand Rapids, Michigan: William. B. Eerdmann Publishing, 2002), 37. The orphan may be orphaned daughter because her ability to inherit her father' was

protection extended to the widow is the same as those extended to orphans, the poor and resident aliens in the BC.

4.2.1. Aliens in the Book of the Covenant

What ancient West Asia literature and Israelite codes have in common is their content. The forms through which the content is conveyed differ. Ancient West Asia literature normally expresses its concern for the deprived in forms like confessions, instruction, and hymn-petitions, rather than through legal statements. Another problem is raised by the social setting of the ancient West Asia references. They are regularly based on a royalty abominated social structure. Do the Israelite laws derived from the same settings?

Noth believed that some of these laws derive from the early tribal period of Israel's history.[364] Waldow explains the similar context of Near Eastern and Israelite statements by showing that the substance of some Near Eastern and Israelite writings both originated among ancient Semetic clans.[365] Moreover, he demonstrates that there was always a need for some laws on social justice, because there were always some in Israel who were not economically secure, namely, the alien, widow, and fatherless child. He asserts that: "some laws of the deprived were added to the codes when extremes of poverty and wealth developed under the Monarchy."[366] Exod 22:21b and 23:9b supports this. So it is likely that the laws being analysed in this chapter developed during a long period of Israel's history extending from its beginnings to the monarchic period. The laws arose from quite different social settings, including an early period of relative equality and a late period of great economic disparity.

In fact, the protection of the poor, widow, and the fatherless was a common Near Eastern policy. It was prevalent in Mesopotamia from Sumerian times,[367] throughout Egyptian history,[368] and at Ugarit.[369] In the oldest Biblical

---

limited (Num.27:7-11) where as the orphaned son could have inherited the father's estate (Deut. 21:15-17). The stranger (*gër*) is an immigrant who is accepted within the Israelite community but maintains a distinctive ethnic or cultural identity. Benneth, *Injustice made legal...,* 48; and Rolf Rendtorff, "The *Gër* in the Priestly Laws of the Pentateuch," 77-88.

364 Martin Noth, *The Laws in the Pentateuch and other Studies* (Philadelphia: Fortress, 1966), 33, 60. Cf. H. E. Von Waldow, *Social Responsibility and Social Structure in Early Israel* (Catholic Biblical Association, 1970), 184-185.

365 Von Waldow, "Social Responsibility and Social Structure in Early Israel," 184-85.

366 Von Waldow, "Social Responsibility and Social Structure in Early Israel," 194-199.

367 F. Charles Fenham, "Widow, Orphan and the Poor…129. Cf. H. Eberhard Von Waldow, "Social Responsibility and Social Structure in Early Israel," *CBQ* 32 (1970), 184-185.

368 Samuel Krammer, *The Sumerians* (Chicago: University of Chicago, 1963), 264. Fensham, "Widow, Orphan and the Poor," 130-131.

369 J. P. Prichard, *ANET,* 407-410, 412-419, 421-424, 441-444.

code, called the covenant code (Exod 20:22-23:19),[370] and in early narrative the גר seems to be an outsider who is resident in a locale, either permanently or temporarily. The person could be either an Israelite or from a non-Israelite ethnic group. Inside/outside was defined by membership in the clan. The provision in the code (Ex 22:21; 23:9, 12) prohibit oppressive or exploitative treatment in general and by the court in particular, and includes the alien along with work animals and slaves among those granted Sabbath rest. The Motive clauses recall the experience of Israelites in Egypt to arouse empathy with the situation of the alien, servants and work animals as recipients of Sabbath rest. The assumption behind including גר among the beneficiaries of a Sabbath rest is that they are dependents of the clan patriarchs addressed in the code.

גר were not only socially poor and weak, they especially were without rights. They were unable to have their own voice in a trial at the gate. Like women, children and slaves, they were unable to express their rights there and enforce them. The alien theme deals with gaining rights for those who have none. Other social groups included in Exod 22:20 and 23:9, the poor (22:24ff), widows and orphans (22:21, 23), were likewise legally handicapped. Nevertheless, what was a problem for them was magnified in the case of foreigners, because there were also women and children among the foreigners. Crusemann has rightly said: "Justice for those who had none was to be given at the place of justice. We do not fine the measure of the judiciary in how it deals with those who were permitted to appear before judges nor were they provided for."[371] The protection of aliens, without respect to their ethnic and religious background, is among the most important commands of the same God who demanded that he alone be worshiped. And this command to protect foreigners could not be ignored.

The three references to theגר in the Book of the Covenant occur in Exod. 22:20; 23: 9, 12. Interestingly, the first two are quite similar, and instruct the Israelites not to mistreat the alien, while the last is the Sabbath command amplified to include the animals, slaves and the alien. The Book of the Covenant is part of the Sinai narratives, but it is clear that it has been inserted

---

370 Scholars assigns 8th cent B.C.E. as the date for the Covenant Code because of the word order. Martin Noth, *A History of Pentateuchal Traditions,* translated by B. W. Anderson (Chico, California.: Scholar Press, 1981), 36, 139. Noth comments, "It is probably that this collection once formed an independent book of law which has been inserted into the Pentateuchal narratives as an already self-contained entity.... No clear relationship to any one of the Pentateuchal narrative 'source' is recognizable". Martin Noth, *Exodus* (Philadelphia: Westminster Press, 1962), 173. Cf. J. Blenkinsopp, *The Pentateuch: an introduction to the first five books of the Bible* (London: SCM Press, 1992), 200-201. F. Crusemann, *The Torah: Theology and SocialHistory of the Old Testament Law,* 184.

371 Grusemann, *The Torah: Theology and SocialHistory of the Old Testament Law,*183.

here. The narrative breaks off at Exod. 20: 21 and resumes in Exod. 24:1.[372] The law collection which is set within this framework seems to have existed independently in some form prior to its incorporated into the narrative.[373]

Sprinkle, adopted 'literary approach'[374] in contrast looks at the text in a synchronic rather than a diachronic way. This approach, used increasingly in recent years is associated with such names as Alter, Berlin, Brichto, and Sternberg. It is akin to the approach to literature called New Criticism, traceable to the 1920s, that centers on a 'close reading' of the text itself, with an eye to its inner coherence, rather than its historical development or production. Others have (less happily) used the term rhetorical criticism for this approach.[375]

The Covenant Code presents the requirement of a separation from foreign populations, especially those of Canaan. These measures are dictated by anti-idolatrous concerns aiming to preserve Israel from syncretism and contamination with local deities and ordered around the exclusive principle of the Lord (Ex 25: 25a). Prohibition of idolatry (Ex 23: 24a) implies the need

---

372 Otto Eissfeldt, *The Old Testament: An Introduction,* translated by P. R. Ackroyd (New York: Harper & Row, 1965), 213. Fohrer, *Introduction to the Old Testament,* 133 and B.S. Childs, *The Book of Exodus: A Critical, Theological Commentary* (OTL; Philadelphia: Westminster Press, 1962), 453-54., for a presentation of how the Book of the Covenant was incorporated into its present context. They argue that the original narrative sequence was Ex 20:8-21; 20:1-17; 24:3. The references in Exod 24:3 to the 'words and laws' are attributed to the redactor. Furthermore, it is argued that the phrase 'all the words' referred only to the Dacalogue, which formed the basis for the following covenant renewal ceremony. Source oriented scholars have posed many question regarding Ex 20: 22- 23:23 Cf. Boecker, *Law and the Administration of Justice in the Old Testament and Ancient East,* 135-75; Patrick, *Old Testament Law,* 63-96. Most literary-critical studies of the Covenant Code accept the view that the code is the product of a long redactional process.

373 Martin Noth, *Exodus: A Commentary,* translated by J. S. Bowden (Philadelphia: Westminster Press, 1962), 169.

374 Joe M. Sprinkle, *'The Book of the Covenant' A literary Approach,* JSOT Suplt 174 (Sheffield: JSOT Press, 1994), 12. Sprinkle approach is in contrast with structuralist, reader-oriented, feminist, and deconstructionist approaches. These approaches sometimes agree together with the kind of literary approach adopted here against source-oriented approaches.

375 In the Old Testament interpretation, Rhetorical criticism was introduced by James Muilenburg through a presidential address in 1968 to the Society of Biblical Literature. Muilenburg defines in this way "The limits or scope of the literary unit, to recognize precisely where and how it begins and how it ends". Secondly to recognize the structure of the composition and to discern the configuration of its component parts, to delineate the warp and woof out of which the literary fabric is woven, and to note the various rhetorical device that are employed for making, on the one hand, the sequence and movement of the periscope, and on the other, the shifts or breaks in the development of the writer's thought. Cf. J. Muilenburg, 'Form Criticism and Beyond', *Journal of Biblical Literature* 88 (1969):1-18 though his inadequate definition of rhetorical criticism as a methodology has allowed various interpretations. M. Kessler, 'A Methodological Setting for Rhetorical Criticism', in *Art and Meaning,* JSOT Sup 19 (Sheffield: JSOT Press, 1982), 1-2.

to differentiate between the children of Israel and the Canaanites in practice ("You shall not do according to their works" 23: 24b). The researcher will look at the precepts in favour of the aliens (Ex 22: 20-26 and 23:9).

4.2.2. Identity of Israel vis-à-vis Egypt

On the journey from Egypt to Sinai the voice of the Israelites were a voice of murmuring and rebellion. The voice of the people's complaining gives access to a pro-Egyptian ideology which the present narrative attempts to subdue by casting it as a form of rebellion against the deity. Just before reaching Sinai, a counter example to this voicing of an explicit pro-Egyptian perspective is offered in the person of Jethro. The narrative thus draws its audience into choosing sides for or against Israel's anti Egyptian identity. One of the instances of resistance or rebellion occurs on the miraculous deliverance at the sea. Hardly three days in the wilderness, at a place named Marah where the water is too bitter to drink, the people complain to Moses: "What shall we drink?" (Exo 15:24). "Moses cried to the Lord, and the Lord showed him a piece of wood, and the water became sweet". The incident becomes an occasion for YHWH to set a condition, described in the text as, a "statute and an ordinance and, he put them to the test" (Exo: 15: 25). The Lord continues to describe:

> If you will listen carefully to the voice of the Lord Your God, and do what is right in his sight, and give heed to his commandments and keep all his statutes, I will not bring upon you any of the diseases that I brought upon the Egyptians; for I am the Lord who heals you (Exo 15:26).

What is striking about these words is the return of Egypt into the discourse of Israel's identity. As Greifenhagen asserts: "YHWH'S words continue to emphasize the polarity between Egypt and Israel; Egypt is associated with disease while Israel is associated with divinity that heals. But at the same time, this polarity is threatened in that if Israel disobeys, it will be treated just like Egypt, and the distinction between the two will collapse."[376] In other words the identity of Israel as not Egypt is here exposed, by constantly obedience to the world defining rules to YHWH. YHWH becomes the term that mediates between Israel's foreign origin and Israel's indigenous claims.

Secondly, Israel's resistance occurs in the wilderness of Sin, where the whole congregation of the Israelites complained against Moses and Aaron in the wilderness:

376 Greifenhagen, *Egypt on the Pentateuch's Ideological Map Constructing Biblical Israel's Identity*, 138-39. The formula of divine disclosure in Exodus simply states "I am YHWH" (6:2, 6, 8, 29; 7:5, 17; 10:2; 12:12).

> If only we had died by the hand of the Lord in the land of Egypt, when we sad by the flashpots and ate our fill of bread, for you have brought us out into this wilderness to kill this whole assembly with hunger (Exo.16:3).

Again, the resistance of the people is described with the verb לון "to murmur, grumble."[377] From the perspective of Israel, Egypt is highlighted as a place of plenty while the wilderness is typified as a place of lack.[378] In fact death in Egypt, even at the hand of YHWH, is preferred to death in the wilderness by famine.

Thirdly, the same terminology of complain לון are expressed in Exo 17:2, 7, however YHWH does not test the people, but the people are described as testing YHWH (17:2, 7). From the narrative perspective of Israel, the lack of water in the wilderness highlights an uncertainty about YHWH's presence. In contrast Egypt is associated with plenty of food (16:3), and here, implicitly, with abundand water. According to this perception of relative lack and plenty, Israel doubts whether YHWH is present in the wilderness; the people seem to think that surely YHWH is back in Egypt. In this connection Greifenhagen remarks: "If Egypt is connected with plenty and the present of the deity, while the wilderness is connected with lack and the absence of the diety, then the very wisdom and necessity of leaving Egypt is brought into question."[379] The logic of the dominant ideology of the narratives, would damage the reputation of the very existence of Israel as a distinct people separated from Egypt. So the narrative present a counter example the person of Jethro, who confess YHWH as the one who delivered the people from the power of Egypt and who is therefore greather than all other gods (Exo 18:9-11).[380] The narration

377 Schunck, "לון lun, תלנות telunnot," in *TDOT*, V11, edited by G. Johannes Botterweck, Helmer Ringgren and Heinz-Josef Fabry (Grand Rapids, Michigan: William B. Eerdman Publishing Company,1995), 509-10.

378 Greifenhagen, *Egypt on the Pentateuch's Ideological Map Constructing Biblical Israel's Identity*, 139. One recalls the status of Egypt in the ancestral account of Genesis as a place of plenty in the times of famine.

379 Greifenhagen, *Egypt on the Pentateuch's Ideological Map Constructing Biblical Israel's Identity*, 141.

380 Exo 18:11 in the MT literally reads: "Now I know that YHWH is greater than all the gods; indeed (or because of) in the matter in which they acted presumptuously or rebelliously against them." The problem is to ascertain the antecedents of the pronouns 'they' and 'them'. *BHS* textual notes suggests a "lacuna" in the text while NRSV the clause because… Egyptian has been transposes a phrase from 18.10 in order to make the phrase mean that Egypt acted presumptuously against the Israelites (an interpretation that seems also to be found in Neh. 9.10). As it stands in the MT, the phrase seems to refer to the other gods, presumably the gods of Egypt as "they", acting presumptuously against the Israelites, thus connecting with the notice in 12.12 that YHWH will execute judgments on the gods of Egypt "them", acting as they have against Israel, have been rebelling toward Yahweh,

allows the voice of Israel to come to expression. It is a voice that longs for its former identity in Egypt, and associates Egypt with plenty and the presence of YHWH. In this voice, the pro-Egyptian ideology that the text is attempting to combat is made manifest, but it is cast as a rebellions and complaining voice.

In the Decalogue, marking the beginning of the list of covenant stipulation begins by identifying the covenant sovereign as 'YHWH your Gods, who brought you out of the land of Egypt' (20:2). It is only at Sinai the people will finally confirm their new identity apart from Egypt in the form of an agreement or covenant with YHWH. At Sinai YHWH designates Israel as a distinct and special people, and the people assent to a relationship with YHWH that is premised on their distinct Identity.[381] This provides an understanding of identity formation.

In other words the legal tradition that defines and undergirds the identity of Israel as a people is rooted in separation from Egypt. YHWH the covenant Lord is identified primarily as the God who effected this separation. From the perspective of the dominant ideology of the text, without an exodus or separation from Egypt, the entire promise for the existence of Israel as a people in a covenant relationship with YHWH would not exist.[382]

Firstly, in Ex 22: 20, for the first time in Israelites history *gerim* were acknowledge, together with widows and orphans, to be an integral part of the *personae miserae* in the Israelite society according to Noth.[383] Waldon maintains that the Israelite monarchy worsened the condition of the *personae miserae*

---

who has in turn proven his superiority by defeating them. This is the interpretation of John I, Durham, *Exodus* WBC 3 (Waco, TX: Word Books, 1987), 239-40. The LXX, reading 'because of this, that they attacked them', seems to refer to the attack of the Amalekites, narrated just previously (17.8-16). These textual difficulties do not significantly affect Jethro's basic affirmation of YHWH as the God who separated Israel from Egypt.

381 The Hebrew word בריה "Covenent" is used to describe the agreement reached between Israel and YHWH at Sinai.

382 The repeated appearance of the phrase "I am YHWH (Your God) who brought out /up from the land of Egypt (with minor variations) throughout the legal material of the Pentateuch, particularly in the Holiness Code of Leviticus with its emphasis on the separateness of Israel: Exod 29:46; Lev 11:45; 19:36; 22:33; 25:38; 26:13: Num 15:41; Deut 5;6.

383 Martin Noth, *Exodus*: *A Commentary,* 186. *Personal miserae,* a class of persons "who did not enjoy the status of full citizenship". Cf. Mark E, Briddle, *Deuteronomy,* Smyth and Helwys Bible Commentary (Macon, Ga: Smith and Helwys, 2003), 182. Or who had "no rights of their own in the law court", Cf. J. G. Conville, *Deuteronomy* Apollos Old Testament Commentary 5 (Leicester: Apollos; Downers Grove, 111: Inter Varsity, 2002), 201. Or simply were "open to economic and judicial oppression." Cf. Andrew D. H. Mayes, *Deuteronomy,* NCB (London: Oliphants, 1979), 210-11.

class in ancient Israel.[384] In the narrative Egypt is mentioned specifically in connection with legislations regarding the treatment of the גר (resident alien):

> "A resident alien you (Sing) will not ינה (*yanah*= afflict/humble) nor will you לחץ(*lachatz* = oppress/squeeze) him; for resident aliens you (pl) were in the land of Egypt" (Exod. 22: 20; [21]).

> "A resident alien you (Sing) will not לחץ (*lachatz* = oppress/ squeeze) you know the life of the resident alien; for resident alien you were in the land of Egypt" (23:9).

In Ex 22: 20 it is said: "You shall not wrong or oppress a resident alien, for you were aliens in the land of Egypt". The two verbs ענה,[385]it appears in Covenant Code, which prohibits "oppressing" or wronging a resident alien (*gër*). לחץ *oppress* heightened the severity of the prohibition, to connote defrauding.[386] The Second verb לחץ, of which the strict sense is 'press' (press a door against someone pushing it), 'squeeze up' (squeeze up against a wall), in this context denotes the oppression of one people by another. We find them again in parallel with the verb 'make to stumble', and this evokes the situation in which Israel found itself in Egypt. At one time a stranger itself, Israel has no better way of keeping that memory alive than by not oppressing the stranger.[387]

The narrative, Numbers and Deuteronomy fairly and consistently present in a negative terms and support the ideology of Exodus that insist on the separation of Israel from Egypt that allows for not possibility of return. Howevere there are various complications and confusion cloud the sharp distinction or boundaries that the text wishes to draw between Israel and Egypt. Already in Exodus, the legal prescriptions pertaining to the relatively equal status of the גר (*gër* = resident alien) and the אזרח (*'azerah* = native, indigene) revealed that the boundary between Israel and Egypt is more interesting than the ideology of the Pentateuch wishes to allow. Similar prescriptions in Leviticus confirm and extend this analysis. אזרח refers to someone who is part

384 H. Eberhard Von Waldow, "Social Responsibility and Social Structure in Early Israel," *CBQ* 32 (1970): 182-204.

385 Ringreen, "יָנָה" in *TDOT,* Vol. V1 (Grand Rapids, Michigan: Wiliam B. Eerdmans Publishing Company, 1995), 104-105.

386 Reindl, "לָחַץ Lahas" in *TDOT,* Vol. V11 (Grand Rapids, Michigan: William B. Eerdmans Publishing Company, 1990), 550.

387 Cited by Leon Epsztein, *Social Justice in the Ancient Near East and the People of the Bible* (Paris: SCM Press Ltd, 1983), 117. The verb לחץ is not random; it was chosen referring to Ex 3:9. Since *ger* is a foreign-born permanent resident and could not fall back upon local family and clan ties, he lacked the social and legal protection. Being dependent on the goodwill of others, he could easily fall victim to discrimination and exploitation. Cf. N. M. Sarna, *Exodus*: *The Traditional Hebrew Text with the new JPS translation* (Philadelphia: Jewish Publication Society, 1991), 137.

of the established and dominant kinship group of the sons or house of Israel, and thus has access to the family's landed property. גר, in contrast, lives in the same territory but is not a member of this dominant kinship group, and has no guaranteed or permanent access to the land, and is thus vulnerable to exploitation and dependent for protection on patrons from the dominant kinship group.

The גר (resident alien) refers to settled or temporary resident who have no familial or tribal affiliation with the dominant residents of a territory, and therefore usually lack full rights and are dependent on a portion for protection from abuse. For Greifenhagen this legislation presumes that: "Israel occupies the role of the dominant kinship group settled in the land, and so stands as a collective over against the resident aliens in its midst. In that situation, Israel's own experience in Egypt is to provide the motivation and the measure for its non-abusive treatment of the resident alien."[388]

Giving the narrative's dominant interest in portraying Israel's Egyptian experience as oppressive, Israel's experience is easily interpreted as a negative example of the maltreatment of the resident alien.[389] Israel is thus enjoined not to repeat such maltreatment when it itself achieves a position of dominance. However, Israel's Egyptian experience in this legislation could also be interpreted as a positive example that Israel is to emulate. The Patriarch Jacob had settled in Hebron and was accustomed to distributing his flocks among his sons to graze the central highlands according to seasonal cycles and grazing customs (Gen 35:1-27).[390] Aharoni agrees saying such area fertile for grazing was Shechem and the valley of Dothan (Gen 37:12-17) the southern pass, as defined by Thutmose 111 (1482 BCE),[391] through the Carmel mountain range to the Sharon Plain where Joseph met his brother to inquire of their welfare. Goshen, in the northeastern Nile Delta, was Joseph's destination. There the Midianites sold Joseph's to Potiphar, a high Pharaonic officer (Gen 37:36). The Josephs story provides a positive example of how Egypt treated the resident alien. To a lesser extent Abraham's experience in Egypt (Gen 12) and the plundering motif in the exodus narrative point to Egypt as a place

---

388 Greifenhagen, *Egypt on the Pentateuch's Ideological Map Constructing Biblical Israel's Identity.* 145.

389 The verb לחץ and ינה have been used previously of the Egyptian oppression of Israel (Exod 1:11-12; 3:9). Both verbs are brought together to describe Egypt's oppression of Israel in the Credo of Deut 26:5-9.

390 Paul H. Wright, *Greatness, Grace & Glory: Carta's Atlas of Biblical Biography* (Jerusalem: carta, 2008), 15.

391 Yohanan Aharoni, Michael Avi-Yonah, Anson F, Rainey and Ze'ev Safrai, *The Macmillan Bible Atlas* 3rd eds (New York: Macmillan, 1993), 31-32.

where resident aliens become enriched.[392] Similarly Abraham lives and indeed enriched, but Pharaoh and his household were stuck with plague.

The Israelite as resident alien in Egypt implies that Israel was not and can never be fully at home there but in reality belonged elsewhere. In Egypt Israel can never be a אזרה ('native, indigene'), only a גר. Because undergirding the separation of Israel from Egypt and the view that Israel's origins are to be found outside of Egypt. Thus, other legal traditions in the Pentateuch call the distinction between אזרה and גר into question. For Example, Israel is specifically enjoined that the same legal code is to apply to אזרה and גר alike,[393] and various legal stipulation are directed to both אזרה and גר.[394] Israel is even commanded to collapse the distinction between אזרה and גר precisely on the basis of its experience in Egypt. The alien who resides with you shall be to you as the citizen among you; you shall love the alien as yourself, for you were aliens in the land of Egypt (Lev. 19:34a).

That the distinction between אזרה and גר is thus problematized by Israel's legal tradition itself,[395]has two implication. Firstly, it suggest that Israel is recognized on at least a certain implicit level of the text to be not the homogenous and rooted kinship group (אזרה) that the image 'sons of Israel' portrays it to be, but rather a collection of originally various elements, including גרים. Secondly, it suggests that the image of Israel as a resident alien in Egypt does not strongly imply the separate and foreign status of Israel there as it might seem at first. If the אזרה and גר are equated in at least some of the Pentateuchal traditions, then the difference force of the assertion that Israel was a resident alien in Egypt is a least theoretically subdued and it becomes possible to find concealed in the text on Israel that is more at home in Egypt that the manifest text will allow.[396]

The concern for separation from Egypt is increasingly generalized into a concern for separation or distinctiveness from all other peoples. For instance the legal stipulation seems more interested in differentiating Israel from the

---

392 Greifenhagen, *Egypt on the Pentateuch's Ideological Map Constructing Biblical Israel's Identity.* 145.

393 Exod 12:49; Lev 24:2.

394 Exod 12:9; Lev 16:29; 17:8-16; 18:26.

395 The legal tradition does differentiate between אזרה and גר, but such explicit distinctions are rare. E.g. in Deut 14:21 in which Israel is prohibited from eating anything that has died of itself but it allowed giving it to the resident aliens. However, the similar law in Lev 17:15 stipulates that both native and alien resident become unclean if they eat that which has died of it.

396 The ancestors of Genesis are regularly described as resident alien in Palestine (e.g. Gen 23:4; 36:6-7), and Jacob and his family are described as resident aliens when they migrate into Egypt (Gen 47:4). However, the story of Joseph is in Genesis portrays Israel as obtaining land in Egypt (Gen 47:11, 27) a step toward gaining the status of אזרה.

tribes in Canaan, than from Egypt (23:23-33; 34:11-26). This generalization is explicitly voiced in Moses' words of YHWH: "we shall be distinct /separate, I and your people from every people on the face of the earth" (33:16b).[397] Thus, gradually the concern for differentiation from Egypt is opening up to include new foci for constructive identity.

4.2.3. Exodus 22:20-27 and Other Passages

The choice of including a regulation about aliens (Exod. 22:20b) is related to the narrative. The text clearly mentioned back to the alien in Egypt: 'for you were גרים in the land of Egypt' (cf. Lev. 19:34). The inclusion of 22:21-23, the case of the widow and the fatherless, and 22:24-26, the case of the poor, may also be related to the Exodus narrative. The verb for oppression in v. 21 ענה (*'anah* = afflict) is used to describe the harsh treatment of Israel by the Egyptian taskmasters (Exod. 1:11-12). The motive clause of vv. 22-23 warns that if a widow or orphan whom they afflict cries out to God, God will become angry and punish Israel, which is exactly what God did to Egypt when he saw Israel's עֳנִי (*'oniy* = affliction) and heard their cry (Exod. 3:7,9). Similarly in v. 24 God will hear the cry of the poor/afflicted הֶעָנִי (*he'oniy* = the affliction) whose garment is seized as pledge (v. 26b). In Lev. 25:35-38 and Deut. 23:20-21 expand on the prohibition of loans at interest. Deut. 24: 13-14 repeats the command encouraging the lenders to return the poor man's pledged garment (cf. Amos 2:8).

4.2.4. Social Justice: Oppression and Loans

A גר could be an Israelite living outside of his own tribe (cf. Judg. 17:7-9; 19:16), but more often as here it refers to a resident, non-Canaanite foreigner. Such a person would likely have at one time worshipped foreign gods in violation of Exod. 22:19, though while he lives among the Israelites he must follow Israel's religious practices: The גר among the Israelites who eats leavened bread at Passover is to be 'cut off', and if he wants to celebrate Passover he and his household must be circumcised (Exod 12:19, 48-49; cf. Num. 9:14). He must also keep the Sabbath (Exod 20:10) and the Day of Atonement (Lev 16:29). He may offer sacrifice but only to YHWH with proper offering of the blood and is unclean if he eats anything torn by animals (Lev. 17:8-15; 22:18; Num 15:14-18). If he touches anything dead, he must remove his impurity by ritual (Num. 19:10). He can be put to death for offering his children to Molech (Lev. 20:2), or for 'showing disrespect for the Name' (Lev. 24:16). Sacrifice for the 'unwitting' sins of Israel are valid for aliens (Num 15:26-30) and he may use cities of refuge (Num 35:15).

397 The LXX here reads 'we will be glorified beyond all the nations,' a translation perhaps based on the verb פלא instead of פלה.

The Book of the Covenant (22:18-23:19) is expressed in apodictic form, as is the brief introductory section in 20:22-26. Apodictic laws are direct commands stated in the second person: "you shall..." or "you shall not..." They content no statement of punishments or consequences. Rhetorical exaggeration and exhortations, however, frequently appear. As in Exodus 22:21: "You shall not wrong or oppress a resident alien, for you were aliens in the land of Egypt." These apodictic laws include laws, as opposed to the casuistic laws borrowed from the common legal tradition of the ancient Near East, were uniquely Israelite in origin.

Joe Sprinkle's literary analysis aims to demonstrate the literary coherence and artistry of the present sequence of the Books law.[398] Sprinkle proposes three cases of oppression in Exodus 22:20-26.[399]

Case A. Oppression of Aliens (22:20)

1. Command: No oppression (v. 20a)
2. Motive clause: empathy (v. 20b)

Case B. The oppression of widows and the Fatherless (22: 21-23)

1. Command: No affliction (v.21)
2. Motive clause: Threat of Divine wrath (vv. 22-23)

Case C. Oppression of the poor (22: 24-26)

1. Command (vv. 24-25)
   a. No taking of interest from poor
   b. Return of needed items taken as pledge
2. Motive Clauses (v. 26)
   a. Sympathy
   b. Threat of Punishment

Generalizing Summary (Exodus 22: 27)

A. Do not show disrespect for the standards of heaven (v. 27a)
B. Do not show disrespect for the moral standards of earth (v. 27b).

There is a clear, parallel structure for the three cases: each includes a command or commands, and a motive clause or a clause that gives Israel reason for obeying the imperatives. Verse 27 in itself shows poetic parallelism[400] which thereby underscores this principle that underlies all biblical regulations: respect for God and his human agents. The most controversial aspect of this

398 Sprinkle, *The Book of the Covenant, A Literary Approach,* 168-172.

399 Sprinkle, *The Book of the Covenant, A Literary Approach,* 167.

400 Patrick, D, *Old Testament Law,* 87.

statement is including v. 27 with percept demanding humanitarian treatment of disadvantaged classes. Verse 27 is usually rendered as an independent precept, 'Do not revile God, nor curse a ruler of your people.'

4.2.5. Exodus 22:20-27: Law or Morality

Upon close examination, it is clear that Exod. 22:20-27 is essentially moral rather than legal in nature. The calls to empathy (you were aliens in Egypt', 22:21b) and sympathy ('for it may be your neighbour's only clothing to use as cover' v. 27), appeal to conscience which is more a moral than a legal category. The threatening punishment (vv. 23, 26) comes not from the state to enforce a law, but from God himself to enforce his morality, though a hint of state enforcement is found in v. 27b with mention of a human leader. According to Sprinkle The use of first person and second person, I/me/you, places these precepts in the category of moral exhortation rather than law.[401]

Several poetic features here are more appropriate as literary art than legal precision: the allusion to the Exodus narratives in v. 20, the irony of the poetic justice in vv. 22-23 in which Israelites who tolerate the oppression of widows and orphans are threatened by divine punishment with having their wives become widows and their son's orphans. As Cassuto remarks, "a word-play" in v. 24 among עַמִּי (*'imi* = my people), and עִמָּךְ (*'immek* = with you)[402] and the poetry-like parallelism in v. 27.

The various types of oppression which is described always as immoral can sometimes be legal. For example, an employer who takes advantage of a desperate poor man by paying extremely low wages would not be acting illegally in a society without a minimum wages law, but the act is condemned morally by these precepts. A seller who charges an exorbitant price to foreigners simply because he thinks them to be ignorant of the fair market value of his commodity would also be acting legally-he can charge whatever he wishes and yet he falls under the condemnation of these precepts.

In connection to loan Maloney asserts: "these guidelines are intended to avoid the economic enslavement and affliction of the poor and to prevent the wealthy from profiteering from their plight. It is not just that interest rates were high, though they often were in ancient times."[403] Rather, interest-taking is seen by the lawgiver as a device for trapping the poor into permanent poverty.

401 Sprinkle, *The Book of the Covenant' A Literary Approach,* 170.

402 U. Cassuto, *A Commentary on the Books of Exodus* (Jerusalem: The Magnes Press, 1951), 292.

403 Maloney shows that ancient West Asia legal collections try to limit the amount of interest which could be charged. For various periods the legal limits were: Old Babylonian 20% for money and 33.3% for grain; Middle Assyrian 25% for money and 50% for grain; Neo-Babylonian and Persian 20% for both money and grain. Despise these 'legal' limits, Maloney notes that abundant examples of even more exorbitant interest-taking occur. R. P.

A wealthy Israelite, according to the text, should give loans to the poor as an act of charity rather than for his own economic gain.

Sprinkle in relation to these regulations confirm their non-legal nature. First, unlike laws, no civil penalties are specified for the violation of these norms. The only penalty for non-compliance described here is divine rather than human: 'I will not acquit the guilty' (v. 7b). Second, the personal, 'apodictic' form of the address (with its I-thou language), the appeal to a sense of fairness ('a bribe blinds the officials', v. 8) or empathy ('you know the hearts of an aliens', v. 9) are all better suited to admonition than law. Third, the literary artistry through word-play, figurative language, and double phrase observed above is more appropriate for literature than it is for a law code.

Fourth, v. 9 in context denounces oppressing a גר by means of the legal system. Such oppression could be 'unlawful', for example, paying off judges, or hiring false witnesses. On the other hand, an oppression could be of such a nature that thought it is morally wrong, it is not covered under any legal stature enforceable by the state, and is, therefore, in the narrow sense, 'legal' (e.g., exploiting the aliens lack of familiarity with a country's language and custom).

A גר could perhaps also be 'oppressed' by a strictly legal, but pitiless, application of a civil law in which there is a heartless insensitivity for the alien's difficult plight. Exod. 23:9, read this way, could well condemn an Israelite plaintiff even if he has every legal right to his judgement against the sojourner, if, given the circumstances, he ought rather to have shown mercy. Hence, it is possible to read v. 9 as advocating a standard of justice higher than the legal.[404]

Thus one justification for taking 22:20-23:9 together as a unit is because it is bracketed by precepts on גר having identical motive clauses: 'for you were aliens in the land of Egypt' (22:20 and 23:9). Moreover, the 'exodus' theme also holds the subunits together. From the example suggested above of the so-called laws of Exod 22: 20-23:9 is not a law code, but moral comments on some legal and non-legal subject conveyed in a manner more appropriate for literary art than for settlement.

4.2.6. Inclusive Laws: Widow Exod. 22:21-24 and Deut. 24:17-22

Exodus 22:21-24 prohibits the abuse of any widow or orphan. The protections extended to the widow are the same as those extended to orphans, the poor, the resident aliens in the BC even though the specific formula of 'the stranger, the orphan, and the widow'.

Maloney, "Usury and Restrictions on Interest-Taking in the Ancient near East", *CBQ* 36 (1974), 1-20.

404 Sprinkle, *The Book of the Covenant A Literary Approach,* 184-186.

Continuing the protections offered in Exodus, Deuteronomy prohibits depriving the resident alien or orphan of justice and taking the widow's garment in pledge (Deut 24:17-18). Similarly, gleaning of the field are to be left for the alien, widow, and orphan (Deut 24:19-22). Another reference to these groups is found in Deuteronomy 26:12-15: the third year of tithes is to go to the Levites, the aliens, the orphans, and the widows. If that were the case, then, these laws would eliminate class distinctions. There is every reason to believe however, that in their socio-economic context, these laws were of minimal help to the widow, orphan, and stranger.

The legal protection of the *gerim* is the same as it is for the orphan of Israel- Deuteronomy 24: 17: "You shall not deprive a resident alien or an orphan of justice". There is a universal principle expressed in the above verses, the need to assure that they are treated fairly in court is often reiterated because their situation, like that of widows and the poor, exposes them to exploitation. Concerning the aliens Tigar argues: "in court the alien is at disadvantages because he is neither a fully integrated member of society nor a peer of the judges or of his adversary and the fatherless may have no adult male with the experience and eloquence to represent them capably."[405] Concerning the food supply, the *gerim* enjoy the same right as the poor Israelites, who are allowed to share the superfluous parts of the harvest; Deuteronomy 24: 19: "When you reap your harvest in your field and forget a sheaf in the field, you shall not go back to get it; it shall be left for the alien, the orphan, and the widow."[406] The Economic Rights of the Labourer Deuteronomy legislation sought to ensure daily workers of fair wages.

The element that unites each of these groups is that they have no means of support through kinship patterns and/or the possession of landed property.[407] To understand that common element, a redefinition of the term 'widow' is needed. In the Bible, a 'widow' is not just a woman whose husband has died; Heibert exclaim, "she is a woman who had no male relatives such as sons or a father-in-law to support her financially."[408] Similarly, גר is a person whose ties with family had been disconnected. Lohfink argues that: "It is through that the *gër* refers to the northerners who migrated to the southern kingdom after

405 Jeffrey H. Tigay, *Deutronomy,* The JPS Torah Commentary (Philadelphia: Jewish Publication Society, 1996), 228.

406 R. Achenbach,"ger-nokhri-tishav-zar" in *The Foreigners and the Law: Perspective from the Hebrew Bible and the Ancient Near East,* edited by Achenbach, Reinhard, Rainer Albertz, and Jakob Wöhrle (Wiesbaden: Harronowitz, 2011), 32.

407 Lohfink, 'Poverty and the law the Ancient Near East and of the Bible," 44.

408 Paul S. Hiebert, "Whence Shall Help Come to Me?" The Biblical Widow", edited by Peggy L. Day, in *Gender and Difference in Ancient Israel* (Minneapolis: Fortress Press, 1989), 137.

the fall of Samaria but that cannot be known with any certainty."[409] Regardless of the particular circumstances that led to the displacement, the גר is one who lives outside of his or her own geographical area and so is without relatives or land. Therefore, the widow and the alien share a common plight because they are without kinship ties in a society where such ties provided identity.

The Hebrew words '*almanah*' has a completely negative tone. It means a woman who has been removed of her male protector (husband, sons, often also brothers). As a person without a living relatives, money, or influence, the widow is often mentioned together with the orphan, the alien and the poor.[410]

The Hebrew '*almana*' then, like the *gër*, existed on the fringe of society. In a society where kinship ties gave one identity meaning and protection, both the '*almana* and the gër had no such ties. Unlike the *gër*, however, the '*almana* lives in this luminal zone as a woman.[411] Steinberg challenges the basic for the romantic universalizing depiction of the widow's circumstances based on sympathy and shows instead the harsh realities of the economic distinctions rejected in the use of the word '*almana*, a woman with limited economic resources, in contrast with other terms for widows. Steinberg argues that: "the use of '*almana* in the Hebrew Bible indicates the plight of the lowest end of the financial spectrum of widows in biblical Israel."[412]

Hiebert states that the widow suffers more 'on the fringes of society' than the *gër* because not only was she bereft of kin, but she was also without a male who ordinarily provided a woman with access to the public sphere.'[413] Similarly, Bird argues that the concern expressed for the poor in biblical legislation and the prophetic literature is for their brother'-males who are disadvantaged-and, with the exception of the widow, not females.[414] Epsztein compares the Israelites widow with the ancient near East as follows:

---

409 Lohfink, "Poverty and the laws of the Ancient Near East and of the Bible," 41; Cf. Crüsemann, *The Torah Theology and Social History of Old Testament Law,* 184.

410 Hoffner, "אַלְמָנָה" 'almanah; אַלְמָנוּת 'almanuth" in *TDOT,* Vol. 1 (Grand Rapids Michigan: William B. Eerdmans Publishing Company, 1974), 287-88.

411 Cheryl B. Anderson, *Women, Ideology, and Violence Critical Theory and the construction of Gender in the Book of Covenant and the Deuteronomic Law,* JSOT Supl 394 (London, New York: T&T Clark International, 2004): 29-31; Cf. Paul, S Hiebert, "Whence Shall Help Come to Me? the Biblical Widow," edited by Peggy L. Day, in *Gender and Difference in Ancient Israel.* (Minneapolis: Fortress Press, 1989), 130.

412 Naomi Steinberg, "Romancing the Widow: The Economic Distinction between the '*almana,* the *'issa-hammet* the '*Eset-Hammet,*" in *God's Word for Our World,* Vol. 1 edited by J. Harold Ellens, Deborah L. Ellens, Rolf P. Knierim, et. al, JSOT Sup 388 (London; New York: T&T Clark International, 2004), 327.

413 Hiebert, "Whence Shall Help Come to Me? the Biblical Widow," 130.

414 Phyllis A. Bird, 'Poor Man or Poor Woman: Gendering the poor in Prophetic Texts,' in *Missing Persons and Mistaken Identities: Woman and Gender in Ancient Israel* (Minneapolis: Fortress Press, 1997), 67-80.

> the Israelite widow had fewer resources with which to survive on her own than a comparable Mesopotamian widow. According to the code of Hammurabi and the Assyrian laws, the formal situation of the widow would seem to have been better than in Israel. In Babylon she had a right to some of her husband estates. The widow or the repudiated wife could even in some cases enjoy part of the estates equivalent to that received by a child and regain full control over her dowry. The Assyrian laws seem to contain analogous dispositions. By contrast, the Israelite widow did not enjoy any right of succession and the estates fell entirely into the hands of the sons of the death man, and if he had none, those of his daughters. If he did not have any children, the estate went to his brothers, his father's brothers or the nearest relative.[415]

A good example of this usage is Deut 14:29, which says in regard to reserving every third year tithe, "the Levites because they have no allotment or inheritance with you, as well as the resident aliens, the orphans, and the widow ('almana) in your town, may come and eat the fill so that the Lord your God may bless you in all the work that you have taken."

Consequently, the laws taken together construct gender indirectly because the widow cannot inherit her husband's property, a fact that contributes to her economic marginalization. Considered by themselves, though this specific biblical laws do not treat the widow differently than males in these marginalized groups. As argued by Lohfink, "the deuteronomic law envisioned a situation where these groups who were not in a position to live off their own land would be supported."[416] According to him, these laws were intended 'to create a world in which one can be a stranger, an orphan, or a widow without being poor.[417] Because the categories, then of Widow, orphan, and stranger necessarily include both male and female, these laws concerning the widow do not create differences between her treatment and that of a similarly situated male.

Thus, national identity defines who the people of Israel are as a community, as distinct from other communities, is the final identity constructed by the inclusive laws of the BC and DL. Famous anthropologist, Barth, identified the maintenance of cultural (or social) boundaries that distinguish one group from another as an important dynamic for any ethnic group.[418] That the elements of a national identity can be detected in these humanitarian laws is seen in the

415 Leon Epsztein, *Social Justice in the Ancient Near East and the people of the Bible,* 113-14.

416 Lohfink, "Poverty and the laws of the Ancient Near East and of the Bible," 44.

417 Lohfink, "Poverty and the laws of the Ancient Near East and of the Bible," 44.

418 Fredrik Barth, ed., "Introduction," *Ethnic Group and Boundaries: The Social Organization of Culture Difference,* edited by Frederik Barth (Boston: Little Brown and Company 1969), 9-38.

use of the motive clause: 'Remember that you were slave in Egypt'. In the humanitarian provision of Deut. 24: 17-22, for example, that motive clause is found twice, to remind the population of their history is to remind them of who they are as a covenant community, and therefore shapes identity.[419] Because of its laws that are geared to the protection of the marginalized, the redactors are able to depict Israel as a just society in the same manner as its regional neighbours. At the same time, the laws convey that the Israelites, as well as the Israelite laws, are different from their neighbours. One difference is that the Israelites laws are not just 'civil laws' but are 'the blending of ritual and social obligation.'[420] According to Pleins, these laws convey the message that "social well-being is not simply a product of royal or judicial fiat but finds its deepest roots in the community's worship response to Israel's divine sovereign."[421] In these ways, the laws serve to construct identity for the Israelites by distinguishing themselves from others.

4.2.7. The Aliens in Deuteronomy

Since the law in Deuteronomy are more comprehensive than those in the Book of Covenant, especially in relation to aliens, we can get a more comprehensive picture of the legal treatment of aliens by focussing on Deuteronomic Code.[422] According to Seter: "Deutronomic Code is viewed as a revision of the Covenant code."[423] Scholars like, de Vaux, Spina, Van Houten show that a long standing discussion is present among scholars of the Hebrew Bible on the delineation and rights of the גר in the Deutronomistic code. The debate about this type of person has several main points:

(a) He/she immigrated from one location and settled in another in the biblical communities;
(b) He/she was a member of a different ethnic group;
(c) He/she was landless, impoverished and an unequal member of Israelite society; and

419 Theodore E. Mulen, jr, *Ethnic Myth and Pentateuchal Foundations: A New Approach to the Formation of the Pentateuch* (Semeia St. Atlanta: Scholar, 1997), 12.

420 J. David Pleins, *The Social Vision of the Hebrew Bible* (Louiseville, Kentucky: Wesminster John Knox Press, 1985), 43-44.

421 Pleins, *The Social Vision of the Hebrew Bible,* 44.

422 W. M. L. de Wette (1805) first proposed that Deuteronomic Code was composed in 7th cent B. C. E. and his opinion is affirmed by many scholars. Cf. G.Von Rad, *Deutronomy: A Commentary* (London: SCM Press, 1988), 14-15. Albrecht Alt, "The Origins of Israelite Laws," in *Essay on Old Testament History and Religion* (Oxford: Basil Blackwell, 1966), 81-132. A. Rofe, *Deutronomy: Issues and Interpretation,* OTS (London: T&T Clark, 2002), 4-5.

423 John Van Seters, *A Law Book for the Diaspora: Revision in the study of the Covenant Code* (Oxford, New York: University Press, 2003), 29.

(d) He/she either agreeably or disagreeably, became a protected citizen in the host community.

The "aliens", "foreigner" or "stranger", occurs twenty-two times in Deuteronomy, two of which refer to the Israelites, who once lived as גר in Egypt (10: 19b; 23:8). All the other occurrences refer to aliens. The following broad areas are discussed in relation to *gër*:

1. Judicial justice and equal treatment for the *gër* (1:16; 24: 178; 27:19), including payment of wages (24:14);
2. Sabbath rest for the *gër* (5:14);
3. Caring for the *gerim* by taking care of their basic needs (10;18) and allowing them to glean in the fields (24:19; 20,21);
4. Allowing the *gër* to share in the consumption of the triennial tithe (14: 29; 26:12,13);
5. Allowing the *ger* to participate in the celebration of religious festivals (16:11,14; 26: 11);
6. The *gër,* together with the Israelites, entered into a covenant relationship with God (29:10). *Gerim* are required to obey the Torah (31: 12).

In Deuteronomy *gerim* enjoy a great deal of privileges and protection under the law. The focus seems to be on their legal status. The view expressed among the literary prophets, in stories in the Deutronomistic History, and in the Deuteronomic concern to make the 'oppressed' the social equals of the propertied classes.[424]

Houten argues that two distinct views of the alien are found in Deuteronomy: first, that found within the law code (Deuteronomy 12-26) and the Decalogue (Deut 5:12-15), and second, the view found in the covenant ceremony of Deut 29:10 (cf. Deut 31:12). Houten views the first group of texts, dated from the late monarchy, identifies the alien as a non-Israelite (Deut 14:21) who has no option of becoming Israelite. Like the laws in the Book of the Covenant, these laws presuppose that the alien is economically vulnerable and probably landless, although unlike the alien in the Book of the Covenant, the Deuteronomic alien is not necessarily a member of the patriarchal household. The laws are aimed at creating a permanent support system for the alien, the widow and the orphan.

Rad interprets the alien in Deut 29:10-15 is in the context of a new speech of Moses-the third in the book, which is made on the occasion of ratifying

424 B. Halpern, "Jerusalem and the Lineages in the seventh Century BCE: Kingship and the Rise of Individual Moral Liability," in *Law and Ideology in Monarchic Israel,* Supl series 124, edited by Baruch Halpern, Deborah W. Hobson (Sheffield: JSOT Press, 1991), 89-90.

a covenant in Moab.[425] Following Mayes suggests that the Deuteronomistic redactor sought to identify the alien with the Gibeonites of Joshua 9. The aliens in Deuteronomy 29 are described as "hewers of wood and drawers of water," a phrase used elsewhere only in reference to the Gibeonites.[426] Mayes argument was that one of the goals of the redactor of Deutronomy 29 was to cast the Gibeonites as aliens, and thereby bring them into a closer relationship with the Israelites. This was important because in Joshua 9 the Gibeonites are connected with temple service, and the Deutronomist is concerned that foreigners should not be involved in the sanctuary. By means of the connections we have noted, it makes clear that Gibeonites are not foreigners, but are aliens.[427]

The Deutronomic code (Deut 12-26) increases the number of provisions concerning with aliens and is more specific in its instruction. Houton regarded this code as deposit to several layers of tradition which can be identified by distinctive formulae.[428] Most references of aliens list them along with widows and orphans, social classes legally vulnerable and economically dependent on the well to-do landowners to whom the code is addressed. Aliens are labourers who need their wages and must supplement their earnings by gleaning. They are to be included, along with widows, orphans and Levites, in the harvest feasts (but not Passover) and receive foodstuffs from the food bank set up from the triennial Tithe.[429] One of the features of the legislation in Deuteronomy is its concern for the unity of the people and their land. Various positive steps are planned in the Deuteronomic Code.

Three categories of individuals appear in Deut 14: 21a, the *ger* and *nokri,* and the '*am qados.*' Two groups, namely, the *gër* and *nokri,* could eat animals that died a natural death; the holy people, however, could only consume these corpses. The rational is that the former two groups were not members of the holy community. Anthropologist Douglas has argued that: "purity laws are part of a social symbol system that classifies boundaries within the realm of nature in order to protect the society from destructive powers. Unclean animals are those who in some way mix or cross over perceived boundaries; fish without fins or scales, flying insects with multiple rather than just two legs, animals

425 Von Rad, *Deutronomy: A Commentary,* translated by D. Barton (Philadelphia: Westminster Press, 1966), 179.

426 A. D. H. Mayes, "Deutronomy 29, Joshua 9, and the place of the Gibeonites in Israel," in *Das Deutronomium,* edited by N. Lohfink (Leuven: Leuven University Press 1985), 321-25.

427 Mayes, "Deutronomy 29, Joshua 9, and the place of the Gibeonites in Israel," 323.

428 Van Houten, *The Alien in Israelites Law A Study of the Changing Legal Status of Stranger in Ancient Israel,* 68-77.

429 Van Houten, *The Alien in Israelites Law A Study of the Changing Legal Status of Stranger in Ancient Israel,* 80-99.

that either do not cud or do not have divided hooves."[430] The implication of this issue is noteworthy. What becomes probable is that the *gër* and *nokri* enjoyed religiousness and an ethos that differed from the same phenomena in the '*am qados'* or at least from these features of social life among the individuals in the in-group. Deut 14: 21 lends support to the idea that ethnocentric phenomena differentiated social group on the Deutronomic Code, and that the *gër* did not assimilate into the mainstream.[431] *Nokri* are passing stranger. "Outside of the family" in other texts the focus is on the family or clan, so *Nokri* means "unfamilial" i.e. standing outside the family. Someone outside a family has not only no emotional and social ties with the family but also no legal ties.[432]

The *Nokri* is exempt from the law and does not even share the privileges of the *gerim*. If somebody enjoys familial protection in another society, he is considered for a limited time as *gër,* even if ethnically and geographically this person belongs to another people or nation. But the *nokri*-person usually does not intend to reside or stay permanently in the area where he or she may enjoy hospitality for a certain time (cf. Ex.2: 22; 18: 3). They consider themselves as someone who originally belongs to another distinct legal system. This is the reason why it is forbidden to sell an Israelite young woman debt-slave, who

430 Cf. Mary Douglas, *Purity and Danger: An Analysis of Concept of Pollution and Taboo* (London: Routledge and kegan paul, 1966), 53. Douglas has refined her works on the biblical purity laws in a number of subsequent publications. Douglas, *Implicit Meanings: Essay in Anthropology* (London: Routledge and Kegan Paul, 1975). One of the obstacles applying Douglas's Anthropological work to the biblical text is the question of the level at which she is working. Does this classification scheme reflect ancient Israelite society? In what period? And for whom? Are the regulation of clean and unclean foods and its rationalizations a product of the Priestly writers of Leviticus that the writers of Deuteronomy have subsequently taken over? David P. Wright, "Ethical Foundations of the Biblical Dietary Laws," in *Religion and Law: Biblical, Judaic and Islamic Perspectives,* edited by E. Firmage, J. Welch, B, Weiss (Winona Lake, IN: Eisenbrauns, 1990), 196. Some few comments on the debate between Milgrom and Douglas, that these classifications developed over time and had multiple origins: economic competition and preference for some domestic animals over others, hygiene simple aversions, nationalism, and resistance to the practice of other religion or peoples. The question that has not been adequately addressed is what happened to this purity an dietary laws in Deuteronomy. What effect does the placement of Deuteronomy 14 under the rubic of the second commandment and the misuse of the name of God have on the meaning of the dietary laws?

431 Harold V. Bennett, *Injustice Made Legal: Deutronomic law and the Plight of Widows, Stranger, and Orphans in Ancient Israel* (Grand Rapids, Michigan: William B. Eerdmann Publishing, 2002), 47. Cf. David M. Carr, *The Formation of the Hebrew Bible: A New Reconstruction* (Oxford: Oxford University Press, 2011), 300.

432 Ringgren, "רבנ נבר, נֵבָר nekar, נָכְרִי; nokri," edited by G.Johannes Botterweck, Helner Ringgren, Heing-Josef Fabry, in *TDOT* Vol. 1X (Grand Rapids, Michigan: William B. Eerdmann publishing Company), 423-432.

was designated for her master, to *nokir* (Ex 21: 8), because she is a person from outside the scope of the Israelites law (cf. Gen 31: 15).[433]

The priestly rules and the Holiness Code do not refer to *nokri*, because they consider them as excluded from the cultic and religious community. In contrast to this exclusivist position, the prayer of 1 Kings 8: 41-43 is remarkable for its universalistic view and its inclusive attitude. In blatant opposition to this concept stand the exclusive traditions around Ezra and Nehemiah (Ezra 10; Neh 13: 26-27), which seem to be the background to the reluctance in the priestly codes to refer to any sort of religious integration of non-residential alien. The area of the holy mount and the temple remained closed for them.[434]

Thirdly, in the third and sixth year of each seven-year cycle, the tithe was to be deposited "in your towns," that is, at the place of the local assembly where it was used to support "the Levite...the resident aliens, the orphans, and the widows in your towns" (Deut 14: 29). Together with the Levites, the fatherless and the widows, the *gerim* have the right to take a part in the third year tithes (cf Deut 26: 11-12).[435] "*Come and eat their fill*" this seems to imply that the recipients of the tithes would receive food daily as needed, rather than quantities to store for longer periods.[436] Sharing the products of the soil with the aliens means to recognize that the Israelites God donated everything to the children of Israel (Deut 26: 11) and specially the land. We understand why at the end of the Deuteronomic law (Deut 26: 1-11), the sharing of the first fruits of the earth with the Levite and the alien, performed in the presence of the priest, is associated with the profession of faith: "A wandering Aramean was my ancestor; he went down into Egypt and lived there as an alien,...and the Lord brought us out of Egypt... and brought us into this place" (Deut 26: 5-9). Solidarity with the stranger is a very concrete way for Israel to preserve the memory of what was its status as a foreigner and a slave in Egypt, liberate by the Lord, and remembered that its establishment in the land is the consequence of the gift of God, which is to share.

4.2.8. The Rhetoric of Deuteronomy

From a rhetorical perspective, when the audience changes, so does the rhetorical situation and therefore the message- the "whom" and the "what," and sometimes even the "who" has changed in the question, "who is persuading whom and

433 R. Achenbach, "ger-nokhri-tishav-zar," 44.

434 R. Achenbach, "ger-nokri-toshav-zar," 44-45; Cf. C. Nihan, "Resident Aliens and Natives in the Holiness Legislation," in *The Foreigner and the Law: Perspective from the Hebrew Bible and the Ancient Near East,* Band 16, edited by R, Achenbach, R. Albertz, J. Worhle (Weisbaden: Harrassowitz Verlag, 2011), 128.

435 R. Achenbach, "ger-nokri-toshav-zar," 32.

436 J. H. Tigay, *Deutronomy,* The JPS Torah Commentary (Philadelphia: Jewish Publication Sociaty, 1996), 144.

what?" Rhetorical analysis can investigate every subsequent interpreter and interpretive community for which we have evidence to discover how this text, or the whole scripture, was/is used to convey a persuasive message from human and/or divine speakers to particular audiences. Who then, are these "non-natives?" On what basis do they enjoy legal privileges and protection in Israel?

The earlier scholarly consensus views the *ger* as non-Israelites. Ridderbos states that: "*ger* is a "semi-citizen"[437] Begg says that the *ger* in the Old Testament refers to a non-Israelite who has the status of Semi-permanent resident.[438] Mayes states that the *ger* in Deuteronomy is a non-Israelite.[439] If *gër* in Deuteronomy indeed refers to non-Israelite, one wonders on what basis they are allowed to participate in the religious ceremonies, including the covenant renewal. It also seems somewhat strange that they are allowed to share in the consumption of the tithes, which is considered as sacred.

Houten[440] argues that the *gër* is allowed to consume the tithes and participate in the festivals simply due to Deuteronomy's humanitarian concerns for marginal groups, but this argument is not convincing.

4.3. Deuteronomy and the Rights of Indigenous People

Deuteronomy is often seen to advocate justice for the widow, orphan, alien and the poor (cf. Deut 10:18; 14:29; 16:11, 14; 24:17-21; 26:12-13; 27:19). According to the rhetoric of Deuteronomy as a speech of Moses at the edge of the promise land, these are foundational aspects of a society that Israel is to establish in Canaan, the so-called promise land, and the approach to justice in similar in the rest of the Old Testament/Hebrew Bible.

The rhetoric of Deuteronomy (and the rest of the Pentateuch) the experience of Israel is all about liberation from oppression by those more powerful than them in Egypt and this is the reason why there should for example be no slaves among the Israelite? (Deut 15: 12-15; 23:15-16; 24:17-22). Even the archaeological record from the Early Age speaks for an egalitarian society, which however then appears to move towards social stratification during Iron Age 11.[441]

However, Deuteronomy also contains banning to destroy indigenous peoples in the process of establishing the ideal society it advocates. Na'aman classifies the indigenous people into so called seven nations in the presentation

437 J. Ridderbos, *Deuteronomy* (Grand Rapids: Zondervan, 1984), 58, 175.

438 T. Christopher Begg, "Foreigner," in *ABD* 2 (New York: Doubleday, 1992), 829-30.

439 A. D. H. Mayes, *Deuteronomy* (Grand Rapids: Eerdmann, 1979), 124-25.

440 Van Houten, *Alien in Israelite Law: A Study of the Changing Legal Status of Strangers in Ancient Israel,* 77-108.

441 W. G. Dever, *Who Were the Early Israelites and Where Did They Come* From? 194-98.

of the books.[442] They are considered a threat, a corrupting presence that has to be eliminated (Deut 7). If the Israelites allow the indigenous people to exist, the Israelite will end up following their customs and religious practices, something that is contrary to the ideals that Deuteronomy advocates (Deut 7).

We should also note here that the justice to the marginal group is allowed by the book only within a specific Yahwistic religion political framework. This becomes clear in particular from the command given in Deut 13, where no mercy is to be shown even to those who are part of one's own family if they do not proscribe to a Yahwistic worldview and Yahwistic worship practices, showing complete allegiance to Yahweh in their attitude to the divine. In case of what Deuteronomy calls idolatry, even those of one's own family are to be eliminated by killing them.

The rhetoric of Deuteronomy about destroying indigenous peoples and other non-Yahwists (closely associated with the concept of *herem* which have been much studied) is then seen for example, as heightened rhetoric for devotion to Yahweh, as attested e.g. as attested by Josiah's reform which was about the destruction of non-Yahwistic religious objects with any killing being marginal,[443] as a fictional construction of past guilt of not destroying the Canaanites, the guilt then serving as justification for the exile,[444] or and culture map which cannot be compared with genocide, terror or total war.

Pitkanen on genocides exclaim, "the ideology of Deuteronomy does not really seem to have been directly compared with ideologies accompanying genocides."[445] Several studies had been done on genocide during recent years. The UN definition of genocide serves as good overall starting points,

442 One of the possible identification of these indigenous people Cf. N. Na'aman, "The 'Conquest of Canaan' in the Book of Joshua and History," *From Nomadism to Monarchy Archaeological and Historical Aspects of Early Israel,* edited by I.Finkelstein and N. Na'aman (Jerusalem: Israel Exploration Society, 1994), 218-81 (239-40).

443 R. W. L, Moberly, "Towards an Interpretation of the Shema," in Theological Exegesis Essay in Honor of Bervard S. Child, edited by C.Seith and K. Greene –Mc Creight (Grand Rapids: Eerdmann, 1999), 124-144.

444 N. Lohfink, "חָרַם *haram*, חֵרֶם, *herem,*" in *Theologica Dictionary of the Old Testament* (Grand Rapids, Michigan: William B. Eerdmans Publishing Company, 1986), 180-99. *Herem* belong to the fixed framework of a generally constant narrative schema found in Deuteronomistic texts. It appears regularly in wars of conquest against enemy cities. The only weapon mentioned is the sword. In political context the weapons vary: sword (Isa 34:5-8), bow (Jer 51:3) hand raised to strike (Isa 11:15). Cf. *BDB,* 356.

445 Pekka Pitkanen, "Dr. Jekyll and Mr. Hyde: Deuteronomy and the Rights of Indigenous peoples," *Political Theology* 11/3 (2010): 403; Cf. M. Prior, "fabricating Colonial myth," in *The Bible and Colonialism: A Moral Critique* (Sheffield: Sheffield Academic Press, 1997), 177-84.

as follows General Assembly Resolution 260A (III) Article 2, 1948.[446] In the present convention, genocide means any of the following acts committed with intent to destroy, in whole or in part, a national, ethnical, racial or religious group, as such.

(a) Killing members of the group;
(b) Causing serious bodily or mental harm to members of the group;
(c) Deliberately inflicting on the group conditions of life calculated to bring about its physical destruction in whole or in part.
(d) Imposing measures intended to prevent births within the group,
(e) Forcibly transferring children of the group to another group.

It is immediately clear that Deuteronomy and the Israelites conquest tradition relate to item (a)-(c).

Leven asserts that: "Genocides are accompanied by thinking where one group see another as a threat, even if they may have a complete control of the other (they can sometimes be practically powerless, as with disabled people)."[447] Those others are seen as a threat means that a group sees them as not fitting their plans and ideals.

One could say that Deuteronomy's rhetoric might only be rhetoric; one may also say that the rhetoric of Deuteronomy is fully compatible with the rhetoric of genocides. In fact, it does plausibly fit with the idea of an external group entering another land and attempting to take over based on a particular ideology that exclude any other groups. In other words we catch a glimpse of a society that felt uneasy or threatened by the intrusion of outsiders, and there is a notc of anxiety towards גר. Deuteronomy has a specific attitude towards nation that are outside the land of Canaan and thus outside the purview of the Israelites society.

4.4. Complicating the Insider-Outsider Boundary

In Deuteronomy, the fact that the *gerim* enter into a covenant relationship with Yahweh (29:10-11) and are to observe the Torah (31:12) suggests that they are members of the Covenant community. Similarly the fact that the *gerim* are allowed to consume the sacred portion (14:29; 26:13) and participate in the national festivals (16:11, 14) at the single sanctuary is better explained on the ground that they are viewed as members of the Covenant people. Houten's explanation that the *ger* is treated favourably simple due to Deuteronomy's humanitarian concerns misses the point. Humanitarian concerns in

446 The International Convention of the Prevention and Punishment of the Crime of Genocide on December 9, 1948 set the United Nations definition of genocide http://www.teachgenocide.org (accessed on 20th July 2014).

447 M. Leven, *Genocide in the Age of the Nation State: The Meaning of Genocide* (London: I. B. Tauris, 2005), 35-89.

Deuteronomy are primarily directed towards members of the Covenant community. This is clearly seen in the sabbatical community, but the debts of foreigners' *nokri* are unaffected by the remission (15:3). There is a clear insider's outsider's mentality.

As Lohfink[448] notes that scholars generally explain the association of the *gër* with orphans and widows in connection with the massive migration from the northern Kingdom to Judah after the fall of Samaria. This identification of the *gër* with fellow-Israelites also finds its support in other parts of the Old Testament. In Judges 19:16, an Ephraimite who settled in Gibeah among the Benjaminites is called *gër.*[449] *Second Chronicle 15:9 described the inhabitants from Ephraim, Manasseh, and Simeon who migrated to Judah during the reign of Asa as gerim.* In addition, *gerim* from Israel who lived in Judah participated in Hezekiah's Passover festival (2 Chr 30:25). If *gerim* denotes the immigrants from the Northern Kingdom, it helps explain their favourable treatment, in Deuteronomy, as opposed to the harsher treatment of genuine outsiders.[450]

In Deuteronomy, with its clear insider-outsider mentality, there is a need to define the status of the גר from the other Israelite tribes who have come to settled in Judah, especially with the influx of refugees after the fall of Samaria. These newcomers are described as having the status of a *gër*. It is a boundary marker that distinguishes the status of the local inhabitants, the new immigrants, and genuine outsiders. This boundary marker is necessary in order to protect the political and religious integrity of the nation. The *gerim* enjoy certain privileges and protection under the law, but this does not mean that they are identical with the Israelites (which here ironical refers to inhabitants of Judah) in all aspects. There are differences between the *gër* and the Israelites as well. For instance, the Israelite are forbidden to consume the meat of any animal that dies of itself, but the *gër* has no such restriction placed on him/her (14:21). In addition dealing with curses and punishment, it is stated that disobedience to the covenant will result in the *gër* gaining power over the Israelites.

Deut 28:43-44 result in a reversal of social order: "Aliens residing among you shall ascend above you higher and higher, while you shall descent lower and lower. They shall lend to you but you shall not lend to them; they shall be the head and you shall be the tail."

This emblematic consequence of breaking YHWH's covenant is followed by the explanatory proposition: "these entire curses shall come upon you, pursuing and overtaking you until you are destroyed, because you did not obey the Lord your God...Because you did not serve the Lord your God with joyfulness and with gladness of heart, for the abundance of everything" (vv. 45-

448 Lohfink, "Poverty in the Laws of the Ancient Near East and of the Bible," 34-50.

449 Roland de Vaux, *Ancient Israel: Its life and Institutions,* 74.

450 Yu Suee Yan, "The Alien in Deuteronomy," *BT* 60/2 (April, 2009), 133.

47). Most importantly, vv. 43-44 must be read as the negative counterpart of vv. 12b-13, which is likewise followed by an explanatory proposition.[451]

The lexemes recur in parallel symmetry:

A - You will lend to many nations (v. 12b)
B - but you will not borrow (v. 12c)
C - YHWH will make you the head, not the tail (v. 13a)
D - You will go up and not down (v. 13b)
E - If you obey the commandments of YHWH (vv. 13c-14)
E - Since you did not obey YHWH's voice to keep his commandments (vv. 45-47)
D - Aliens residing in your midst shall ascend above you higher and higher, while you will descend lower and lower (v. 43)
C- He will be the head, you will be the tail (44) (c-d)
B- but you will not lend to him (v. 44b)
A- He will lend to you (v. 44a)

This text envisages the insiders submissive to the outsiders. The direct context of both texts, vv. 12-13 and vv. 43-44, is neither political nor cultic, but economic. Preceding vv. 12-13 YHWH causes material prosperity, fertile humans and livestock, and bountiful Promised Land (v. 11). He issues seasonal rain to bless the majority population's agrarian labors (v. 12). Likewise the preceding context vv. 43-44 is economic: due to covenant disloyalty "Locusts will inherit each of your trees and the fruit of your ground" (v. 42). YHWH's material bounty is also the context of the parallel antecedent language of 15:6: "When the Lord your God has blessed you, as he promised you, you will not borrow; you will rule over many nations, but they will not rule over you." Reading Deut 28:12-13 as blessing and vv. 43-44 as counterpart curse illuminates how vv. 43-44 conceive of the ethno-geographical origins of the גר. "You will lend to many nations" (v. 12b) is inverted by the statement "He (גר in v. 43) will lend to you" (הוא ילוו; v. 44a). In this text the גר residing in Israel did not have a monolithic origin, but came from multiple nations.

4.5. Detecting Ethnicity: Israelite, Judahite, or Non-Israelite/Non-Judhahite

Is the גר who is reflected in the language of Deuteronomy's legislation ethnically Israelite or Judahite or non-Israelite/non-Judahite? Deuteronomy 14:21 closes the unit enumerating clean and unclean foods: "you must not eat anything that dies of itself; you may give it to aliens residing in your towns

451 Weindfeld, *Deuteronomic in Deuteronomic School,* 119.

for them to eat, or you may sell it to a foreigner. For you are a people holy to the Lord your God." Douglas represents a common semantic fallacy that the גר, a noun without inherent ethnic connotations, "is not a foreigner or a fully enfranchised member" in part because Hebrew uses a separate word for "foreigner" נכרי.[452] Houten offers a better alternative: both גר anנכרי are of foreign origins in the book of Deuteronomy, but the "difference between the alien and foreigner that emerged here (in 14:21) is an economic one. The alien needs economic support; the foreigner has means and is expected to pay for what he gets. Both are the same, however, in that the food laws do not apply to them."[453]

Deuteronomy probably also distinguishes the גר and נכרי on religious ground. Na'aman asserts: "Deut 24:1-21 he means 14:1-21 shows the influence of the Priestly source, and the entire paragraph is influenced by the Book of Leviticus 11."[454] The concern over cleanness and uncleanness is not original to the DC and therefore "v. 21 is extraneous to the discussion about the status of the sojourner during the First Temple period."[455] Against Na'aman, 14:21 cannot be the product of priestly authorship or redaction because it neither correlates with priestly idiomatic phraseology for the גר, nor with the priestly (H) *prohibition* of the גר native from eating a carcass. Instead, 14:21 permits both גר (*gër* = aliens) and נכרי (*nokir* = foreigner) to eat a carcass, but prohibits the Israelite addressees from the same. The Israelites are called "a holy people to YHWH your God." The גר and נכרי must be of non-Israelite and non-Judahite origins. In addition, the interconnection with 14:21 and 14:29 may be suggestive, as McConville observes that a redactor has conjoined these units: "our examination of the immediate context of Deuteronomy's tithe-law (14.22-29) leads us to conclude that, along with the food laws (vv. 3-21), it represents a logical development from the statement in 14.1f, of Israel's chosenness and holiness to Yahweh."[456] On this plausible editorial level, 14:28-29 presumes

452 Mary Douglas, "The Stranger in the Bible," *Archives Europeennes de Sociologie* 35 (1994): 284. Cf. Nadav Na'aman, "Sojourners and Levites in the Kingdom of Judah in the Seventh Century BCE," *ZABR* 14 (2008), 256.

453 Van Houten, *Alien in Israelite Law: A Study of the Changing Legal Status of Strangers in Ancient Israel,* 81. Cf. Frank Anthony Spina "Israelites as *gerim,* 'Sojourners,' in *The Word of the Lord Shall go Forth*, edited by C. L. Meyem & M. O. Conner (Winona Lake, IN: Eisenbrauns, 1983), 321-35, contends that the majority of the גר referents in the Hebrew Bible are non-Israelites.

454 Na'aman, "Sojourners and Levites in the Kingdom of Judah in the Seventh Century BCE," 248-49.

455 Na'aman, "Sojourners and Levites in the Kingdom of Judah in the Seventh Century BCE," 249.

456 J. G. McConville, *Law and Theology in Deuteronomy* JSOT Sup 33 (Sheffield: *JSOT,* 1985): 78-81.

the גר in 14:28-29 shares the same non-Israelite/non-Judahite ethnicity as the גר in 14:21. In addition, the lexemic overlap and probably framing the tithe regulations of chs 14 and 26 might, by extension, indicate the same non-Israelite and non-Judahite גר in 26:10-13.
In Deuteronomy 24: 14-15 states:

> You must not withhold the wages of poor and needy laborers, whether other Israelites or aliens who reside in your land in one of your towns. You shall pay them their wages daily before sunset, because they are poor and their livelihood depends on them; otherwise they might cry to the Lord against you, and you would incur guild.

The best explanation for the גר in 24:14-15 is that he was either a Northern Kingdom Israelite, or in the light of the other DC laws, a non-Israelite and non-Judahite. YHWH was inclining to cry in 24:15, not because he was a native, but because he resided in Israel as a "poor and needy" person, vulnerable to oppression (10:17-19).

Legal protection and gleaning provisions for the גר, orphan, and widow in Deut 24:17-18, 19-22; and 27:19 might be considered the strongest evidence for the indigenous ethnicity of the גר.[457] As Na'aman explain "anyone who argues that the sojourner was a foreigner must explain why the Book of Deuteronomy presents a set of laws designed to protect aliens, and does not apply them to the needy of the Judahite origin."[458] Yet, this question totally neglects the vision of Deut 15:11: "For there will never cease to be poor in the land. Therefore I command you, 'you shall open wide your hand to your אח (brother) to the needy and to the poor, in your land.'" The solidarity and benevolence of Israelite or Judahite kinsfolk infused with a social identity defined by YHWH's redemption (15:15) was the DC's mechanism to meet local Judahite or Israelite needs. Deut 24:14-15 also ensures the local Judahite fair compensation.

As for the *reason* for the various laws that protect the non-Israelite or non-Judahite, this becomes much clearer when we reexamine their intent. Lohfink shows that biblical texts before D, chiefly the BC, use various terms that "had been mixed up without any clear distinction," but in D are now reduced and bifurcated into two groups: firstly, אביון and עני, both terms continue to be used for the poor; secondly, the גר orphan-widow triad, which is never combined

---

457 Reading Josh 8:30-33, one discovers that the priestly (H) interpretation of the enacting of the Schechemite Decalogue juxtapose the אזרח "native Israelite" with the גר, suggesting the גר mentioned here and in Deut 24:17 is a non-Israelite.

458 Na'aman, "Sojourners and Levites in the Kingdom of Judah in the Seventh Century BCE," 256.

with group one.[459] Lohfink once thought the Deuteronomic laws, formulated during Josiah's era, were fixated on meeting the needs of the poor, but then he realized the words for "poor" in D (group one) never occur in any of the *personae miserae* triad (or composite) passages. Thus, D's laws do not add new subgroups, the גר, orphan, and widow (and Levite), to the impoverished class, but restructure society in order to support groups that do not have the capacity to live off the land; in line with the Exodus narrative, D creates "a world in which one can be a stranger, an orphan, or a widow without being poor."[460] Therefore, as Houten states, the laws dealing with the גר, orphan, widow, and sometimes slaves and Levites, "are providing for the economic maintenance of groups of people who have no land. If that system worked, members of these groups would not be poor."[461] Na'aman understands this quite well,[462] but does not make the connection that local Judahites (or Israelites) were already protected by working the land that YHWH gave to them or working the land of one of their countrymen (6:10-12; 8:7-10; 24:14-15). Judahites or Israelites who were disassociated from a landowning *paterfamilias* – the orphan, widow and Levite – were protected by various laws. This discredits Na'aman's contention, "The mention of the sojourner alongside the Levite reinforces the conclusion that he originates from the kingdom of Judah."[463] Rather, Levites are often associated with the גר, orphan, and widow because they did not own property in Israelite or Judahite territory (12:12, 19; 14:29; 16:11, 16; 18:1-2; 26:11-13).

4.6. Conclusion

The text begins by setting up the classic ethnic polarity between 'us' and 'them', between Israel and Egypt, and then expends its rhetorical effort in persuading its audience to comply to this binary opposition. And finally the focus for constructive identity begins to shift from Egypt to the tribal people of Canaan, although differentiation from Egypt remains the underlying paradigm. The key values the researcher suggests are these:

Firstly, Exodus 22:21-27 is essentially moral rather than legal in nature. The calls to empathy (you were aliens in Egypt 22:21b) and sympathy (for it may be your neighbour's only clothing to use as cover v. 27) appeal to conscience which is more moral than a legal category. Exod 22: 20-23:9 which

459 Norbert Lohfink, "Poverty in the Laws of the Ancient Near East and of the Bible," 34-50.

460 Norbert Lohfink, "Poverty in the Laws of the Ancient Near East and of the Bible," 44.

461 Van Houten, *Alien in Israelite Law: ...* 95.

462 Na'aman, "Sojourners and Levites in the Kingdom of Judah in the Seventh Century BCE," 254.

463 Na'aman, "Sojourners and Levites in the Kingdom of Judah in the Seventh Century BCE," 256.

is so called law code, but moral comments on some legal and non-legal subject conveyed in a manner more appropriate for literary art than for adjudication.

Secondly, redefinition of the term widow is needed in Exod 22:21-23, it is not just a woman whose husband has died; she is a woman who had no male relatives such as sons or a father-in-law to support her financially. Thus, the widow and the גר share a common plight because they are without kinship ties in a society where such tie provides identity.

Thirdly, Deuteronomy law do not add new groups, the גר, orphan, and widow (and livites) to the impoverished class, but restructure society in order to support groups that do not have the capacity to live in the land: in line with the Exodus narratives. Deuteronomy creates "a world in which one can be a stranger, an orphan, or a widow without being poor.

Fourthly, in the rhetoric of Deuteronomy, we may think of a society that is just to remember of its own group and an example to others outside its purview, but at the same time destroy those within its purview that do not follow its ideals. Moving on toward contemporary application, we first note that the concern of justice within a society is probably universal.

The rhetoric of Deuteronomy is one passage speaks of protection of the poor and the needy as on the other hand destroying the indigenous people. It is pointed out that the ideology of Deuteronomy is very exclusive and its treatment of indigenous peoples compatible with the ideologies that accompany genocides and conquest. The Deuteronomy's rhetoric establishes the rights of the Indigenous peoples to the protection of their cultural property and identity.

Fifthly, Legal protection and gleaning provisions for the גר, orphan, and widow in Deut 24:17-18, 19-22; and 27:19 might be considered the strongest evidence for the indigenous ethnicity of the גר. The researchers disagree with Houten concluding remark: "the alien's identity was forged by an act in the past which would not be repeated, and which separated them from all other people; there are no ways for non-Israelites to become Israelites. Aliens were considered non-Israelites, and there was no way that status could be changed."[464]Anyone who argues that the aliens was a non-Israelites must explain why the Book of Deuteronomy presents a set of laws designed to protect aliens, and does not apply them to the needy of the Judahite origin. Yet, this question totally neglects the vision of Deut 15:11: "For there will never cease to be poor in the land. Therefore I command you, 'you shall open wide your hand to your brother (אח), to the needy and to the poor, in your land.' The solidarity and benevolence of Israelite or Judahite kinsfolk infused with a social identity defined by YHWH's redemption (15:15) was the DC's mechanism to meet local Judahite or Israelite needs. Deut 24:14-15 also ensures the local Judahite fair compensation.

464 Houton, *Aliens in Israelite Law...,* 108.

Chapter 5

Aliens in the Holiness Code

5. Introduction

The first half of Leviticus the focus is indeed wider and includes texts discussing the relationship between Israelites and their fellow Israelites as well as their relationship with aliens. Unlike the גר laws in the Covenant Code and the Deuteronomistic Code, it includes both, the Israelite and the גר have sanction (Lev 17:8, 12, 13, 15, 18:26; 20:2; 24:16, 22). The fundamental common element to all these laws is their primary concern with the matter of holiness. Ramirez Kidd argues that in the Holiness Code the noun גר is mentioned in two kinds of laws: (1) laws given to the Israelites for the protection of the *ger* and (2) laws addressed equally to the Israelites and the *ger* for the preservation of holiness. In other words, when the laws deal with the subject; of the preservation of holiness, the *gër* is subject to the law just as the Israelites.[465] The *gër* were identified as Israelites.

The purpose of this chapter is to study the text of Leviticus 17, 24 and 25 anew to tell whether and to what extent it deserves its status in constructing the identity of the land. We cannot avoid the questions which have to be asked about any text that claimed, to mediate justice; what kind of justice does it offer and to whom; whose interest are represented by the text; what understanding

465 In the Holiness Code, the resident alien is subordinated to laws of rituals purity lest by transgressing them he should pollute the land; in Deutronomic Code, the resident alien is not subordinated to purity laws Cf. Kidd, *Alterity and Identity, the ger in the Old Testament,* 57-58.

of the social world does it embody, and how close is that to anything we might recognize? The question what's just about the Jubilee? The question is what kind of justice and for whom. By means of the tools of ideological criticism the researcher will attempt to reconstruct that stage in this process, and the situations to which the laws were responding.

5.1. From Cult to Community: The Two Halves of Leviticus

Traditionally in Old Testament redactional criticism, a distinction is made between the first half of Leviticus (Lev. 1-16) and the second half (Lev. 17-26). In historical critical jargon, the first half is usually regarded as part of the Priestly text (P) and the second is called (H) by some after the Holiness code. Some have argued that the Lev. 1-16 is mostly concerned with what we would call rituals, where the second half (or H) is concern with 'ethics,' among other things.

According to many scholars, this section (Lev. 17-26) probably once existed independently as a law code. There is no unanimity of opinion among scholars regarding the origin of this code. Some scholars argue for its exilic origin while the others argue for the pre-exilic origin, probably during Josiah's time. The name 'Holiness Code' was given to chapters 17-26 of Leviticus by Klosterman in 1877[466] and Wellhausen supported this by maintaining that Lev. 17-26 occupied a unique position in the whole of P document.

Since the Holiness code is believed to have been in combination of smaller individual collections, it is not possible to give dating to each of the collection. For Rendtorff it is not clear that the Holiness Code ever existed as a separate document,[467] nor is it clear from the text that a distinct collection has been incorporated.[468] Even those who argue for the existence of the Holiness Code as an independent document at one time, claim that it was thoroughly

---

466 Rolf Rendtorff, "Is it possible to Read Leviticus as a Separate Books? *Reading Leviticus a Conversation with Mary Douglas*, edited by John F. A. Sawyer, JSOT Supl 227 (Sheffield: Sheffield Academic Press, 1996), 27.

467 Rolf Rendtorff, *The Old Testament: An Introduction,* translated by J. Bowden (Philadelphia: Fortress Press, 1986), 145. There is lack of internal order to the uneven stress on holiness and to the fact that this is not unique to the Holiness Code. Fohrer, *Introduction to the Old Testament,* 138, point out what seem to be separate collections within the Holiness Code. None of these arguments alone decisively demonstrates that the Holiness Code did not exist as an independent document at one time. In fact, most of this statement could also be applied to the Covenant Code. However, the decisive difference is that the Covenant Code has a clear beginning and end in the text, whereas the Holiness Code does not.

468 Milgrom argue that Lev. 17 is not an opening chapter since it is connected thematically and verbally with what precedes it. J. Milgrom, "Leviticus," in *IDB Sup* (Nashville: Abington Press, 1976), 541-45; Cf. G. J. Wenham, *The Book of Leviticus* (Grand Rapids: Eerdmanns, 1979), 7.

edited when it was incorporated into the Priestly laws.[469] Priestly document are among the most disputed in Old Testament scholarship.

Things have radically changed in the last few decades, with more and more scholars agreeing that H was created later than Leviticus 1–16. There are two groups of scholars who support this view. On the one hand, there are (mostly) Jewish scholars who belong to what one could call the 'Kaufmann School,'[470] of which Milgrom and Knohl would probably be the foremost examples. For both Milgrom and Knohl, H was produced by a Holiness School that consisted of priests, but who belonged to a later generation than those who produced the bulk of the earlier Priestly source (P), of which Leviticus 1–16 forms part. In Europe, similar arguments are followed by scholars belonging to the 'redactional critical'[471] school, of which Otto, Achenbach and Nihan would probably be the best examples. These two groups differ on the dating of these texts, but they agree on the chronological relationship between P and H. For all of them, H was written after P.

Kaufmann takes aim at the central thesis of Wellhausen and observes that, "fixity in times and rites and absence of 'natural spontaneity' characterize the festival of ancient Babylonia, Egypt, and all known civilization. Annual purification is likewise ubiquitous… that these elements are found in P rather than in JE or D is, in itself, no indication of lateness."[472] So he argued that P is pre-exilic but not Mosaic. Knohl is one of those scholars who could be regarded as following in the footsteps of Kaufmann, who responded to Wellhausen's

469 One area which need not concern us is whether or not P was initially a narrative source into which the laws were inserted at a later date, or whether P was ever an independent document. P. R. Ackroyd, *Exile and Restoration* (Philadelphia: Westminster Press, 1968), 91. Fohrer, *Introduction to the Old Testament,* 138-42. Blenkinsopp argues that it was first an account of the founding events into which the laws were inserted at a later stage. Cf. J. Blenkinsopp, "The structure of P," *CBQ* 38 (1976): 275; Cf F. M. Cross, "The Priestly Work," in *Canaanites Myth and Hebrew Epic* (Cambridge, MA: Harvard University Press, 1973), 293-94, conclude that P is a trident, but not an independent narrative.

470 "Yehezkel Kaufmann" I refer to the scholars who argue that the priestly texts are pre-exilic. Cf. E. E. Meyer, "Dating the Priestly text in the pre-exilic period: Some remarks about anachronistic slips and other obstacles," *Vebum et ecclesia* 31/1 (2010): 1-6, for an overview and critical discussion, or especially the debate between Milgrom "The antiquity of the Priestly source: A reply to Joseph Blenkinsopp" *ZAW* 111 (1999): 10-22, and Joseph Blenkinsopp "An Assessment of the Alleged Pre-Exilic Date of the Priestly material in Pentateuch," *ZAW* 108 (1996): 495-518.

471 J. Stackert, "The Holiness legislation and its Pentateuchal sources: Revision, supplementation, and replacement," in S. Schectman & J. S. Baden eds., *The Strata of the Priestly Writings. Contemporary Debate and Future Directions*, ATAN 95 (Zurich: Theologischer Verlag, 2009), 187-201.

472 Yehezkel Kaufmann, *The Religion of Israel,* translated by M. Greenberg (Chicago: University of Chicago Press, 1960), 178.

rather negative portrayal of P by arguing for a pre-exilic dating of P.[473] Knohl is also the one of those scholars who argue that H came after P and who has clearly shown that the focus of the Holiness School (HS) is more ethical than that of Priestly Torah (PT).

Joosten asserts: “determining the historical background of Holiness is problematic. It relates words and events from the period after the Exodus when Israel was camping at Mount Sinai. It is not, however an eye witness report and the text itself gives indications of being written, when the people of Israel were already established in the land.”[474]

There are others scholars who place the Holiness Code before Deuteronomy. The common arguments for the earlier date for the Holiness Code or the Priestly source is that a number of questions from Leviticus are found in Ezekiel[475] Out of five references,[476] the two in Ezekiel 22 reflect the traditional image of aliens as dependent, vulnerable people. Ezekiel 22:7 groups them with the fatherless and widow; and Ezek. 22:9 with the poor and the needy. Wenham argues that: “the language does not resemble a late Biblical Hebrew.”[477]

Because of the similarities in contents and language, it has been even thought that Ezekiel might be the compiler of the Holiness Code, or else both Ezekiel and compiler of Holiness Code might have used the same source.[478]In Ezek 14:1-11 we have a unit framed by a narrative introduction and concluding formula.[479] The addressees of this law are the house of Israel, which is repeated and expanded in v.7 by the addition of ומהגר אשׁר־יגור בישׂראל (an from the alien who resides in Israel). As Zimmerli explains, ‘this phrase occurs, with minor variations, in Lev. 17:3, 8, 10, 13; 20:2; 22:18.”[480] This similarity

473 Knohl talks of the Priestly Torah (PT) and the Holiness School (HS). The latter were the people who produce the Holiness the Holiness code and they also added other text in the first four books of the Pentateuch, which is then often described as HS. Cf. Israel Knohl, *The Sanctuary of Silence: The Priestly Torah and the Holiness School* (Minneopolis: Fortress Press, 1995), 104-106.

474 Jan Joosten, *People and Land in the Holiness Code: An Exegetical Study of the Ideational Framework of the Law in Leviticus 17-26* (Leiden: Brill, 1996), 9.

475 Lev 18:3; Ezek 20:11; Lev 26; Ezek 34.

476 Ezek. 14: 7; 22:7, 29; 47: 22, 23.

477 Wenham, *The Book of Leviticus,* 12-13.

478 Eissfeldt accepts the possibility of the two using the same sources and said that the idea of Ezekiel being the compiler of the Holiness Code can be thought only with the recognition that both came into being in roughly the same period, in the same environment and serve the same end. O. Eissfeldt, *The Old Testament: An Introduction*, 238.

479 W. Zimmerli, *Ezekiel,* translated by R. E. Clement (Philadelphia: Fortress Press, 1979), 302.

480 W. Zimmerli, *Ezekiel,* 303.

points to the close contact that exists between the author(s) of Ezekiel and the Holiness Code. Fohrer[481] objects to this view and claim that Ezekiel and the redactor of Holiness Code worked independently and that the Holiness Code must have come to being toward the end of the pre-exilic period and been known to the prophet while he was still in Jerusalem. Its further revision and final codification however took place only in the exilic period. Whybray generally held to be postexilic in date.[482]

Otto takes us to a totally different time, namely the Persian period. In short, Otto argues that during the exilic period, two important works were written engaging with the Israel; identity. The first considered of a priestly code that extended from Genesis 1 and end somewhere in the Sinai periscope. The second started with Deuteronomy 5 and concluded in Joshua 23 dates this Hexateuch to the time of Nehemiah. In the Hexateuch, the land is the most important gift to Israel. Later, the Hexateuch was changed to a Pentateuch by cutting off the Book of Joshua at the time of Ezra; this was done for the sake of Jews living in the Diaspora and in response to their quest for identity.[483] Israel's identity should not be constituted by living in the promise land but by the Torah given at Mount Sinai in the desert outside the promise land: Jews should be those all over the world who kept YHWH's Torah, regardless of whether they lived in the promise land or the diaspora.[484] With the argument stated above Holiness Code written in the Persian period, post-exilic 5th century text,[485] holiness is fundamentally understood as a separation from the non-Jewish populations.

The researcher would like to support Otto's argument rather than Knohls simply because majority of the scholar who argue that Holiness texts are exilic and post-exilic. The most attractive part of Otto's hypothesis is obviously the construction of an identity which is not dependent on land, but closely connected to a way of living, or in other words to a kind of ethics as found in the Holiness code.

---

481 Fohrer, *Introduction to the Old Testament,* 142.

482 R. Norman Whybray, *Introduction to the Pentateuch* (Grand Rapids, Michigan: William B. Eerdmans Publishing Company, 1995), 123.

483 E. Otto, "The Holiness Code in diachrony and Synchrony in the Legal Hermeneutics of the Pentateuch," in *The strata of the Priestly writings. Contemporary Debate and Future Directions*, ATAN, edited by S. Schectman & J. S. Baden (Zürich: Theologischer Verlag, 2009), 135–156.

484 Otto, "The Holiness Code in diachrony and synchrony in the legal hermeneutics of the Pentateuch," 171-72.

485 The historical and literary context for Holiness Code is sought in a first edition of the Torah in the Persian period , early 5th cent B.C.E. Cf. C. Nishan, *From Priestly Torah to Pentateuch: A Study in the Composition of the Book of Leviticus* (Tübingen: Mohr Siebeck, 2007), 545-548.

The Holiness Code גר a postexilic, non-indigenous- maybe ethnically non-Israelite many affirms that the postexilic Jewish congregation integrated. Many affirms that the postexilic Jewish congregation integrated circumcised גרים (Exod.12:48-49), but who exactly were they?[486] Perhaps they were like D's גרים, Northern Kingdom Israelites who yielded to Judean domination after Samaria fall. Or were they Samaritan hierarchs,[487] that is, Israelite who stayed in Palestine and joined the exiles who returned?[488] Or conversely, Judean exiles who returned to Jerusalem or instead were they diasporas Jew travelling to Jerusalem to celebrate the Festival? As Wienfeld asserts: "that the different between the status of the גר in each law corpus may not be the result of different historical conditions or distinct referents or meaning for the term גר, but may be simply the theological and ideological differences between one corpus to another.[489] With different ideological debate given above, now let us see the extrinsic analysis.

5.2. Extrinsic Analysis on Holiness Code

The researcher assumes that most date for the composition of Holiness Code was the Persian period. The Persian period, also called the Achaemenid period, which refers to matters concerning an empire of Southern and South Western Asia during 539-333 B.C.E whose empires their lineage to the family of a certain Achemenes.[490]

The term 'Jew/Judaean' seems to have been taken for granted as an ethnic and geographical destination for the inhabitants of Judah. Yehud[491] (plural Yehudim) was the term used to refer to those who were seen as natives of Judah. Furthermore, in the common phrasing of the time, those who originated in Judah were also called 'Jews/Judaeans' even when they lived elsewhere.

---

486 Ross H. Cole "The Sabbath and the Alien," *AUSS* 38 (2000): 223-29, argues with John Calvin, that the Sabbath participants enumerated in Exod 23:21 and Deut 5:21 would have included *uncircumcised* גרים. If so, then weekly Sabbath provides an exception to the norm of only permitting circumcised aliens to observe Israel's sacred customs.

487 Van Houten, *The Aliensin Israelite law...,* 156.

488 J. G. Vink, "The Date and Origin of the Priestly Code in the Old Testament," in *The Priestly Code and Seven Other Studies,* edited by P. A. de Boer Old Testament Studies 15 (Leiden: Brill, 1969), 1-44.

489 Weinfeld, *Deuteronomy and Deuteronomic School,* 230-231.

490 John L. Berguist, "Constructing of Identities in Postcolonial Yehud," edited by Oded Lipschits and Manfred Oeming, in *Judah and the Judean in the Persian Period* (Eisenbrauns: Winona Lake, Indiana, 2006), 53.

491 The term "Yehud" reflects the Persian name for the province or area that included Jerusalem and its environs. The use of this term differentiates Jerusalem and "Judah" during the post exilic period from the independent Judah of the monarchy as well as from Judah in other periods. Also "Yehud" restricts the analysis to the period of Persia rule (539-333B. C.E).

Berquist question, 'Who, then, counts as Judean? What criteria can we use to ascertain who is a Judean and who is not? What are the limits of this group, and what kind of group would they be? These designations could apply to communities that had not lived in the homeland for generations, such as the Jewish community in Elephantine. The members are called 'Jews, Judaeans' (Aramaic Yehudin, Yehudaya) in the documents.[492] They are interchangeable used.

5.2.1. Colonial Israel: A Foreign Tributary Mode of Production

Persian imperial policy is fairly short as the goal is not to engage in a detailed history of Yehud and the Archaemenid Empire. At times, there was direct imperial intervention in Jerusalem and Yehud but also period of little Persian influence; there were imperial funding for building projects (money coming in) but also times of heavy taxation (money going out). Persians preferred to rule its province including Yehud, through governors and possibly religious leaders. In Yehud those with ethnic ties to the land were send back with imperial power to implement imperial policies which were favorable to the empire.[493]

With an agrarian based economy the vast majority of Jews were engaged in some sort of livelihood relating to agriculture. There was probably not a lot of social differentiation among the peasants class. Much farming seems to have been done by individual families on small holdings. Their lifestyle and style and status are likely to have been much the same, whether they own their own land or rented it. We get a glimpse of people like this in such passages as Hag 1:2-11 and Nehemiah 5. Rather lower on the social scale would have been itinerate workers and day laborers. We know of them by reference in some of the law collections that probably date from the Persian period (e.g. Deut 24:14-15). As Neh 5:2-5 shows, those who owned land might have to sell it to pay debts and thus become renters. One presumes that the next stage would be to become a hired worker, though this is not specifically mentioned here. The worst situation was to sell one's family or oneself into slavery, as Neh 5:5 envisages. The social conditions had change dramatically from being dependent laborers working for landowners according to Covenant and

492 Lester L. Grabbe, *A History of the Jews and Judaism in the Second Temple period,* Vol. 1 (London, NY: T&T Clark International, 2004), 167.

493 Sources for Persian history and Yehud: Blenkinsopp, *The Pentateuch: An Introduction to the First Five Books of the Bible* (New York: Doubleday, 1992), 239-42; Berquist, *Judaism in Persian Shadow a Social and Historical Approach,* 23-120; Josef Wiesehöfer, "The Achaemenid Empire in the Fourth Century B.C.E: A Period of Decline? In *Judah and the Judeans in the Fourth Century B.C.E,* edited by Oded Lipschits, Gery N. Knoppers and Rainer Albertz (Winona Lake: Eisenbrauns, 2007), 11-32; Israel Finkelstein, "Jerusalem in the Persian (and Early Hellenistic) period and the wall of Nehemiah," *JSOT* 32/4 (2008): 501-20.

Deuteronomic tradition; in the Holiness Code the גר would appear to have increase in their self sufficiency.

Likewise, there is great ambivalence towards aliens in the Holiness Code, at times bordering on opposition (18: 24-30; 24: 10-16). Nevertheless, in chap. 19, respectful treatment of foreign workers and residents is clearly enjoined, an injunction that bears the same weight as the text's call for just weights and measures in the passages that immediately follow:

> When an alien resides with you in your land, you shall not oppress the alien. The alien who resides with you shall be to you as the citizen among you; you shall love the alien as yourself, for you were aliens in the land of Egypt: I am the Lord Your God (Lev 19:33).

The laws pertaining to the alien as well as the bulk of the Holiness Code are illuminating when they are understood as a creative response to the crisis brought about by the exile, and the subsequent reuniting of the returnees (golah) with those who had remain in Judah (*am ha'ares*). The exile was a crisis of mammoth proportions for the Jews. It involved coming to grips with being defeated, with losing their homeland to pagan conquerors, with being deported, with losing their identity as citizens, with being a minority people who were dominated by their conquerors. In exile they survived by fashioning 'mobile identities' through a variety of survival strategies. As Smith describe "they refined themselves, and became an ethnic minority, and a confession community. When they returned, they had to become integrated with a group who claimed the same religious heritage, but had not undergone the profound ideological and sociological transformation as the group that had survived the Babylonian exile."[494] Mullen argues that Tetrateuch was composed in the post-exilic era by those Persian 'returned to Jerusalem'. Mullen content that: "Persian imperial policy entailed resettling peoples from elsewhere in the empire into strategic cities, Jerusalem among them. A group, possibly made up of descendants of exiled Judeans, possibly not, was moved to Jerusalem in order to further Persian political and economic interest through unifying and local people around a common identity, and through the administration of the rebuild temple. Persian policy even required some sort of written 'charter' for subject peoples, codifying their laws and recording their history. Mullen contends that Temple scribes, part of these transplanted 'returnees', created the Tetrateuch in order to provide this mix of 'returnees' and native inhabitants

---

494 Smith argues the survival strategies of other refugees who have maintained their distinct identities. D. L. Smith, *The Religion of the Landless: A Social Context of the Babylonian Exile* (Bloomington, IN: Meyer Stone Books, 1989).

with such a 'charter' for a common ethnic identity."[495] The economic policy of the Persian served to divide the Jewish community; between those already inhabiting there and the exiles.

The monarchical period, from the eight century onward, had witness a society that was increasingly drifting apart. Essential elements of continuity lay at the heart of a divided society. All the elements of indebtedness, oppression, and impoverishment that can be observed in the late monarchical period are found also in the Persian era; the tendency to impoverishment appears to have increased. Thus Haggai and Zechariah name bad economic conditions as the reason for the slowness in beginning to rebuild the temple. In drastic terms: "you that earn wages to put them into a bag with holes" (Hag. 1:6). Kessler asserts: "even though general economic misery says nothing in particular about social relationships, the text shows that there were not only farming families, but day-laborers as well, that is, people without land who had to hire themselves out for wages."[496]

Text likes Isaiah 58: 6-7; 61: 1-2 which are probability to be dated to the Persian era, the picture become much sharper. The book of Malachi speaks of people "who oppress the hired workers in their wages, the widow and the orphan… who trust aside the alien" (Mal 3:5). A keen awareness of economic and political oppression comes out most clearly in Third Isaiah (Isaiah 58). Sweeney asserts that: "Isaiah 58 falls in the section of Third Isaiah 56-59 that is devoted to the "issue of proper observance of YHWH's covenant."[497]

As a restored community in Palestine and as permanently dispersed enclaves abroad, Israelites fell under a foreign tributary mode of production by allowing home rule among Palestinian Jews, the Persian tribute-takers granted the operation of a native tributary mode of production headed by Jewish elite. Gottwald rightly said: "The beneficiaries of this native tributary apparatus, functioning through the temple economy, fought stubborn battles with communitarians, extending on into Hellenistic and Roman periods. It is evident that it was the heirs of the Old Judahite elite, restored from Babylon by the Persians, who gained the upper hand in Palestine, although they could not do so without coming to some terms with the indigenous Jewish populace that had never left Palestine."[498]

---

495 E. T. Mullen, *Ethnic Myths and Pentateuchal Foundations: A New Approach to the Formation of the Pentateuch,* SBLSS (Atlanta: Scholar Press, 1997), 327.

496 Rainer Kessler, *The social History of Ancient Israel An Introduction,* 135.

497 Sweeney, Marvin A, "The Reconceptualization of the Davidic Covenant in Isaiah," *Studies in the Book of Isaiah* (Festschrift Willem Am Beuken, 1997), 206-224.

498 Norman K. Gottwald, "Sociology method in the Study of Ancient Israel," in *The Bible and lLiberation: Political and Social hermeneutics,* edited by Norman K. Gottwald (Maryknoll, New York: Orbis, 1983), 85.

Another important view on economic and social realities of the community of this period is proposed by Weinberg[499] postulate the existence of this community based on the leadership of various *Bet 'Abot.* He believes that the *Bet 'Abot* was a social institution a collective within the citizen-temple community of the sixth-to fourth century B.C.[500] Weinberg's thesis of citizen temple community has been criticized by many scholars. Smith criticized him for taking the biblical documents for relating external politics because biblical document from this period are understood as documents exclusively about the internal politics of the community.[501] Williamson rejects citizen temple community theory for many reasons. He criticized Weinberg for taking the list in Ezra as the source for this type of community, because most scholars consider it as the reflection of the population of Judah including both, returnees and remainees. Similarly, the temple had not played the central economic role in the society as Weinberg explained.[502]

5.2.2. Social Conflict

There were social conflicts between the Judean repatriated from Babylon and those who were living in Judea when they returned. Considering themselves as a "cultic community" whose character were marked by observance of the Torah under the supervision of the priest of the Jerusalem cult of Yahweh, the returnees want to separate them from others. In this interpretation Bedford remarks: "The antagonists of the repatriates are identified by some scholars as Judeans who never went to exile and by others as the inhabitants of Samaria."[503]

Another understanding of the social conflict in the Jewish community of Persia focuses on the different views of the restoration of Judah. Hanson describes this conflict in the book *The Dawn of Apocalyptic.* He named these two groups as "visionaries" and "hierocratic party." According to Hanson, the visionaries are the group consisted of the Levites who did not go to exile along with some of the returnees who stood in the tradition of Deutro Isaiah in rejecting the restoration of monarchy.[504] Hierocratic party is identified with the Zadokite priests who claimed the legitimate priesthood with the support

499 Joel Weinberg, *The Citizen-Temple Community,* translated by Daniel L. Smith-Christopher (Sheffield: Sheffield Academic Press, Ltd., 1992), 53.

500 Joel Weinberg, *The Citizen-Temple Community,* 53.

501 Smith, *The Religion of the Landless...,* 108.

502 H. G. M. Williamson, "Exiles and After: Historical Studies," in *The Face of Old Testament Studies; A Survey of Contemporary Approaches,* edited by David W. Baker and Bill T.Arnold (Grand Rapids/ Michigan: Baker Academic, 1999), 249-50.

503 Peter R. Bedford, *Temple Restoration in early Achaemenid Judah* (Leiden: Brill, 2001), 11-12.

504 Paul D. Hanson, Paul Hanson, *The Dawn of Apocalyptic: The Historical and Sociological Roots of Jewish Apocalyptic Eschatology* (Philadelphia: Fortress Press, 1979), 32ff.

of Persian rule.[505] He placed Trito Isaiah with visionaries and Haggai and Zechariah 1-8 with the hierocratic group. Hanson projects two rival groups, each with a plan for restoration and each vying with the other for domination.

Smith gives a different interpretation of the social conflict in this period. According to him the conflict is between "Yahweh-alone" party and the "syncretist" party. He identified at least three groups in the early Persian period Judah: a local party and two important groups of repatriates. Local party was the adherents of syncretic cult. Majority of the returned exiles were devoted to Yahweh alone. But a second group of returned exile was the priest of Jerusalem temple who had economic interest in its restoration.[506]

Horsley says about multiple conflicts in Yehud under Persian rule. He observed four conflicts that persisted in Yehud throughout the Persian rule. They are:

1. The division between the immigrant elites and the people who had remained in the land;
2. The division between the peasants in the villages and the wealthy and powerful elite in Jerusalem;
3. The struggle between various priestly groups; and
4. The struggle for power between local magnates and between local magnates and Persian governors.[507]

However, some criticisms have leveled against this conflict theory. Based on the archeological study, Hoglund states that: "the presumption of a class struggle between exiles and the 'remainees' over land rights do not fit the evidence of the pattern of these Persian period village."[508] Scholars like Japhet and Bedford question the exact period when this conflict emerged in Yehud. They are among those who sharply distinguish Haggai and Zachariah from Ezra-Nehemiah, and thus argue that the conflict in it's most extremely exclusive from started only with the communities represented by the latter composition; that is by the fifth and perhaps even the fourth centuries.[509]

505 Hanson, *The Dawn of Apocalyptic...,* 220ff.

506 Morton Smith, *Palestinian Parties and Politics That Shaped the Old Testament* (New York: Columbia University Press), 107-108.

507 Richard A. Horsley, *Scribes, Visionaries and the Politics of Second Temple Judea* (London, Loisville: Westminster John Knox Press, 2007), 37.

508 Cited in Williamson, "Exiles and After: Historical Studies," 225, and Charles E. Carter, *The Emergence of Yehud in the Persian Period A Social and Demographic Study,* JSOT Suplt Series 294 (Sheffield: Sheffield Academic Press, 1999), 214-215.

509 Sara Japhet, "People and Land in the Restoration Period," in *Das land Israel im biblischer Zeit: Jerusalem-Symposium 1981 der Hebraischen Universitat Und der Georg-August-Universitat,* edited by G. Strecker, GTA, 25 (Gottingen: Vanden-hoeck & Ruprecht, 1983), 103-25. Cf. Bedford, *Temple Restoration*...42-61. H. G. M. Williamson, "The concept of

According to Bedford, the crucial conflict was that with the Samarians, in the fourth century B.C.E, and this was anachronistically retrojected (in Ezra 3:1-4:5) into the early Persian period, to the time of Zerubbabel and Joshua; to the time of Zechariah the repatriate and Haggai the not exiled.[510] This conflict aspect confirms that Jerusalem temple was at the centre of struggle among competing groups for power because the diversity of opinion and a measure of conflict.

The researcher would like to go with this theory because "Israel –Diaspora relationship has engendered lively and complicated discussions over the last hundred years. But, in fact, scholars have often traced back contemporary homeland-Diaspora conflict to the division drawn between "Jerusalem" (i.e the entire land of Israel) and "Babel" in rabbinic literature. Or even as far back as the conflict of the Persian period.

Secondly, it is argued that biblical texts of the Neo-Babylonian and the early Persian period show fierce adversarial relationship between the Judean group. We find no expressions of sympathy to the deported community for its dislocation, no empathic expression towards the people who remained under Babylonian subjugation in Judah. The opposite is apparent, hostile, superior, and denunciating language characterizing the relationship between resident and exiled Judean throughout the sixth and fifth centuries. The question is why and how did this Babylonian Diaspora community develop such hostile relations with its homeland community? And vice-versa; Why and how did the homeland community left in Judah following the Babylonian deportations re-establish its community life by delegitimizing those Exile that had been forced to leave their homeland? What needs and ends were served by such intra-community divisions and hostility? Post exilic, Judaism, therefore, displayed a tangle of conflicting and contradictory practices and ideologies along the spectrum of tributary vs communitarian modes of production.

5.2.3. Identity, Inclusion and Exclusion: The *Golah* and the Development of Jewish Identity

During the post exilic or Persian period which dates from 539-333 B.C.E the Bible reports that members of the exilic community in Babylonia, who moved to Jerusalem restored the temple and revived the cultic practices and eventually set up a government there. Ezra, Nehemiah, Haggai and Zechariah, which contain the only biblical stories directly pertaining to the period in the

---

Israel in Transition," in *The World of Ancient Israel: Sociological, Anthropological, and Political Perspective: Essay by Members of the Society for Old Testament Study,* edited by R. E. Clements (Cambridge: Cambridge University Press, 1989), 141-61, who founded the first seeds of exiles exclusively in Deutero-Isaiah (Isa 40-55, see especially pp. 146-47).

510 Bedford, *Temple Restoration in early ...*,278-79.

land, offer detailed information about only a limited group of people, mainly immigrants to Jerusalem from Babylonia. As Moor asserts: "these returnees (as the Bible sees them) or immigrants (a more neutral term) then became the focus of the biblical story of the period, and it follows that traditionally they were (and still usually are) the focus of historian's as well.[511] Berquest uses terms such as *ha-golah* and *am-ha-'aretz* to signify identity.[512]

There are many scholars who find the presence of diverse communities and traditions in this period. Kessler observes many diverse yet related communities tracing their origins to the earlier kingdoms of Israel and Judah. He summarizes this complex group as (1) *golah* returnees in Yehud, (2) *golah* remainees in Babylon, (3) Yehudite remainees, (4) Israelite/Judean residents in Egypt, (5) Israelite/Judean inhabitant in the province of Samaria and (6) other Israelite/ Judeans in the various regions of the Levant.[513]

According to redactor, the '*am ha'ares* were the descendant of Judeans who had escaped Babylonian captivity. They consider them to be poor, downtrodden, and newly disenfranchised by the returning *gola.* Grabbe asserts that: "the '*ame ha'ares, peoples* of the land,' who are identified as foreigners. He concludes saying "many, if not all, these 'people of the land' were Jewish descendants of those who were not deported. In the eyes of the author of Ezra, these peoples were no longer kin; the only 'people of Israel' were those who had gone into captivity."[514] For Fried "the identity of the '*am ha'ares* does not seem to have changed, except that now the ones who control the land are foreign."[515]

Historians today are faced with a number of unanswered questions about the biblical sources that would help them evaluate the limited information they do provide. These include question on when Ezra, Nehemiah, Haggai and Zechariah were compiled, what sources their authors used, when those sources

511 Megan Bishop Moore and Brad E. Kelle, *Biblical History and Israel's Past: The Changing study of the Bible and History* (Grand Rapids, Michigan/Cambridge, U.K: William B. Eerdmans Publishing Company, 2011), 397.

512 Jon L. Berquest, "Constructions of Identity in Post Colonial Yehud," 55.

513 John Kessler, "Diaspora and Homeland in the Early Achaemenid Period: Community, Geography and Demography in Zechariah 1-8" in *Approaching Yehud-New Approaches to the Study of the Persian Period,* edited by Jon L. Berquist (Atlanta: Society for Biblical Literature, 2007), 141.

514 Lester L. Grabbe, *Ezra-Nehemiah.* Old Testament Reading (London and New York: Routledge, 1998), 135.

515 Lisbeth S. Fried, "The 'am ha'ares in Ezra 4:4 and Persian Imperial Administration," in *Judah and the Judeans in the Persian Period,* edited by Oded Lipschits and Manfred Oeming (Winona Lake, Indiana: Eisenbrauns, 2006), 129.

were composed, how the authors altered the sources they used.[516] In whose interest and ideas serves a particular group, especially a dominant group.

5.2.4. Movement Towards Inclusion

There are specific questions about the social-political make up of the *golah* community that precisely supports the framework in this section. In what sense was the *golah* community autonomous, authoritative, or exclusive? Also in what sense, if at all, did the religious ideologies of the *golah* community dictate social, economic, and political actions in Yehud or even more in Jerusalem? Does Ezra-Nehemiah reflect an ideal situation one in which the leaders of the *golah* community were able to dictate the flow of the social, economic, and political system in Yehud? The researcher view Ezra-Nehemiah as originally produced by representatives of a particular social group that, while portraying an idealized vision of a society, affirm to react to certain social realities in Yehud.

The so called Golah list of Ezra 2 and Nehemiah 7, however, suggest that the *golah* community defined itself with a stronger sense of exclusivity. The *golah* community appears to base membership on a collection of certain bloodlines, and possibly more importantly on a shared experience of exile (cf. Ezra 6:19-22). As the passage from Ezra 6:21 suggest, it appears possible that some people who may not have emigrated from Babylon were granted honorary membership in the community after they professed loyalty to it and its god.

The rhetoric of Ezra-Nehemiah presents its readers with an ideal image of a social space that is divided into two categories based on religion, those who are members of a sacred community and those who are not members (Ezra 10:2, 10-11; Neh 13:3, 26-27). According to Schults interpretation "those who were deported were the true remnant, while those who remained in the land were of no significance."[517] Prophets like Jeremiah (Jer. 24:1-10), Ezekiel (Ezek.11:33; 23-24, 27-28) and Isaiah (Isa 43: 28; 49:6; 51:3; 52:2, 9) share this opinion. Scholars like Dyck, Hanson, and Wellhausen suggests that "the meaning behind such rhetoric in Ezra-Nehemiah as an adequate representation of Yehud has suggested to some that a theocracy existed in the province."[518] One cannot escape the deep-rooted presence of religious agenda and ideology

516 Megan Bishop Moore and Brad E. Kelle, *Biblical History and Israel's Past*...398.

517 C. Schultz, "The Political Tensions Reflected in Ezra-Nehemiah," in *Scripture in Context,* edited by C. D. Evans, W. W. Hallo and J. B. White (Pittsburgh: The Pickwick Press, 1980), 223.

518 Jonathan E. Dyck, *The Theocratic Ideology of the Chronicler,* Vol. 33 (Leiden: Brill, 1988), 1-4. Paul Hanson, *The Dawn of Apocalyptic*... 211-220. Julius Wellhausen, *Prolegomena to the History of Israel* (Atlanta: Scholars Press, 1994), 411-22.

within Ezra-Nehemiah. Ezra-Nehemiah is above all, a religious text, defined by the text itself and limited to the *Golah* community.

Such an inclusive policy would have served the interests of *golah* returnees' charter group,[519] the *golah remainees,* and the Persian in a number of ways. Porter considers a Charter Group to be elite (or composite of elites) with certain distinctive features. He defines a Charter Group as "an ethnic elite that moves into a geographical region, establishes its power base, and creates a sociological and cultural structure distinct from the one already existing in that region. Thus, a Charter Group is "the first ethnic group to come into a previously unpopulated territory, as the effective possessor,"[520] noting as well as "a Charter Group may have to conquer an indigenous group to established its claim."[521]Most significant among these would be speedy reconstruction of the temple, social cohesion under the leadership of the *golah* returnees', and demographic and economic development.[522] In the case of *golah* returnees, they were an ethnically defined group (based upon connections with the previous rulers of Judah) send by the Persians to establish a community in Jerusalem around the central shrine and worship of YHWH.[523] They carried out this mission under the authority of, and for the benefit of, the Persian Crown. As those in a position of power, they played an important role in shaping the identity of Yahwists in the post-exilic period. Kessler sees this identity taking shape as the elite group emphasized ritual purity (Ezra 6:21), observance to the law of Moses, and action against foreign wives.

5.2.5. Movement Towards Exclusion

Having said about the inclusive policy of the *golah* returnees however as Kessler remarks that "at the same time such as exclusivist orientation would have generated forces of exclusion, specifically when it threatened to dislodge the charter group's hegemony over the social, political and religious life of the

519 Kessler draws upon the work of sociologist John Porter. A 'charter group' is an ethnic elite that moves into a geographical region, establishes its power base, and creates a sociological and cultural structure distinct from the one existing in that region. John Kessler, "Persia's Loyal Yahwists: Power Identity and Ethnicity in Archaemenid Yehud," in *Judah and the Judeans in the Persian period,* edited by Oded Lipchits and Manfred Oeming (Winina Lake, Indiana: Eisenbrauns, 2006), 99.

520 John Porter, *The Vertical Mosaic: A Study of Social Class and Power in Canada* (Toronto: Buffalo, 1965), 60.

521 Porter, *The Vertical Mosaic...,*60.

522 Kessler, "Persia's Loyal Yahwists: Power Identity and Ethnicity in Archaemenid Yehud," 110.

523 Kessler, "Persia's Loyal Yahwists: Power Identity and Ethnicity in Archaemenid Yehud," 106.

province, or perhaps more importantly, its own sense of identity rooted in the common shared historical experience of exile."[524]

The Neo-Babylon and Persian period biblical text generally reject those who remained in the land after the exiles. Ezekiel 11:1-25, for related example, does no less than reduce these, rather unfairly, to an offence group of syncretistic self-deceivers who wrongly believed they had right to the land.[525] Similar kind of rejection of "foreigners" is seen in Ezra-Nehemiah (cf. Ezra 10: 1-44, Neh 13:1-3), with 'foreign' being synonymous with 'profane.'

One group especially sensitive to this inclusive stance would have been the Babylonian *golah* remainees, who risked the loss of a significant measure of control over the life inYehud. Ezra (Ezra 9:4-5; 10:10) and Nehemiah (Neh 13:23-27) may be seen to be representative of *golah* remainees who were clearly threatened by the more open stance towards marriage with the people of the land practiced by the returnees. Similarly Nehemiah (Neh 13:4-9, 15-22, 28) stands opposed to the locals' willingness to accommodate the economic and religious practices of other non-golah Yahwists who frequented the temple.[526] The dramatic reaction to intermarriage in Ezra-Nehemiah may indeed reflect significant lines of stress within a social group, i.e., the golah.[527]According to Esler, Ezra-Nehemiah as a narratives intended to create ethnic identity. He relies heavily on Barth's understanding of ethnicity and on Cornell's work on the role of narratives in the formation and maintenance of ethnic identity. He focuses on the roles of share history and collective memory. Cornell contends that when people reflect upon their identity, they create or adopt a narrative that expresses important components of what it means to be a part of their group. Key stages in this process include selecting events and their plot for the group's identity. Such a narrative can be changed as new historical circumstances force the group to rethink their place within a new setting. Narratives related to ethnic identity are also tied to issue of power. In-groups will often struggle over the shape of these narratives, since the outcome will determine which group's claims to power receive legitimation.[528] Thus, history and collective memory plays an important role in shaping identity.

524 Kessler, "Persia's Loyal Yahwists: Power Identity and Ethnicity in Archaemenid Yehud," 110.

525 Mary Joan Winn Leith, "Israel among the Nations: The Persian Period," in *The Oxford History of the Biblical World,* edited by Coogan Michael D. (Oxford: Oxford University Press, 1998), 297.

526 Megan Bishop Moore and Brad E. Kelle, *Biblical History and Israel's Past...,*111.

527 David, J. A Clines, *Ezra, Nehemiah and Easter*, New Century Bible (Grand Rapids: Eerdmans, 1984), 247.

528 P. F. Esler, "Ezra-Nehemiah as a Narrative of (Re-Invented) Israelite Identity," *Biblical Intepretation* 11 3/4 (2003a), 413-26.

5.2.6. Persian Colonial Ideology

The law pertaining to the alien, as well as the entire priestly corpus were edited and revised during this period, and certainly many of the concerns and emphases of the laws can be understood as a creative response to this new situation. Smith asserts that: "the rituals and laws prescribed by the priestly law functioned as an effective mechanism for maintaining boundaries which separated the Jews from foreigners. By insisting on the requirement of purity, and claiming that purity is lost upon contact with the unclean and can be restored through ritual, the priestly laws helped to preserve the distinct identity of the Jews."[529] Despite the conflict's ideological construction, the text shows that the exile elevated role is properly constructed. In the simplest terms, we may say that the Persian-era Judah the returnees from the exile assumed the role of the upper class and that the social contrast between the upper and lower classes was at least partly equivalent to that between the returnees and those who has remained in the land.[530]

No matter how much the fundamental social conflict in the Persian era can thus be described as a conflict between those who had remained in the Land and those who returned from exile, it can be no means reduced solely to that. Not all those who returned from exile were members of the upper class. The polarizing tendencies even increased, so that we must posit a growing impoverishment on the lower end of the social scale. But there were shift in the composition of the social strata originally connected with the fact that it was primarily the Judean upper class that were exile took over the leading role in the Persian province of Yehud.

As could be seen in the Babylonian *golah's* submission and reverence to the Persian rulers. There are traces of influence of religious policies of the Persian Empire upon the Babylonian exile group. For example, the Babylonian *golah* returnees' are expected to offer prayers for Darius and his son as a proof of their loyalty to the Persian ruler to gain their support for the rebuilding of the temple.[531] Therefore, Persian religious policy no doubt re-instated religious pluralism in the empire but at the same time rejects pluralistic and inclusive dialogue among the various communities and instead plays a back stage part

529 Smith, *Religion of the Landless*...10, 80, 81, and 140-43.

530 Joseph Blenkinsopp, "Temple and Society in Achaemenid Judah," in *Second Temple Studies 1: Persian period,* edited by Philip R. Davies, JSOT Sup 117 (Sheffield: Sheffield Academic, 1991), 22-53. Carter concludes that "the traditional view of intra-province struggle between returnees and those who had remained on the land" can be no means is regarded as having been refuted. (248). Cf. Carter, *The Emergence of Yehud in the Persian Period A Social and Demographic Study,* 214-48.

531 Rainer Albertz, *Israel in Exile: The History and Literature of the Sixth Century B.C.E,* translated by David Green (Atlanta: Society for Biblical Literature, 2003), 129.

in the intra-community conflicts which benefited none other than the colonial empire.

Ideology critics question the identification of Judean in Babylonian exile as Israel as a socio-ideological construct of the elites that try to legitimate their connection with the land.[532] Davies contends such view as "Judah and Israel were two separate kingdoms and cultures and sees that such identification is a product of the Persian period to Mizpah and other religions."[533] For Kessler, the question of what the people of Israel is and who belongs to it becomes acute in the Persian period. He argues that from a purely external view point, the most obvious group was the Babylonian exile. He argued that the inhabitants of the provinces of Judah and Samaria were also a subset that belonged to the domain, even though their claim was questioned by the exile community. Kessler specifically mentions the Jews of Elephantine, who he says, turned time and again to Jerusalem in important religious matter.[534] Therefore, this shows a sign of their acknowledgement of Jerusalem as their centre for worship.

The Cyrus Cylinder is a primary source demonstrating the policy of Persia but it must be remembered that the evidence on the Cyrus cylinder indicates that during this period Cyrus interest focused solely on bringing the border land between Persia and Babylon back under cultivation. Tucker argues that: "the portrayal of Cyrus as a kind of savior and model of the benign tolerance of Persian policy suggest that while the Cyrus cylinder may have been directed only to Babylonian audience originally, subsequent communities familiar with Archaemenid imperial ideology appeared to appropriate its ideology in their own attempts at restoration."[535]

For Albertz the version of Cyrus edict found in Ezra 1:2-4 is clearly fictive. To him it is formulated entirely in the language of the author of the book of Ezra; second it is in many ways highly improbable. Cyrus had just hailed himself as chosen by Marduk, so to find him describing himself as called by YHWH at the same time and in the same place seem improbable even impossible.[536] Further, the analysis of the Marasu text pointed out that the economic policy served to divide the Jewish community; between those already inhabiting there and the exiles. The Samaritan schism was a result of a division and dismissive attitude of the exile towards the inhabitants.[537] The fact

532 Megan Bishop Moore and Brad E. Kelle, *Biblical History and Israel's Past...*,380.

533 Philips R. Davies, *The origin of the Biblical Israel,* LHBOTS 485 (New York and London: T&T Clark, 2007), 108-11.

534 Rainer Kessler, *The Social History of Ancient Israel...,* 130.

535 W. Dennis Tucker Jr, *Constructing and Deconstructing Power in Psalms 107-150,* Society for Biblical literature 19 (Atlanta: SBL Press, 2014), 57.

536 Rainer Albertz, *Israel in Exile...*, 121.

537 Geo Widergren, "The Persian Period," in *Israelite and Judean History,* edited by John H. Hayes and J. Maxwell Miller (London: SCM Press Ltd, 1977), 312.

that the land was described as 'empty' by the Chronicler stemmed from the fact that there was no ideological prejudice of the exiled communities against those who were left behind.[538] Thus, one observe the significant changes brought forth by the Persian Empire and spread the conflict within the community that had a long lasting impact on the history of the people of Israel in its latter development.

Thus, the laws pertaining to the alien, as well as the entire priestly corpus were edited and revised during the period, and certainly many of the concerns and emphases of the laws can be understood as a creative response to this new situation. For example, in order to deported people to maintain their separate identity, they may address the issue of self-identification, and create pattern to preserve it. As Rom-Shiloni rightly said "expulsion from God's land in retribution for violating his covenant this partial exile presented fundamental questions of religious and national identity: should exile actually signify the exclusion of the deportees from the people of God, and should those who remained be considered the sole remnant, or vice versa? Such question had major implications for the two communities' hope for restoration."[539] However this intra-community conflict began only with the return to Yehud, whether early or late. Is this internal conflict really only a late sixth; or even fifth or fourth phenomenon? And did it emerge initially in Persian Yehud? Although different scholars have mention passages in Ezekiel and Jeremiah to show that deliberations over identity issues among Judean communities started at an earlier juncture, there is still a need for a thorough overview of these conflict and intra-connection, from the earliest stages to the latest attested forms in Ezra-Nehemiah. During the Persian period, Judea or Yehud existed as a colony in the Persian Empire. Specially beginning with the reign of Darius 1 (522-486 BCE), the empire shifted from conquest as a primary mode of resource extraction from its territories to more long-term strategies of imperial colonization.[540] Part of this process included the authorization and support

---

538 Daniel Smith, Christopher, *A Biblical Theology of Exile* (Minneapolish: Fortress Press, 2002), 46; Cf. Peter R. Bedford, "Diaspora: Homeland Relation in Ezra-Nehemiah," *Vetus Testamentum* 52.2 (2002): 149-150. This conception of the land as a "Vaccum" (commonly called "the empty land"), from the time of the exile to the return-conveniently ignores the ongoing presence of Non-exiled Judean as well as any other peoples. This metaphorical construction, which turns invisible all other occupants of the land, indeed distinguishes Zechariah from Ezra-Nehemiah; as we have seen, the "people of the land" are insistently present in the rhetoric of the book. This distinction further validates the suggestion that the empty land metaphor is an ideological construction, not based on historical circumstances.

539 Dalit Rom-Shiloni, *Exclusive Inclusive: Identity Conflicts Between the Exiles and the People who Remained (6th-5th Centuries BCE)* (New York, London: Bloomsbury T&T Clark, 2013), 2.

540 Jon L. Berguist, 'Postcolonialism and Imperialism Motives for Canonization,' *Semeia* 75 (1996), 17-18, 15-35.

of the codification and standardization of local legal traditions in the various provinces and colonies, which would then be understood as the king's law. Berguist contents that "the mission of Ezra has been interpreted in light of this imperial policy, leading to the suggestion that the 'law of your god and the law of the king' (Ezra 7:26) which Ezra is instructed to teach and administer is a reference to a similar codification of Israelite law undertaken under Persian imperial auspices; and furthermore, that this codification is to be associated in some way with the Pentateuch."[541] The production of the Pentateuch is thus a product not only of the internal need of the community of Yehud to construct a sense of cultural and religious identity, but also, significantly, of the external pressure exerted by the Persian empire for standardized law.[542] The historical authenticities of the biblical traditions concerning Ezra are subject to debate. However, whether it is authentic or not, the biblical tradition places the figure of Ezra in the fifth century BCE, and associate him widely known as authoritative Torah.

Smith has suggested a sequence of events in the post-exilic period which would explain chronologically the two emphases of separation and integration. He points to Ezra and to the fact that Ezra did not even consider the possibility that aliens, among whom Smith includes the foreign wives, could become purified and be granted the status of proselytes, as evidence that much of the legislation of P, especially the laws referring to the alien, had not been formulated. He characterizes the time from Zerubbabel to Nehemiah as a time dominated by the question of purity to the extent that it could not envision incorporating the impure. He claims that the author of Isaiah 56:1-8, writing when Nehemiah was governor, introduced the notion that outsiders could join the holy people. Smith concludes that his prophecy was fulfilled much later in the legislation of P found in Exodus 12: 43-50, Numbers 9:14, 15:1-31, 19:10, Deuteronomy 29:10 and Joshua 20:9.[543] Therefore, this law will be discussed more in detail as individual laws are considered.

5.3. Intrinsic Analysis of Leviticus 17:8-15 and 24:16, 22 and 25

Leviticus 17: 8, 10, 12, 13, 15 repeatedly includes the גר in its sacrificial regulations, and so the Septuagint changes "of the house of Israel" (ישראל

541 Jon L. Berguist, *Judaism in Persian's Shadow*...110-12, 138-39. Cf. Joseph Blenkinsopp, "The Mission of Udjahorresnet and those of Ezra and Nehemiah,' *JBL* 106/3 (Sept. 1987): 409-21.

542 Gottwald refers to the same internal and external factors, adding that the internal need included the necessity of compromise between different tradition (a P Torah and a D Torah) resulting in a 'new consensus Torah'. Norman K. Gottwald, 'Social Matrix and Canonical Shape,' *Theology Today* 42:320.

543 Smith, *Religion of the Landless*...,179-82.

מבית)[544] to τωνυωνσραηλ (of the sons of Israel) in order to add or of ἥτων προσηλῦτων των προσκειμενων ενυμιν (the aliens/proselytes who resides among you). Joosten claims "the MT rules that, to the Israelites, all slaughter of domestic animals is forbidden except as *zebah slamin* (peace offering) at the end of tent meeting (Lev 17:3, 4). However the rule does not apply to the resident alien, which implies that to them profane slaughter is permitted (though it is not encouraged)."[545] Joosten interprets this omission of the גר as evidence that the גר was religiously free, not obligated to present offerings to YHWH.[546] Jacob Milgrom clarifies that H's concern is that the גר, residing in Israel but in covenant with YHWH, had the ability to pollute the land:

> The *ger* is bound by the Noahide law to drain the blood (Gen 9:4), but since he is required to worship Israel's God, he need not bring the blood to his alter...it is incumbent on the *ger* to obey only YHWH's prohibitive commandments, since their violation generates impurity that pollutes the land and ultimately results in Israel's exile. The violation of performative commandments, however, is characterized not by action, but by neglect. No pollution is generated by inaction, and the ecology is not upset...Thus in H's view, the *ger* does not belong in this law.[547]

This is a interesting reading, except for the major problem that Leviticus 17:8-9 includes the גר and regulates performance of sacrifice; it is not a prohibitive command.

5.3.1. Laws Concerning Aliens

Leviticus 17 does not only function as an introduction to chapter 18-22, but is also (like Deuteronomy 12) the main law of the code. Otto states that there are "many links in Leviticus 17 which point forward to what follows in the rest of the code. Another forward-pointing technique identified in Leviticus 17 has to do with the way in which Leviticus 17:15 reinterpreted Exodus 22:30 and 14:21."[548]

---

544 Baruch A. Levine, *Leviticus.* JPS Torah Commentary (Philadelphia: Jewish Publication Society, 1989), 112.

545 Jan Joosten, *People and the Land...* 65-66.

546 Joosten, *People and the Land....*, 65-66. "The *ger* is an exceptional situation: not an Israelite yet entitled to live as a free man among the people. Taking account of this, the sacral law does not oblige him to behave like and Israelite; he is not required to bring sacrifices to other gods or the eating of the blood. A transgression against those prohibitions would bring guild on the whole people; it must not be tolerated."

547 Jacob Milgrom, *Leviticus...*, 230-31.

548 E. Otto, "The Holiness Code in Diachrony and Synchrony in Legal Hermeneutics of the Pentateuch," in *The Strata of the Priestly Writings: Contemporary Debate and Future*

Lev15-16 is the law regarding carcasses that concerns the גר and אזרה "natives" Israelites. Ex 22: 30 states that carcasses should be discarded as dog meat; Deut 14: 21 claims that the *gër* (and the foreigner) may benefit from carcasses; and Lev 17: 15-16 insists that the *gër* who eats of a carcass must undergo purification. In this connection Milgrom asserts "the position of Exodus (JE) is unclear; since it is addressed to the Israelites, it may benefit from carcass. Deuteronomy (D), in its concerns for the underprivileged, including the *ger* (e.g. Deut 10: 18; 24: 17, 19, 20, 21; 26: 12-13) recommends that the carcass be given to the *ger.* Leviticus (H) obsessed with the fear that the land may be polluted by its inhabitants concedes the carcass to the *gër* on condition that he purify himself."[549] Therefore irrespective of ethnicity or status, all are required to obey YHWH's law. Weinfeld explain "failure to do so automatically defiles YHWH's land, and only by "constant physical purification and sanctification" can holiness be restored and maintained."[550] This explain why priests, because of their closer proximity to YHWH's presence, are prohibited from eating the נבלה וטרפה (carcass of torn animals) Lev 22:8. Whereas the same code presume that lay persons, the גר and אזרה to eat a נבלה (Carcass) or טרפה (forbidden food)[551] (Lev 17: 15-16).

In the first case of carcass consumption both text from Exodus and Deuteronomy we find statement that the people are to be holy. This is not repeated in Leviticus 17:15, although 17:15 is clearly correcting these two earlier verses. One does not fine any reference to "being holy" in all of Chapter 17, which is after all the Holiness Code. This leaves a kind of gap in the text which points forward to the framework of the Holiness Code, which starts in chapter 18, although the actual command to be holy only starts to be appeared in chapter 19. Leviticus 17 not the starting point of the Holiness Code since we do not fine any reference to Holiness. Leviticus 17 is the start of the Code and it is the main law, but it is no point of entry.

Secondly, Gleaning is mentioned only rarely in the ancient West Asia texts, which have been discovered, though the information available suggests it was not uncommon. There is an explicit reference in the harvest section of the Sumerian Farmer's Almanac (lines 73-86):

> The gleaners must do not damage; they must not tear apart the sheaves. During your daily harvesting, as in 'days of need', make the earth supply the sustenance of the youth and the gleaners according to their number, (and) let them sleep (in your field) as (in)

Direction, edited by Schectman & Baden, ATHANT 95 (Zurich: Theologischer Verlag Zurich, 2009), 144.

549 Milgrom, *Leviticus...,* 1485.

550 M. Weinfeld, *Deuteronomy and Deuteronomic School,* 226.

551 *BDB,* 383.

the (open) marshland. (If you do so) your god will show everlasting favour.

The first sentence assumes there will be gleaners at harvest time, and sets limits to their activity, while the next two sentences specifically encourage the practice. The harvester is exhorted to leave fallen ears of barley on the ground for needy children and gleaners, and this is considered a charitable deed for which he will receive divine blessing.[552]

Leviticus 19: 9-10 commands the Israelite landowners to leave the remains of the harvest and of the vineyard to the "poor" and to the *gër*. This passage takes up the corresponding prescription is repeated once, in the case of harvest, in Leviticus 23:22. In the majority of passages, however, the *gër* appears in H as a person, who in spite of his foreign origins is nonetheless *economically independent,* as some of the authors correctly remarked. Several passages presuppose, for example, that the *gër* is *wealthy enough to offer animal sacrifice* on his own (Lev 17: 8-9; 22: 18-19; see Num 15:14-16) including burn offerings. Likewise, one passage of the jubilee legislation (Lev 25:47-54) addresses in some detail the case of resident alien who are economically well enough to lend money to Israelites, and may therefore eventually treat them as debt-slaves (Lev 25: 47a). As Levine remarks: "such a representation of the *gër* is a complete novelty and was considered in the former legal traditions-except, significantly, in the context of the curses sanctioned the non-observance of the Deuteronomic legislation (cf. Deut 28: 43-44)."[553]

There is a significant development in the status of alien at the time. The older laws in Exodus and Deuteronomy maintained distinction between aliens and natives; but in Leviticus such distinction is no longer, maintained, equal treatment has been given to aliens and Israelites. The גר is allowed to offer sacrifices and burnt offering. They are equally required with the אזרח to bring it to the entrance of the tent.

In connection with the dietary law we have seen that an animal found death may be eaten by any Israelite, it may not be sold but given to an alien as an act of charity but it may be sold to a foreigner (Deut 14: 2) should be given to the dog (Exod 22:30). In Leviticus the native and aliens are treated equally with regard to the eating of an animal found dead for whoever eats the meat, Israelites or aliens shall be cut off. They shall wash their clothes and bathe

552 According to the interpretation of Samuel Noah Kramer, *The Sumerians: Their History, Culture, and Character* (Chicago, IL: University of Chicago Press, 1963), 108, 341, whose translation I have used above.

553 B. A. Levine, *Leviticus.* JPS Torah Commentary (Philadelphia: Jewish Publication Society, 1989), 180, cf. C. Nihan, "Resident Aliens and Natives in the Holiness Legislation," 116-17.

themselves and remain unclean till the evening and both Israelites and aliens who fail to do this will bear their guild.

But it is not clear whether the inclusion of the גר in the food law is indicates their inclusion in the cultic community. It is possible that without necessary being circumcised or accepted as full members in the cultic community, aliens were expected to follow and conform to the main rules of Israelites society.[554] To love the aliens are expressed as follows:

> When an גר resides with you in your land you shall not תונו (oppress/ suppress) him. The גר who resides with you shall be to you as the citizen among you; you shall love the aliens as yourself, for you were aliens in the land of Egypt; I am the Lord your God (Lev. 19:33, 34).

Inclusion of גר in the community Perdue asserts that: "the most comprehensive and inclusive statement is found in Leviticus 19:33-34, which not only proscribes the mistreatment of the resident alien but also instructs that the marginalized members of the household be treated as a native Israelites and "loved as one self."[555] Thus, Lev 19: 33-34 are used in an inclusive term.

The law requires that an alien who lives among the Israelites should not be oppressed. Here the word used for oppressed is ינה the term is frequently used in connection with the oppression of the poor Israelite by the powerful Israelite,[556] and here its use applies also to a גר. The term ינה (*yanah* seems to connote oppression) in the ideological sense, where as the term לחץ (*lachats* = which is used more in connection with foreigners oppressing Israelites)[557] seems to refer to oppression in the sense of physical ill-treatment. The two verbs are used in the Exodus text but only ינה is used in Leviticus. However, their marriage may not be limited to physical oppression alone; any kind of oppression either of an alien or an Israelite is against the moral will of God.

The development of the law from Exodus 22:21 can be seen in the phrase, "the alien who resides with you shall be to you as citizen among you; you shall love the alien as yourself." The law demands that the alien should be treated

554 This view is supported by G. J. Wenham who claims that while remaining outside the cultic sphere of Israel's community, the aliens were expected to conform to their rules and regulation. *The Book of Leviticus,* 244; Cf. M. Smith, *Palestinian Parties and Politics That Shaped the Old Testament* (New York: Columbia University press, 1971), 93. Christiana Van Houton, *Aliens in Israelite Law...,* 148.

555 Leo G. Perdue, et al., "The Israelite and Early Jewish Family: Summary and Conclusions," *Families in Ancient Israel* (Louiseville, Kentucky: Westminister John Knox Press, 1997), 198.

556 Lev. 19:33; 25:14,17; Deut. 23:17; Jer. 22:3; Ezek. 18:7,12,16; 22:7, 29; 45:8.

557 Exod. 3:9; Jud.2:18; 4:3; 6:9; 10:12; 1 Sam 10:18; 2 Kgs 13:4, 22; Amos 6:14; Jer 30:20; Ps 106:42.

equally as the native-born Israelite. Houten notes that "the demand to treat the alien as the Israelite citizen is not referring to cultic equality, but is speaking of justice at the gate, being paid fair wages, not making immoral demands of the alien or his family and so on."[558] Thus, the law requiring equal treatment speaks of aliens in a new way. In this context the meaning of the word גר has changed quite drastically to the point that its original meaning of a socially and economically dependent person has been superseded.

5.3.2. The Role of Blood in the Kipper-Act: Blood as Symbol of Life and Death

Leviticus 17: 8-9, prohibits other types of sacrifices people might wish to offer somewhere other than the tabernacle area. The wisdom of such a restriction can be quickly gathered from reading the subsequent history of the nation of Israel. Disobedience to command, such as these led to idolatry on practically every high hill in Judah and Israel it was the trap that finally destroyed both the northern and southern Kingdoms. In regards to prohibition Milgrom asserts that "the prohibition applies to the resident alien as much as it does to any Israelite. The reason for this rule is the same as for Israel: to discourage the aliens from sacrificing to pagan gods."[559]

The consequences of (v 10) which prohibits eating, blood, has been recast from the impersonal third person to direct divine address stated twice "I shall set my face against," and "I shall cut off" in order to give it greater rhetorical force. The clue that it has been reworked is that the case is still in the third person singular (v. 10a).[560]

Verses 10-12 find several chiastic patterns:

V.10 Prohibition A

V.11 V.11a Reason

V.11b Institution by Yahweh B

V. 11c Reason

V.12 Repetition of prohibition A

V. 11 the center of the larger chiasm, has its own chiasm. The center and the point of emphasis in 11b Schenker[561] finds a chiasm in the meaning of נפש (*nepes* = life, person).

V.10 person

---

558 Van Houten, *Aliens in Israelite law...,* 142.

559 Milgrom, *Leviticus 17-22: A New Translation with Introduction and Commentary* (New York: Doubleday, 2000), 1463.

560 John E. Hartley, "Leviticus," in *WBC,* Vol. 4 (Dallas, Texas: Word Books, Publisher, 1992), 265-69.

561 Schenker, "Das Zeichen Des Blutes Und Die Gewissheit Der Vergebung Im Alten Testament," *Munchener Theologishe Zeitschrift* 34 (1983), 197-98.

V11a life
V.11b person
V.11c life
V.12 person

Further vv. 10-12 stand at the center of the laws in chap 17. The preceding two laws treat the slaughter of domesticated animals (v. 2-9) and following two laws concerning eating from animals that may not be sacrifice (vv. 13-16).

When these laws are assembled in this speech, reasons were added to encourage compliance with them. These motivations enhance greatly the speech's rhetorical quality. Thus the rhetorical force of this speech is enhanced by taking the audience back to the time of the origin at Sinai as a covenant people through the use of archaic wording, "one who is offering up a whole offering or a sacrifice."[562]

In v.10 just as they are forbidden to worship other gods (vv 8-9), so are they forbidden to ingest blood. The alien is subject to all the prohibitive commandments. Milgrom suggest "another reason for specifying the *gër* is that the non-Israelite world of which he was a part not only lacked a blood prohibition, but savored blood in its diet."[563] In the Holiness retrojection, in the wilderness the "landless" *gër* would have been the aliens who attached themselves to Israel when they left Israel (Ex 12: 38, 48; Num 11: 4; Cf. Lev 24: 10).

Why is there so strong prohibition? Two explanations are given in this text. The first is for the life of a creature is in the blood: the word translated "life" is נפש (nepes), which has a wide assortment of meanings, such as "throat," "soul," "appetite," "life" and "person."[564] The word translated "creature" is בשר (*basar* =flesh) which also has a wide range of meaning, including "flesh," "body," "the male reproductive organ," and "creature."[565]

Leviticus 17: 13-14 wild animals can be killed away from the tabernacle, but the blood prohibition still applies. Wild animals are not subject to being considered for sacrifices at the altar; therefore, it does not matter where they are butchered. However, they must be thoroughly drained of all blood because the reasons cited in v.11 still holds. One reason is repeated in v.14 "because the life of every creature is its blood" (occurring twice in this verse).

---

562 John E. Hartley, "Leviticus," 209.

563 Milgrom, "Leviticus"... 1470. Leviticus 17:10-12, deals with the prohibition on eating blood. Again, the resident alien is as much obligated to keep this law as is the Israelite. This rule has been in force ever since God allowed Noah to eat meat; it was on the condition that he would thoroughly drain the animals' blood before eating it (cf. Gen 9: 4). This is not the only place where this law reappears (see Lev 7:26-27; Deut 12: 16, 23; 15: 23; 1 Sam 14: 32-44).

564 *BDB,* 659.

565 Kaiser, *The Book of Leviticus...,* 1119. Cf. Noth, *Leviticus...,* 132.

Anything that is found dead, is killed by another animal or expires naturally is not to be eaten, since its blood would have coagulated in its veins and arteries and the one who ate that meat would be guilty of violating life itself. Only strangers and resident aliens are allowed to eat such meat (Deut 14: 21) but Israelites and Proselytes are to refrain from doing so.[566] The rule does not contradict the rule in Leviticus but adds a provision not mentioned in Leviticus. Both texts agree that Israelite should not eat any meat in the category mentioned here.

In conclusion, the researcher would like to view the work of at least two scholars who have argued differently, namely Milgrom and Douglas. Both of them have attempted to attribute theological value of P, especially dealing with Leviticus 11. Milgrom places the blood prohibition first. Not only is it the most important of the dietary laws in the Bible, seen as binding on all humanity, but it offers the clearest example of what he wishes to prove, for its rational is stated in the biblical text several times over (Gen 9: 4; Lev 17: 11, 14; Deut 12: 23): "the blood is the life" of the animals. The implicit message is "Mankind has the right to nourishment, not to life."[567] Milgrom interprets the prohibition in the context of priestly narrative of creation and flood, in which human beings are intended at the start of the vegetarian (Gen 1: 29), but after the flood are given the concession of animal food, but only on condition that they do not eat the blood (Gen 9: 3-4); and he notes that in Israel's case according to H (Lev 7: 3-4), there is the further condition that the domestic animals must be brought to the sanctuary for sacrifice. If this is not done, the act is equavelent to murder, as Lev 17: 4b distinctly states. Milgrom includes a detail argument,[568] which need not detain us, that the atonement stated in v.11 to be worked by the blood is for the crime of killing the animal itself.[569]

Milgrom most extensive exposition of his position can be found in his commentary on Leviticus. Milgrom thus argues that the Priestly authors of Leviticus at some stage attempted to limit the number of animals that could be eaten by the Israelites. This was their purpose with this law and in order to do that they came up with two criteria. Milgrom understands, one could thus describe the Priest as predecessors of today's "green movement." They attempt to protect certain animals from ending up on Israelites table.[570]

---

566 Kaiser, *The Book of Leviticus...,* 1120.

567 Milgrom, *Leviticus 1-16,* in The Anchor Bible (Doubleday, 1991), 713.

568 J. Milgrom, "A Prolegomenon to Leviticus 17:11," JSOT (1971): 149-156.

569 Cf. Walter J. Houston, "Towards an Integrated Reading of the Dietary Laws of Leviticus," edited by Rolf Rendtorff and Robert A. Kugler, in *The Book of Leviticus Composition and Reception* (Leiden, Boston: Brill, 2003), 147-48.

570 Esias E. Meyer, "Respect for Animal life in the Book of Leviticus. How Green were the Priestly Authors? *Old Testament Essay* 24/1 (2011), 142-158. (Hereby OTE.).

Douglas in her book *Leviticus as Literature* her work of 1999 argued that the whole of Leviticus could be projected on the grand plan of the tabernacle. This is a kind of literature structure superimposed into the whole book. This is similar to what she proposed in 1993.[571]

With regard to land animals, Douglas starts off by drawing attention to the fact that one point is never made in Leviticus, namely "what is bad for the health of the body to eat any of the forbidden animals."[572] Like Milgrom she is thus not a supporter of the "hygienic" theory. She continues her discussion on this animals by questioning the common notion of the meat of the forbidden animals is "abominable, detestable, or unedifying, in one way or another."[573] She then said: "Taking account of the full context, which is the rest of the Pentateuch, it would be difficult to overlook one biblical principle: God is compassionate for all living things; not only to the humans, is he good to his entire creature."[574]

While dealing with the carcass of the death animals she asserts: "in effect the rule against touching a death animal protects it in its lifetime. Since its carcass cannot be skinned or dismembered, most of the ways in which it could be exploited are ruled out, so it is not worth breeding, hunting, or trapping.... The rule is a comprehensive command to respect the dead body of every land animals.[575] She classified unclean ought to be "an advantage for the survival of the species."[576] This is rather optimistic statement in the light of the penalties for such transgression.

Douglas concludes with a plea that the term "unclean" should not be understood as pejoratively as usual: "Unclean is not a term of psychological horror and disgust; it is a technical term for the cult, as commentators has often pointed out. To import feelings into the translation falsifies, and creates more puzzles."[577] Both, Milgrom and Douglas thus offer similar arguments to the effect that the objective of these laws was to protect animals. Milgrom argued that the priestly author set out to limit the amount of meat consume by Israelites and Douglas similarly thinks that for an animals to be on either the טמא (*tama* = impure) or שקץ (*saqash* = moving) she eventually proposes that a

571 Mary Douglas, "The forbidden animals in Leviticus," *JSOT* 59 (1993): 3-23.

572 Mary Douglas, *Leviticus as Literature* (Oxford: University Press, 1989), 134.

573 Douglas, *Leviticus as Literature...,* 135.

574 Douglas, *Leviticus as Literature...,* 135. Her argument in the subsequent two chapters then amounts to this: the categories of "impure" for land animals and "abomination" for the other creatures do not necessarily have the pejorative connotations which modern-day readers attribute to them. These classifications should rather be seen as attempts to *protect* these creatures.

575 Douglas, *Leviticus as Literature...,* 141.

576 Douglas, *Leviticus as Literature...,* 142.

577 Douglas, *Leviticus as Literature...,* 151.

more neutral translation such as "to shun" should rather be used.[578] This would have been to the advantage of that species. Both of them it sounds as if the Priestly authors were early conservationist who attempted to protect certain species.

5.3.3. The Nature of the Blasphemer's Transgression

Lev 24:16, 22, both this passage dealing with alien who blasphemes against the name of God. The narrative concerning blasphemes extends the ideal of a sanctified Israelite community living under God's rule, symbolized within Lev 24:1-9, to everyday life within the Israelite community. Milgrom recognizes that an analysis of Lev. 24 must "answer two nettling question: The placement of this anomalous chapter, and the relationship between two parts vv.1-9 and vv.10-23."[579] He attempts to answer the first question by claiming that there is no meaningful relationship between vv.1-9 and vv. 10-23.[580] Trevaskis propose an alternative explanation for the position of Lev 24: 10-23 which admits thematic coherence between the two parts of the Lev 24. The narrative concerning the blasphemer extends the ideal of the sanctified Israelite community living under God's rule, symbolized within Lev 24: 1-9, of everyday life within the Israelite community.[581]

Most scholars argue that the tension within the narrative surrounds the blasphemer's mixed pedigree. Though it remains unclear, they acknowledge that these references to this mixed ethnicity provide a clue to the relationship between the narrative (vv 10-12, 23) and the legal material it frames in (vv.13-22).

According to Leuchter, "Lev 24:10-23 is the lone narrative in the otherwise exclusively legislative Holiness Code (H; Leviticus 17-26) about a man mixed ancestry who engages in an act of blasphemy and received punishment after Moses consult with YHWH regarding his blasphemous act."[582] They propose that this "mixed lineage" introduces a note of ambiguity

578 Douglas, *Leviticus as Literature...,* 166-69. In this regard she differs from *Milgrom Leviticus 1-16...,*656. His understanding to the word שִׁקֵּץ is closer to the traditional understanding. Doughlas interpretation of her argument is not very convincing.

579 J. Milgrom, *Leviticus 23-27*: *A New Translation with Introduction and Commentary* (New York: Doubleday, 2000), 2081.

580 Milgrom, *Leviticus 23-2,* 2082.

581 Leigh M. Trevaskis, "The purpose of Leviticus 24 within its Literary context," *Vetus Testamentum* 59 (2009), 307.

582 Mark Leuchter, "The Ambiguous Details in the Blasphemer Narrative: Source and Redaction in Leviticus 24:10-23," *JBL* 130/3 (2011): 431-450. Modern researcher dealing with the formation of the Pentateuch distinguishes between Holiness Code and Priestly Code in and beyond the Book of Leviticus, though there is lack of agreement regarding the purpose and role of Holiness in relation to other collection of pentateuchal

concerning the relationship of "sojourners" (gër) and the law. This give rise to the "rules of talion" which confirm that the jurisdiction of the law extends to the "sojourner." The persuasiveness of this interpretation is increase when it is [583]observed that the "rules of talion" begin and end with references to an "aliens" (gër vv. 16, 22).

In the second part the chiastically arranged laws in Lev 24: 17-21 (beginning and closing with parallel formulae in v.16 and 22) preserve and indeed highlight this understanding:[584]

24: 16	A reference to resident alien and native Israelite. (כגר כאזרח)
24: 17	B homicide (יכה כל נפש אדם)
24:18	C destruction of animals' property (ומכה נפש־בהמה)
24: 19-20	D personal injury/defacement (ואיש כי־יתן מום בעמיתו)
24: 21a	C destruction of animals' property (ומכה בהמה)
24: 21b	B homicide (ומכה אדם)
24: 22	A reference to resident alien and native Israelite (כגר־כאזרח)

The ruling of for blaspheme and homicide contain equal treatment for aliens and the Israelites. Both the RSV and NRSV render 'law' for משפט (*mishpath*) implying thereby equal legal status. "You shall have one משפט (*mishpath* = judgment) for the alien and for the citizens". Other version renders standard and Penalty.

The rendering of 'one judgement or penalty or standard' is more appropriate for משפט (*mishpath*) than 'law' because the passage does not seems to speak about having one law in legal sense, but equal judgement/punishment. This may also relate to the prohibition to have 'partiality' in judgement (cf. Exodus 23:3. Lev. 19:15). Both the alien and the native Israelites should be given the same punishment when they blaspheme God. They are put on equal

---

law. Cf. Israel Knohl, *The Sanctuary of Silence*... 124-98. Cf. Also Baruch A. Levine, "Leviticus: Its Literary History and Location in Biblical Literature," in *The Book of Leviticus: Composition and Reception,* edited by Rolf Rendtorff and Robert A. Kugler, VT Supt 93 (Leiden, Boston: Brill, 2003), 21-22.

583 Leigh M. Trevaskis, "The purpose of Leviticus 24," 295-312.

584 The chiasmus in Lev. 24:10-23 and its literary effects has long been established. For example, see Michael Fishbane, *Biblical Interpretation in Ancient Israel* (Oxford: Clarendon, 1985), 101; see Milgrom, *Leviticus,* 3:2128-30, Wenham, *Leviticus,* 311-12. For the role of diminishing length of syntactical unit towards the centre of the chiasmus in bringing focus to the formula, see Mark Leuchter has demonstrated the role of the chiasmus in the assimilation of blasphemy to the register of the physical injuries in Lev 24:10-23 "The Ambiguous details in the Blasphemy narrative… 431-50 (443). Within this scheme the choice of קלל for the act of verbal denigration, with its connotation of physical violence (e.g. Gen 8:21; Lev. 19:14; 2 Sam 16:7), instead of the expected חלל ('to desecrate') is apt.

footing in punishment. The priestly gives the גר and Israelites equal legal status. This is found in connection with the Passover legislation.

The symmetry and balance of this structure reinforces the points made explicitly in the text, namely, that in these cases the same penalty must be applied to both resident alien and native Israelite (vv. 16, 22) and that in all cases the punishment must match the offence: *If a man injures his fellow citizen, whatever he did must be done to him* (v. 19).

5.3.4. Ideological and Ethical Reflections on Leviticus 25

Leviticus 25 is a composition consisting of two halves related in content but stylistically inconsistence. Verses 2-22 ('A') is mainly in the style of a decree: it mandates the community to take certain measures which have a universal effect. Verses 23-55 ('B'), on the other hand, is set out as a series of laws (so called casuistic laws), detailing the way in which individual should behave in particular situations.

Both these types of material are paralleled in the ancient West Asia. To take a later type first, in Mesopotamia not only legal codes such as Hammurabi's but also working legal documents, case records, contracts, wills, etc., are preserved in great quantity, and it is recognized that rarely if ever do the working documents refer to the codes. Jackson has argued that the same applies to the way in which the biblical codes work.[585] Where instructions are given specifically to Judges (e.g. Deut 16:18-19), they are not told to apply a written code.

Mesopotamian records also include administrative decrees, such as the decrees known as *misarum* decrees of equity. *Misrum* means equity and justice, and it is the process by which law is made to function uniformly. This was an institution known in Mesopotamia during the Old Babylonian period, but, probably, going back to the later period of the early dynasty. This was meant for the kings to promote equity and justice. It was concerned mainly with the release of debts, reversion of land holdings to their original owners, and the release of slaves taken as pledge on debts.[586] In this connection Weindfeld asserts: "this typically provides for the remission of debts, the release of slaves, the return of security for debts, and the remission of taxes: in a word, everything provided for by the Jubiles law."[587] On the other hand there are two

585 B. S. Jackson, "Ideas of Law and Legal Administration: A Semiotic Approach," in *The World of Ancient Israel,* edited by R. E. Clements (Cambridge: Cambridge University Press, 1989), 187-88.

586 Cited by Gnana Robinson, *The Origin and Development of the Old Testament Sabbath: A Comprehensive Exegetical Approach* (UTC, Bangalore: ISPCK, Delhi, 1998), 109-110.

587 M. Weindfeld, Social *Justice in Ancient Israel and in the Ancient Near East* (Jerusalem: Magnes/Minneapolis: Fortress, 1998). It largely devoted to detailed comparison between these decrees and the biblical law of social justice.

major differences between the jubilee law and the *misarum* decrees. The first is obvious and has frequently been observed. The *misarum* decree was issued unexpectedly, at irregular intervals, to be applied immediately. No one could anticipate such a decree and discount it. By contrast, the jubilee is ordained to occur at regular intervals which can be calculated. The owners of property and credit can allow for it in advance, and abolish its effect.

5.3.5. Subject and Object of the Law

To whom, then these words addressed, and whom do they concern? Who is expected to implement them, or at least to listen to them, and who may be affected by them? The formal audience here (v. 2) is the Israelites. It is Israel that must proclaim the jubilee, and it is the whole people that must, each individually, return to their native place and possess once more their allotted fields. It is however, sufficiently clear that once we get down to details it is only the secure possessors of property who are in a position to ensure that the law is obeyed.

> If your brothers become יָמוּךְ (*yamuk* = poor) and stretches out his hands towards you, you shall support him; he shall live with you as a גר (*gër*=alien) and as a תושב (*toshab*=sojourn). You shall not take from him נשך (*neshek*= interest) and תרבִית (*tarbiyth* = profit), but you shall fear your God; let your brother live with you. You shall not give to him your money at interest; you shall not give your food at a profit. I am Yahweh your God, who brought you out of the land of Egypt, to give you the land of Canaan, to be your God (Lev 25:35-38, cf. Ex 22:25, Deut 23:19-20).

In (Lev 25: 25, 35, 39, and 47) the case that addressee, the 'you' who is the subject of the law, is the secure proprietor who is in a position to help his 'brother' who had fallen on evil days.[588] The language of 'brotherhood is important. The compassionate actions mandated in this section were the prime responsibility of the family, 'your brother' actually means 'your fellow-Israelites', for 'your brothers' in 25:46 is explained as 'the Israelites'; and that is clear what the similar language in Deuteronomy means. But there is a tension in the use of this motif;[589] the law uses language demanding in principle that

588 The Hebrew term for 'poor' is seldom used in the Holiness Code, this is not because there are no 'poor,' but the term 'poor' has become more or less synonymous with 'brother.' This also implies that the 'poor' addressed in the Holiness Code is a fellow Israelite. 'Brother' is a typical Deuteronomic expression for the 'poor' and there is a renewal emphasis in this legislation that the 'poor' is a 'brother.'

589 W. J. Houtson, "Open your Hand to your Needy Brother:" Ideology and Moral formation in Deut 15:1-18," in *The Bible in Ethics,* edited by John Rogerson, Margaret Davies and M. Daniel Carroll R (Sheffield: Academic Press, 1995), 304.

people treat each other as equals, as 'brothers,' but at the same time envisages a situation of inequality, which may be expected to continue until the jubilee: this is particularly clear in vv. 35 and 40.

But the jubilee, in theory offers a term to the situation of inequality. The chapter does not say with Deuteronomy 15:11 that 'the poor will not cease from the land'; for the return of each man to his *'ahuzza,* his ancestry holding (v. 41) marks the end of his state of need which required the sale of the land or of himself (vv. 28, 40, 54). As Noth rightly observed: "Since the land was ultimately Yahweh who leased out to them as he willed, Israelites were not allowed to sell or dispose of the land as if his individual property. In this regard, the Israelites were merely in the position of *gerim* and *toshabhim* "who could be entrusted only with the use of something without establishing a claim to ownership."[590] Division of YHWH's people into sellers and buyers, patrons and clients, masters and servants marks the period between jubilee; at the jubilee each one return, takes up his holding and the nation once more becomes equal. At that point the poor cease from the land.

According to Habel, "the society is not truly egalitarian in the modern sense of the word. Labourers, servants, immigrants and urbanites are excluded from gaining the same level of social standing as landholding peasants and priest… the rural workers at the bottom of the order remain dependent on the landed peasant farmers."[591] But while the text is perfectly explicit on the subject of foreign slaves and the *gerim,* the resident aliens, who have no right to redeemed, nor do they posses *'ahuzza,* so that they have nowhere to return to at the jubilee, it does not admit the existence of rural Israelite workers without an ancestral holding. In the real world there may have been a class of landless labourers and permanent slaves who could show no connection with any ancestral land.

On the other hand, it is clear as could be that foreigner and *gerim*, though not a class, since they may include masters as well as slaves, are yet a group without any rights of the trueborn Israelite. They may be enslaved in perpetuity and worked as slaves, whatever precisely that may mean. We may reasonably suppose that they include people who had lived in Judah for generations and knew no other home. We certainly cannot speak of a truly egalitarian society in such condition. It is also clear enough that even among Israelites this justice only applies between adult males, who are the possessors of land. Women and children are entirely invisible. Wright argues: "that the adult male subject of the law is not functioning as an individual but as a family head and the land to which he returns serves as the livelihood for an entire family unit including all

590 M. Noth, *Leviticus* OLT (Philadelphia: Westminster Press, 1965). 189.

591 Norman. Habel, *The Land is Mine: Six Biblical Land Ideologies* (Minneapolis: fortress, 1995), 112.

his dependants."[592] In Nehemiah 5:5 it is read that the Israelite peasant would sell his children, particularly his daughters, into slavery before he would abandon his land.

> The background for this self-description as *gerim,* may be sought in the political situation of Palestine during the post-exilic period. Under the Persian rule Israel became *gerim* in its own land; foreigners now possess their land as said in Nehemiah 9:36-37.
>
> Here we are slave to this day, slaves in the land that you gave to our ancestors to enjoy its fruit and its good gifts. Its rich yield goes to the kings whom you have set over us because of our sins; they have power also over our bodies and over our livestock at their pleasure, and we are in great distress.

This situation has created in them a sense of foreignness in their own land and made them to call themselves *gerim* under the direct protection of Yahweh. They transfer their hopes, formerly pinned on the land, now directly to Yahweh. This dependence on God empowered them to overcome the uncertainties of their condition.

Each family has its own inheritance, which may not be sold or bought, "in perpetuity." Undergirding the principal of a family's right to its inheritance stands the theology that God himself holds title to the land. The people are "resident aliens" or "tenants" with God. The phrase "with me" may carry the meaning "under my protection."[593] To be Yahweh's *gerim* means to have a right to dwell on his land. יִמְּדִי (*yamdi* = with me) probably implies God's presence with them and therefore the Israelite are under his protection. Just as an alien who is the guest of an Israelite comes under the protection. The close relationship between *Yahweh* and the families in Israel as well as the security that this great God offers them is stressed here. Fager rightly notes: "the very fact that Yahweh owned the land called for the distribution of the land that reflected the divine purpose for the people, namely, a people who had access to the means of survival so that they were dependent upon God alone and not upon the whim of a few wealthy humans."[594] The divine owner declares that every property given as an inheritance to the Israelites families under the covenant carries a "right of redemption." Or to say it another way, no land held by an Israelite is to be exempted from the "right of redemption." No legal

592 C. J. H. Wright, *God's People in God's Land: Family, Land and Property in the Old Testament* (Grand Rapids: Eerdmands/Exeter: Paternoster, 1990), 124-125.

593 H. D. Preuss, "אֵת 'eth; עִם 'im," in *TDOT*, Vol. 1 (Grand Rapids, Michigan: William B. Eerdmans Publishing Company, 1974), 450.

594 J. A. Fager, *Land Tenure and the Biblical Jubilee, Uncovering Hebrew Ethics through the Sociology of Knowledge,* JSOT Suppl Series 155 (Sheffield: JSOT Press, 1993), 110.

loopholes are to be devised to circumvent the intention of this law.[595] Thus, the land may be redeemed either by the original owner or his near relatives (go'el) may redeem it for him, so that he might return to his property if he had no sufficient amount of money to redeem it, the land remains to the one who brought it until it is released in the year of Jubilee without any payment (Lev 25:25, 28).[596] In this way, the law protects a poor man from permanent alienation of his ancestor's land.

Today contemporary readers are often upset by the ways in which Israel's theology created distinction between Israelites and non-Israelites. At the same time, some would applaud P's requirement that resident aliens observe certain basic Israelite purity rules. Yet even today, cultural inclusion regularly involves gaining rights within the new group but also added responsibilities. Today many countries accept resident alien, although they are not fully citizen and lack certain rights. It is intellectually incoherent to argue that resident aliens, whether living today or in antiquity, be treated like native while at the same time advocating that it is wrong to impose upon them any legal or cultural norms stemming from the new society in which they now reside.

5.3.6. Who Benefits from the Jubilee?

The above statements clarify whose justice the jubilee is. The group that would clearly benefit from the implementation of the measure, if it were ever been implemented, would be the peasantry, the landholding families of Israelite villages. It would not benefit those without recognized title to land: those identified in the text as 'the aliens residing with you' (v. 45). We have no means of knowing what proportion of the population these were, but it was clearly not negligible, in view of the frequency with which the *ger* is mentioned so frequently as exploiting the peasant and seeking to gain control of his land and his person.

The idea that the fifty years of the jubilee are related to the fifty years of exile and that the law's object is to legitimate the repossession of Judah by the exile. As Habel points out that in its support that 'the sequel in chapter 26 promotes 'the myth of the land' which enjoys its Sabbaths'[597] The context is concerned with impoverishment, not with deportation, and the ancient West parallel also underlining the economic context of measures of this kind.

595 J. E. Harley, *Leviticus...* 437.

596 M. Weinfeld, "Sabbatical Year and Jubilee in the Pentateuch laws and their Ancient Near Eastern Background," in *The Law in the Bible and its Environment,* edited by T. Veijola (Gottingen: Vandenhoeck Ruprecht, 1990), 61.

597 Habel, *The Land is Mine: Six Biblical Land Ideologies,* 113; Cf B. A. Levine, *Leviticus...* 274.

5.3.7. The World of the Text and Social Reality

The question that arises is was the law actually implemented? Or they have been just 'visionary' as some suggested? There are three social groups, none of which are classes: the land holding Israelites, the *gerim*, and the Levites. Poverty and landlessness, which is the motive of the whole system, is in this text not a condition, not a state of life, but a process, an event: 'If your brother becomes impoverished.' It is a temporary misfortune of individuals which will last at most fifty years. None of the Hebrew nouns or adjectives meaning 'poor' appears in the chapter unlike the text we have seen in Exodus and Deuteronomy.

Descriptive texts on the agrarian situation, for example Nehemiah 5, suggest the existence of a relatively small ruling class, which Nehemiah calls 'the nobles and the officers,' who were exploiting the mass of the peasantry who were falling into debt. And on the other hand Hebrew writers generally take for granted that even small proprietor were able to draw for labour on a pool of landless people, men and women, by no means all of whom were *gerim,* whether as slaves or day-labourers at minimum wages.

In the previous chapter, we have categorize אזרח (native) and גר (resident alien) are fluid and contingent upon the ideological interests of the users of these terms. To portray Israel as resident aliens in Egypt and as indigenous in Canaan may suit an ideology that seeks to promote Israel's lack of roots in Egypt and its claim to ownership of Canaan, but the ideology trips over its inherent contradictions, not least with a tradition of origin in Mesopotomia.

The regulation regarding the sale of property a debt-slavery in Lev 25 offer a particular interesting view of how Leviticus further understand the status of the resident alien and the natives in relation to the exodus from Egypt. The chapter contains references to a number of socio-economic strata of society: from the lowest to the highest strata, one finds references to slaves עבדים ('*ebedyim*=slaves) both עבד ('*ebed* = male-servant) and אמה ('*amah* = maid-servant, Lev 25:6, 39, 42, 44), then the שׂכיר (*sakiyr*= hired-servant) and תושׁב (*toshab*=sojourn), 25:6, 23,35,40,50,53), then the גר (*gër*= resident alien, 25:23,35,47), and finally, the land holders, indicated by references to their אחזה (*'achuzzah* = inalienable property, 25:10,13,24,25,27,28,32,33,34,41,45,46).[598] Over-lapping with this list are references to categories of kinship or kin immediacy, such as אח ('*ach* = brother or close relatives, 25:25, 35, 36, 39, 46, 47, 48), and עמית (*'amiyth* = relative or associate, 25:14, 15, 17).

These rules of inalienable property apply to the landholding Israelite alone. While an Israelite may out of need be forced to sell his property and so take on the status of a resident alien, or a tenant or seasonal worker, such as

598 Interestingly, the term אזרח ('native') is not used in this chapter.

situation is not viewed as permanent (25:25-28). While an Israelite out of need similarly sell himself/themselves into indentured servitude, again this situation is not seen as permanent (25:39-41). In contrast, slaves taken by Israel from the surrounding nations, or from the resident aliens born in their midst, are considered slaves in perpetuity and may be inherited in the same way as the family's landholdings (25:44-46). In contradictory view mentioned above Greifenhagen remarks: "the attempt earlier in Leviticus to mandate the equal treatment of resident aliens here breaks down. The contradiction is especially evident if one compares the earlier invocation of Egypt to justify the equal treatment of resident aliens ('love the resident alien as yourself, for you were resident aliens in Egypt', 19:34) with the invocation of Egypt here to justify the differential treatment of the Israelite and the resident alien. The kinship group of the son of Israel (25:46) is immune from permanent enslavement because YHWH claims, 'they are my slaves, whom I brought out from the land of Egypt; therefore they will not be sold as slaves are sold' (25:42 see also 25:55)."[599]

Thus Leviticus 25 presents tensions both internal to the chapter and externally with previous material in the scroll. Internally, the prohibition against charging interest or profiteering from one's kin which is found in Leviticus 25:35-38:

> If your brother becomes poor (ימוך) and stretches out his hands towards you, you shall support him; he shall live with you as a גר and as a תושב. You shall not take from him interest (נשך) and profit (תרבית), but you shall fear your God; let your brother live with you. You shall not give to him your money at interest; you shall not give your food at a profit. I am Yahweh your God, who brought you out of the land of Egypt, to give you the land of Canaan, to be your God.[600]

According to Bergsma, the comparison between the poor Israelite and the "resident alien" is appropriate, because at this stage in the Israelite's progressive impoverishment, he has lost house and land. Without claim to any real property, his socio-economic is quite analogous to that of "resident alien." Both are landless, vulnerable members of society."[601] Porter remarks that in

599 Greifenhagen, *Egypt on the Pentateuch's Ideological Map...,* 193.

600 R. Lianhnuni, *Legal protection for the Poor in Ancient Israel and its significance for Mizo Society* (D.Th Dissertation, 1995), 128.

601 John Sietze Bergsma, *The Jubilee from Leviticus to Qumran,* Supl to Vetus Testamentum Vol. 15 (Leiden, Boston: Brill, 2007), 98.

using 'brother' instead of 'poor' the strength of the concept of family and its common possessions", is seen.[602]

The Phrase "he shall live with you as a גר (*gër* = resident alien) and a תושב (*toshab* = sojourn) is difficult to explain. It probably means like the גר and a תושב the poor brother has to earn his living by trade or daily labour as he stands in more or less similar economic situation.[603]Schenkar question "what did these migrants receive as a loan without interest? Some capital and food are found in (Lev 25:37). And what did they give in return for the permission given them to sojourn in a land which did not belong to them? They work for their hosts. The *gerim* are often mentioned among the labour force, for example, in the Decalogue (Ex 20:10; Deut 5:14). Jacob worked for Laban (Gen 29:15); the Israelites did service in *Corvee* in Egypt for the country and the King. Leviticus 25:40 mentioned the תושב, alongside the hired man (שכיר) since both worked for another man, one for wages and the other for permission to stay in the country, their work being a kind of residence tax. [604] Thus, Leviticus 25:35-38 constitute a special protection for such migrants against exploitation.

Despite the constant complaints against the utopianism of the chapter, attention has rarely given to this truly utopian features as it is surely is. A utopia is a fictive world, particularly a fictive social world. If the jubilee regulation is believed unlikely to work in a real society, which does not make it part of a utopia unless the society in which it does work is also described: there are plenty of unworkable regulations in real societies. Leviticus 25 at least knows that people get poor, fall into debt, and want to sell up, for instance, it is uncertain how far the legislation about the Sabbath year (Lev 25:1-7) and the year of jubilee (Lev 25:8-17, 27:24ff) which were aimed to helping the poor were put into practice. It is certain that the sabbatical year was observed (cf. Ex 23:11). In the time Ezra (Neh 10:31) the people covenanted to forgo the crops of the seventh year and to cancel all debts. Josephus remarks "Caius Caesar, imperator the second time, had ordained, that all the country of the Jews, excepting Joppa, do pay a tribute yearly for the city Jerusalem, excepting the seventh, which they called the Sabbatical

602 Porter, *Leviticus A Commentary,* (Cambridge, 1976), 205.

603 Patrick, *Old Testament Law…,* 184.

604 Adrian Schenkar, "The Biblical Legislation on the Release of Slaves: the Road from Exodus to Leviticus," *JSOT* 78 (1998): 31. Cf. F.Rachel Magdalene and Cornelia Wunsch, "Slavery between Judah and Babylon: The Exilic Experience." *Slaves and Households in the Near East*, edited by Laura Culbertson (Chicago: Illinois, 2011), 119. According to him some of these passages, such as those that prohibit making a Hebrew a chattel slave, the Jubilee Year release, and not returning runaway slaves to their masters, seek to change some aspect of the practice of slavery in the greater ancient Near East by softening certain usual practices.

Year, because thereon they neither receive the fruits of their trees, nor do they sow their land."[605] Snaith[606] states that Josephus testifies to the observance of sabbatical year at the time of Alexander, the great and also during the times of Hasomoneans and Herods.

It is more questionable whether the regulation about the Sabbath year were observed in the context in which it was written and whether it did much for the poor even where it was practiced. As for the year of Jubilee, scholars are skeptical about the implementation. It probably remained a dead letter, a 'utopian law'[607] or a "utopian ideal" that was never designed for observation.[608]A study of Near Eastern laws reveal that there are possible parallels for such Israelite institutions as the Sabbath year and the Jubilee year which regarded as purely utopian construct.[609] The Near Eastern parallel neither explicates the actual functioning of this institution. Therefore, as Tucker[610] asserts whether laws always and everywhere functioned in the way they are presented is a question for critical analysis. However, direct evidence to look to the decisions rendered in the juridical context is very much limited. In an attempt to solve this problem contemporary approach to biblical past has made use ethnographic research as a vital source for examining actual social condition of people.

---

605 Flavius Josephus, *Josephus Complete Works,* translated by William Whiston (Grand Rapids, MI: kregel, 1960), 541.

606 N. H. Snaith, eds., *Leviticus and Numbers,* The Century Bible (London: Thomas and Nelson & Sons Ltd., 1967), 161. Conrad Boerma noted that according to Flavius Josephus, who lived in the second half of the first century C.E., the Sabbath year was observed. How strictly it was observed varied from one place to another, but even the Greek and Roman authentic took it into account. Alexander the Great granted the Jew exemption from taxes every seventh year and Julius Ceasar did the same thing. However, soon after the destruction of the second temple (70 C.E) the law proved impracticable. Cited by Conrad Boerman, *Richman Poor Man and the Bible* (London: SCM, 1979), 33-34 but does not give the reference.

607 Conrad Boerman, *Richman Poor Man and the Bible,* 34.

608 John E. Harley, "Leviticus," in WBC 4 (Texas: Word Books Publisher, 1992), 434. G. J. Wenham, *Leviticus.* Had the Jubilee been observed, such exploitation of the poor as seen in (Is 5:8 and Am 2:6) would have been checked, p. 317. They as a social institution the Jubilee year remained an ideal which was rarely, if ever realized; N. H. Snaith, *Leviticus and Numbers…*, 162.

609 J. J. M. Roberts, "Ancient Near Eastern Environments," in *The Hebrew Bible and its Modern Interpreters,* edited by D. A. Knight & Gene M. Tucker (Chico, California: Scholar press, 1985), 92.

610 Gene M. Tucker, "The Law in the Eight Century prophet," in *Canon Theology and Old Testament Interpreter,* edited by G. M. Tucker et. al (Philadelphia: Fortress, 1988), 212.

5.3.8. The Key Values

The key values by which the whole system is guided, the researcher suggest:

a. The proper ordering of society is to be found in the past. In this belief Leviticus is at one with the ancient West Asia generally. When the Israelites entered Canaan, they received just allocations of land; but the misfortunes of some and the advantage taken by others have led inevitably to the loss of original just ordering. The task of the lawgiver is to ensure that this original justice is restored.

b. The system values the attachment of the rural population to the land and not just of the population generally to the land in general, but to this man or family to this piece of ground. "Everyone shall return to his own possession." The Israelites were time and again reminded of the fact that it is Yahweh who gives them the land[611] and every tribe is allotted a portion of Land by divine degree (Num 32, Josh 13ff) and the Israelite can sell the portion of land that belong to him by this degree. In 1 Kings 21:3 Naboth said to Ahab, "The Lord forbids that I should give you my ancestral inheritance." This is response to Naboth refusal to Ahab's offer of another vineyard better than his own, because the land belonged to his ancestor. No one should underestimate the strength of this sentiment in any peasant population.

According to Weinfeld he argues that the jubilee has its origin in a communal system of landholding,[612]there is no trace of this in the text. This takes individual landholding, presumably through inheritance. By valuing the individual's possession of his own plot on behalf of his family is not the same thing as believing that the individual has an indefeasible property right, including the right of alienation that the community ought not to interfere with. On the contrary, the text denies this in its theory of divine ownership, and specifically denies that anyone can acquire property rights over land other than the ancestral land.

c. It is in keeping with the particularity of this attachment Anthony D. Smith viewed as: "the unique and indispensable setting of events and experiences that moulded the community."[613] In practice, this connection is achieved by:

> ...attaching specific memories of 'our ancestors' and forebears, particularly if they are saintly or heroic, to particular stretches of territory. For example, leaders and educators of the community may locate the deeds

611 Gen 15: 7;17:8; 24:7; Ex 6:4; Lev 20: 24; 25: 2, 38; Deut 5:16.

612 M. Weindfeld, Social *Justice in Ancient Israel and in the Ancient Near East...,* 178.

613 Anthony D. Smith, *Chosen People* (Oxford: Oxford University press, 2003), 134-35

> of heroes and great men at specific sites, 'poetic space' eulogized in the chronicles and ballads recited down the generations, thereby binding their descendants to a distinct landscape lie the 'sites of memory;' the fields of battle, the monuments to the fallen, the places of peace treaties, the temples of priests, the last resting places of saints and heroes, the sacred groves of spirit and gods who guards of land.[614]

Smith draws special attention to the burial sites of ancestor, which make the land a witness to the survival of the community.[615] The researcher has discussed this issue in Chapter 2.

5.4. Aliens in the Post-Exilic Priestly Addition (4th Cent B.C.E)

One of the first consequences of the later reworking of the Pentateuch in connection with a Pentateuch redaction was that the scribes had to find a way to integrate the *gerim* into the very most Israelite ritual, the rituals of Passover. According to the expansion of the Priestly Code (P) in Genesis 17:9-14, circumcision was the distinguishing mark of those who were integrated into the covenantal religious rights of the heirs of Abraham. Consequently, Exodus 12:48-49 requires circumcision for those *gerim* who want to share the Passover ritual. The text creates the possibility of an integration of the *gerim*.[616]

Secondly Numbers 9:14b "you shall have one statute (sacral law) for both the resident alien and the native." The sacral law refers to various cases: aliens-cursed the name of God (Lev 24:10-23), he can be struck by uncleanness through touching a corpse (Num 9:6-14), he can observe but also violate the commandments unconsciously and without intention (Num 15:26, 29, 30), and he can even be received into in the cities of asylum (Num 35:15). They are even allowed to present offerings, where it was the privilege of the high-priest to share the meal with God and no other Levitical priest or laymen were allowed to attend (Num 15:14).[617]

Thirdly, in the latest layers of the priestly tradition of Numbers we find the most far-reaching rule of integration concerning *gerim*, namely in Num 15:16 "you and the alien who resides with you shall have the same law and the same ordinance."[618] The גר and the Israelite are the same before the Lord. There is to be one law for both.

---

614 Anthony D. Smith, *Myths and Memories of the Nation* (Oxford: Oxford University Press, 1999), 151-52.

615 Smith, *Myths and Memories...,* 151.

616 Achenbach, "*ger-nakhri-toshav-zar,*" 40-41.

617 Achenbach, "*ger-nakhri-toshav-zar,*" 41-42.

618 The LXX in the 3rd century translates the term *ger* from the late 5th and 4th century texts with proselytes, but this term describes the status of new members of the Jewish communities who intentionally wanted to be taken up into the Qahal, but who did not necessarily ask for political or social protection. Cf. Achenbach, "*ger-nakhri-toshav-zar,*" 43; J. Milgom,

5.4.1. Aliens in Numbers

The later insertions of priestly scribe into the Pentateuch, especially in the book of Numbers make additional requirements for alien in the realm of sacral distinction as in Numbers 19:10 the section concerning the cleansing of someone who has become 'unclean' through contact with a dead body has only a very shaky connection with the context in which it is set and is probably an addition, [619] where alien is included at the end of the instruction which tell the Israelite how to make purifying water. Here the ritual of making ashes of a red heifer פרה אדמה (*parah adumah)* for the purpose of making 'lustral water' or 'water of impurity' for the removal of sin and uncleanness (19: 9). The red heifer פרה אדמה (*parah adumah)* was a cow reddish in colour without defect or blemish and never used under a yoke.[620] In this chapter, the Israelites are instructed on how to purify themselves after contact with death. This necessitated not castrating animals in Lev. 22:24, and here it requires purification rituals after being in contact with a corpse. The introductory phrase of Lev 16: 29 is similar, but not identical to this phrase. On the basis of content, the inclusion of aliens in a law regarding contact with a corpse makes more sense than inclusion in a law providing for the making of cleansing water. It is clear that in these verses the alien is crucially integrated into Israel.

In Numbers 15:13-16, 26, 29, and 30, this section contains further instructions on offering various sacrifices, especially for sins committed unintentionally or unconsciously. One highlight of this periscope is the text which says that there should be one statute both for the Israelites as well as for the aliens living among them. These indicate that the alien has become a full member of the community.

In Num 15:13-14 Olson indicates that "this theme of broadening or widening not only to issue of time but also to the groups of person responsible for obeying the law. The law on sacrifice conclude with a note that the laws apply to 'every native Israelites' (v. 13) and also to 'an alien who lives with you' who wishes to make an offering (v. 14). Numbers 15:15-16, goes on in

---

Numbers, The JPS Torah Commentary (Philadelphia: Jewish Publication Society, 1990), 121. This is only one of a whole series of statues that put the native and the sojourn on par; cf. (Ex 12:19; Lev 16:29-31; 17:8, 10-12, 15-16; 18:26; 20:2; 22:18-20; 24:6; Num 9:14; 15:26, 30; 19:10-12; 35:15). Cf. T. R. Ashley, *The Book of Numbers,* NICOT (Grand Rapids: W. B. Eerdmans, 1993), 281; Cf. P. Joseph Titus, "Concern for the Migrants: An opening Toward Universalism in the Hebrew Bible," *Indian Theological Studies* 50 (Sept & Dec 2013), 283.

619 Martin Noth, *Numbers A Commentary* (London: SCM Press Ltd, 1968), 141; Cf. Wenham, *Leviticus*, 245-46.

620 Sebastian Kizhakkeyil, *The Pentateuch An Exegetical Commentary* (Mumbai: St Paul Society, 2009), 386.

strong term to accentuate the widening of the sojourner or non-Israelite into the obligations of the assembly or community."[621]

"As for the assembly, there shall be for both you and resident alien a single statute, a perpetual statue throughout your generations; you and your alien shall be alike before the Lord. You and the alien shall who resides with you shall have the same law and the same ordinance." (Num 15:15-16).

Numbers 15 broadens the scope of the alien's participation and obligation to include all sacrifices and offerings. Such offering are made at the tent of meeting at the heart and centre of the camp. Any non Israelite groups within the holy war camp of Israel were apparently located on the fringes of Israel's camp.[622] In any case this non-Israelite group are welcome into the centre to offer their sacrifices and offering. This way they are given the same statute as native Israelite before God.

In the following section (Num 15:22-30), aliens are again mentioned in vv. 26, 29, 30. This section deals with the atonement for offences committed unintentionally, inadvertently, 'unwittingly' against a divine command. As Fishbane asserts: "this law is related to Lev 4:13-31. The nature of the relationship has long been debated, but he concludes that Numbers 15 is an expansion of Leviticus 4.[623] In vv. 22-26 it explore unintentional corporate sin. If an act of transgression is committed without the people's knowing it, corporate forgiveness of both native Israelite and resident aliens is possible.[624]

Fishbane notes that Number 15:22-31 do not ascribe the law to God or Moses, since it speaks of both in the third person. Instead, according to the text, the speaker is a preacher of the law as given to Moses. It is beginning, Fishbane claims, of a new stage in exegesis in which human exegesis is allowed to change the divine revelation and adapt it to new circumstances. It is the beginning of new form, the exegetical legal discourse.[625] Because of the equal status given to the alien, and because of the new manner of reforming the legal tradition, it is clear that it represents a late stage in the redaction of the Pentateuch.

In summing up today contemporary readers are often upset by the ways in which Israel's theology created distinction between Israelites and non-Indigenous resident. At the sametime, few westerners would applaud P's requirement that resident aliens observe certain basic Israelites purity rules,

621 Dennis T. Olson, *Numbers: Interpretation A Bible Commentary for Teaching and Preaching* (Louisville: John Knox Press, 1996), 92. Dozeman explain how the priestly writers also extend the law to the resident alien. If they choose to participate cf. Thomas B. Dozeman, *The Book of Numbers,* in NIB, Vol.11 (Nashville: Abingdon Press, 1998), 127-128.

622 Dennis T. Olson, *Numbers...,* 93.

623 Michael Fishbane, *Biblical Interpretation...,* 190.

624 Thomas B. Dozeman, *The Book of Numbers...*, 127.

625 Michael Fishbane, *Biblical Interpretation...,* 190-92.

even though this is an act of cultural inclusion. Leviticus does not portray the גר as religiously neutral, but as one governed by covenant with Yahweh, and by implication as one required to relinquish allegiance to other deities. The גר was a cultic participant and was accountable to preserve the purity of Yahweh's land, temple, and people as holy dwelling for Yahweh's presence. On the other hand, the גר *bound* himself to Yahweh and experience coextensive membership in Israel's religious community. On the other hand, the גר was *unbound* with respect to his ethnicity: he was not, and would never be considered indigenous to the region or to the Israelites community. This means the גר called Yahweh אלהיו ('*elhyu* = his God) and was therefore obliged to uphold the sanctity of his God's reputation. It also means that גר was free to celebrate Israel's redemptive history, but not required to. It is likely, if not probable, that the גר was free to retain his custom of nonsacred slaughter of domestic animals as a means of hunger. That the גר had bound himself in covenant relationship to Yahweh is enforced by chapters. 18-20 where compassion toward גרים (*geryim* = non-indigenous residents) is contrasted with abhorrence for the customs of the nations הגרים (*hageryim*). Christopher Wright reminds us:

> we ourselves, like every generation of Christians, standing as we do between Pentecost and the Parousia, are a part of the story-line. We stand in organic spiritual continuity with the biblical people of God in both Testaments, a continuity which transcends the varying degrees of cultural discontinuity. Our story is part of their story. This was the principle by which New Testament writers could apply the ethics of the Old Testament to their Christian readers, even before the formation of the New Testament canon.[626]

Yet even today, cultural inclusion regularly involves gaining rights within the new groups but also added responsibilities. Today, many countries accept resident alien, although they are not fully citizen and thus lack certain rights. It is intellectually incoherent to argue that resident aliens, whether living today or in antiquity, be treated like native while at the same time advocating that it is wrong to impose upon them any legal or cultural norms stemming from the new society in which they now reside.

There is however another strand in postmodernist thought that a more promosing for an approach to biblical ethics. Deconstruction is famously concerns with difference, or as Derrida would say, "difference."[627] Derrida declares that the "first rule" is "respect for the others, that is, for the right

626 Christopher. H. Wright, *Walking in the Ways of the Lord: The Ethical Authority of the Old Testament* (Downers Grove, Ill: Inter varsity, 1995), 25.

627 Jacues Derrida, "Difference," in *Speech and Phenomena, and Other Essay on Husserl's Theory of Signs* (Evanston: Northwestern University Press, 1973), 129-60.

to difference, in his relations to others but also in his relation to himself."[628] It is certainly true that postmodernist scholarship is especially sensitive to voice from the margins, and it takes a negative view of any claims that might be considered hegemonic or totalizing. Torah demands care for the גר, the widows and the orphans.

5.5. Conclusion

Most of the studies on the Persian period deal with the time of Nehemiah and Ezra, which was nearly one hundred years after the return of first group from exile. The social setting of the people of Judah in the early period was a complex one and they suffered from severe social fragmentation. There were many attempts among the scholars to understand these complexities of the society.

Secondly, it is not possible to sum up what we have discovered and suggest possible answers to our initial question. The laws associating the alien with the poor and the temporary resident were mostly integral to their context. As their identity does not seems to have changed, except that now the ones who control the land are now aliens.

Thirdly, the laws requiring equal treatment speak of aliens in a new way. They have become part of the chosen people. In this context the meaning of the word גר has change quite drastically to the point that its original meaning of a socially and economically dependent person has been superseded.

Fourthly, we have also seen that the aliens who were treated as equals were not poor and dependent. This is most obvious in the Passover legislation in Exodus 12:48, 49. Which presumes that they were households and responsibility? Whereas the slaves, the temporary resident and the hired the workers are not. This change in their social status, that refers to the Israelites who had remained in the land and who joined the community of the returnees.

Fifthly, the rhetorical aim is to persuade the audience that they have no right to appropriate themselves what Yahweh has claimed for himself. Neither land nor people are to be used for personal profit, which is what sales and perpetuity implies. Land must provide the means of life, and not, through exploitation, produce the means of death.

Thus, in general aliens are perceived as a threat, whether they speak a different language or not, whether their appearance is different or not, whether they came from far away or from the next village. However, Ashby remarks: "the Biblical laws concerning aliens exclude all exploitation of aliens, all apartheid, all ethnic cleansing, all forced removals, all racial prejudice,

628 Derrida, "Deconstruction and the Other," in *Dialogue with Contemporary Continental Thinkers,* edited by Richard Kearney (Manchester: University of Manchester press, 1984), 107-26.

these things are unworthy of Gods people. It is true that the scale of the issue addressed by the Biblical law is smaller than that of the modern world."[629] One could take the treatment of the גר in the Holiness code and ask about the ethical values or ethos that lies behind there text, and the amount of space they are given as an example of how we could treat גר in our society. The book of Acts 11:18ff records a hesitant but gradual acceptance of gentiles converts into the Christian community initially consisted of Jews. Yet in our days, aliens, even in small numbers, stand little chance of being accepted and cared for in most countries.

629 G. W. Ashby, *Go Out and Meet God: A Commentary on the Book of Exodus,* ITC (Grand Rapids: W. B. Eerdmann, 1997), 107.

Chapter 6

Struggle for Identity as גר in North-East India

6. Introduction

The North East India region has eight states- Assam, Arunachal Pradesh, Manipur, Meghalaya, Mizoram, Nagaland, Tripura and Sikkim. The tribal communities of the North East India have spread throughout the region stretching over a vast area bordering Myanmar, China, Bangladesh, Bhutan, Nepal and the Indian State of West Bengal. The vastness of the area, the diversity of the communities and the accessibility of the neighbouring foreign countries of India, tribal communities are potentially vulnerable to develop fluidity in their cultural life and expressions. At the same time, there is no doubt that there are too many varied ethnic groups which possess unique and distinctive cultural heritage including countless of different linguistic identifying communities that follows particular customs and traditions despite being a part of a nation state with different values and ethos. Most of the identities in the North East India seem to basically be the colonial ethnic and social constructs during the period of British rule in the region. Wati Longchar on the Spirituality of the Indigenous People starts by asking "Who are we?" According to Longchar, many people have confusion over the identity of indigenous people. He asserts: "they are identified as tribal, ethnic minorities, native, aborigines or 'Indians.' These names are given by colonizers, western missionaries and anthropologists. Sometimes indigenous people in some countries are also identified as cultural minorities, hill tribes, mountain peoples, forest/remote area dwellers and so forth. All these identities are given by western missionaries, anthropologists and colonial administers, urban settlers, and later by the respective Government. However, none of the indigenous community identified themselves with those names. Indigenous people identify themselves by their own names, e.g. Hakka, Amis, Thao, Aos, Changs, Chin, Mizos, Khasis, Ainus, etc."[630] Thus, indigenous people are those who are considered to be original inhabitant of the land, prior to the arrival of the colonizers, who has a historical continuity with a certain region or area.

Having discussed the aliens in AWA and in the ancient Israelite laws, this chapter will be in two parts. The first part will be on the experience of the people of North East India as alien in their own land and how they struggle for their identity. Secondly, on the ancient Israelite laws concerning aliens and the North East Indian society.

6.1. Defining Indigenous People

The UN Declaration on the Rights of Indigenous Peoples begins with three affirmations of the status of indigenous people followed by one reaffirmation that in the exercise of their rights, indigenous people should be free from discrimination of any kind. That is followed by recognizing the needs to respect the rights and values of the indigenous peoples, and the concern is expressed by way of emphasizing the urgent needs that UN should play its role.

The Universal Declaration on the Rights of Indigenous People contains 46 Articles covering a wide range of personal and social aspects of life. The Articles 3-6[631] gives special attention towards the freedom of the indigenous

630 However they are all imposed and constructed terms by the colonizers and rather they identify themselves by their own names. Cf. Wati Longchar, *Returning to Mother Earth Theology, Christian Witness and Theological Education An Indigenous Perspective* (Kolkota: SCEPTRE, 2013), 19-20. Datta Ray in his book *Tribal Identity and Tension in North-East India* writes people from the plain could not grasp their name correctly; they gave the tribal communities some name of their own convenience. Thus the Monpa and Sherdukpen who come in the market of Udalgiri in Assam were often referred to as Buthia by the locals. The tribes of Arunachal Pradesh insist on being called by their names. Similarly the Aka who are found in the Thrizino subdivision of West Kameng and lower Subansiri district were called as Daflas by the plain people. The people concerned consider this term derogatory. Cf. B. Datta Ray, *Tribal Identity and Tension in North-East India* (New Delhi: Omsons Publications, 1989), 31.

631 *Article3:* Indigenous people have the right to self-determination. By virtue of that right they freely determine their political status and freely pursue their economic, social and cultural development.
Article 4: Indigenous peoples, in exercising their rights to self-determination, have the right to autonomy or self government in matters relating to their internal and local affairs, as well as ways and means for financing their autonomous functions.
Article 5: Indigenous people have the right to maintain and strengthen their distinct political, legal, economic, social and cultural institutions, While retaining their rights to

people. Article10[632] talks about possession of land and that they should not be removed from their lands. No relocation shall take place without the free, prior and informed consent of the indigenous peoples' concerned.

The word "indigenous" is defined as originating in and characteristic of a particular region, place or country.[633] A more detail definition of the word can be found in the words of H. Srikanth where he identified the indigenous people as those who are the descendants of the original inhabitants of the land, who had been marginalized and made subordinated at a particular time of history by the communities who have migrated or colonized the land and who follows a particular customs and traditions despite being a part of nation state with different values and ethos.[634] Most of the identities in the North East India seem to be basically the colonial ethnic and social constructs during the period of British rule in the region.

6.2. Colonisation: The Tribes are Created

The term "ethnicity" sometimes confuses one with other terms like tribe, people, cultural group, linguistic group, religious group, community, etc. In the context of North East India, the term "ethnic group is a recent sociological alternative to the term "tribe"," this is considered to be out of date and a derogatory term. But these terms to the same set of confused facts and units of "original people" as differentiated from units of "newer people" occupying the same space. Definition of the term "tribe" may vary from time to time depending upon who are the "newer people."

As Oppitz remarks: "the British officers, who in many cases were responsible for the nomenclature of the North East Indian tribes, showed a boisterous lack of concern when naming the societies they encountered on their way to the East in the aftermath of the First Anglo-Burmese war in the

---

participate fully, if they so choose, in the political, economic, social and cultural life of the State.

632 Indigenous people shall not be forcibly removed from their lands or territories. No relocation shall take place without the free, prior and informed consent of the indigenous peoples concerned and after agreement on just and fair compensation and, where possible, with the option of return.

633 "Indigenous," *Oxford English Dictionary,* edited by Sara Hawker (New Delhi: Oxford University Press, 2011), 352.

634 H. Srikanth, "Who in North East are Indigenous People," *Economic & Political Weekly* 69/20 (May, 2014): 42. Irica-Irene Daes, the founding Chairperson of the United Nation Working Group on Indigenous population (UNWGIP) says that indigenous people are those descendents of groups that were in the territory of the country at the time when other groups of different culture or ethnic origins arrives.

1820s."[635] This may have been somehow justified in the case of advice of the Indian sub-continent.

The first usage of the term "tribe" was with specific references to the biblical people of Israel as well as to certain divisions of political units of ancient Rome from Latin '*tribus.*' It was very clear that it referred to a certain group of people without any emotive connotations. It was with its appearances in Middle English that has brought about vagueness and plurality of meaning in the usage. This coincided with the age of British colonialism. The colonial administrators began to apply the term pejoratively to people in colonial area by calling them as primitive, uncivilized, conservative, and inferior. The "original people" were then looked down upon by "newer people" only because the traditions and loyalties of the former were quite different from the traditions and loyalties of the latter. Colonial scholars also took up the cue and understood these "people" as such.[636] As Oppitz argues:

> The problem behind the haphazard and woolly nomenclature came from applying the notion of the *tribe* to the ethnic groups in the hills of Northeast India. This may have been somehow justified in the case of *adivasis* tribes of the Indian subcontinent: the Santal, which is the largest homogenous tribe in India in terms of pure numbers, control, along with the culturally and linguistically closely related Munda, Uraon and Ho, a territory that is unbroken for long stretches across the present day states of Jharkhand, West Bengal and Orissa. Much the same is true of the numerous smaller tribes of Central India. But applied to the population of Northeast India, the term was inappropriate from the very start.[637]

The term "tribal" invites serious discussion among the scholars as it carries derogatory connotations in the history of its usage in the Indian Sub-continent.[638] Whatever may be the original meaning of the term, as it

---

635 Michael Oppitz, et al., *Naga Identities Changing Local Cultures in Northeast of India* (Snoeck Publisher Gent, 2008), 16-17.

636 B. Pakem, "The Question of Ethnic Formation among the Hill People of North-East India," in *Nationality, Ethnicity and Cultural Identity in North-East India,* edited by B. Pakem (Guwahati: Omsons Publication, 1990), 110.

637 Michael Oppitz, et al., *Naga Identities Changing Local...,* 16-17.

638 For more detailed discussion on the term "tribals" see K. Thanzauva, *Theology of Community: Tribal Theology in the making* (Bangalore: Asian Trading Corporation, 2004), 1-9; Brightstar J. Syiemlieh, "The Viability of the term 'Tribe' in the light of Post modernity," in *The Search of Identity and Tribal Theology: A Tribute to Dr. Renthy Keitzar,* edited by A. Wati Longchar (Jorhat: TSC, 2001), 17-28. Lalsangkima Pachuau, *Ethnic Identity and Christianity: A Socio-Historical and Missiological Study of Christianity in North East India with Special reference to Mizoram* (Frankfurt am Maim: Peter Lang,

has been used by the European imperialists, the Indian Government and the "mainstream Indians" the term stands for "uncivilized," "backward," "poor," and "illiterate." The term was imposed upon the communities concerned by others and the former had been carrying the heavy burden of alienation, loss of self-esteem and confidence under the umbrella of this term in spite of the fact that the Government has safeguarded their interest and existence by providing special protections and provision.[639]Anthropologist, Missionaries, and the Constitution of India imposed this term on those people who lived in hills and forests. Most often this term is used in a derogatory way by the public to refer to those who are confined to the margins, totally cut off from the world of science and modern technology. The indigenous people themselves have never willingly accepted the name as a common generic term applicable to them but prefer to be identified by the name of their respective communities (such as Mizo, Naga, Khasi, etc).

Thanzauva and Wati Longchar strongly argue for the imposed and derogatory nature of this term.[640] However, from a constructive point of view, they understand this term in a redeemable manner affirming their primitiveness, history of suffering and alienation, giving a common identity to them. It needs to be admitted and accepted that there is no universally accepted definition of the 'indigenous'. Vashum uses the term 'tribal' and 'indigenous' interchangeably. For him this usage shows that all tribalgroups are integral members of the World's Indigenous Community.[641] Nowhere in the Indian constitution has the term, 'tribe', been defined. The Indian constitution, on the other hand, seems to have accepted 'tribe' as a stage in the evolution of human civilization. The fifth and sixth schedules of the constitution have placed certain politically and economically backward communities of the plains and the hills under special categories for administration. The constitution has empowered the president to appoint a commission after every ten years to review the situation of the scheduled tribes and declare by public notification the tribes or tribal

---

2002), 34-43.Cf. V. V. Thomas, *Dalit and Tribal Christians and India Issues and Challenges* (Malapuram: Focus India Trust, 2014), 73-74.

639 Vanlalnghaka Ralte, "Critical Re-Look at the Tribal Heritage: A New Testament Perspective," in *Theologizing Tribal Heritage: A Critical Re-Look,* edited by Hrangthan Chhungi (Delhi: CWM, ISET-ECC, PCI, 2008), 261.

640 K. Thanzauva, *Theology of Community: Tribal Theology in the Making*... 10; Cf. Wati A. Longchar, *Returning to Mother Earth Theology*..., 20.

641 Ahao Vashum, "Emerging Vision of Indigenous/Tribals Theology," in *Dalit-Tribal Theological Interface: Current Trends in Subaltern Theologies,* edited by James Massey and Shimreingam Shimray (New Delhi, Jorhat: CDS and TSC/WSC, 2007), 16-17; Cf. Shimreingam Shimray, "Towards A New Paradigm of Human Rights in the Context of North East India," *Asian Journal of Theology,* vol. 28 (April, 2014), 71.

communities.[642] The term constitutionally carries certain privileges and since no appropriate alternative term is at hand, the term "tribal" may be used as the common name for this specially categorized group of people. It is also worth noting that today not all communities involved can be labelled with the derogatory connotation as the term used to carry before. Also the fact remains that the North East Indian tribal groups had always been quite different in many ways from their counterparts residing in the plains of central India.

6.3. Aliens in Our Own Land

The death of Nido Tania, a 19-year old young man from Arunachal Pradesh, in Delhi on 29th January 2014 after a racially-inspired assault has brought the issue of racism into the spotlight. To put it simply, 'they look different from the other people of India.' They are not viewed as yet another ethnic group in the vast Indian milieu; they are an exceptional ethnic population. For most respondents, racism in Delhi is expressed by the epithet "Chinky." As McDuie-Ra remarks: "they are constantly subject to the epithet as they move about the city, in their workplace from colleagues, from other students in their classes at university and even from friends. Importantly, "chinky" is not used by North East Indians to refer to themselves or each other. In other words they have not claimed ownership of the epithet. Other groups are subject to this derogatory term: Bhutanese nationals, Burmese refugees and migrants, Chinese nationals, Ladakhis, Nepalis from certain ethnic group (Limbus, Magyars and Rais), and Tibetans. All of these groups are present in Delhi. They share some of the same places of work, education and neighbourhood as the North East Indian migrants, but for the most part they occupy different niches in the city."[643]

Epithets matters because they reflect embedded stereotypes about North East Indians. Their stereotyping is layered. In other words, the stereotypes that North East Indian are subject to in Delhi have multiple layers, multiple effects, and multiple origins, stereotype are not always negative and have enabled the growth of the labour niche for North East Indian migrants, yet North East

642 Alexander Mackenzie, *History of the Relations of the Government with the Hill of the North-East Frontier of Bengal* (Calcutta: Government of India, 1884), 245. Article 366 (25) that the "ST" are as "such tribe or tribal communities or parts of or groups within such tribes or tribal communities as are deemed under 342 to be scheduled tribes for the purposes of this constitution. Definition of the "Schedule Tribes" in the constitution of India cited in http://tribal.nic.in/ (accessed on 4th March, 2015).

643 Duncan McDuie-Ra, "The 'North-East' Map of Delhi," *Economic and Political Weekly* XLV11/30 (28th July 2012): 17. The word, Momos,' 'Chinkis,' Chinese,' 'Chichi Chu Chu' or any other derogatory remarks relating to race, culture, identity or physical appearances for instance, is used widely to refer to the people of the North East India by not just elders and youngsters but also kids in play schools of North India. All such perceptions about people from the North East India can be pointed towards the ignorance of many Indians about the latter, and also on the silence adopted by the North East states on the subject.

Indians do not have control over the ways they are represented whether positive or negative. The recent report release by the North East India support centre and Helpline (NESC&H 2011) also reflects the uneasiness regarding the terms "migrant." To quote from the report:

> The term migrant is used when a citizen of the country goes and lives in another country. But terming the same citizen who goes and lives in another city of different states within the country, the term becomes questionable.[644]

They are cast as backward and exotic. As Barbara rightly said: "Colonial era classifications have been reproduced in the systems of governing the North-east region in contemporary Indian,"[645] and in popular representation of North East Indian especially tribal communities in museums, tourism campaigns, guidebooks, schoolbooks and national parades. According to Echtner and Prasad tribal communities are represented using:"the three "un" myths: "unchanged", "un restrained" and "uncivilized." This carries over into everyday life in the city and tribal communities must constantly challenge the notion that they are from a premodern society "untouched" by modernity. Further, they are cast as anti-national."[646]

Here, the backward frontier dweller meets the violent anti-national separatist bent on destroying India. Most significantly, they are cast as immoral and trouble makers. This affects North East India women and men in different ways. The women are cast as loose in morals and sexually promiscuous. Many of them work in highly visible occupation where their sexuality is emphasized. According to 'The Hindu' 14-year-old Manipuri girl working as a domestic help was raped in South Delhi's Munirka as she was returning from a medical store. The rapist, her landlord's son was photographed by some CCTV cameras as he cruelly dragged the girl, leading to his arrest. But Munirka has a Khap panchayat which met along with members of the Resident Welfare Association; and instead of condemning the rape by a young man of their community and finding ways to make the colony safer for women, they decided to evict tenants from the North-east India: their resolution was

644 Babu P. Remesh, "Strangers in their own land Migrants from the North-East in Delhi," *Economic & Political Weekly* XLV11/22 (2 June 2012), 38.

645 Sanjay Barbara, "Autonomous Districts and/or Ethnic Homelands: An Ethnographic Account of the Genesis of Political Violence in Assam (North-East India) against the Normative Frame of the India Constitution," *International Journal on Minority & Group Rights* 15 2/3 (2008), 313-34.

646 Charlotte Echtner and Pushkola Prasad, "The Contest of Third World Tourism Marketing," in *Annals of Tourism Research* 30/3 (2003): 660-82. Cf. Vrushali Patil, "Narrating Political History about Contrast Space: Tourism Websites of India's Northeast," *Annals of Tourism Research* 38/2 (2011), 989-1008.

reportedly to clean up the colony by throwing out from it the North-easterner 'trash': the word used was *gandagi.*[647] *In the recent "India's Daughter" documentary the defence lawyer Sharma remarks: "India has the best culture. No place for a woman in our culture."*[648] If Delhi is a very safe city, it is also known as the rape capital. Acknowledging the present scenario, true state of India, and then pushed into making it safe not only for women, but for everyone is imperative. It will have to start with acceptance at the government level. Men are also subject to some of the loose and immoral assumption but are also cast as heavy drinkers, unpredictable and potentially violent.[649] Today there is rampant sexual harassment and violence faced by young North East Indian women, random hade violence against North East Indian men, barbs by classmates, work colleagues, landlords and strangers, and bias in police stations, classroom and surprisingly hospitals. The cold uncomfortable word they used to describe the discrimination they routinely face was 'racism.'

Today, even the rich culture heritage of the native North East India are not spared. The recent controversial remark by Lok Sabha MP Shahshi Tharoor[650] refer the Naga Headgear as "Outlandish" and "hilarious" which has irrevocably hurt the sentiments of the Nagas. The Naga traditional headgear depicts the patriotic valour and the rich cultural heritage of the Nagas forefathers it was a symbol of respect and status accorded to an honoured guest or revered person of a certain community. Another incident (June 26, 2017) where a North East Indian woman shunted out of Delhi Golf Club for wearing *Jainsem* (a dress worn by the indigenous Khasi women in Meghalaya).[651] She had been turned out of the dining room of the Delhi Golf Club because her traditional Khasi attire looked like a "maid's uniform" to the staffers. The incident is purely a case of racial discrimination; judging a person by what she wears and calling someone a 'dustbin.' Even in the wake of global coronavirus pandemic which have caused many lives globally, people from North East India have also been facing hate. Many North East Indian students living outside of their home states have reported being called "corona" or "coronavirus" after the virus broke out in Wuhan, China. They hav been denied entry into apartment complexes, forced to evict their flats, and even asked to leave restaurants as their presence was making others uncomfortable.

647 Harsh Mander, "Capital fears," *The Hindu* 9th March 2014, 3.

648 www.Scoopwhoop.com/news/banned-bbc-nirbhaya. Documentary, (accessed on 17th September, 2015).

649 Duncan McDuie-Ra, "The 'North-East' Map of Delhi," 72.

650 *Nagaland Post*, August 8, 2018.

651 The attire comprises of two pieces of fabrics which are either tied or pinned at the shoulders and is worn either below the knee or ankle length. The *Jainsem* is generally worn with a blouse and a petticoat underneath, which showcased ethnic apparel of the Kashis of the North East India.

Are you from Japan or from China? These are some questions which sometimes makes majority of North Eastern people doubtful about their origin as an Indian. India is such a vast country and some cultural misunderstandings are ought to happen. Racists' attacks against the people of North East India have proliferated throughout India.

The experience of racism by the North East Indian of Mongoloid racial stock in other parts of central, western and southern India is of different order. Because of observed ethnic/racial appearance in the form of different skin colour and looks, language, cultural barriers and alien sounding. As Jamir remarks: " …, during the last fifty years or so, several developments and shifts have taken place in the tribal societies of North East India, such as, first, a whole generation of the tribal people who were educated outside the tribal society. They were art of the Indian and Western educational system, following Indian or Western culture. But they were not able to be fully a part of the Indian or Western environment, because they were yellow in colour!"[652]

Young people from North East India feel wounded by the routine ignorance and how they are not regarded to be Indians. Classmates and colleagues do not take the trouble to learn and pronounce their names correctly, assume they are Chinese or Nepalese, sometimes actually ask them if they need passports, and called them 'chinky.'

Recently when the BJP read out their manifesto: "North-eastern immigrants to be protected"[653] has erupted a protest in most of the North East Indian states. The BJP manifesto calling North East Indian citizens as "immigrants" is not by mistake. Discrimination at its highest and should not be tolerated. The BJP manifesto for the recent held Delhi Assembly Election is a grim example of racism.[654] This has further alienated the people of the region on the basis of their racial and geographical origin.

Unlike other parts of the country, North East India holds an important position from a strategic point of view as this state's share their border with other countries like Bangladesh, China, Myanmar and Bhutan. The terrain, the state of socio-economic development and historical factors such as language/ ethnicity, tribal rivalry, migration, ownership and control over local resources and a widespread feeling of exploitation and alienation have resulted into a fragile security situation in the North East Indian States. This has resulted into violence and diverse demands by various Indian insurgent groups.

---

652 L. Imsutoshi Jamir, "Who is not Us: The Politics of Tribal Identity," in *Gardening Tribal Resources for Doing Tribal Christian Theology,* in Tribal Studies Series 16, edited by Razouselie Lasetso (Jorhat: ETC Programme Coordination, 2008), 60.

653 Sushanta Talukdar, "Protest in Assam over 'immigrant' reference," *The Hindu,* 5th February 2015, 7.

654 "Mounting Trouble: The 'Immigrant' Gaffe could Cost the BJP dear in the Northeast," *The Week,* 22nd February 2015, 26.

Unless development happens in North East India, insurgency problems will keep aggravating. The Government's objective should be long term gain and not short term one. North East India is notorious for militancy resulting mainly from lack of development and corruption. The region has also faced negligence for many years, and it is only in recent time that the development work has taken up by the Central Government. The Special Economic Zones Act (SEZs) was passed by the Government of India in May 2005 and it received Presidential assent on the 23rd of June, 2005. The bill came into effect on 10 February 2006, providing for drastic simplification of procedures and for single window clearance on matters relating to central as well as state governments. There were about 143 SEZs (as of June 2012) operating throughout India, by June 2013 this has risen to 173.[655] This initiative is welcoming so that it will bring all round development of the North East Indian State.

6.4. The Racist Experience of the North East India

Increasingly the Tribal communities from the North East India are targeted in the big cities such as New Delhi and Bengaluru because they look different and their profiles do not conform to the specification of "Indians." They are subjected to verbal and physical attacks. Systematically they are ridiculed, abused and thus undergo psycho-somatic tortures with clear warnings that they should quit and get back to their domiciles.[656]

Migration from Northeast India to large metropolitan cities like Bangalore, Kolkata, Mumbai, and more so Delhi has increased rapidly in the last decade and limited livelihood prospect, changing social aspirations, and armed conflicts (in certain areas) push migrants out of the region. The transformation of Indian cities through neo-liberal reforms have led to rapidly expanding employment opportunities in the retail and services sector, labour recruitment, and growing networks based on clan-kin and ethnic ties pull migrants to particular jobs, neighbourhoods and colleges. The migrants' experience in these cities includes racism, violence and discrimination.[657]Along with this city-bound exodus, there has also been some movement of youth towards smaller towns and suburbs of far-off states within the country.[658]

Determinants of outmigration the unparalleled city-bound migration of youth from the North East India in recent times is understood to be determined

655 http://en.wikipedia.org/wiki/Special_economic_zone (accessed on 30th September, 2015).

656 John Mohan Razu, "Racisms, Casteim & Classism Looms: Rage from the Margins," *Nagaland Post,* 17 December, 2014. 5.

657 Duncan McDuie-Ra, "The 'North-East' Map of Delhi," 69-77.

658 Kalyan Das and Dadul Chutia, "Outward Bound,'*Assam Tribune* 6 February, 2011.

by a multitude of factors, of which the most important are "educational and employment considerations." An analysis of data from the NSS 64th round (2007-08) suggests that migration "for studies and employment" assumes much more significance in the case of North East Indian states compared to the rest of India. Despite a high literacy rate,[659] the North East region is characterized by a visible lack of adequate avenues for higher or technical education or vocational training. Further, there is a felt mismatch between the demand in the job market and the potential of the local educational system – especially to meet the requirements of the new economy occupations and professional service sectors.[660] The educational base of the region is an important factor that prompts migration decisions of educated and ambitious youth to urban centres for higher learning. The relatively brighter human resource profile of these migrants prompts one to see this outmigration as a process of "brain-drain,"[661] since a good proportion of the youth often opt to continue in urban centres after education, for employment.

The bleak employment prospect in the local labour markets is perhaps the most important determinant of migration of youth from North East India Region to urban centres. Increasing educated and youth unemployment in the North East Indian States owe considerably to the terribly lower level of industrialization and lower expansion of modern service sector occupation in the region. The saturation in the Government public/sector job also intensified the unemployment situation. Lower labour absorption capacity of local labour markets and perceived employment prospects in the urban centres together prompt the aspirant youth in North East India to migrate to cities (at least for sometimes) to explore better opportunities.

As Ramesh opined that: "The political unrest, violence and poverty of the region also often influence the decision of the youth in favour of migration." Most of the States in North East India have unrests and tensions (which includes: religious/ ethnic/communal clashes, tension between people and army, insurgency and so on). Due to this tension, the normal life of the people of the region is affected."[662] As report suggests that life in Manipur in recent years have become difficult for the ordinary people. With 100 days of public

---

659 In terms of literacy rate, most states in the region are ahead of the national average (64.8%)- e.g. Mizoram (88.8%); Tripura (73.2%); Manipur (70.5%); Sikkim (68.6%); and Nagaland (66.6%). Government of India, *Union Budget and Economic Survey,* National Informatics Center. Cf. http://indiabudget.nic.in/, viewed on 2 January 2015.

660 Biloris, Lyndem and Utpal Kumar De, eds., *Education in North-East India: Experience and Challenge* (New Delhi: Concept Publishing Company, 2004).

661 Singh, M. Prakash, "Brain Drain and the North-East (2007)," http://www.kanglaonline.com/?template=kshow&kid=245, accessed on 2 January 2015.

662 Babu P. Ramesh, *Migration from North-East to Urban Centres: A Study of Delhi Region* (Noida: V. V. Giri National Labour Institute, 2012), 4.

strikes a year, market shut, school closed and public transportation off the road, the people find it very difficult to pursue their studies and livelihood in the state. Such tension with bleak educational infrastructure and employment prospect in the region are found prompting the youngsters to try their luck in urban centres in other parts of the country.

A survey released by the North East Support Centre and Helpline (NESCH) in 2011 puts the number of migrants outside the North East India is 14,850. The same report cites a 12-fold increase in migration out of the North East India from 2005 to 2011, of the migrants leaving the North East India 48% migrate to Delhi; making for a population of around 2,00,000. Survey figures are likely to be underestimates, as movement back and forth between the North East India and Delhi is constant and periods of stay very dramatically from a few months to several years.[663] Recent research suggests that there are 8000 Assamese youth working in plywood factories in Perumbavoor, a town in far off Kerala.[664]

Kuku, an Afro-American doctoral research at the Delhi School of Economics writes:

> Racism in India is systemic and independent of the foreign of any hue. This climate permits and promotes this lawlessness and disdain for dark skin. Most Indian pop icons have light-damn-near-white skin. Several stars even promote skin-bleaching cream that promise to improve one's popularity and career success. Matrimonial advertisements boast of fair, very fair and very fair skin alongside foreign visas and advanced university degrees.[665]

---

663 Duncan McDuie-Ra, "The 'North-East' Map of Delhi," 70.

664 Kalyan Das, & Chutia, Dadul, "Outward Bound," 3.

665 Diepiriye Kuku, "India is Racist, And Happy About It. A Black American's first-hand Experience of Foothpath India: No One Even Want to Change," *Outlook Magazine* (June 29, 2209), http://www.outlookindia.com (accessed on Nov 18, 2015). Cf. Liang, Lawrence and Golan Naulak, "Cultural Ignorance and Prejudice," *The Hindu,* 4 February, http://www.thehindu.com/todays-paper/tp-opinion/cultural-igno-rance-anprejudice/article5650955. accessed on 20 February, 2015. Thangkhanlal Ngaitt, "Nido Taniam and the Fraught Question of Racism in India" in *Economic and Political Weekly* XL1V/11 (March 15, 2014): 15. Lawrence Liang and Golan Naulak made a distinction between two level of racism, viz. "footnote racism" and "Front Page racism. As for Thangkhanlal Ngaihte: "footnote racism" implies racial prejudice experienced in subtle forms in everyday life. This type of racismhappens at everyday interactions with random people in the streets, at neighborhood markets, alleyways and other interactions with essential utility providers. Secondly "Headline racism" refers to overt physical, racist hate attacks which occupy newspaper headlines and hence the characterization.

Kuku rightly identifies the malice among the Indians: "It is shocking that people wear liberalism as a sign of modernity, yet revert to ultra-conservatism when actually faced with difference."[666]

North East India migrants experience high levels of racism in Delhi. They are seen as racially distinct from other groups that make up India's diverse citizen and physical appearance is central in interaction with members of other communities. Features denoting Thai Tibeto-Burman, and Mon-Khmer lineage mark them as separate. In fact, race routinely leads to the nationality and citizenship of migrants being questioned by other city dwellers. India contains many communities earmarked as "others" based on religion, caste, and even ethnicity, yet the nationality and origin of these communities are not questions at every turn.

The people of North East India bear a Mongoloid look because of which people of other parts of India think of them as foreigners. This Indian attitude based on colour and caste has made a huge irreparable damage to the lives of many young aspiring students in Delhi and other Indian cosmopolitan cities. The existing laws and online reporting offices are not enough to tackle the issue and so a concrete decision should be taken which would make things feasible. From the perspective of human rights, one can without hesitation say that tribal people are the victims of alienation, exploitation, discrimination and oppression in India. As Thanzauva rightly said "They have suffered at the hands of Aryan invaders, the Muslim rulers, the British administrators and the privileged people of Indian today."[667] In his key note address on "Tribal Theology and the Bible" he asserts:

> The hill tribe in the North East India, will tell a similar story and say as Deuteronomist had said, 'wandering hunter was my father and he went to Myanmar and sojourned there, there his descendants were multiplied then became great in number and they were oppressed and exploited by the Burmese. The king of Myanmar, (Siampahranga) forced them to work very hard in the construction of his palace when the burden became too heavy for them they left Myanmar in search for a new place. Then they came in peace. But the British invaded them and made them aliens. For the convenience of their administration the British rulers divided them, since then they became a divided people. Now they are scattered in Myanmar, Bangladesh and India. Their dreams and aspirations to become

666 Diepiriye Kuku, "India Is Racist, And Happy About It."

667 K. Thanzauva, "Human Rights: The Tribal Theological Perspective," in *Theological Tribal Heritage: A Critical Re-Look*, edited by Hrangthan Chhungi (Delhi: ISPCK, 2008), 202.

one nation remain as an ideal hope, but in reality they continue to remain as alien.[668]

The tribal communities in the North East India are aliens in India. The tribal communities of the North East India will be reduced to "second class citizen."

It is inspiring to learn that the Ministry of Home Affairs has accepted the recommendation of the M.K. Bezabaruah panel- a panel appointed in 2014 to suggest ways of curbing racial bias against people from the North East India and has decided to amend the Indian Panel Code (IPC) to strengthen the legal framework against racial discrimination. IPC to be amended to punishment.[669]

This decision of the Ministry of Home Affairs has been long awaited, especially by the people from the Eight sister states, and could usher in a new era of peaceful co-existence between citizens from different ethnic backgrounds. The Ministry of Home Affairs is in process finalizing a comprehensive bill for insertion of new sections of 153A of the IPC which deals with "promoting enmity between groups." "The Ministry of Home Affairs is in process finalizing a comprehensive bill for insertion of new sections of 153C and 159A in Indian Penal Code which will be introduced in parliament after inter-ministerial consultations" progressive step towards harmonious living and is greatly appreciated.

Racism is a deadly virus in our system despite the existence of laws to curb such acts. As long as, the alienation of people by birth, colour culture, language, region and religion exists among us, there is a long way to go into making a pragmatic society of "unity and diversity" in our land. Therefore, racism should be fought by all because it is dehumanizing behaviour towards humanity regardless of the victims.

But when we look at the Israelite legal concern for גר, the law simply commands that the Israelite should be kind to aliens, they should show hospitality to them, and should not illtreat or abuse them. There is no indication anywhere in the Old Testament that the aliens were illegal migrants, the issue of legal and illegal aliens does not arise at all. Without considering their status of alienhood, the Israelite law demands that since the aliens are not citizens, they have no social, political or legal rights. Therefore, care and concern must be shown to them. We have also seen that in the latter period there was a tendency to include the גר into full membership of Israelite community and that they should have one law for the natives and the aliens (e.g. Lev. 24:22).

668 K. Thanzauva, "Tribal/Indigenous Interpretation of the Bible: A key note Address," in *Tribal Theology and the Bible: A Search for Contextual Relevance,* edited by Yangkahao Vashum (Jorhat: Tribal Study Centre, 2011), 23.

669 *Nagaland Post*, July 9, 2015.

In Deuteronomy we find that since the Israelite they were once גר in their own land (24:18, 22; cf. Exod. 22:22; 23:19). גר should be helped (Deut. 14:28, 29; 24:19, 20, 21, 22), they should not be oppressed (Deut. 5:12-15), they should be allowed to participate in Covenant ceremonies and worship (29:9, 10; 31:12). Justice must be done to the גר (Deut. 24:14, 17, 19, 21, and 22). The message of the Israelite law that the poor and needy aliens of North East India without considering their status of alien hood, should be given care and protection. The Israelite law provides a biblical and theological basis for showing care and concern to them.

6.5. The Ancient Israelite Laws Concerning Aliens and the North East Indian Society

The second part of the chapter attempts to compare the significant ancient Israel laws concerning aliens with the North East Indian society. There will be lot of differences and a direct application with the Israelite law may not be possible. However, like any portion of the Bible which requires proper interpretation for any given situation, it is a hermeneutical interpretive to interpret the legal protection of the aliens in the Old Testament with the North East Indian Society. The method of applying the findings to North East India is a hermeneutical application to critically analysis the challenges that the tribal communities are struggling for their existence and perseveration of their own identity. The researcher has no intention to make specific suggestion for legal reforms. However, like any other portions of the Bible which require proper interpretation for any given situation, it is a hermeneutical imperative to interpret the legal protection of the alien in the Old Testament for the North East Indian community. It is the researcher's intention to interpret the ancient Israel legal protection for the alien in the context of the North East Indian community.

6.5.1. Gleaning Grain Behind Reapers: A Resonant Rural Image of North East India

Gleaning grain behind reapers in Leviticus and Deuteronomy is something familiar with rural farmers of North East India. Leviticus says:

> When you reap the harvest of your land, you shall reap to the harvest of your land; you shall not reap to the very edge of the field, or gather the gleanings of your harvest. You shall not strip your vineyard bare, or gather the fallen grapes of your vineyard; you shall leave them for the poor and the alien. I am the Lord your God (Lev 19:9-10).

To the mind of the researcher this is one of the finest laws of the Bible which shows a delicate sensitivity to the feelings of the poor and the alien. It is a way of helping the poor and the needy people at the same time avoiding embarrassing them for the help they get. It makes the poor feel as if they are gathering some grain from the fields out of their own labour, not because of the charity of the others. Before Christianity the, Ao (Naga) have been practicing *Tsukdok Shim* which means 'one cannot collect the fallen grain from the field which is kept aside for the alien and the poor.'[670] Among the Rengma Nagas during the harvesting, the edges of the field are always kept aside for the landless farmers and the strangers.[671] The injunction of Leviticus to make this part of the holiness code is an example holiness or spirituality that is very much down to earth and humanely human.

Similar things happen in rural areas of North East India when the owner of paddy fields know that the poor or alien without fields. They do leave some grains of paddy behind purposely un-harvested so that the poor may benefit out of it. Like many of the parables of Jesus, gleaning of grain behind the reapers teaches the care and concern of God through simple rural imageries. The tribal communities of the North East India have an egalitarian society. The values are taught and inculcated for generations. We find the values illustrated or taught in a story, a myth, festival, or in the institutions. Peter Haokip asserts that: "the value of anti-greed taught a Naga Feast of Merit, in which a rich Naga, instead of hoarding his wealth, spend it for the benefit of the community,[672] which clearly illustrates the value of anti-greed. The Kukis too have similar festivals like *chang-ar*,[673] and *Sa-ar*.[674]

The 'Feast of Merit' is understood as generous philosophy of feeding the poor and sharing of wealth with the entire population. The term is used by Anthropologists and sociologists to articulate the true English equivalent of the Naga perception of the ceremony grant feast given by the rich men for the acquisition of status and is accompanied by wild merry-making.[675] The feasts of merits were a means of distributing wealth for the community. Today, we suffer because wealth is not shared and distributed. Only when wealth is

670 Interviewed with Mr. Aokumba Pongen, 18 August 2015.

671 Interviewed with Rev. Wekhenu Kath, 27 August 2015.

672 Peter Haokip, "Tribal Theology: Sources, Methodology and Hermeneutics," in *Search for a New Society Tribal Theology for North East India,* edited by Yankahao Vashum, Peter Haokip, Melvil Pereira (Guwahati: North Eastern Social Research Center, 2012), 34.

673 It is a festival of abundance harvest celebration by women who do the bulk of cultivation

674 *Sa-ar* is festival celebrated by a man who is adept in hunting and who has killed a considerable number of animals including tiger, bear or Janga (wild mithun); Cf. Haokip, "Tribal Theology: Sources, Methodology and Hermeneutics," 34.

675 Joseph S. Thong and Phanenmo Kath, *Glimpses of Naga Legacy and Culture* (Kottayam: Society for Naga Students' Werlfare Kerala, 2011), 137.

distributed to one and all, then will there be the fulfilment of the material need of the people. It is wrong to accumulate lands and wealth when some are on the verge of starvation. Social justice demands that all people have a share in the wealth of the Land. When there is inequality, we cannot expect peace and harmony in the land.

6.5.2. Socio-ethical Practices of the People of North East India

Today we live in a culture, in which people live increasingly isolated, seldom reaching out beyond a narrow circle. Let us remember Abraham, the great גר= 'alien'. He had God in his tent, but he did not know it. However he was hospitable to the three strangers who stood before his tent. This is why the author of the letter to the Hebrews writes: "Do not neglect to show hospitability to strangers, for by doing that some have entertained angels without knowing it" (Heb 13:1-2).

It has been mentioned that the nature of legal protection for the poor in ancient Israel is more an instruction which aims at persuading the Israelites to act kindly and graciously by their own choice. It is more of a preaching or instruction rather than a civil law legislated by an authentic body of legislatures to be executed by the judicial and executive bodies. Though certain execution were to be carried out by elders or by the royal court in *Mishpatim* Yahweh himself is the executor in the commandments. He directly protects the cause of the poor and needy certainly there is serious doubt among the scholars about the actual implementation of the laws in ancient Israel. Perhaps there is little evidence of legal actions taken for the implementation of the laws.

Does this means that the legal protection of the poor and the alien remains an ideal and a dream which is never realised? Without evidence it is difficult to answer this question in absolute term. However, it may be said that though the ideas expressed in the laws might not be fully realised in the full sense of the laws, but a study of Israelites society has revealed that the laws had far reaching impact on their social life.

The North East Indian tribal communities and ancient Israelite society faced similar social problems, despites the crudities and technical problems of the law in the application; it has significance for North East Indian tribal communities today. The laws of Israel and some of the customary laws of North East India like the Mizos, Nagas, Garos and others are comparable to a certain extent. On account of certain similarities in the nature of the laws of both societies, the researcher will discuss the significance of Israel laws for the aliens in the context of North East Indian community.

6.5.3. Sobaliba (Ao Naga) and Tlawmngaihna (Mizo) Code of Ethics

Among the Tribal communities of the North East India especially there are certain practices underlying the principle of the tribal communitarian way of living such as *Sobaliba* by the AoNagas and *Tlawmngaihna* by Mizos, *Gun-gnangani*by Garos[676] *Keng-Alia Ahea* (Tangsa tribe) of Arunachal.[677]

*Tlawmngaihna/ Sobaliba/Gun-gnangani*and *Keng-Alia Aheais* a social ethical principle of the tribal community which provides the basis for a communitarian society to exist and function effectively. The word *sobaliba* is a unique word that describes the human being. Ao word *sobaliba* however means pregnant. It contains a wide range of implications for both individual and community life. As Longchar listed several terms and phrases such as extending help to the poor, needy and strangers, willingness to share ones' belongings with others, respect for elders and parents, selflessness, truthfulness, self-control, integrity and obedience, being hospitable, industriousness, vicariousness, tactfulness, dedication, commitment, frugality, simplicity, sustainable use of resources, sociable and so forth."[678] Relational consciousness becomes a possibility for the Ao Naga because of *sobaliba.* Imsong argues that: "It is the medium of *sobaliba* that the Ao Naga has an intimate relationship with the 'land and spirit.'"[679] The rhythmic movement of the land can be synchronized with the human creative force because of *sobaliba.*

It is the ethical principle of *sobaliba* that kept the socio-economic equality of the people and turned down the steep mountains and the difficult *Jhum* cultivation into paradise that people were not aware of the problem of poverty. "The essence of humanity is *sobaliba* which makes humans distinct from animals." The AoNagas highly esteems those who practice *sobaliba* in a sense, Ao communitarian society cannot be sustained without *sobaliba.* This precept of sobaliba makes people to be selfless towards others in times of famine, misfortune, death, sickness, etc. The poor, needy, and those with disabilities, old folks are protected and taken care of. It advocates individual freedom but rejects individualism, selfishness and dishonesty. The practice

676 Interviewed with Rev. Krickwin Ch. Marak & Rev. Lalmithanggi Ch. Marak on 15th Oct. 2016 Time 9:00 am. By Garos it means Diligent and determined, helpful and self-sacrificing to the needs of others. Well mannered, self-disciplined, soft-spoken, modesty, honesty Humbling oneself to others, one who loves the own tradition and culture Being simplicity, dignity, hospitable, and kindness towards other.Well mannered, self discipline, soft-spoken, modesty, honesty Humbling oneself to others, one who loves the own tradition and culture Being simplicity, dignity, hospitable, and kindness towards other.

677 Interviewed with Mr. Ralth Baimin Mungray on 14th October, 2016.

678 Wati Longchar, "Sobaliba," *Good News for North East India,* edited by Renthy keitzar (Guwahati: Christian Literature Center, 1995), 160.

679 Mar Imsong, *God-Land-People: An Ethnic Naga Identity* (Dimapur: Heritage Publishing House, 2009), 210.

of *sobaliba* has been deteriorating in the present day society based on the principle of competition within the tradition of independence, traditional personal *sobaliba* and piety became more and more insignificant and is difficult to practice in a different way. It may be difficult to codify *sobaliba* in legal terms, but the law can be formulated in such a way that the spirit of *sobaliba* translates into reality and practiced in the society.

So also among the Mizo community, *Tlawmngaihna* is an ethical principle which binds the people together and protect the poor people in the tradition of Mizo society. *Tlawmngaihna* literary means a resistance to being help by helping others who are in need.[680] The emphasis is on a denial of self rather than an effort to be independent. The fundamental principle of *Tlawmngaihna* is denial of self to serve the community as well as individual person who are in need of help. Without the principle of *Tlawmngaihna*, it would not be possible to build a harmonious society where members of the community practiced 'decision by consensus', sharing their sorrows and caring one another.[681] The capitalistic as well as the modern communist system do not have this kind of basis to build a community on. But for the tribal societies of the North East India, such a basis is provided by *Sobaliba/Tlawmngaihna* which means creating a conducive system to protect גר = 'aliens' from discrimination and exploitation.

Among the tribal community, there exists the nature/culture of sharing and hospitability. Neither individuals nor family remains out of place in a tribal setting, since, in the case one lacks in something like material, they receive requirements from the one who has these; helping hands for those who requires for manual works and so on. Both from within and neighbouring communities, such help and hospitability are extended. In the tribal understanding, when one is hospitable, then it is a sign of receiving God into their homes or lives. Therefore, extending community with 'hospitability without borders' could be a model in interpreting texts from a tribal lens.

6.5.4. Attitudes Towards Gër

Thanzauva and Hnuni indicates how tribal people in India are understood as 'aliens for the following reasons: (a) they do not belong to the dominion racial groups of the Dravidians; (b) they do not belong to the major religious communities of the Hindus and the Muslims; (c) they are a vulnerable minority; (d) landless; (e) dependent upon the assistance of the Central Government, and

680 Thanzauva, *Theology of Community: Tribal Theology in the Making...*, 152.

681 Thanzauva, *Theology of Community: Tribal Theology in the Making...*, 153.

(f) victims of alienation, oppression and exploitation.[682] As indicated above, the North East India tribal communities are understood as aliens
The text identified above may be understood and applied to the tribal context in India: the Government policy towards tribal communities should combine both legal protection and promotion. The British administration adopted a policy of protection, isolation the tribalcommunities and protecting them from the interference of others in tribal affairs. This policy has been continued until recently. The Central Government's intention today to lift *The Inner Line Permit Regulation* (ILP) introduced in Arunachal Pradesh, Nagaland and Mizoram for the purpose of protecting the tribal people from others could well lead to even greater hardships for the tribal communities. This will be a radical change in the tribal policy. Any weaker section of any society will need a certain degree of protection, without which no emancipation will take place. Protection must be seen as an integral part of the development process.

Protection, however, important as it may be, is not sufficient in itself. True protection means empowering the people, caring, teaching training and organizing the people to enable the tribal to protect themselves. Empowering the tribal communities would also involve letting them participate in the formulation and execution of the laws. It would also involve economic development, because economic vulnerability is one of the primary factors which has allowed oppression of the tribal people. Moving beyond protection to empowerment might take beyond the legal vision of Deuteronomy to encompass Ezekiel's radical exhortation to allow resident aliens an inheritance within the boundaries of the land (Ezek 47:22-23); thereby allowing aliens to participate in the theology of promise land.

6.5.5. Tribal Communities' Attitude Towards Land

For tribal people, land is life. A major chunk of livelihood and socio-economic activities are land-centric.Their whole life activity revolves around the land and its surroundings. It is central to their identity, history, spirituality, economic and their very survival. Land is life because it is believed that the land has her own distinct life; the land is never a dead object. It is a living entity endowed with spirits. "In a non-literary society the land is their scripture through which they read about the spirits and God and create myths and songs."[683]

682 Thanzauva and R. L. Hnuni, "Ethnicity, Identity and Hermeneutics: An Indian Tribal perspective," edited by Mark G. Brett in *Ethnicity and the Bible* (Boston, Leiden: Brill Academic Publishers, INC, 2002), 356.

683 Thanzauva, *Theology of Community*...130. For a detail discussion on tribal concept of land refer to Yangkahao Vashum, "Theology of Land: A Naga Perspective," in *The Tribal Worldview and Ecology,* Tribal Studies Series no. 2, eds., A. Wati Longchar and Yangkahao Vashum (Jorhat: Tribal Study Centre, 1998), 69-94.

Secondly, the importance of land to the indigenous people lies in the fact that even the Supreme Being is understood in relation to the land. A number of the North East Indian tribes including the Aos, Sangtams and Chang Nagas call their Supreme Being, *Lijaba, Li* means "soil" and *Jaba* means "enter", meaning "the one who enters" or 'indwells in the soil."[684] It is the belief of the people that *Lijaba* enters into the earth with the seeds and rises up again along with the crops. Hence, for the people, the blooming flowers, trees bearing fruits and rice signify the presence of the creator.

People's ethical life is against closely related and based on the land. As long as one lives on this earth, one is expected to live an honest and truthful life. Honesty, truthfulness, sincerity and faithfulness are highly valued virtues among the tribal people. In the tribal society, the land is owned by the community in general. For example the land tenure in Naga society is well reflected in the report:

> In Nagaland, each tribe had a well demarcated territory within the villages inhabited by that tribe were located, with well-defined boundaries. Though the practice of each tribe differed, the village land was generally classified as (a) common village land, (b) clan land, (c) individual land, and (d) *morung* land. The village council was responsible for the management. Clan land was mostly jhum land owned by a particular clan certain areas, usually terraced lands were owned by individuals. Some portion of the village land was designated for *morung* where the young people slept there.[685]

Similar system is also found among the khasi-Jaintias of Meghalaya. The land is classified into *Ri Kynti* (clan land) and *Ri Jati* (community land).[686] One of the reasons for the classification of the land system is that no one in the village is made landless and poor. In the past landlessness and beggars were unknown to the tribal society.

The land tenure systems are related to the production of technology of a given society and are therefore, best understood in relation to the prevalent systems which for the North East India happen to be the Jhum or the shifting cultivation system. In such a system there exists the individual and community ownership of land. However, the concept of ownership of land is somewhat

---

684 A. Wati Longchar, "A Creation-Poem of the Ao Nagas: A Theological Exploration," in *The Tribal Worldview and Ecology,* Tribal Study Series no. 2, eds. A. Wati Longchar and Yangkahao Vashum (Jorhat: Tribal Study Centre, 1998), 16.

685 Planning Commission, *The Report of the Working Group on the Land System Among Tribals in the North Eastern India,* May, 1984.

686 R. T. Rymbai, "The Traditional Ecological Concept of the Khasi-Pnars," in *The Tribal Worldview and Ecology,* Tribal Study Series no. 2, eds. A. Wati Longchar and Yangkahao Vashum (Jorhat: Tribal Study Centre, 1998), 16.

diffused because of the very nature of the Jhum system of cultivation. As Alemtemshi opines: "Since the Jhum involves only a maximum cycle of only two years of cultivation in a particular plot, the land can be cultivated by anyone with all the agriculture rights for that period. Such cultivation however, can be possible with the permission of the original owner. It means that the system recognizes the ownership but also permits its temporary use by others."[687] At one point of time there was a strong thinking that Jhum practice should be eradicated and accordingly the Government of India introduced Jhum control programs have been discontinued because of certain reasons including the realization that there are something good in the Jhum system. As there are no landless laborers category of people in a Jhum society and therefore no abject poverty exists.

However, the imperative of modernization of the North East Indian society and adapting the people to the process of globalization is also perceived as a historical process as evidence through the scale of urbanization that is taking place in North East India today and the change in the mindset of the people, of the educated young. The Jhum Cultivation which was once the main economic base, is no longer economically viable as the gap of following the land in the *cycle of Jhum* cultivation decreases. Interestingly almost all the families in the villages find difficult to maintain their living in the traditional Jhum cultivation eventually compelling them to migrate to the towns in search of livelihood opportunities.

In most of the North East Indian villages, the village chief holds the nominal ownership of the land.[688] The village chief is normally assisted by the village council, the people representatives. However, the ultimate power rests in the hands of the people as a whole, who empower the chief and the council to carry out the task on behalf of the village. As Vashum points out that there are a number of ways by which the tribal people conserved and preserved their land.

a) Terrace cultivation method which is widely practiced in the region protects the land from erosion and landslides.
b) Shifting/Jhum cultivation which takes place after 6-8 years; leaves the land fallowed in between the period of the cycle year for rejuvenation and rest of the land. Of course, it needs to be pointed out that in recent years the length of cycle years has drastically shortened

687 Alemtemshi Jamir, "Land Tenure and Reform in Nagaland," in *Challenges of Land Development in Nagaland,* edited by Takatemjen (Aolijen, Mokokchung: Clark for Peace Research and aAction, 2015), 183.

688 Tribes like Kukis of Manipur and the Sumis of Nagaland where land holding is in the hands of the village chiefs.

due to a number of factors including increase in populations, logging business, etc.[689]

Land system is based on traditional village set up. The change of village system and economy certainly necessitates certain changes in the land system. Privatization, to some certain extent, is necessary for economic development and it requires the right to use and own the land privately for certain period of time. But today the problem with the existing system is that whether one uses it or not he owns the land by legal fiction. Rich people, political leader and bureaucrats simply own a vast area of land without utilizing it. If privatization is meant for increasing economy, there is no justice in simply owning the land permanently without any utilization.

Tribal communities conceive that land owns the people and gives them their identity. The tribal rhetoric states: "Land is the Supreme Being's land"; "One cannot become rich by selling land"; "Do not be greedy people"; "The earth is truth; do not lie to the earth."[690]

In this connection, the legal sanction of Yahweh's ownership of land in the jubilee legislation becomes a hermeneutical point for the society. The traditional tribal community's ownership of the land is in accord with the theological implication of the land. God is the real owner of the land and individuals are granted the right to use the land freely but not to exploit it. "The land shall not be sold in perpetuity, for the land is mine; with me you are but aliens and tenants" (Lev. 25:23). This principle highlights primarily divine ownership on earth. Philips argues that: "if fallow land was for the sustenance of the poor there would need to be some land left fallow every year."[691] Kaiser opines that: "by repossessing, symbolically, of the promise land, the Lord gives equality to all its inhabitants: owners, Hebrew slaves or laborers, all are only "aliens and tenants" in earth. All during this jubilee year becomes dependent on divine providence for their own subsistence."[692] Artus argues that: "this first principle has an aim to reduce in the Persian period social

---

689 Yangkahao Vashum, "Space, Creation and Land: An Indigenous/Tribal Eco-Theology of the Northeast India," *Journal of Tribal Studies* Vol. XVII/1 (January-June 2012), 38.

690 A. Wati Longchar, *The Tribal Religious Tradition in North East India: An Introduction* (Jorhat: The Author, 2000), 108.

691 Anthony Philips, *Ancient Israel's Criminal law* (Oxford: Blackwell, 1970), 75. It is questionable "whether a fallow year once in seven years would be of much real benefit to the poor. What did they eat in the other six years? For this reason, some scholars reckon that this earliest form of the law was not prescribing a universal fallow over the whole land of Israel in a single sabbatical year for all."

692 Walter C. Kaiser, "The Book of Leviticus," in *The New Interpreter's Bible,* edited by L. E. Keck, Vol. 12 (Nashville: Abingdon Press, 1994), 983-1174, 1174-1175.

tensions and establish equality between members of the Israel community."[693] With the help of this principle, a clear limit is raised, not only for the property of the Israelites but also for that of the resident aliens. Temporary possession is not ownership. This limit is set within Israel, to maintain social cohesion, but also to criticize the legitimacy of foreign ownership at the time of (the Persian period) where they find themselves in a dominant economic position. This attitude will check the accumulation of wealth and lands in the hands of the few rich. Divine ownership of everything on the earth warns the Indian Government not to deprive the small farmers from any means of support by selling their lands to the multinational companies. Even the transfer of land among the tribal people should be prohibited.

6.5.6. Protection of People in North East India in the Indian Constitution/Law

Trade and commerce had been controlled by outsiders in most part of the North East India. It is necessary that the people be protected from encroachment by the neighbouring people. The tribal communities are struggling for their existence and preservation of their own dignity.

Looking at the history the British enacted Bengal Eastern Frontier Regulation way back in 1873, much before their physical entry into Naga territory, it was a time when they had no clear knowledge of, or dealing with the Nagas, least of all consider protecting the welfare, traditions and customs of the Nagas. This enactment was therefore more of mechanism to effectively protect their crown's commercial interest from all other internal competition in tea, oil and elephant trade in the fertile Eastern frontier. As Khekiye rightly stated that: "the Inner Line Permit (ILP), which is the off shoot of the regulation, did not originate with a specific intention of protecting the tribal culture and welfare as is often expounded, it had nevertheless served a side purpose of preventing most of the North East Indian tribes from the outright outsiders' exploitation."[694] The Government of India in its post-Independence era continued with the British policy of restriction in the "Protected Areas" in 1950's by simply replacing the reference of "British subject" to that of "citizen of India" while retaining the same restrictive contents for application in Nagaland in particular and elsewhere in the North East India in general.

With regard to Mizoram, the Chin Hills Regulation (Regulation V) of 1896 was enacted to protect the Mizo people from the exploitation of outsiders;

---

693 O. Artus, "Sabbath Year and Jubilee in Lev 25," *Indian Theological Studies 50/3-4* (September & December, 2003), 235.

694 Khekiye K. Sema, "Setting Up of Nagaland Special Disaster Zones (NSDZs)!" in *Challenges of Land Development in Nagaland,* edited by Takatemjen (Aolijen, Mokokchung: Clark Center for Peace and Research and Action (CCPRA), 2015, 216.

the regulation authorized the superintendent of Lushia Hills (now Mizoram) to order an 'undesirable outsider' to leave the area and to tax the residents. The Government of India Act of 1919 did not change the policy of protection. The Simon Commission was formed to examine the matter for further constitutional reforms and the recommendation was embodied in section 91 & 92 of the Government of India Act of 1935, and declared Mizoram as excluded area.[695] The protection of the weaker section has been regarded as essential component of tribal development.

Recently the publication of the final National Residential Certificate (NRC) draft has once again brought to fore how sensitive the North East Indian are of the illegal migration, and that they consider migration a grave threat to the identity and political rights of the ethnic group residing in the region.

The news of over 40 lakhs applicants (out of total 3.29 Crore) being left out of the final draft, neighbouring North East India states of Meghalaya, Arunachal Pradesh, Nagaland and Manipur which share boundaries with Assam raised the alarm that those left out of the final NRC draft would flock to their states to avoid detention and deportation in Assam. The NRC in Assam is being updated in view of the burning problem of illegal migration from Bangladesh so that it becomes easier to differentiate between genuine Indian Citizen and illegal migrants who had sneaked into the state after 24th March, 1971 which is the cut-off date mentioned in Assam accord for detection of illegal migrants.

Few years back in 31st August, 2015 The Manipur state assembly had passed the protection of Manipur People Bill, 2015, the Manipur Land Revenue and Land Reform (Seventh Amendment) Bill, 2015 and the Manipur shop's and establishments (2nd Amendment) Bill, 2015.[696] which was been slammed by the Chief Minister of other neighbouring states asserting that the bill were intended to protect the original settler of Manipur, and harming the interest on any indigenous community in the state.

Above all the tribal communities in the plains who were not protected from their neighbour's traders are victims of exploitation and discrimination. They lost their land, culture and identity in the process of assimilation. One concrete example in North East India is Tripura where the tribal population which formed majority, just before Indian Independence was reduced to minority. The Tripura population in 1951 was only 6.42 lakhs which shot up to 11.42 lakhs increase by 78.71%. In the same year the rate of population growth in India was 21.64%. Population in this century (1901-1981) was increased

695 R. Lianhnuni, *Legal Protection for the Poor in Ancient Israel...*, 339.

696 *Nagaland Post,* September 15, 2015.

by 1,084.51% against 187.05% increase in the whole of India.[697] The 2011 Census the population size is 3673917.[698] Even in Meghalaya the population has reported highest decadal growth not only among all the North East Indian states but also among all the special category states and even states with vast international borders like Punjab and Rajasthan. The state with a population of 29, 64,007 recorded 27.82 percent of decadal growth, higher than the national average in the provisional report of Census 2011. In the last Census, the state has a population 23, 18,822.[699] No reason can be given for the high decadal growth of population in Meghalaya it is believed that large number of illegal immigrants from neighbouring Bangladesh is believed to have counted in the state. Many such foreigner are entering from neighbouring Assam since they cannot go to other North East Indian states Arunachal Pradesh, Nagaland and Mizoram because of the inner line permit.

The legal protection of גר in the ancient Israel provides a hermeneutical clue to affirm the existing inner line regulation and other legal provisions for the protection of the North East Indian community. The question of lifting the laws of protection does not arise; rather the provision must be properly implemented.

6.5.7. Protection of Residence Alien

The issue of alien in North East India is not an isolated issue; it is a burning problem in all countries of the world, and particularly in the first world. The issue of aliens in North East India can be compared to the aliens in the laws of Israel. Just as there are two groups, *gerims* and *nokri* in the Old Testament. The *nokri* of the Old Testament who were probably involved in trade and commerce, as such are not poor and needy may be compared with Bengali traders who tried to control trade and commerce in Mizoram, or Bangladesh and Pakistan in Assam, *Meyas* of Bangladesh in Nagaland, they are not focused in this paper.

As Lianhnuni asserts: "The *Lai and Mara* who have been participating in the social and political life of Mizoram are ethnically regarded as Mizo, they are treated as alien. Their social and economic condition is more or less the same with the rest of population. In this work *Chakma, Bru* and the people coming from Burma are treated as the aliens in Mizoram."[700] The word *Bru* (earlier known as Reang) means 'person' or 'human being' and it is the

697 *Basic Statistic of North East Region* (Shillong: North Eastern Council, 1990), 6; A. K. Agarwal, *Economic Problem and Planning in North-East India* (New Delhi: sterling Publishers Private Limited, 1987), 56-57.

698 www.censusindia.gov. in/2011, accessed on 15th September, 2015, time: 10:07 P.M.

699 "Meghalaya records highest decadal growth in NEI Nagaland only state with negative growth (-0.47%). In *The Shillong Times*, 1st April, 2011.

700 R. Lianhnuni, *Legal Protection for the Poor...*, 373.

favourite identifying term of the Bru of Mizoram.[701] Refugee languishing in different, Tripura relief camps since October 1997, after the murder of a Mizo forest warden. *Chakma* or *Chukma* comes from the word 'Ma,' 'Mi,' (Mian) which refers to pronoun 'I' or to noun or to nation in the Burmese and the Arakanese language. In other words Ma, Mi (Mian) connotes man or people. Therefore the word *Chawngma* or *Sawngma* or *Chakma* or *Chukma* means people of *Tsak*or *Thek* clan who are the progenitor of the Burmese race.[702]

The *Chakma* and *Bru* who gradually came to live in Mizoram do not ethnically belong to Mizo tribe; they are distinct tribal groups. Since they were not Mizo they have been house tax of Rs 5/- was collected from them while Rs 2 was fixed for Mizo.[703] Another group of aliens who came from Burma is difficult to categorize. They belong to Mizo-Chin group, but they lived in Burma for many years and some of them for generations that many of them cannot speak proper Mizo anymore. Due to political and economic crisis with the Burmese government, they were drawn to Mizoram in search of better living conditions.

Similar to Mizoram, in Arunachal Pradesh *Chakmas* and *Hajongs*who settled for generations have raised many questions. The indigenous people living in the area where the refugees are settled have raised their voice against the central government's initiative of settling them there. Though apparently there is no physical displacement of the indigenous population due to the settlement of these refugees, the indigenous people seem to feel threatened by their presence.

The *Chakmas* and *Hajongs* were displaced from the Chittagong Hill tracks and Mymensingh district of present day Bangladesh due to religious persecution and installation of the Kaptai Dam in that area. As Panigrahi asserts: "the first batch of these refugees was settled in Arunachal Pradesh then known as the Tirap Division of North East Frontiers Agency (NEFA) in 1964.[704] The decision was unilateral by nature, and the indigenous people were neither taken into confidence nor consulted.

September 20, 2015 was a relief for the *Chakma* and *Hajong* refugees as the supreme Court has directed the Center and Arunachal Pradesh government to grant citizenship within three months to *Chakma* and *Hajong* tribals who had migrated from Bangladesh in 1964-69, saying they cannot be discriminated in any manner. A bènch of Justice Dave and Goel said: "They could not be

701 T. Vanlaltlani, *A Study of Religious Identity Among the Bru of Mizoram* (Delhi: ISPCK, 2007), 46.

702 S. P. Talukdar, *The Chakmas Life and Struggle* (Delhi: Gian Publishing House, 1988), 6.

703 Lianhnuni, *Legal Protection for the Poor*..., 372.

704 P. K. Panigrahi, "Displacement and Refugee Issue in Arunachal Pradesh," in *Blisters on their Feet Tales of Internally Displaced Person in India's North East,* edited by Samir Kumar Das (New Delhi: Sage Publication, 2008), 57.

discriminated against in any manner pending formal conferment of rights to citizenship. Their status also stands duly acknowledged in the guideline of the election Commission of India."[705] The apex court said that the *Chakmas* have the right to be granted citizenship as it is even "recognized by judicial decisions that they cannot be required to obtain any Inner Line permit as they are settled in Arunachal Pradesh."

The Israelites were themselves once aliens in the land of Egypt. In the later period after Israel's settlement, *gerim* refers to those non-Israelites who have found a home in Israel. The presence of *gerim* among the Israelites was not unique to them as there were also analogies in ancient near eastern literature. It is the commandment of God that they should not oppress the aliens within their own community

6.5.8. The Question of Women, Land and Identity

It is a common phenomenon in all the patriarchal, male dominated society that women are poor in terms of their discrimination and underprivileged condition on the basis of gender. In the context of land and identity, gender land relationship within the scope of customary law unequivocally points akin to that of stranger in the village who, even though given the rights to cultivate and reside, are never accorded proprietary right of control and ownership. While women cannot be considered as גר or stranger on account of their kinship ties yet they were neither given the status nor rights of full citizenship. Denial, thus, of land rights to women under North East Indian culture effectively renders them secondary citizenship equating them in a sense with resident aliens within their own society, negating their identity unless used as an addendum to a male's. So, women were not included among the privileged group.

Today it is a widely acknowledged fact that the systematic exclusion of a category of people from any sphere of social activity is symptomatic of social discrimination. The lack of land rights by North East Indian women indicates that they are victims of discrimination since land is considered the most fundamental resources to women's living conditions, economic empowerment and to some extent; they struggle for equity within a patriarchal society.

Customary laws defines gender relations to that they delineate the roles of men and women. Gender refers to a structural relationship of inequality between women and men based on perceived sex differences, which is manifested in society, politics, economy, ideology and in culture.[706] Khasis

705 "Grant citizenship to Chakma, Hajong tribals in 3 months: SC," *Nagaland Post,* Septemper 21st 2015.

706 Benerjee Paula, "The Space Between: Women's Negotiation with Democracy," in *Dimensions of Development in Nagaland,* edited by C. Joshua Thomas and Durudas Das (New Delhi: Regency Publication, 2002), 52.

and Garo women in the state of Meghalaya, the other parts of the North East India practices patrilineage wherein inheritance occurs through the male line.

The exclusion from societal governance has multiple implications on social, political and economic status of women in North East Indian society. For one, though apparently unrelated, it renders them vulnerable to domestic violence among other forms of gender based discrimination. Property and land rights can strengthen a woman's fallback position and her bargaining power within marriage, which likely serves to deter violence. And because this right can enhance a women's self-worth, they can thereby reduce her tolerance to violence. Marginalization in decision making institutions severely negates their political presence making them voiceless, and their valuable productive contribution to the economy becomes invisible due to their dispossessed status. Women's lack of title to landed property and inheritance means less access to agricultural services and credit as well which serves to perpetuate the cycle of dependency and poverty.

In Mizoram ownership of land had never been an issue for women and men in the past because there was no privatization of land. The community owned the land and the chief was the guardian. As time passed by, lack of ownership of land had become an issue for women as privatization of land set in. With the coming of the British and later the Indian rule, families began to have their own land. Women do not have their own land nor do they inherit property unless they are widowed.

As Ralte question: "Since the Mizo community land holding pattern was destroyed and was replaced by a permanent land-holding system called 'patta-system,' a few new question arise as to whether women should claim land as with men? Is land right an emerging issue at all since she can be divorced by one word? Can she manage agriculture, house and shops by herself? Since the patta system was introduced land has become the prime asset, and land ownership has unequal implication for men and women."[707] Thus, the concept needs to be reconstructed.

Even among the Naga customary laws Naga women have no right to own or inherit the most vital segments of land in the Naga villages and their territories,[708] namely, the village owned land, clan owned land, ancestral clan owned land and land owned by individual families.[709] The first three categories

707 Lalrinawmi Ralte, "A Feminist Critique of Land Holding Patterns in Mizoram," 243.

708 Imsong, *God-Land-People*, 169.

709 Pangernungba, "Land and *Ali-Rongsen* (Cultural-Political Economy): An Ao Naga Perspective," in *Tribal Ecology: A Search for Ecological Values from the Cultures and Practices of the Tribes of North East India,* Tribal Study series, No. 20, edited by Razouselie Lasetso, Marlene Ch. Marak and Yangkahao Vashum (Jorhat: ETC Programme Coordination, 2012), 166ff.

of land constitute 80-90% of the total land of a village land.[710] Naga women are not entitled to hold or own all the categories of the land of the village. "The right to ownership of land, whether private, clan or community land, always rests with men and is never owned by women"[711] While women cannot be considered as foreigners or גר in their own states, but rejection, of land rights to women under NE culture effectively render them secondary citizens equating them in a sense with resident aliens within their own society.

The Israelite law does provide hermeneutical point for challenge and improving the condition of women in the social circle. Outside the legal text occasional references to women in positions of leadership both in religious and social circle such as, Miriam, Deborah, and Huldah may be used as hermeneutical challenge. When occasion demands Israelite did not hesitate to appoint women as leader both in social and religious circle.

6.6. Conclusion

As North East Indian societies are largely tribal/community based, their norms of social behaviour are distinctly different from the North also other parts Indian communities, which are essentially shaped by caste based and patriarchal norms. These cultural deviations when juxtaposed with other divergences (such as food habits, faith, physical features and personal traits) result in undesirable social labelling of the migrants. For example, social relations in North East Indian societies are more egalitarian and the resultant friendly mingling and free social assimilation of women is often mistaken for lack of moral values. These misconception leads to discrimination and atrocities in the public space.

To some extent, the discriminations could be attributed to the lack of exposureof the local community to the richcultural heritage and social norms andvalues of tribal communities of the North East India. The images created by popular media about tribal societies (highlighting distinct traditional outfits and folk dances) are in contradiction to the modern and stylish outfits of the migrant youth.

Tagging the migrants as "terrorists "and "anti-nationals" citing insurgencies back home is yet another aspect of social labelling that the migrants have to endure. In many cases, the wrong portrayal of facts by the media and erroneous conceptualizations by the urban residents – especially the middle classes– are factors that have added to such misconceptions. On the whole, the findings of the study suggests an apparent "cultural gap"

710 Imsong, *God-Land-People,* 168.

711 Lanusashi Longkumer and Toshimenla Jamir, *Status of Adivasis/Indigenous peoples Land Series 6: Nagaland–Land Alienation: Dynamics of Colonialism, Security and Development* (Delhi: AAKAR Books, 2012), 32.

between the migrant and local societies, which is central to the hardships of people from the North East India Region in the city. This calls for efforts towards highlighting the rich cultural heritage and ethos of the North East Indian societies, along with providing various support systems for migrants in the city.

It is evident from our description that a common thread that connects all the ethnopolitical movements of the region is the people's fear of losing the power to control their destiny in the hands of "outsiders." The people identity consciousness has been largely shaped by the fear of being suppressed by larger groups.This is what called xenophobia.[712] This is not an exaggeration. Facts defy the perception that we Indians are tolerant group of people.

There are reasons to be concerned as immigrants have outnumbered the indigenous people and have ousted them from the political and economic authority in states like Tripura. In this situation, maintenance of distinctive social and cultural tradition appears to have grave social-economic and political consequences. Some of the key problems among the tribes of North East India are:

1. Problems of communication
2. Negligence of educational programme
3. Ignorance of cultural values
4. Non implementation of programme on time.

Though we do not have sabbatical or Jubilee law, etc., but the customary law, the land system, the Gleaning law, legal protection and the development policies may be framed from the perspective of the גר, so that the message of justice and liberation, development of the migrants may be made the content of these laws and system. This will be the way in which the significance of the legal protection of the גר in ancient Israel may be drawn meaningfully in the context of גר in North East India.

712 Xenophobia: a negative attitude and behavior against people and groups and outsiders of all types who are aliens and different. Xenophobes hate the language, culture, clothing, and nationalities of others. Racism on the other hand, hates the 'race' and 'descent.' Whereby both naturally can go hand in hand. They mostly do, but it does not have to be the case." Cf. Thomas Schirrmacher, *Racism,* The WEA Global Issue Series, Vol. 8 (Bonn: Verlag fur Kultur und Wissenschaft Culture and Science Publisher, 2011), 17.

Conclusion

Though Israel defined herself as "God's treasured possession" (Deut 7), she cannot be charged as particularistic, because, as the study shows, she had opening towards others. Particularly Israel's concern for the *Gër, Nokri, Toshab* and *Sakir* is a great witness for her universalistic attitude.

In comparison with Ancient West Asia question is still one of sources, but it takes us one level deeper. These ideologies make a further contribution to the on-going debate about the writing of the history of ancient Israel. What come into the mind of the reader what were the sources for the provisions in these law collections. This is where scholarship diverges and disagreements are keen. The starting point is usually the idea that the codes are the product of the same pseudo-scientific efforts that gave us other collections or lists. As explained above different societies of Ancient West Asia reacted differently to the challenge of incorporating newcomers.

Aliens and ethnic identity of ancestral narrative of Genesis serves an important function in the construction of an *ethnie,* helping to clarify the ideological map of the text by colouring certain locations with shades of alienation and others with shades of belonging. As the patriarch move through the land of Canaan and its surrounding regions, the narrative uses the theme of alien to describe their relationship with the land. Residing as anגר in Canaan is positioned as the homeland, the location of belonging and destiny. This is clear in the stories of both Abraham and Jacob. In contrast to this position stand Egypt and Paddan-aram, where the patriarchs resides as alien temporarily, with clear structural emphasis on their eventual return. On the other hand Egypt is excluded from the chosen lineage, but keeps threatening to enter in. The ancestral account thus portrays a dominion negative orientation towards Egypt in contrast to a more positive orientation towards Mesopotamia.

Secondly, the above study shows, the consideration for גר appears constantly in the legislative texts of the Torah, either out of a generosity recalling the deliverance from slavery in Egypt granted by God in Deut 16:11-12. It is the Holiness Code, however, that formulates the most audacious rules concerning the גר. The גר is no longer an 'exclusive' of the law; he becomes an 'inclusive', responsible together with the local inhabitants of the land for its holiness and its purity. Local inhabitants and 'aliens' are therefore united in a common responsibility and by a bond described by the vocabulary of love (cf. Lev 19:33-34). The Holiness Code then legislates for the integration of גר, or at least of migrants, into the community of the children of Israel. Old Testament does not propose a temporary solution for the problem of migrants; it creates a permanent solution by formulating laws to welcome them, to treat them with dignity and respect, and to give them love and their rights, and to integrate them into the community.

Thirdly, the law articulated in the Hebrew Bible concerning the גר can be arranged under two categories. On the one hand, there are laws formulated to protect the *gerim.* Prohibition is made for Israel to explore and oppress the גר (Ex 22: 20; 23:9; Lev 19:33-34; Deut 24:14; Jer 22:3). Israel has an obligation to respect the custom of leaving the fields for gleanings by the poor and the *gerim* (Lev 19:10; 23:22; Deut 24:19-21). An example of this is given in the book of Ruth chapter 2. The triennial tithe is entirely devoted to the poor, which includes the גר (Deut 14:29; 26:12-13). The Jew has no right to cheat the law of the גר (Deut 24: 17; 27:19).

The rhetoric of Deuteronomy is one passage speaks of protection of the poor and the needy as on the other hand destroying the indigenous people. It is pointed out that the ideology of Deuteronomy is very exclusive and its treatment of indigenous peoples compatible with the ideologies that accompany genocides and conquest. The Deuteronomy's rhetoric establishes the rights of the Indigenous peoples to the protection of their cultural property and identity. Legal protection and gleaning provisions for the גר, orphan, and widow in Deut 24:17-18, 19-22; and 27:19 might be considered the strongest evidence for the indigenous ethnicity of the גר. The researchers disagree with Houten concluding remark: "the alien's identity was forged by an act in the past which would not be repeated, and which separated them from all other people; there are no ways for non-Israelites to become Israelites. Aliens were considered non-Israelites, and there was no way that status could be changed."[713]Anyone who argues that the aliens was a non-Israelites must explain why the Book of Deuteronomy presents a set of laws designed to protect aliens, and does not apply them to the needy of the Judahite origin. Yet, this question totally neglects the vision of Deut 15:11: "For there will

713 Houton, *Aliens in Israelite Law,* 108.

never cease to be poor in the land. Therefore, I command you, 'you shall open wide your hand to your brother (אח), to the needy and to the poor, in your land.' The solidarity and benevolence of Israelite or Judahite kinsfolk infused with a social identity defined by YHWH's redemption (15:15) was the DC's mechanism to meet local Judahite or Israelite needs. Deut 24:14-15 also ensures the local Judahite fair compensation.

Fourthly, the researcher argued that Deuteronomy has revised certain גר laws from the Covenant Code, but has diverged both lexically and often conceptually from גר laws from the Holiness collection. The inner-biblical analyses have uncovered Deuteronomy's theological and sociological tendencies displayed in its גר laws.

Fifthly, Hebrew Bible has laws to integrate the migrant into the community of Israel. The migrant, if circumcised, can celebrate the Passover (Ex 12:28; Num 9:14). He has the ability to offer a sacrifice at the entrance of the tent of the meeting (Lev 17:8), he can offer a holocaust in the condition that the animal chosen is a male without blemish (Lev 22:18), he also has the right to make vegetable offerings (Num 15:14-16). During the rituals atonement for unintentional mistakes, forgiveness is granted to all including the גר (Num 15:26). The possibility for the migrant to flee to one of the six refuge cities is granted him (Num 35:10; Josh 20:9). Above all there is only one law in Israel, for the גר as for the natives (Lev 4:22; Deut 31:12), the reading of the law is made before all people, גר and natives (Josh 8:33, 35) as, One ritual of the Passover (Num 9:14), One law for sin, the same for all (Num 15:30). All this law are made to integrate them.

In all human societies, foreigners are perceived as a threat, whether they speak a different language or not, whether their appearance is different or not, whether they come from far away or from the next village. However, the Biblical laws concerning גר exclude all exploitation, all apartheid, all ethnic cleansing, all forced removals, all racial prejudice. These things are unworthy of God's people. It is true that the scale of the issue addressed by the Biblical law is smaller than that of the modern world.[714] Israel never forgot its origins. It remembered that its ancestors were גר. And so its laws always insisted that גר were to be treated kindly and with respect. Much later in Israelite history, the prophet Zechariah expected whole nations to attach themselves to the Hebrews in order to seek their God (Zech 8:20-23). The book of Acts records a hesitant but gradual acceptance of Gentile converts into the Christian community, which initially consisted of Jews. Yet in our days, גר even in small numbers, stand little chance of being accepted and cared for in most countries.

---

714 G. W. Ashby, *Go out and meet God: A Commentary on the Book of Exodus,* ITC (Grand Rapids: Eerdmans, 1997), 107.

Simarlarly, care and concern shown to the poor and needy, widow, orphans and aliens in society expressed in various form in the Israelites law are directly applicable to the North East Indians. Laws which are directly applicable to the North East India like hospitability shown to the stranger, daily wages should not be withheld, laws like charity in the gleaning law, the granting of rest to the daily labourers or servants on Sabbath day (in the context on Sunday) are important messages to the people of the North East India. Hermeneutically all these laws become very much relevant for the whole of India and particularly for the North East Indians.

Bibliography

A: Books, Dictionaries, and Commentaries

Achenbach, R. "ger-nokhri-tishav-zar." In *The Foreigners and the Law: Perspective from the Hebrew Bible and the Ancient Near East.* Edited by Achenbach, Reinhard, Rainer Albertz, and Jakob Wöhrle. Wiesbaden: Harronowitz, 2011.

Ackroyd, P. R. *Exile and Restoration.* Philadelphia: Westminster Press, 1968.

Agarwal, A. K. *Economic Problem and Planning in North-East India.* New Delhi: Sterling Publishers Private Limited, 1987.

Ahlstrom, Gosta W. "The Role of Archaeological and Literary Remains in Reconstructing Israel." In *The Fabric of History: Text, Artifact and Israel's Past.* Edited by D.V. Ede lman, JSOT Sup127. Sheffield: JSOT Press, 1991.

________. *The History of Ancient Palestine from the Palaeolithic Period to Alexander's Conquest.* Edited by D. V. Edelman, JSOT Sup 146. Sheffield: JSOT Press, 1993.

________. *Who is the Israelites?* Winona Lake, Ind.: Eisenbrauns, 1986.

Albertz, Rainer. *A History of Israelite Religion in the Old Testament Period.* Vol.1. London: SCM, 1992.

Albertz, Rainer. *Israel in Exile: The History and Literature of the Sixth Century B.C.E.* Translated by David Green. Atlanta: Society for Biblical Literature, 2003.

Albright, W. F. *Yahweh and the Gods of Canaan.* London: University of London Press, 1978.

Alt, A. *Essay on Old Testament History and Religion.* Garden City, New York: Doubleday, 1968.

Alt, Albrecht. "The Origins of Israelite Laws." In *Essay on Old Testament History and Religion.* Oxford: Basil Blackwell, 1966.

Alter, Robert. "Sodom as Nexus: The Web of Design in Biblical Narrative." *The Book and the Text: The Bible and Literary Theory*. Edited by Regina Schwartz. Cambridge: Basil Blackwell, 1986.

Amin, Samir. *Class and Nation, Historically and in the Present Crisis*. New York/London: Monthly Review, 1980.

Anderson, Cheryl B. *Women, Ideology, and Violence Critical Theory and the Construction of Gender in the Book of Covenant and the Deuteronomic Law.* JSOT Supl 394. London, New York: T&T Clark International, 2004.

Ashby, G. W. *Go Out and Meet God: A Commentary on the Book of Exodus.* ITC. Grand Rapids: W. B. Eerdmans, 1997.

Ashley, T. R. *The Book of Numbers.* NICOT. Grand Rapids: W. B. Eerdmans, 1993.

Awabdy, Mark Abraham. "He Loves the Immigrant: Deuteronomy's Theological and Vision for the גר." Ph.D dissertation, Asbury Theological Seminary, 2012.

Awabdy, Mark A. *Immigrants and Innovative Law.* Tubingen, Germany: Mohr Siebeck, 2014.

Barr, James. *History and Ideology in the Old Testament: Biblical Studies at the End of the Millennium.* Oxford: University Press, 2005.

Barth, Frederik. "Introduction." In *Ethnic Groups and Boundaries: The Social Organization of Culture Difference.* Edited by Frederik Barth. Boston: Little Brown and Company, 1969.

Bauman, Zygmunt. "From Pilgrim to Tourist-or a Short History of Identity." In *Questions of Cultural Identity.* Edited by Stuart Hall and Paul du Gay. New Delhi: SAGE Publications, 1997.

Bedford, Peter R. *Temple Restoration in Early Achaemenid Judah.* Leiden: Brill, 2001.

Begg, T. Christopher. "Foreigner." *Anchor Bible Dictionary* 2. New York: Doubleday, 1992: 829-830.

Bergsma, John Sietze. *The Jubilee from Leviticus to Qumra.* Suplt to Vetus Testamentum Vol. 15. Leiden, Boston: Brill, 2007.

Berquist, Jon L. *Judaism in Persia's Shadow: A Social and Historical Approach.* Eugene, Oregon: Wipf and Stock Publishers, 1995.

Berquist, Jon L. "Constructions of identity in Postcolonial Yehud." In *Judah and the Judeans in the Persian Period,* edited by Oded Lipschits and Manfred Oeming. Eisenbrauns: Winona Lake, Indiana, 2006.

Biddle, Mark E. *Deuteronomy.* Smyth and Helwys Bible Commentary. Macon, Ga: Smyth and Helwys, 2003.

Bird, Phyllis A. "Poor Man or Poor Woman: Gendering the poor in Prophetic Texts." In *Missing Persons and Mistaken Identities: Woman and Gender in Ancient Israel.* Minneapolis: Fortress Press, 1997.

Blenkinsopp, Joseph. "The Pentateuch." In *The Cambridge Companion to Biblical Interpretation.* Edited by John Barton. Cambridge: University press, 2011.

________. "Constructions of Identity in Postcolonial Yehud." In *Judah and the Judeans in the Persian Period.* Edited by Oded Lipschits and Manfred Oeming. Winona Lake, Indiana: Eisenbrauns, 2006.

________. *The Pentateuch: An Introduction to the first Five Books of the Bible.* London: SCM Press, 1992.

________. "Temple and Society in Achaemenid Judah." In *Second Temple Studies 1: Persian period.* Edited by Philip R. Davies, JSOT Sup 117. Sheffield: Sheffield Academic, 1991.

________. *Gibeon and Israel.* SOTSMS, 2. Cambridge: Cambridge University Press, 1972.

Boadt, Lawrence. *Reading the Old Testament: An Introduction.* New York: Paulist Press, 1984.

Boecker, H. J. *Law and the Administration of Justice in the Old Testament and the Ancient East.* Minneapolis: Augsburg, 1980.

Boerman, Conrad. *Richman, Poor Man and the Bible.* London: SCM, 1979.

Bodie, Daniel. *The Demise of the Warlord: A New Look at the David Story.* Hebrew Bible Monographs 26. Sheffield: Sheffield Phoenix, 2010.

Breet, M. G. "Interpreting Ethnicity." *Ethnicity and the Bible.* Edited by M. G. Breet, Biblical Interpretation Series 19. Leden: Brill, 1996.

Brettler, Marc Zvi. *The Creation of History in Ancient* Israel. London and New York: Routledge, 1995.

Briddle, Mark E. *Deuteronomy.* Smyth and Helwys Bible Commentary. Macon, Ga: Smith and Helwys, 2003.

Bright, John. "Hebrew Religion, History of." *Interpreter's Bible Dictionary 2.* Nashville: Abingdon Press, 1962.

Brown, Francis, S. R. Driver, and Charles A. Briggs. *A Hebrew and English Lexicon of the Old Testament.* Oxford: Clarendon Press, 1979.

Calhoun, Craig. *Critical Social Theory: Culture, History, and the Challenge of Difference.* Oxford: Basil Blackwell, 1995.

Carr, David M. *The Formation of the Hebrew Bible: A New Reconstruction.* Oxford: Oxford University Press, 2011.

Carter, Charles E. *The Emergence of Yehud in the Persian Period A Social and Demographic Study.* JSOT Suplt Series 294. Sheffield: Sheffield Academic Press, 1999.

Cassuto. *A Commentary on the Book of Genesis.* Jerusalem: The Magnes Press, 1984.

Cassuto, U. *A Commentary on the Books of Exodus.* Jerusalem: The Magnes Press, 1951.

Chalcraft, David J. *Social-Scientific Old Testament Criticism: A Sheffield Reader.* Sheffield: Academic Press, 1997.

Childs, B. S. *The Book of Exodus: A Critical, Theological Commentary.* OTL; Philadelphia: Westminster Press, 1962.

Christopher, Daniel Smith. *A Biblical Theology of Exile.* Minneapolish: Fortress Press, 2002.

Clements, Ronald E. "The Book of Deuteronomy." In *the New Interpreter's Bible A Commentary.* Vol. 2. Nashville: Abingdon Press, 1998.

Clements, R. E. *Deuteronomy: Old Testament Guides.* Sheffield: JSOT Press, 1976.

Clement, Ronald ed. *The World of Ancient Israel: Sociological Anthropological & Political Perspective.* Cambridge: Cambridge University Press, 1989.

Clifford, Geertz. *The Interpretation of Culture.* New York: Basic Books, 1973.

Clines, David, J. A. *Ezra, Nehemiah and Easter.* New Century Bible. Grand Rapids: Eerdmans, 1984.

________. *Interested Parties: The Ideology of Writers and Readers of the Hebrew Bible.* Edited by David J. A. Clines and Philip R. Davies, JSOT Supp 205. Sheffield: Sheffield Academic Press, 1995.

________. *What Does Eve Do to Help? And Other Readerly Question to the Old Testament.* JSOT Supplement 94. Sheffield: Sheffield Academic Press, 1990.

________. *The Theme of the Pentateuch.* JSOT Sup10. Sheffield: Sheffield Academic Press, 2004.

Coats, G. W. "A Threat to the Host." In *Saga, Legend, Tale, Novella, Fable: Narrative Forms in Old Testament Literature.* Edited by G. Coat. JSOT Supt 35. Sheffield: JSOT Press, 1985.

________. *Genesis with an Introduction to Narrative Literature*. Vol. 1. Grand Rapids, Michigan: William B. Eerdmans Publishing Company, 1983.

Conville, J. G. *Deuteronomy* Apollos Old Testament Commentary 5. Leicester: Apollos; Downers Grove, 111: Inter Varsity, 2002.

________. *Law and Theology in Deuteronomy.* JSOT Sup 33. Sheffield: *JSOT*, 1985.

Cook, L. Stephen. *The Social Roots of Biblical Yahwism*. Atlanta: SBL, 2004.

Coote, Robert B. & Keith W. Whitelam. *The Emergence of Early Israel in Historical Perspective.* Sheffield: Sheffield Phoenix Pres, 2010.

Craigie, Peter C. *The Book of Deuteronomy, The New International Commentary on the Old Testament.* Grand Rapids, Michigan: Wm. B. Eerdmans Publishing Company, 1976.

Cross, F. M. *Canaanite Myth and Hebrew Epic: Essay in the History of the Religion of Israel.* Cambridge, MA: Harvard University Press, 1973.

Crüsemann, Frank. *The Torah Theology and Social History of Old Testament Law*. Translated by Allan W. Mahnke. Edinburgh: T&T Clark, 1996.

Davies, Philips R. *In Search of 'Ancient Israel.* JSOT Sup 148. Sheffield: JSOT Press, 1992.

________. *The origin of the Biblical Israel.* LHBOTS 485. New York and London: T&T Clark, 2007.

de Vaux, Roland. *Ancient Israel: Its life and Institution.* Translated by John McHugh. London: Darton, Longman & Todd, 1961.

________. *Ancient Israel.* New York: Mc Graw-Hill, 1961.

Derrida, Jacques. "Difference." In *Speech and Phenomena, and Other Essay on Husserl's Theory of Signs*. Evanston: Northwestern University Press, 1973.

________. "Deconstruction and the Other." In *Dialogue with Contemporary Continental Thinkers.* Edited by Richard Kearney. Manchester: University of Manchester press, 1984.

Dever, W. G. *Who Were the Early Israelites and Where Did They Come* From? Grand Rapids, Michigan: Eerdmans, 2003.

________. *Recent Archaeological Discoveries and Biblical Research.* Seattle: University of Washington Press, 1990.

________. *What Did the Biblical Writers know and When Did They Know it?* Grand Rapids, Michigan: William B. Eerdmans Publishing Company, 2001.

________. "Archaeology and the Emergence of Early Israel." In *Archaeology and Biblical Interpretation.* Edited by J. R. Bartlett. London: Routledge, 1997.

Dever, William G. "Israel, History of (Archaeology and the Conquest)." *Anchor Bible Dictionary.* Vol. 3. New York: Doubleday, 1992, 545-558.

Douglas, Mary. *In the Wilderness: The Doctrine of Defilement in the Book of Numbers.* Sheffield: JSOT Press, 1993.

________. *Purity and Danger: An Analysis of Concept of Pollution and Taboo.* London: Routledge and kegan paul, 1966.

________. *Implicit Meanings: Essay in Anthropology.* London: Routledge and Kegan Paul, 1975.

________. *Leviticus as Literature.* Oxford: University Press, 1989.

Dowd, Ryan O. *The Wisdom of Torah: Epistemology in Deuteronomy and the Wisdom Literature.* Gottingen: Vandenhoeck & Ruprecht, 2009.

Dozeman, Thomas B. *The Book of Numbers.* In *New Interpreters Bible.* Vol. 11. Nashville: Abingdon Press, 1998.

Durham, John I. *Exodus. Word Biblical Commentary*. Vol. 3. Waco, TX: Word Books, 1987.

Dyck, Jonathan E. *The Theocratic Ideology of the Chronicler.* Vol. 33. Leiden: Brill, 1988.

Cohn, Robert L. "The Second Coming of Moses: Deuteronomy and the Construction of Israelite Identity." In *Proceeding of the Twelfth World Congress of Jewish Studies.* Jerusalem: World Union of Jewish Studies, 1999.

Cross, F. M. *Canaanite Myth and Hebrew Epic.* Cambridge: Harvard University Press, 1973.

CycK, Jonathan E. "A Map of Ideology for Biblical Critics." In *Rethinking Contexts, Rereading Texts Contribution from the Social Sciences to Biblical Interpretation.* Edited by M. Daniel Carroll R. Sheffield, England: Sheffield Academic press, 2000.

Croix, G. E. M. De Ste. *The Class Struggle in Ancient Greek World from the Archaic Age to the Arab Conquests*. Ithaca, New York: Cornell University Press, 1981.

Eissfeld, Otto. *The Old Testament: An Introduction.* Translated by P. R. Ackroyd. Oxford: Basil Blackwell, 1966.

Eliott H. John. *What is Social-Scientific Criticism*? Minneapolis: Fortress Press, 1993.

Epsztein, Leon. *Social Justice in the Ancient Near East and the People of the Bible.* Translated by John Bowden. London: SCM Press, 1986.

Exum, J. Cheryl. "Who is Afraid of the Endangered Ancestress?" In *The New Literary Criticism and the Hebrew Bible.* Edited by J. Cheryl Exum and David J. A. Clines. JSOT Supt 143. Sheffield: JSOT Press, 1993.

Fager, J. A. *Land Tenure and the Biblical Jubilee: Uncovering Hebrew Ethics Through the Sociology of Knowledge.* JSOT Suppl Series 155. Sheffield: JSOT Press, 1993.

Finkelstein, Israel. *The Archaeology of the Israelite Settlement.* Jerusalem: Israel Exploration Society, 1988.

________. *The Bible Unearthed: Archaeology's New Vision of Ancient Israel and the Origin of Its Sacred Texts.* New York: Simon and Schuster, 2001.

Fishbane, Michael. *Biblical Interpretation in Ancient Israel.* Oxford: Clarendon, 1985.

Fohrer, Gorge. *Introduction to the Old Testament.* Translated by David Green. London: SPCK, 1970.

Foster, Benjamin R. *Before the Muses: An Anthology of Akkadian Literature.* Bethesda, MD: CDL Press, 1996.

Frick, S. Frank. *The City in Ancient Israel.* Missoula, Montana: The Society of Biblical Literature, 1977.

Fretheim. "The Book of Genesis." In *The Interpreter's Bible.* Edited by Leander E. Keck, Thomas G. Long, David L. Petersen et al. Nashville: Abingdon, 1994.

Frick, F. S. *The City in Ancient Israel.* Society of Biblical Literature Dissertation Series 36 . Missoula, MT: Scholar Press, 1977.

Fried, Lisbeth S. "The 'am ha'ares in Ezra 4:4 and Persian Imperial Administration." In *Judah and the Judeans in the Persian Period.* Edited by Oded Lipschits and Manfred Oeming. Winona Lake, Indiana: Eisenbrauns, 2006.

Fritz, Volkmar. *The Emergence of Israel in the Twelve and Eleventh Century BCE. Biblical Encyclopedia* 2. Atlanta: SBL, 2011.

Fuhs, H. F. "עָלָה ala." *Theological Dictionary of the Old Testament.* Vol. V1. Edited by G. Johannes Botterweck, Helmer Ringgrenn and Heinz-Josef Fabry. Grand Rapids, Michigan: William B. Eerdmans Publishing Company, 2001: 77-79.

Gardiner, Alan H. *Egypt of the Pharaohs.* Oxford: Oxford University Press, 1961.

Gnuse, Robert. *You Shall Not Steal: Community and Property in the Biblical Tradition.* Maryknoll. New York: Orbis Books, 1985.

Goetze, Albrecht. "The Laws of Eshunna." In *Ancient Near Eastern Texts Relating to the Old Testament.* Edited by James B. Pritchard. Princeton. New Jersey: Princeton University Press, 1969.

Golden, Jonathan M. *Ancient Canaan and Israel: An Introduction.* Oxford: Oxford University Press, 2004.

Goldingay, J. "The Patriarchs in Scripture and Tradition." In *Essay on the Patriarchal Narrative.* Edited by A. R. Millard & D. J. Wiseman. Leicester: IVP, 1980.

Gottwald, Norman K. *The Hebrew Bible in Its Social World and in Ours.* Atlanta: Scholars Press, 1993.

________. "Sociology (Ancient Israel)." *Anchor Bible Dictionary* 6. New York: Doubleday, 1992: 79-89.

________. *The Tribes of Yahweh: A Sociological Study of the Religion of Liberated Israel 1250-1050 BCE*. Maryknoll, N.Y.: Orbis Book, 1979.

________. "Sociological Method in the Study of Ancient Israel." In *The Bible and Liberation: Political and Social Hermeneutics.* Edited by Norman K. Gottwald. Maryknoll, New York.: Orbis, 1983.

________. "Early Israel and the Canaanite Sociological System." In *Palestine in Transition: The Emergence of Ancient Israel.* Edited by D. N. Freedman and D. F. Graf. Sheffield: Almond, 1983.

________. *The Tribes of Yahweh.* Maryknoll, New York: Orbis, 1979.

Grabbe, Lester L. *A History of the Jews and Judaism in the Second Temple period.* Vol. 1. London, NY: T&T Clark International, 2004.

Grabbe, Lester L. *Ezra-Nehemiah.* Old Testament Reading. London and New York: Routledge, 1998.

Gracia, J. E. George. *How Can We Know What God Means?: The Interpretation of Revelation.* New York: Palgrave, 2001.

Greenberg, Moshe. "Jewish conceptions of the Human factors in Biblical prophecy." In *Justice and the Holy: Essay in Honor of Walter Harrelson.* Edited by Douglas A. Knight and Peter J. Paris. Atlanta: Scholars, 1989.

Greifenhagen, F. V. *Egypt on the Pentateuch's Ideological Map Constructing Biblical Israel's Identity*. JSOT Supplement Series 361. Sheffield: Sheffield Academic Press. 2002.

Grintz, Yehoshua M. "Gerar." *Encyclopaedia Judaica.* Vol. 7. New York: Thomas Gales, 2007: 505.

Gunkel, H. *Genesis*. 3rd edn. Gottingen: N.p., 1910.

Habel, Norman. *The Land is Mine: Six Biblical Land Ideologies.* Minneapolis: Fortress, 1995.

Halpern, B. "Jerusalem and the Lineages in the seventh Century BCE: Kingship and the Rise of Individual Moral Liability." In *Law and Ideology in Monarchic Israel.* Edited by Baruch Halpern and Deborah W. Hobson Sup series 124. Sheffield: JSOT Press, 1991.

Hallow, W. W. and K. L. Younger, eds. *The Context of Scripture: Canonical Composition from the Biblical World.* Leiden: Brill, 1997.

Hanson, Paul. *The Dawn of Apocalyptic: The Historical and Sociological Roots of Jewish Apocalyptic Eschatology.* Philadelphia: Fortress Press, 1979.

Haokip, Peter. "Tribal Theology: Sources, Methodology and Hermeneutics." *Search for a New Society Tribal Theology for North East India.* Edited by Yankahao Vashum, Peter Haokip and Melvil Pereira. Guwahati: North Eastern Social Research Center, 2012.

Harrison, R. K. *Introduction to the Old Testament with a Comprehensive review of Old Testament Studies and a Special Supplement on the Apocrypha.* Grand Rapids, Michigan: William B. Eerdmans Publishing Company, 1969.

Harold V. Bennett. *Injustice Made Legal: Deutronomic law and the Plight of Widows, Strangers, and Orphans in Ancient Israel.* Grand Rapids, Michigan: William B. Eerdmans Publishing, 2002.

Hartley, John E. "Leviticus." In *Word Biblical Commentary.* Vol. 4. Dallas, Texas: Word Books, Publisher, 1992.

Hawker, Sara "Indigenous." *Oxford English Dictionary.* New Delhi: Oxford University Press, 2011.

Hiebert, Theodore. *The Yahwist's Landscape: Nature and Religion in Early Israel.* Oxford: Oxford University Press, 1996.

Hiebert, Paul S. "Whence Shall Help Come to Me?" The Biblical Widow." Edited by Peggy L. Day. In *Gender and Difference in Ancient Israel.* Minneapolis: Fortress Press, 1989.

Hoffner, "אַלְמָנָה" 'almanah; אַלְמָנוּת 'almanuth." *Theological Dictionary of the Old Testament.* Vol. 1. Grand Rapids Michigan: William B. Eerdmans Publishing Company, 1974: 287-291.

Holladay, J. S. "Religion in Israel and Judah under the Monarchy: An Explicitly Archaeological Approach." In *Ancient Israelite Religion: Essays in honor of Frank Moore Cross*. Edited by P. D. Miller Jr., P. D. Hanson and S. D. McBride. Philadelphia: Fortress, 1987.

________. "The Kingdoms of Israel and Judah: Political and Economic Centralization in the Iron 11 A-B (ca. 1000-750 B.C.E)." In *The Archaeology of Society in the Holy Land.* Edited by Thomas E. Levy. New York: Facts and File, 1995.

Hopkins, David. "Bare Bones: Putting Flesh on the Economic of Ancient Israel." In *Origin of the Ancient Israelite States*. Edited by Volkmar Fritz and Philip R. Davies. JSOT Sup 228. Sheffield: Sheffield Academic Press, 1996.

Hornby, A. S. *Oxford Advanced Learner's Dictionary.* 8th Edition. Oxford: University Press, 2010.

Horowitz, David L. "Ethnic identity." In *Ethnicity: Theory and Experience.* Edited by N. Glazer and D. P. Moynihan. Cambridge, Mass: Harvard University Press, 1975.

Horsley, Richard A. *Scribes, Visionaries and the Politics of Second Temple Judea.* London, Loisville: Westminster John Knox Press, 2007.

Houston, Walter J. "Towards an Integrated Reading of the Dietary Laws of Leviticus." Edited by Rolf Rendtorff and Robert A. Kugler. In *The Book of Leviticus: Composition and Reception.* Leiden, Boston: Brill, 2003.

Houston, Walter J. "Open your Hand to your Needy Brother: Ideology and Moral formation in Deut 15:1-18." In *The Bible in Ethics.* Edited by John Rogerson, Margaret Davies and M. Daniel Carroll R. Sheffield: Academic Press, 1995.

Houten, Christiana Van. *Alien in Israelite Law: A Study of the Changing Legal Status of Strangers in Ancient Israel.* JSOT Suplt 107. Sheffield: Sheffield Academic Press, 1991.

Hutchinson, J. and Anthony D. Smith, eds. *Ethnicity.* Oxford Readers: Oxford University press, 1996.

Imsong, Mar. *God-Land-People: An Ethnic Naga Identity.* Dimapur: Heritage Publishing House, 2009.

Israel, Knohl. *The Sanctuary of Silence: The Priestly Torah and the Holiness School.* Minneapolis, MN: Fortress, 1995.

Jackson, B. S. "Ideas of Law and Legal Administration: A Semiotic Approach." In *The World of Ancient Israel.* Edited by R. E. Clements. Cambridge: Cambridge University Press, 1989.

Jameson, Fredric. *The Political Unconscious: Narrative as a Socially Symbolic Act*. Ithaca: Cornell University Press, 1981.

Jamir, Alemtemshi. "Land Tenure and Reform in Nagaland." In *Challenges of Land Development in Nagaland.* Edited by Takatemjen. Aolijen. Mokokchung: Clark for Peace Research and Action, 2015.

Jamir, L. Imsutoshi. "Who is not us?: The Politics of Tribal Identity." In *Garnering Tribal Resources for Doing Tribal Christian Theology.* Tribal Studies Series 16. Edited by Razouselie Lasetso. Jorhat: ETC Programme Coordination, 2008.

Janzen, J. Gerald. *Abraham and All the Families of the Earth: A Commentary on the Book of Genesis 12-50*. Grand Rapids: Wm. B. Eerdmans Publishing Co., 1993.

Japhet, Sara. "People and Land in the Restoration Period." *Das land Israel im biblischer Zeit: Jerusalem-Symposium 1981 der Hebraischen Universitat Und der Georg-August-Universitat.* Edited by G. Strecker, GTA, 25. Gottingen: Vanden-hoeck & Ruprecht, 1983.

Jobling, David. "'Very Limited Ideological Options:' Marxism and Biblical Studies in Postcolonial Scenes." In *Postcolonial Biblical Criticism: Interdisciplinary Intersections*. Edited by Stephen D. Moore and Fernando F. Segovia. London and New York: T&T Clark, 2005.

Jones, Sian. *The Archaeology of Ethnicity, Constructing Identities in the Past and Present*. London, New York: Routledge 1997a.

________. "Identities in practice: Towards an Archaeological Perspective on Jewish Identity and in Antiquity." In *Jewish Local Patriotism and Self-Identification in the Graeco-Roman Period.* Edited by Sian Jones and Sarah Pearce. Sheffield Academic Press, 1998.

Joosten, Jan. *People and Land in the Holiness Code: An Exegetical Study of the Ideational Framework of the Law in Leviticus 17-26.* Leiden: Brill, 1996.

Josephus, Flavius. *Josephus' Complete Works.* Translated by William Whiston. Grand Rapids, MI: kregel, 1960.

Joy, Joseph. "'Re-Lecturing' of Deuteronomy (Chapter 12-26) in the Post Exilic period." D.Th Dissertation, Munchen University, 1997.

Kaiser, Walter C. "The Book of Leviticus." *The New Interpreter's Bible.* Edited by L. E. Keck, et al. Vol. 12. Nashville: Abingdon Press, 1994.

Kalekin-Fishman, Devorah. "Community and Ethnicity in Israel: interrelationships of theory and practice." In *"Race" Ethnicity and Nation: International perspective on Social Conflict.* Edited by Peter Ratcliff. London: Routledge's, 1994.

Kaufmann, Yehezkel. *The Religion of Israel.* Translated by M. Greenberg. Chicago: University of Chicago Press, 1960.

Kellermann, D. "גור *gur*; גר *ger*; גרות *geruth;* מגורִים *meghurim.*" In *Theological Dictionary of the Old Testament.* Vol-11. Edited by G. Johannes Botterweck and Helmer Ringgren. Grand Rapids, Michigan: William B. Eerdmans Publishing Company, 1975: 439-449.

Kennedy, Elisabeth Robertson. *Seeking A Homeland: Sojourn and Ethnic Identity in the Ancestral Narratives of Genesis*. Leiden: Brill, 2011.

Kessler, M. "A Methodological Setting for Rhetorical Criticism." In *Art and Meaning,* JSOT Sup 19. Sheffield: JSOT Press, 1982.

Kessler, John. "Persia's Loyal Yahwists: Power Identity and Ethnicity in Archaemenid Yehud." In *Judah and the Judeans in the Persian period.* Edited by Oded Lipchits and Manfred Oeming. Winona Lake, Indiana: Eisenbrauns, 2006.

Kessler, John. "Diaspora and Homeland in the Early Achaemenid Period: Community, Geography and Demography in Zechariah 1-8." In *Approaching Yehud-New Approaches to the Study of the Persian Period.* Edited by Jon L. Berquist. Atlanta: Society for Biblical Literature, 2007.

Kessler, Rainer, *The Social History of Ancient Israel: An Introduction.* Translated by Linda M. Maloney. Minneapolis: Fortress Press, 2008.

Kidd, José E. Ramírez. *Alterity and Identity in Israel: The* גר *in the Old Testament. Beiheft zur Zeitschrift fur die Altestamentliche Wissenichaft* 283. Berlin: Walter de Gruyter, 1999.

Killebrew, Ann E. *Biblical People and Ethnicity: An Archaeological Study of Egyptian, Canaanites, Philistines, and Early Israel 1300-1100 B.C.E.* Atlanta: Society of Biblical Literature, 2005.

King, P. J. & L. E. Stager. *Life in Biblical Israel.* Library of Ancient Israel; Louisville, Kentucky: Westminster John Knox, 2001.

Kitchen, K. A. *Ancient Orient and Old Testament.* London: The Tyndale Press, 1966.

Kizhakkeyil, Sebastian. *The Pentateuch: An Exegetical Commentary.* Mumbai: St Paul Society, 2009.

Kline, Meridith G. *Treaty of the Great King-The Covenant Structure of Deuteronomy: Studies and Commentary.* Grand Rapids, Michigan: William B. Eardmans Publishing Company, 1963.

Knierim, R. P. "Customs, Judges and Legislator in Ancient Israel." In *Early Jewish and and Christian Exegesis: Studies in Memory of W. H. Brownlee.* Edited by C. A. Evans and F. Stinespring. Atlanta, Georgia: scholar press, 1987.

Knight, Douglas A. "The Pentateuch." *The Hebrew Bible and the Modern Interpreters.* Edited by D. A. Knight and G. M. Tucker. Philadelphia: Fortress, 1985.

________. "Village Law and the Book of the Covenant." In *A Wise and Discerning Mind: Essay in Honor of Burke O. Long.* Edited by Saul M. Olyan and Robert C. Culley. Province RI: Brown Judaic Studies, 2000.

Knohl, Israel. *The Sanctuary of Silence: The Priestly Torah and the Holiness School.* Minneopolis: Fortress Press, 1995.

Koch, K. *The Growth of the Biblical Tradition.* London, 1969.

Kooy, V. H. "Hospitality." *Interpreter's Dictionary of the Bible.* Vol. 11. Nashville: Abingdon Press, 1976: 654.

Krammer, Samuel. *The Sumerians.* Chicago: University of Chicago, 1963.

Kramer, Samuel Noah. *The Sumerians: Their History, Culture, and Character* Chicago, IL: University of Chicago Press, 1963.

Kunin, Seth Daniel. *The Logic of Incest A Structuralist Analysis of Hebrew Mythology.* JSOT Sup 185. Sheffield: Sheffield Academic Press, 1995.

Leith, Mary Joan Winn. "Israel among the nations: The Persian Period." In *The Oxford History of the Biblical World.* Edited by Coogan Michael D. Oxford: Oxford University Press, 1998.

Lemche, N. "The History of Ancient Syria and Palestine: An Overview." In *Civilization of the Ancient Near East.* Edited by Sasson J. Vol. 11. New York: Charles Scribner's sons, 1995.

________. *Early Israel: Anthropological and Historical Studies on the Israelites Society before the Monarchy.* VT Sup 37. Leiden: Brill, 1995.

________. *The Israelites in History and Tradition.* Library of Ancient Israel; Louisville, Kentucky: Westminster John Knox, 1998.

________. *The Cannanites and their Land: The Tradition of the Canaanites.* Sheffield England: Sheffield Academic Press, 1991.

________. "Israel, History of (premonarchic Period)." *Anchor Bible Dictionary.* Vol. 3. New York: Doubleday, 1992: 527-545.

Lenski, G. E. *Power and Privilege: A Theory of Social Stratification.* New York: McGrw-Hill, 1966.

Lester L. Grabbe, A *History of the Jews and Judaism in the Second Temple Period 1; Yehud: A History of the Persian Province of Judah.* London and New York: T&T Clark International, 2004a.

Leven, M. *Genocide in the Age of the Nation State: The Meaning of Genocide.* London: I. B.Tauris, 2005.

Levine, Baruch A. "Leviticus: Its Literary History and Location in Biblical Literature." In *The Book of Leviticus: Composition and Reception.* Edited by Rolf Rendtorff and Robert A. Kugler, VT Supt 93. Leiden, Boston: Brill, 2003.

________________. *Leviticus. JPS Torah Commentary*. Philadelphia: Jewish Publication Society, 1989.

Levinson, Bernard M. *Deuteronomy and the Hermeneutics of Legal Innovation.* New York: Oxford University Press, 1997.

Levinson, Bernard M. "The Human Voice in Divine Revelation: The Problem of Authority in Biblical Law." In *Innovation in Religious Tradition: Essay in the Interpretation of Religion Change.* Religion and Society 31. Edited by Michael A. Williams, Collett Cox, and Martin S. Jaffee. Berlin/New York: Mouton de Gruyter, 1992.

Lianhnuni, R. *Legal Protection for the Poor in Ancient Israel and its Significance for Mizo Society.* D.Th Dissertation, 1995.

Lipinski, E. "נָחַל *nahal;* נַחֲלָה *nahala.*" *Theological Dictionary of the Old Testament*. Vol. XI. Edited by G. Johannes Botterweck, Helmer Ringgren and Heinz-Josef Fabry. Grand Rapids, Michigan: William Eerdmans Publishing Company, 2001: 260-261.

Lohfink, N. "חַרַם *haram*, חֵרֶם, *herem.*" *Theological Dictionary of the Old Testament*. Grand Rapids, Michigan: William B. Eerdmans Publishing Company, 1986:180-199.

Long, V. P. D. W. Baker and G. J. Wenham, eds. *Windows into Old Testament History: Evidence, Argument, and the Crisis of 'Biblical Israel.'* Grand Rapids, Michigan: Eerdmans, 2002.

Longchar, Wati A. *Returning to Mother Earth Theology, Christian Witness and Theological Education: An Indigenous Perspective.* Kolkota: SCEPTRE, 2012.

________. "Sobaliba." In *Good News for North East India.* Edited by Renthy keitzar. Guwahati: Christian Literature Center, 1995.

________. "A Creation-Poem of the Ao Nagas: A Theological Exploration." In *The Tribal Worldview and Ecology.* Tribal Study Series No. 2, edited by A. Wati Longchar and Yangkahao Vashum. Jorhat: Tribal Study Centre, 1998.

________. *The Tribal Religious Tradition in North East India: An Introduction.* Jorhat: Author, 2000.

________. "Tribal Theology-Issues, Method and Perspective." In *Visioning New Life Together Among Asian Religion.* Edited by Daniel S. Thiagarajah and A. Wati Longchar. Hong Kong: CCA, 2002.

Longkumer, Lanusashi and Toshimenla Jamir. *Status of Adivasis/Indigenous peoples Land Series 6: Nagaland–Land Alienation: Dynamics of Colonialism, Security and Development.* Delhi: AAKAR Books, 2012.

Lyndem, Biloris and Utpal Kumar De, eds. *Education in North-East India: Experience and Challenge.* New Delhi: Concept Publishing Company, 2004.

Machinist, Peter. "Outsider or Insiders: The Biblical View of Emergent Israel and its Contexts." In *The Other in Jewish Thought and History Constructions of Jewish Culture and Identity.* Edited by Laurence J, Silberstein and Robert L. Cohn. New York: University Press, 1994.

Mackenzie, Alexander. *History of the Relations of the Government with the Hill of the North-East Frontier of Bengal.* Calcutta: Government of India, 1884.

Magdalene, F. Rachel and Cornelia Wunsch. "Slavery Between Judah and Babylon: The Exilic Experience." In *Slaves and Households in the Near East.* Edited by Laura Culbertson. Chicago: Illinois, 2011.

Maisuangdibou, M. "Marginality Reconstituted: Rethinking National-Transnational Identities." A Paper Presented at National Seminar on Diaspora/Migration Studies at Mar Thoma Theological seminary, Kottayam, February 17-19, 2015: 6.

Malesevic, Sinisa. *Identity as Ideology: Understanding Ethnicity and Nationalism.* New York: Palgrave Macmillan, 2006.

________. *The Sociology of Ethnicity.* London, New Delhi: Sage Publications, 2004.

Manley, G. T. *The Book of Law: Studies in Date of Deuteronomy.* London: The Tyndale Press. 1957.

Marvin, Sweeney A.."The Reconceptualization of the Davidic Covenant in Isaiah." *Studies in the Book of Isaiah.* Festschrift Willem Am Beuken, 1997.

Marx, Karl and Friedrich Engels. "The German Ideology" (1845). In *Cultural and Theory: An Anthology.* Edited by Imre Szeman and Timothy Kaposy. West Sussex: Wiley-Blackwell, 2011.

Massey, James Ear. "Reading the Bible from Particular Social Locations: An Introduction." In *The New Interpreters Bible.* Vol. 1. Nashville: Abingdon Press, 1994.

Mathews, Victor H. and Don C. Benjamin. *Old Testament Parallels Laws and Stories from the Ancient Near East.* New York/Mahwah, New Jesey: Paulist Press, 2006.

Matthews, Victor H. "An Anthropology of Slavery in the Covenant Code." In *Theory and Method in Biblical and Cuneiform Law Revision Interpolation and Development.* Edited by Bernard M. Levinson. JSOT Suppl 181. Sheffield: Sheffield Academic Press Ltd., 1994.

Matthews, Victor H. *Studying the Ancient Israelites: A Guide to Source and Methods.* Grand Rapids, Machigan: Baker Academic, 2007.

Mauch, T. M. "Sojourner." *The Interpreter's Dictionary of the Bible.* New York: Abingdon Press, 1962: 397-399.

Mayes, Andrew D. H. *Deuteronomy. New Century Bible.* London: Oliphants, 1979.

________. "Deutronomy 29, Joshua 9, and the place of the Gibeonites in Israel." In *Das Deutronomium.* Edited by N. Lohfink. Leuven: Leuven University Press 1985.

Mayer, G. "יָרַד; yarad." *Theological Dictionary of the Old Testament.* Vol. V1. Edited by G. Johannes Botterweck and Helmer Ringgrenn. Grand Rapids, Michigan: William B. Eerdmann Publishing Company, 1990: 315-322.

McAfee, Gene. "Chosen People in a Chosen Land: Theology and Ecology in the Story of Israel's Origins." In *The Earth Story in Genesis.* Edited by Norman C. Habel & Shirley Wurst. Sheffield: Sheffield Academic press, 2000.

McConville, J. G. *Law and Theology in Deuteronomy.* JSOT Sup 33. Sheffield: JSOT, 1985.

Meek, T. J. "The origin of Hebrew law." In *Hebrew Origins.* New York: Harper & Row, 1936.

Mendenhall, G. E. *The Tenth Generation.* Baltimore: Johns Hopkins University press, 1973.

________. *Ancient Israel's Faith and History: An Introduction to the Bible in Context.* Edited by Gary A. Herion. Louisville/Westminster: John Knox, 2001.

________. *The Tenth Generation the Origin of biblical Tradition.* London: The John Hopkins University Press, 1973.

Meyers, Carol. *Discovering Eve: Ancient Israelite Women in Context.* Oxford: Oxford University Press, 1988.

Meyers, Carol. "The Family in Early Israel." In *Families in Ancient Israel.* Edited by Don S. Browning and Ian S. Evison. Louisville, Kentucky: Westminster John Knox Press, 1997.

Meyes, A. D. H. *Judges.* Sheffield: JSOT Press, 1988.

Miller, J. M. “Israelite History.” In *Hebrew Bible and Its Modern Interpreters.* Edited by D. A. Knight and G. M. Tucker. Philadelphia: Fortress 1985.

Miller, Patrick D. Jr. “Israel as Host to Strangers.” In *Israelite Religion and Biblical Theology: Collected Essays.* Sheffield: Sheffield Academic Press, 2000.

Milgrom, Jacob. *Numbers: The Traditional Hebrew Text with the New JPS Translation.* JPS Torah Commentary. Philadelphia: Jewish Publication Society, 1990.

________. *Leviticus 1-16. Anchor Bible* 3. New York: Doubleday, 1991.

________. *Leviticus 17-22. Anchor Bible* 3. New York: Doubleday, 2000.

________.“Leviticus.” *Interpreters' Dictionary of the Bible Sup.* Nashville: Abingdon Press, 1976.

________. *Leviticus 17-22: A New Translation with Introduction and Commentary.* New York: Doubleday, 2000.

________. *Leviticus 23-27: A New Translation with Introduction and Commentary.* New York: Doubleday, 2000.

________. *Numbers. The JPS Torah Commentary.* Philadelphia: Jewish Publication Society, 1990.

Miller, J. M. and J. H. Hayes. *A History of Ancient Israel and Judah.* Philadelphia: Westminster, 1986.

Miller, Patric D. *The Religion of Ancient Israel.* Louisville, Kentucky: Westminster John Knox Press, 2000.

Moberly, R. W. L. “Towards an Interpretation of the Shema.” In *Theological Exegesis Essay in Honor of Bervard S. Childs.* Edited by C. Seith and K. Greene –Mc Creight. Grand Rapids: Eerdmans, 1999.

Moore, Megan Bishop and Brad E. Kelle. *Biblical History and Israel's Past: The Changing Study of the Bible and History.* Grand Rapids, Michigan/ Cambridge, U.K: William B. Eerdmans Publishing Company, 2011.

Morris, Ian and Joseph G. Manning. “Introduction.” In *The Ancient Economy: Evidence and Models.* Edited by Joseph G. Manning and Ian Morris. Stanford California: Stanford University Press, 2005.

Mullen, E. Theodore Jr. *Narrative History and Ethnic Boundaries: The Deuteronomistic Historian and the Creation of Israelite National Identity.* Atlanta: Scholar Press, 1993.

________. *Ethnic Myth and Pentateuchal Foundations: A New Approach to the Formation of the Pentateuch.* Semeia St. Atlanta: Scholar, 1997.

Na'aman, N. "The 'Conquest of Canaan' in the Book of Joshua and History." In *From Nomadism to Monarchy Archaeological and Historical Aspects of Early Israel.* Edited by I. Finkelstein and N. Na'aman. Jerusalem: Israel Exploration Society, 1994.

Nicholson, E. W. *Deuteronomy and Tradition.* Oxford: Basil Blackwell, 1967.

Nicol, G. G. *Studies in the Interpretation of Genesis 26:1-33.* D.Phil Thesis, Faculty of Theology, University of Oxford, 1987.

Niditch, Susan. *Underdogs and Tricksters: A Prelude to Biblical Folklore.* San Francisco: Harper & Row, 1987.

Nihan, C. "Resident Aliens and Natives in the Holiness Legislation." In *The Foreigner and the Law: Perspective from the Hebrew Bible and the Ancient Near East.* Edited by R. Achenbach, R. Albertz and J. Worhle. Band 16. Weisbaden: Harrassowitz Verlag, 2011.

Nishan, C. *From Priestly Torah to Pentateuch: A Study in the Composition of the Book of Leviticus.* Tübingen: Mohr Siebeck, 2007.

Noth, Martin. *Exodus: A Commentary.* Translated by J. S. Bowden. Philadelphia: Westminster Press, 1962.

________. *The Laws in the Pentateuch and other Studies.* Philadelphia: Fortress, 1966.

________. *A History of Pentateuchal Tradition.* Translated by B. W. Anderson, Chico, California.: Scholar Press, 1981.

________. *Numbers: A commentary*. London: SCM Press Ltd., 1968.

________. *Leviticus. Old Testament Library*. Philadelphia: Westminster Press, 1965.

Olson, Dennis T. *Numbers: Interpretation; A Bible Commentary for Teaching and Preaching.* Louisville: John Knox Press, 1996.

Oppitz, Michael, et al. *Naga Identities: Changing Local Cultures in Northeast of India.* Snoeck Publishers, 2008.

Orni, Efraim. "Negev." *Encyclopaedia Judaica.* Vol. 15. New York: Thomas Gales, 2007.

Osterud, Nancy Grey. "Land, Identity, and Agency in the Oral Autobiography of Farm Women." In *Women and Farming: Changing Roles, Changing Structures*. Rural Studies Series. Edited by Wava G. Haney and Jane B. Knowles. Boulder, Colo: Westview Press, 1988.

Otto, E. "The Holiness Code in diachrony and synchrony in the legal hermeneutics of the Pentateuch." In *The strata of the Priestly writings:*

Contemporary Debate and Future Directions. Edited by S. Schectman & J. S. Baden. ATHANT. Zürich: Theologischer Verlag, 2009.

Owen, Roger. *The Middle East in the World Economy 1800-1914*. London, NY: I. B. Tauris, 2009.

Pachuau, Lalsangkima. *Ethnic Identity and Christianity: A Socio-Historical and Missiological Study of Christianity in North East India with Special reference to Mizoram.* Frankfurt am Maim: Peter Lang, 2002.

Pakem, B. "The Question of Ethnic Formation Among the Hill People of North-East India." In *Nationality, Ethnicity and Cultural Identity in North-East India.* Edited by B. Pakem. Guwahati: Omsons Publication, 1990.

Pangernungba. "Land and *Ali-Rongsen* (Cultural-Political Economy): An Ao Naga Perspective." In *Tribal Ecology: A Search for Ecological Values from the Cultures and Practices of the Tribes of North East India.* Tribal Study series. No 20. Edited by Razouselie Lasetso, Marlene Ch. Marak and Yangkahao Vashum. Jorhat: ETC Programme Coordination, 2012.

Panigrahi, P. K. "Displacement and Refugee Issue in Arunachal Pradesh." In *Blisters on their Feet: Tales of Internally Displaced Person in India's North East.* Edited by Samir Kumar Das. New Delhi: Sage Publication, 2008.

Parsons, T. "Some Theoretical Consideration on the Nature and Trends of change in Ethnicity." In *Ethnicity: Theory and Experience.* Edited by N. Glazer and D. P. Moynihan. Cambridge: Harvard University Press, 1975.

Patrick, Dale. *Old Testament Law*. Atlanta: John Knox Press, 1985.

Paul, S. M. *Studies in the Book of the Covenant in the Light of Cuneiform and Biblical Law.* Leiden: Brill, 1970.

Paula, Benerjee. "The Space Between: Women's Negotiation with Democracy." In *Dimensions of Development in Nagaland.* Edited by C. Joshua Thomas and Durudas Das. New Delhi: Regency Publication, 2002.

Pedersen, J. *Israel: Its Life and Culture,* I. London: Oxford University Press, 1973.

Perdue, Leo G., et al. "The Israelite and Early Jewish Family: Summary and Conclusions." In *Families in Ancient Israel.* Louiseville, Kentucky: Westminister John Knox Press, 1997.

Philips, Anthony. *Ancient Israel's Criminal Law.* Oxford: Blackwell, 1970.

Planning Commission. *The Report of the Working Group on the Land System among Tribals in the North Eastern India.* May, 1984.

Pitt-Rivers, Julian. *The Fate of Shechem or The Politics of Sex: Essays in the Anthropology of the Mediterranean.* Cambridge: Cambridge University Press, 1977.

Pleins, J. David. *The Social Vision of the Hebrew Bible*. Louiseville, Kentucky: Wesminster John Knox Press, 1985.

Porter, John. *The Vertical Mosaic: A Study of Social Class and Power in Canada.* Toronto: Buffalo, 1965.

________. *Leviticus: A Commentary.* Cambridge, 1976.

Preuss, H. D. "את 'eth; עם 'im." *Theological Dictionary of the Old Tesstament*. Vol.1. Grand Rapids, Michigan: William B. Eerdmans Publishing Company, 1974: 449-463.

Prior, M. "Fabricating Colonial Myth." In *The Bible and Colonialism: A Moral Critique.* Sheffield: Sheffield Academic Press, 1997.

Ralte, Vanlalnghaka. "Critical Re-Look at the Tribal Heritage: A New Testament Perspective." In *Theologizing Tribal Heritage: A Critical Re-Look.* Edited by Hrangthan Chhungi. Delhi: CWM, ISET-ECC, PCI, 2008.

Ramesh, Babu P. *Migration from North-East to Urban Centres: A Study of Delhi Region.* Noida: V. V. Giri National Labour Institute, 2012.

Ray, B. Datta. *Tribal Identity and Tension in North-East India.* New Delhi: Omsons Publications, 1989.

Reindl, "לָחָץ Lahas." *Theological Dictionary of the Old Tesstament*. Vol. V11. Grand Rapids, Michigan: William B. Eerdmans Publishing Company, 1990: 550-555.

Rendorff, R. "The *Ger* in the Priestly Laws of the Pentateuch." In *Ethnicity and the Bible*. Edited by M. G. Brett. Leiden: E. J. Brill, 1996.

________. "Is it possible to Read Leviticus as a Separate Book?" In *Reading Leviticus: A Conversation with Mary Douglas*. Edited by John F. A. Sawyer, JSOT Supl 227. Sheffield: Sheffield Academic Press, 1996.

________. *The Old Testament: An Introduction.* Translated by J. Bowden. Philadelphia: Fortress Press, 1986.

Ridderbos, J. *Deuteronomy.* Grand Rapids: Zondervan, 1984.

Ringreen, "יָנַה" In *Theological Dictionary of the Old Testament*. Vol. V1. Grand Rapids, Michigan: Wiliam B. Eerdmans Publishing Company, 1995:104-106.

________. "רבנ נבר, נבָר nekar, נכֵרי; nokri." *Theological Dictionary of the Old Tesstament*. Vol IX. Edited by G. Johannes Botterweck, Helner Ringgren, Heing-Josef Fabry. Grand Rapids, Michigan: William B. Eerdmann publishing Company, 2000: 423-432.

Robertson, John F. "Social Tensions in the Ancient Near East." In *A Companion To the Ancient Near East*. Edited by Daniel C. Snell. Malden: Blackwell Publishing Ltd., 2005.

Roberts, J. J. M. "Ancient Near Eastern Environments." In *The Hebrew Bible and its Modern Interpreters.* Edited by D. A. Knight and Gene M. Tucker. Chico, California: Scholar press, 1985.

Robinson, Gnana. *The Origin and Development of the Old Testament Sabbath: A Comprehensive Exegetical Approach.* UTC, Bangalore: ISPCK, Delhi, 1998.

Rocca, Samuel. *The Fortification of Ancient Israel and Judah 1200-586 BC.* Oxford: Osprey Publishing Ltd, 2010.

Rofe, A. *Deutronomy: Issues and Interpretation. Old Testament Studies.* London: T&T Clark, 2002.

Rosenberg, Joel. *King and Kin: Political Allegory in the Hebrew Bible.* Bloomington: Indiana University Press, 1986.

Rogerson, John W. *Anthropology and the Old Testament.* Oxford: Blackwell, 1978.

Rogerson, John W. "Anthropology." *A Dictionary of Biblical Interpretation.* Edited by R. J. Coggins and J. L. Houlden. London: SCM, 1990: 26-28.

Rom-Shiloni, Dalit. *Exclusive Inclusive: Identity Conflicts Between the Exiles and the People who Remained (6th-5th Centuries BCE).* New York, London: Bloomsbury T&T Clark, 2013.

Roth, Martha T. *Law Collections from Mesopotamia and Asia Minor.* Society of Biblical Literature. Atlanta: Scholar Press, 1995.

Rymbai, R. T. "The Traditional Ecological Concept of the Khasi-Pnars." In *The Tribal Worldview and Ecology.* Tribal Study Series No. 2. Edited by A. Wati Longchar and Yangkahao Vashum. Jorhat: Tribal Study Centre, 1998.

Sarna, N. M. *Genesis*. The JPS Torah Commentary. Philadelphia: Jewish Publication Society, 1989.

Sarna, N. M. *Exodus: The Traditional Hebrew Text with the new JPS translation.* Philadelphia: Jewish Publication Society, 1991.

Scharbert, Joseph. "ברך *brk*; בְּרָכָה *berakhah*." *Theological Dictionary of the Old Tesstament..* Vol. II. Edited by G. Johannes Botterweck, Helmer Ringgren. Grand Rapids, Michigan: William B. Eerdmans Publishing Company, 1975: 300-308.

Schermerhorn, R. A. *Comparative Ethnic Relations: A Framework for Theory.* New York: Random House, 1970.

Schmid, K. "The So Called Yahwist and the Literary Gap between Genesis and Exodus." In *A Farwell to the Yahwist: The Composition of the Pentateuch in recent European Interpretation.* SBL Symposium Series 34. Edited by T. B. Dozeman and K. Schmid. Atlanta: Society of Biblical Literature, 2006.

Schirrmacher, Thomas. *Racism.* The WEA Global Issue Series, Vol. 8. Bonn: Verlag fur Kultur und Wissenschaft Culture and Science Publisher, 2011.

Schultz, C. "The Political Tensions Reflected in Ezra-Nehemiah." In *Scripture in Context.* Edited by C. D. Evans, W. W. Hallo and J. B. White. Pittsburgh: The Pickwick Press, 1980.

Schunck, "לון lun, תלנות telunnot." *Theological Dictionary of the Old Tesstament.* Vol. V11. Edited by G. Johannes Botterweck, Helmer Ringgren and Heinz-Josef Fabry. Grand Rapids, Michigan: William B. Eerdman Publishing Company, 1995: 509-512.

Scullion, J. J. *Genesis: A Commentary for Students, Teachers, and Preachers.* OTS 6. Collegeville: Liturgical, 1992.

Sema, Khekiye K. "Setting Up of Nagaland Special Disaster Zones (NSDZs)!." In *Challenges of Land Development in Nagaland.* Edited by Takatemjen. Aolijen, Mokokchung: Clark Center for Peace and Research and Action (CCPRA), 2015.

Seters, John Van. *A Law Book of Diaspora: Revision in the Covenant Book.* Oxford, New York: Oxford University Press, 2003.

________. P*rologue to History: The Yahwist as Historian in Genesis.* Louisville: Westminster John Knox, 1992.

________. *Abraham in History and Tradition.* New Haven, Conn and London, 1975.

Seybold, Donald A. "Paradox and symmetry in the Joseph Narrative." In *Literary Interpretations of Biblical Narratives.* Edited by Kenneth R. R. Gros Louis, James S. Ackerman, and Thayer S. Warshaw. Nashville: Abingdon, 1974.

Shea, William H. "Famine." *Anchor Bible Dictionary* 2. New York: Double day, 1992: 770-71.

Shingmila, S. "North-East Migrant Women in Delhi's Service Sector." Paper presented at the National Seminar on Women and Migration organized by Centre for Women's Development Studies. New Delhi, September 2007: 19-20.

Shonin, Teodor. "Peasantry as a Political Factor." In *Peasants and Peasant Society.* Edited by Teodor Shonin. Harmondsworth, Middlex: Penguin Books, 1971.

Skinner, J. *A Critical and Exegetical Commentary on Genesis*. 2nd edn. Edinburgh: N. P., 1930.

Smith, Anthony D. and John Hutchinson. "Introduction." In *Ethnicity*. Edited by John Hutchinson and Anthony D. Smith. Oxford: Oxford University Press, 1996.

Smith, Anthony D. *Myth and Memories of the Nation*. Oxford: Oxford University press, 1999a. 208.

________. "The Politics of Culture: Ethnicity and Nationalism." In *Companion Encyclopedia of Anthropology.* Edited by Tim Ingold. London: Routledge, 1994.

________. "The Politics of Culture: Ethnicity and Nationalism." *Companion Encyclopedia of Anthropology*. Edited by Tim Ingold. London: Routledge, 1994.

________. *Chosen People.* Oxford: Oxford University press, 2003.

________. *Ethno-Symbolism and Nationalism A Cultural Approach*. London/ New York: Routledge Taylor and Francis group, 2009.

________. *National Identity.* London: Penguin Books, 1991.

Smith, Mark S. *The Pilgrimage Pattern in Exodus*. JSOT Supl 239. Sheffield: Sheffield Academic Press, 1997.

Smith, M. *Palestinian Parties and Politics That Shaped the Old Testament.* New York: Columbia University press, 1971.

Smith, D. L. *The Religion of the Landless: A Social Context of the Babylonian Exile*. Bloomington, IN: Meyer –Stone Books, 1989.

Smith. *The Ethnic Origins of Nations*. Oxford: Basil Blackwell, 1986.

Snaith, N. H. eds. *Leviticus and Numbers. The Century Bible*. London: Thomas and Nelson & Sons Ltd., 1967.

Sprinkle, Joe M. *The Book of the Covenant: A literary Approach.* JSOT Sup 174. Sheffield: JSOT Press, 1994.

Sparks, Kenton L. *Ethnicity and Identity in Ancient Israel*. Winona Lake, Ind.: Eisenbrauns, 1998.

Speiser, E. A. *Genesis*. Garden City, New York, 1964.

________. "The Wife-Sister Motif in the Pentateuch Narratives." In *Biblical and Other Studies.* Edited by Alexander Altmann. Cambridge, MA: Harvard University Press, 1963.

Sparks, Kentron L. *Ethnicity and Identity in Ancient Israel: Prolegomena to the Study of Ethnic sentiments and their Expression in the Hebrew Bible.* Winona Lake, Indiana: Eisenbrauns, 1998.

Spina, F. A. "Israelites as *gerim*, Sojourner." In *The Word of the Lord shall go Forth.* Edited by C. L. Meyem & M. O'Conner. Winona Lake, IN: Eisenbrauns, 1983.

Stackert, Jeffrey. *Rewriting the Torah: Literary Revision in Deuteronomy and the Holiness Legislation.* FAT 52. Tubingen, Germany: Mohr Siecbeck, 2007.

________. "The Holiness legislation and its Pentateuchal sources: Revision, supplementation, and replacement." In S. Schectman & J. S. Baden eds., *The Strata of the Priestly writings. Contemporary Debate and Future Directions*. ATAN 95. Zurich: Theologischer Verla, 2009.

Steinberg, Naomi. "Sociological Approaches: Toward A Sociology of Childhood in the Hebrew Bible." In *Method Matters Essays on the Interpretation of the Hebrew Bible in Honor of David L. Petersen*. Edited by Joel M. Lemon and Kent Herold Richards. Atlanta: Society of Biblical Literature, 2009.

________. "Romancing the Widow: The Economic Distinction between the '*almana*,' the *'issa-hammet'* the '*Eset-Hammet.*'" In *God's Word for Our World.* Vol. 1. Edited by J. Harold Ellens, et al. JSOT Sup 388. London; New York: T&T Clark International, 2004.

Syiemlieh, Brightstar J. "The Viability of the term 'Tribe' in the light of Post modernity." In *The Search of Identity and Tribal Theology: A Tribute to Dr. Renthy Keitzar.* Edited by A Wati Longchar. Jorhat: TSC, 2001.

Talukdar, S. P. *The Chakmas: Life and Struggle*. Delhi: Gian Publishing House, 1988.

Taylor, J. P. *Political Geography, World Economy, Nation State and Locality.* London: Longman, 1985.

Thomas L. Thompson. *The Origin Tradition of Ancient Israel, 1: The Literary Formation of Genesis and Exodus 1-23.* JSOTSup. Vol. 55. Sheffield: Sheffield Academic Press, 1987.

Thornier, D. "Peasant Economy as a Category in Economic History." In *Peasants and Peasant Economies.* Edited by T. Shanin. Harmondsworth: Penguin, 1971.

Thanzauva, K. "Human Rights: The Tribal Theological Perspective." In *Theological Tribal Heritage: A Critical Re-Look.* Edited by Hrangthan Chhungi. Delhi: ISPCK, 2008.

________. "Tribal/Indigenous Interpretation of the Bible: A key note Address." In *Tribal Theology and the Bible: A Search for Contextual Relevance.* Edited by Yangkahao Vashum. Jorhat: Tribal Study Centre, 2011.

________. *Theology of Community: Tribal Theology in the Making.* Bangalore: Asian Trading Corporation, 2004.

Thomas, V. V. *Dalit and Tribal Christians in India: Issues and Challenges.* Malapuram: Focus India Trust, 2014.

Thompson, T. L. *Early History of the Israelite People: From the Written and Archaeological Sources.* Leiden: Brill, 1992b.

Thong, Joseph S. and Phanenmo Kath. *Glimpses of Naga Legacy and Culture.* Kottayam: Society for Naga Students' Welfare Kerala, 2011.

Tigay, Jeffrey H. *Deuteronomy.* The JPS Torah Commentary. Philadelphia: Jewish Publication Society, 1996.

Tucker, W. Dennis Jr. *Constructing and Deconstructing Power in Psalms 107-150.* Society for Biblical literature 19. Atlanta: SBL Press, 2014.

Tucker, Gene M. "The Law in the Eight Century Prophet." In *Canon Theology and Old Testament Interpreter.* Edited by G. M.Tucker, et al. Philadelphia: Fortress, 1988.

Vanlaltlani, T. *A Study of Religious Identity Among the Bru of Mizoram*. Delhi: ISPCK, 2007.

Vashum, Ahao. "Emerging Vision of Indigenous/Tribals Theology." In *Dalit-Tribal Theological Interface: Current Trends in Subaltern Theologie.* Edited by James Massey and Shimreingam Shimray. New Delhi, Jorhat: CDS and TSC/WSC, 2007.

________. "Theology of Land: A Naga Perspective." In *The Tribal Worldview and Ecology.* Tribal Studies Series No. 2. Edited by A. Wati Longchar and Yangkahao Vashum. Jorhat: Tribal Study Centre, 1998.

Vink, J. G. "The Date and Origin of the Priestly Code in the Old Testament." In *The Priestly Code and Seven Other Studies.* Edited by P. A. de Boer Old Testament Studies 15. Leiden: Brill, 1969.

von Rad, Gerhard. "The Form Critical Problem of the Hexateuch." In *The Problem of Hexateuch and other Essay.* Translated by E. W. T. Dickens. Edinburgh, London: Oliver and Boyd, 1966.

________. *The Problem of Hexateuch and other essay*. Translated by E. W. T. Dicken. New York: Mc Graw, Hill, 1966.

________. *Old Testament Theology: The Theology of Israel's historical Origins*. Vol. 1. Translated by D. G. M. Stalker. San Francisco: Harper Collins, 1962.

________. *Genesis: A Commentary.* Translated by John H. Marks. London: SCM Press Ltd., 1956.

________. *Genesis: A Commentary*. 2nd edn. London: SCM Press Ltd., 1972.

________. *Deuteronomy: A Commentary.* Philadelphia: Westminster Press, 1966.

________. *Genesis: A Commentary.* Translated by John H. Marks. OTL. London: SCM Press Ltd, 1961.

Weber, Max *Ancient Judaism*. Translated and edited by Hans H. Gerth and Don Martindale. New York: Collier Macmillan Publisher, 1952.

Weinberg, Joel. *The Citizen-Temple Community.* Translated by Daniel L. Smith-Christopher. Sheffield: Sheffield Academic Press, Ltd, 1992.

Weinfeld, Moshe. *Deuteronomy and Deuteronomic School.* Oxford: Clarendon Press, 1972.

________. Social *Justice in Ancient Israel and in the Ancient Near East.* Jerusalem: Magnes/Minneapolis: Fortress, 1998.

________. "Sabbatical Year and Jubilee in the Pentateuch laws and their Ancient Near Eastern Background." In *The Law in the Bible and its Environment.* Edited by T.Veijola. Gottingen: Vandenhoeck Ruprecht, 1990.

Wellhausen, J. *Prolegomena to the History of Ancient Israel.* Cleveland & New York: Meridian Books, 1957.

________. *Prolegomena to the History of Israel.* Atlanta: Scholars Press, 1994.

Wenham, G. J. "Pondering the Pentateuch: the Search for a New Paradigm." In *The Face of Old Testament Studies: A Survey of Contemporary Approaches.* Edited by D. W. Baker and B. T. Arnold. Grand Rapids: Baker, 1999.

________. *Genesis* 1-15. *Word Biblical Commentary*. Vol. 1. Waco, Texas: Word books, 1987.

________. *Genesis 16-50. Word Biblical Commentary*. Vol. 2. Dallas: Word Books, 1994.

________. *The Book of Leviticus.* Grand Rapids: Eerdmanns, 1979.

Westbrooke, Raymond. "The Character of Ancient Near Eastern law." In *A History of Ancient Near Eastern Law.* Edited by Ramond West brook. Vol. 1. Leiden, Boston: Brill, 2003.

________. "Old Babylonian Period." In *A History of Ancient Near Eastern Law.* Edited by Ramond West brook, Vol. 1. Leiden, Boston: Brill, 2003.

Westermann, Claus. *Genesis 12-36: A Commentary.* Translated by John J. Scullion. London: SPCK, 1985.

________. *Genesis: An Introduction.* Translated by John J. Scullion S.J. Minneapolis: Fortress Press, 1992.

Whitelam, Keith W. "Introduction: General Problems of Studying the Text of the Bible in Order to Reconstruct History and Social background." In *The Oxford Hand Book of Biblical Studies.* Edited by J. W. Rogerson and Judith M. Lieu, Oxford: University Press, 2006.

Whitelam, Keith W. *The Just King: Monarchical Judicial Authority in Ancient Israel.* JSOT Sup 12. Sheffield: JSOT Press, 1979.

Whybray, R. Norman. *Introduction to the Pentateuch.* Grand Rapids, Michigan: William B. Eerdmans Publishing Company, 1995.

Wiesehöfer, Josef. "The Achaemenid Empire in the Fourth Century B.C.E: A Period of Decline?" In *Judah and the Judeans in the Fourth Century B.C.E.* Edited by Oded Lipschits, Gery N. Knoppers and Rainer Albertz. Winona Lake: Eisenbrauns, 2007.

Widergren, Geo. "The Persian Period." In *Israelite and Judean History.* Edited by John H. Hayes and J. Maxwell Miller. London: SCM Press Ltd., 1977.

Williamson, H. G. M. "The concept of Israel in Transition." In *The World of Ancient Israel: Sociological, Anthropological, and Political Perspectives: Essay by Members of the Society for Old Testament Study.* Edited by R. E. Clements. Cambridge: Cambridge University Press, 1989.

________. "Exiles and After: Historical Studies." In *The Face of Old Testament Studies: A Survey of Contemporary Approaches.* Edited by David W. Baker and Bill T. Arnold. Grand Rapids/Michigan: Baker Academic, 1999.

Wilson, Robert R. *Sociological Approaches to the Old Testament*. Philadelphia: Fortress Press, 1984.

Wilson, Robert R. "Sociology of Old Testament." *Harper Collins Bible Dictionary.* Edited by Paul J. Achtemeier. Bangalore: Theological Publication in India, 2009: 400.

Wright, Christopher J. H. *Old Testament Ethics for the People of God.* Leicester, England: InterVarsity Press, 2004.

________. *Walking in the Ways of the Lord: The Ethical Authority of the Old Testament.* Downers Grove, Ill: InterVarsity, 1995.

________. *God's People in God's Land: Family, Land and Property in the Old Testament.* Grand Rapids: Eerdmands/Exeter: Paternoster, 1990.

Wright, Paul H. *Greatness, Grace and Glory: Carta's Atlas of Biblical Biography.* Jerusalem: carta, 2008.

Wright, David P. "Ethical Foundations of the Biblical Dietary Laws." In *Religion and Law: Biblical, Judaic and Islamic Perspectives.* Edited by E. Firmage, J. Welch and B. Weiss. Winona Lake, IN: Eisenbrauns, 1990.

Yee, Gale A. "Ideological Criticism: Judges 17-21 and the Dismembered Body." In *Judges and Method New Approaches in Biblical Studies*. Edited by Gale A. Yee. Minneapolis: Fortress Press, 1995.

________. *Poor Banished Children of the Eve Woman as Evil in the Hebrew Bible.* Minneapolis: Fortress Press, 2003.

Zimmerli, W. *Ezekiel.* Translated by R. E. Clement. Philadelphia: Fortress Press, 1979.

Zobel, H. J. "מִשְׁפָּחָה; mispaha." *Theological Dictionary of the Old Testament.* Vol. IX. Edited by G. Johannes Botterweck, Helmer Ringgren, Heinz-Josef Fabry. Grand Rapids, Michigan: William B. Eerdmans Publishing Company, 1998: 79-84.

B: Journals

Alexander, T. D. "Are the Wife/Sister of Genesis Literary Composition Variant?" *VT* XLII/2 (1992): 145-153.

Armstrong, John. "Mobilised and Proletarian Diasporas." *American Political Science Review* 70 (1976): 393–408.

Artus, O. "Sabbath Year and Jubilee in Lev 25." *Indian Theological Studies* 50/3-*4* (September & December, 2003): 233-254.

Awabdy, Mark A. "Green Eggs and Shawarma: Reinterpreting the Bible, Reforming Mission with Leviticus גר as Test case." *Asbury Journal* 66 (2011): 31-45.

Barbara, Sanjay. "Autonomous Districts and/or Ethnic Homelands: An Ethnographic Account of the Genesis of Political Violence in Assam (North-East India) against the Normative Frame of the India Constitution." *International Journal on Minority & Group Rights* 15 2/3 (2008): 313-34.

Bartlett, R. "Medieval and Modern Concepts of Race and Ethnicity." *Journal of Medieval and Early Modern Studies* 31/1 (2001): 39–40.

Bedford, Peter R. "Diaspora: Homeland Relation in Ezra-Nehemiah." *Vetus Testamendum* 52/2 (2002): 147-165.

Bentley, Carter, G. "Ethnicity and Practice." *Comparative Studies in Society and History* 29 (1987): 24-27.

Berguist, Jon L. "Postcolonialism and Imperialism Motives for Canonization." *Semeia* 75 (1996): 15-35.

Biddle, Mark E. "The 'Endangered Ancestress' and Blessing for the Nation." *Journal of Biblical Literature* 109/4 (1990): 599-611.

Blenkinsopp, J. "The structure of P." *Catholic Biblical Quaterly* 38 (1976): 275.

Blenkinsopp, J. "An Assessment of the Alleged Pre-Exilic Date of the Priestly material in Pentateuch." *Zeitschrift fur die alttestmenliche Wissenschaft* 108/4 (1996): 495-518.

Blenkinsopp, J. "The Mission of Udjahorresnet and those of Ezra and Nehemiah.' *Journal of Biblical Literature 106*/3 (Sept. 1987): 409-21.

Block-Smith, Elizabeth. "Israelites Ethnicity in Iron 1: Archaeology Preserves What is Remembered and what is Forgotten in Israel's History." *Journal of Biblical Literature 122*/3 (2003): 402.

Burnside, Jonathan P. "Exodus and Asylum: Uncovering the Relationship between Biblical Law and Narrative." *Journal for the Study of the Old Testament* 34/3 (March 2010): 243-266.

Chaney, Marvin L. "Systemic Study of the Israelite Monarchy." *Semeia* 37 (1986): 67-68.

Clines, D.J.A. "Possibilities and Priorities of Biblical Interpretation in an International Perspective." *Biblical Interpretation* 1 (1993): 67-87.

Cohn, Robert L. "Negotiating (with) the Native: Ancestors and Identity in Genesis." *Harvard Theological Review* 96 (2003): 147-66.

Cole, Ross H. "The Sabbath and the Alien." *Andrew University Seminary Studies* 38 (2000): 223-29.

Coote, Robert B. and Keith W. Whitelam. "The Emergence of Israel Social Transformation and State Formation following the Decline in Late Bronze Age Trade." *Semeia* 37 (1986): 107-47.

Dever, William G. "Archaeology, Ideology and the Quest for an "Ancient" or "Biblical" Israel." *Near Eastern Archaeology* 61/1 (1998): 47-52.

Douglas, Mary. "The Stranger in the Bible." *Archives Europeennes de Sociologie* 35 (1994): 284.

Douglas, Mary. "The forbidden animals in Leviticus." *JSOT* 59 (1993): 3-23.

Echtner, Charlotte and Pushkola Prasad. "The Contest of third World Tourism marketing." *Annals of Tourism Research* 30/3 (2003): 660-82.

Esler, P. F. "Ezra-Nehemiah as a Narrative of (Re-Invented) Israelite Identity." *Biblical Interpretation* 11 3/4 (2003a): 413-26.

Fensham, F. Charles. "Widow, Orphan, and the Poor in Ancient Near Eastern Legal and Wisdom Literature." *Journal of near Eastern Studies* 21/2 (April 1962): 129-137.

Finkelstein, Israel. "The Emergence of Israel in Canaan: Consensus, Mainstream and Dispute." *Journal for the Study of the Old Testament* 2 (1991): 49-59.

________. "The Emergence of the Monarchy in Israel: The Environmental and Socio-Economic Aspects." *Journal for the Study of Old Testament* 44 (1989): 61-70.

________. "The Philistines in the Bible: A late-Monarchic perspective." *JSOT* 27/2 (December, 2002): 132.

________. "Jerusalem in the Persian (and Early Hellenistic) period and the wall of Nehemiah." *JSOT* 32/4 (2008): 501-20.

Gnuse, R. "The Emergence of Monotheism in Ancient Israel: A Survey of Recent Scholarship." *Religion* 29 (1999): 315-36.

Gottwald, N. K. "Social class as Analytical and Hermeneutical Categories in Biblical Studies." *Journal of Biblical Literature* 112/1 (1993): 4-6.

________. "The Participation of Free Agrarians in the Introduction of Monarchy to Ancient Israel: An Application of H.A. Landsberger's Framework for the Analysis of Peasants." *Semeia* 37 (1986): 87-88.

________. 'Social Matrix and Canonical Shape.' *Theology Today* 42: 307-21.

Gressmann, H. "Josiah und das Deuteronomiun." *Zeitschrift fur die alttestmenliche Wissenschaft* 42 (1924): 313-337.

Haokip, Peter. "The tribal People of the Northeast: A Liberating Quest for Identity, Equality and Respect." *Janadeepa* 2/2 (1999): 69-72.

Hauge, Martin Ravndal. "Struggles of the Blessed in Estrangement II." *Studia Theologica* 29 (1995): 114-15.

Hobbs, T. R. "Hospitality in the First Testament and the 'Telological Fallacy.'" *Journal for the Study of the Old Testament* 95 (2001): 20-24.

Hallo, William W. "The Road to Emar." *Journal of Cuneiform Studies* 18 (1964): 57-88. Cited by Donald J. Wiseman. "History and Tradition." *Bibliotheca Sacra* (April-June 1977): 125.

Hoffmeier, James K. "'The Wives' Tales of Genesis 12, 20 & 26 and the Covenants at Beer-Sheba." *TyndaleBulletin* 43/1(1992): 81-99.

Kensky, T. Frymer. "Tit for Tat: The Principles of Equal Retribution in Near Eastern and biblical Law." *Biblical Archaeologist* 43 (1980): 230-34.

Lenchak, Timothy A. "Israel's Refugee Ancestors." *The Bible Today* 35/1 (January 1997): 11-15.

Leuchter, Mark. "The Ambiguous Details in the Blasphemer Narrative: Source and Redaction in Leviticus 24:10-23." *Journal of Biblical Literature* 130/3 (2011): 431-450.

Lohfink, Norbert S. J. "Poverty in the Laws of the Ancient Near East and of the Bible." *Theological Studies* 52 (1991): 40-45.

Maloney, R. P. "Usury and Restrictions on Interest-Taking in the Ancient near East." *Catholic Biblical Quaterly* 36 (1974): 1-20.

Matthews, Victor, H. Abstract of *From Aliens to proselytes: Non-Priestly and Priestly Legislation concerning stranger,* by Rainer Albertz. *Old Testament Abstract* 35 (February 2012): 75-85.

McDuie-Ra, Duncan. "The 'North-East' Map of Delhi." *Economic and Political Weekly* XLV11/30 (July 28, 2012): 69-77.

Mendenhall, G. E. "Ancient Oriental and Biblical Law." *Biblical Archaeologist* 17/2 (May, 1954): 26-46.

Meyer, Esias E. "Respect for Animal life in the Book of Leviticus. How Green were the Priestly Authors? *Old Testament Essay* 24/1 (2011): 142-158.

Meyer, Esias E. "Dating the Priestly Text in the pre-exilic Period: Some Remarks about Anachronistic Slips and Other Obstacles." *Vebum et ecclesia* 31/1 (2010): 1-6.

Milgrom, J. "A Prolegomenon to Leviticus 17:11." *Journal for the Study of the Old Testament* (1971): 149-156.

Miller, James C. "Ethnicity and the Hebrew Bible: Problems and Prospects." *Currents in the Biblical Research* 6/2 (2008): 170-205.

Muilenburg, J. "Form Criticism and Beyond." *Journal of Biblical Studies* 88 (1969): 1-18.

Na'aman, Nadav. "Sojourners and Levites in the Kingdom of Judah in the Seventh Century BCE." *Zeitschrift fur altorentalische und Biblische Rechtsgeschichte* 14 (2008): 256.

Ngaitt, Thangkhanlal. "Nido Taniam and the Fraught Question of Racism in India." *Economic and Political Weekly* XL1V/11 (March 15, 2014): 15.

Nicholson, E. W. "The Meaning of the Expression *'m h'rs* in the Old Testament." *Journal of Semitic Studies* X (1965): 59-66.

N. Postgate J. Review of the *Studies in Biblical and Cuneiform Law.* Westbrook, Raymond. *Vetus Testamendum* 40/3 (July 1992): 431-432.

Patil, Vrushali. "Narrating Political History about Contrast Space: Tourism Websites of India's Northeast." *Annals of Tourism Research* 38/2 (2011): 989-1008.

Peterson, David. "A Thrice-Told Tale." *Biblical Research* 18 (1973): 3-43.

________. "Genesis & Family Values." *Journal of Biblical Literature* 124/1 (2005): 5-23.

Pitkänen. "Ethnicity, Assimilation and the Israelite Settlement." *Tyndale Bulletin* 55/2 (2004): 162-181.

Pitkanen, Pekka. "Dr. Jekyll and Mr. Hyde: Deuteronomy and the Rights of Indigenous peoples." *Political Theology* 11/3 (2010): 399-409.

Polzin Robert. "The Ancestress of Israel in Danger." *SEMEIA* 3 (1995): 81-97.

Provan, Iain W. "Ideologies, Literary and Critical Reflection on Recent Writing on the History of Israel." *Journal of Biblical Literature* 114/4 (1995): 585-606.

Remesh, Babu P. "Strangers in their own land Migrants from the North-East in Delhi." *Economic & Political Weekly* XLV11/22 (June 2, 2012): 38.

Rendorff, Rolf "The Paradigm is Changing Hopes-and Fears." *Biblical Interpretation* 1/1 (1993): 34-53.

Robert B. Coote, and Keith W. Whitelam. "The Emergence of Israel, Social Transformation and State Formation following the Decline in Late Bronze Age Trade." *SEMEIA* 37 (1986): 107-147.

Schenker. "Das Zeichen Des Blutes Und Die Gewissheit Der Vergebung Im Alten Testament." *Munchener Theologishe Zeitschrift* 34 (1983): 197-98.

Schenkar, Adrian. "The Biblical Legislation on the Release of Slaves: the Road from Exodus to Leviticus." In *Journal for the Studies of the Old Testament* 78 (1998): 23-40.

Scott, George, M. Jr. "A Resynthesis of the Primordial & Circumstantial Approaches to Ethnic groups Solidarity: Towards an Explanatory Model. *Ethnic and Racial Studies* 13:147-71.

Shimray, Shimreingam. "Towards A New Paradigm of Human Rights in the Context of North East India." In *Asian Journal of Theology,* vol. 28 (April, 2014): 71.

Skjeggestad's, M. "Ethnic Groups in Early Iron Age Palestine: Some Remarks on the Use of the Term 'Israelite' in Recent Research." *Journal for the Studies of the Old Testament* 6 (1992): 159-186.

Smith, Bloch. "Israelite Ethnicity in Iron Age 1: Archaeological Preserves what is Remembered and what is Forgotten in Israel's History." *Journal of Biblical Literature* 112/3 (2003): 423-425.

Speiser, E. A. "Cuneiform Law and the History of Civilization." *Proceedings of the American Philosophical Society* 107 (1963): 538-39.

Srikanth, H. "Who in North East are Indigenous People." *Economic & Political Weekly* 69/20 (May, 2014): 42.

Stager, L. "Agriculture."*IDBSV;* 13. Cited by Robert B. Coote and Keith W. Whitelam, "The Emergence of Israel Social Transformation and State Formation following the Decline in Late Bronze Age Trade." *Semeia* 37 (1986): 107-47.

Steinberg, Naomi. "The Genealogical Framework of the Family Stories in Genesis." *Semeia* 46 (1989): 41-50.

Stott, Katherine. "Finding the Lost Book of the Law: Re-reaching the Story of 'The Book of the Law' (Deuteronomy-2 Kings) in Light of Classic Literature." *Journal for the Study of the Old Testament 30*/2 (2005): 155-169.

Titus P. Joseph. "Concern for the Migrants: An opening Toward Universalism in the Hebrew Bible." *Indian Theological Studies* 50 (Sept. & Dec. 2013): 269-296.

Trevaskis, Leigh M. "The purpose of Leviticus 24 within its literary context." *Vetus Testamendum* 59 (2009): 307.

Vashum, Yangkahao. "Space, Creation and Land: An Indigenous/Tribal Eco-Theology of the Northeast India." *Journal of Tribal Studies* Vol. XVII/1 (January-June 2012): 25-38.

Wallis, Louis. "Biblical Sociology 11." *American Journal of Sociology* 14/3 (November 1908): 327.

Waldow, H. Eberhard Von. "Social Responsibility and Social Structure in Early Israel" *Catholic Biblical Quarterly* 32 (1970): 184-185.

Weinfeld, Moshe. "The Covenant of Grant in the Old Testament and the Ancient Near East."*Journal of Americal Oriental Studies* 90/2 (1970): 195.

Weinfeld, Moshe. "Deuteronomy- The Present State of Inquiry." *Journal of Biblical Literature* LXXXV1 (Sept, 1967): 249.

West, Gerald. "Tracking an Ancient Near Eastern Economic System: The Tributary Mode of Production and the Temple State." *Old Testament Essay* 24/2 (2011): 511-532.

Westbrooke, Raymond. "Biblical and Cuniform Law Codes." *Revenue Biblique* 92 (1985): 249-56.

Westbrook, R. "Cuneiform Law codes and the Origin of Legislation." *Zeitschrift fur Assyriologie* 79 (1989): 201–22.

Whitelam, Keith W. "The Identity of Early Israel: The Realignment and Transformation of Late Bronze-Iron Age Palestine." *Journal for the Study of the Old Testament* 63 (1994): 57-87.

Whitelam, Keith W. "Israel's traditions of origin reclaiming the land." *Journal for the Study of the Old Testament* 44 (1989): 19-42.

Wilson, J. A. "Authority and Law in Ancient Egypt." *Journal of American Oriental Society* Supp 17 (1954): 5.

Wittenberg, Günther. "King Solomon and the Theologians." *Journal of Theology for Southern Africa* 63 (1988): 16-17.

Yan, Yu Suee. "The Alien in Deuteronomy." *Bible Today* 60/2 (April, 2009): 112-117.

C. New Papers and Magazine

Assam Tribune, 6 February 2011.

Basic Statistic of North East Region. Nongrim Hills: Shillong 1990.

Nagaland Post, 21 Septemper 2015.

Nagaland Post, 9 July 2015.

Nagaland Post, 15 September 2015.

Nagaland Post, 7 February 2015.

Nagaland Post, 17 December 2014.

The Hindu, 9 March 2014.

The Shillong Times, 1 April 2011.

The Week, 22 February 2015.

The Hindu, 5 February 2015.

D. E-Source

Censusindia gov. in/2011, (accessed on 15th September, 2015).

Kuku, Diepiriye. "India Is Racist, And Happy About It. A Black American's first-hand experience of foothpath India: No one even want to change." *Outlook Magazine* (June 29, 2209), http://www.outlookindia.com (accessed on Nov 18, 2015).

Lawrence, Liang and Golan Naulak. "Cultural Ignorance and Prejudice." *The Hindu,* 4 February. http://www.thehindu.com/todays-paper/tp-opinion/cultural-igno-rance-and-prejudice/article5650955.ece, (accessed on 20 February, 2015).

"Schedule Tribes" in the constitution of India cited in http://tribal.nic.in/ (accessed on 4th March, 2015).

Prakash, Singh, M. "Brain Drain and the North-East (2007)." http://www.kanglaonline.com/?template=kshow&kid=245, (accessed on 2 January 2015).

www.Scoopwhoop.com/news/banned-bbc-nirbhaya. Documentary, (accessed on 17th September, 2015).

http://www.teachgenocide.org . (accessed on 20th July 2014).

F. Interview

Interviewed with Mr. Aokumba Pongen, 18 August 2015.

Interviewed with Rev. Wekhenu Kath, 27August 2015.

Interviewed with Mr. Ralth Baimin Mungray on 14th October, 2016.

Interviewed with Rev. Krickwin Ch. Marak & Rev. Lalmithanggi Ch. Marak on 15th Oct. 2016 Time 9:00 am.